German Standards

BEST OF GERMAN INDUSTRY

DEUTSCHE/STANDARDS

Wir danken unseren Industry-Partnern:
We would like to thank our industry partners:

wöhner

German Standards

BEST OF GERMAN INDUSTRY

Herausgegeben von Dr. Florian Langenscheidt
Published by Dr Florian Langenscheidt

Präsentiert von der ZEIT Verlagsgruppe
Presented by ZEIT Publishing Group

Prestel

Munich · London · New York

MITARBEIT
COOPERATION

DR. FLORIAN LANGENSCHEIDT
Herausgeber/Publisher

OLAF SALIÉ
Projektleitung/Project Management

FABIAN WESTKAMP
Leitung Marketing & Kundenkommunikation
Head of Marketing & Customer Communications

ISA FALCKENBERG
Kundenkommunikation
Customer Communications

YVONNE BAUMGÄRTEL
Leitung Projektmanagement, Redaktion und Grafik
Head of Project Management, Editing and Graphics

CHRISTIANE BLASS, DR. KATRIN WEIDEN
Projektmanagement/Project Management

STEPHANIE HANEL, ALEXANDRA VON POSCHINGER, FRANK SKERKA U. A.
Redaktion/Editing

JULIA KÜHN
Schlussredaktion/Final Editing

MAHRT FACHÜBERSETZUNGEN GMBH
Übersetzung/Translation

HAUSER LACOUR KOMMUNIKATIONSGESTALTUNG GMBH
Design

SUSANNE KLUGE
Gestaltung und Satz/Layout and Typesetting

DANK
THANKS

Wir bedanken uns bei unserer Jury und dem Beirat
für die engagierte und konstruktive Unterstützung:

We would like to thank our Jury and Advisory Board
for their dedicated, constructive support:

JURY

YVONNE BAUMGÄRTEL
Redaktionsleitung, Deutsche Standards/Studio ZX GmbH
Editorial Management, German Standards/Studio ZX GmbH

NAEMI DENZ
Geschäftsführerin, Sutco® RecyclingTechnik GmbH
Managing Director, Sutco® RecyclingTechnik GmbH

SVEN HEPPES
Leiter Externe Kommunikation und Standortpresse, BASF SE
Head of External Communications and Site Communications, BASF SE

DR. CAROLA HILBRAND
Leitung Corporate Communication, RITTAL GmbH & Co. KG
Director Corporate and Brand Communications, RITTAL GmbH & Co. KG

DETLEV LEISSE
Head of Direct Sales, Studio ZX GmbH

OLAF SALIÉ
Projektleiter, Deutsche Standards
Project Manager, German Standards

HOLGER SCHULTE
Manager of Corporate Technology Management, Wöhner GmbH & Co. KG

DETLEF SIEVERDINGBECK
General Manager of Corporate Communications & Branding, HARTING Technologiegruppe

FABIAN WESTKAMP
Leitung Marketing & Kundenkommunikation, Deutsche Standards
Head of Marketing & Customer Communications, German Standards

BEIRAT/ADVISORY BOARD

DR. RAINER ESSER
Geschäftsführer, ZEIT Verlagsgruppe
Managing Director, ZEIT Publishing Group

ISABEL GRUPP
Geschäftsleiterin, Plastro Mayer GmbH
Managing Director, Plastro Mayer GmbH

BIRGIT HERAEUS-ROGGENDORF
Aufsichtsratsmitglied, Heraeus Holding GmbH
Member of the Supervisory Board, Heraeus Holding GmbH

DR. FLORIAN LANGENSCHEIDT
Herausgeber, Deutsche Standards
Publisher, German Standards

HENRIKE LUSZICK
Founder & CEO, Bridgemaker GmbH

THORSTEN MEIER
Bereichsleiter Kommunikation,
Verband der Elektro- und Digitalindustrie (ZVEI)
Director of Communications,
German Electro and Digital Industry Association (ZVEI)

RENATE PILZ
Gesellschafterin, Pilz GmbH & Co. KG
Partner, Pilz GmbH & Co. KG

HARTMUT RAUEN
Stellv. Hauptgeschäftsführer,
Verband Deutscher Maschinen- und Anlagenbau (VDMA)
Deputy Executive Director,
German Mechanical and Plant Engineering Association (VDMA)

CHRISTIAN RIEKER
Verlagsleiter, Prestel Verlag
Director, Prestel Verlag

MICHAEL ROSE
Protokollchef, Deutsche Messe AG
Director of Protocol, Deutsche Messe AG

DR. MARK SCHIFFHAUER
Mitglied der Geschäftsleitung, ZEIT Verlagsgruppe
und Geschäftsführer, Studio ZX GmbH
Member of the Management Board, ZEIT Publishing Group,
and Managing Director, Studio ZX GmbH

INHALT
CONTENTS

UNTERNEHMEN STATT UNTERLASSEN

Dr. Florian Langenscheidt

Ob im Fußball oder in der Leichtathletik: Unsere Wettbewerbsfähigkeit sinkt langsam in vielen Lebensbereichen. Wenn wir nicht aufpassen und mit voller Kraft und all unseren Ideen und Fähigkeiten gegensteuern, werden wir von einigen gewohnten Spitzenplätzen in der Welt absteigen. Ich liebe unser Land, aber mache mir ein wenig Sorgen.

Die deutschen Schlüsselindustrien geraten ins Wanken. Wegen chinesischer Konkurrenz, Energiepreisen und strategischen Fehlern. Selbst die Glasscheiben für die Renovierung unserer Nationalgalerie gab es nur noch in China. Unsere Energiepolitik ist ohne System und Verstand. Die CO_2-freie und in Deutschland so sichere Kernkraft wird irrational verteufelt und abgeschaltet. Wichtige und bewährte Energieformen werden radikal reduziert, während Wind, Wasser und Sonne noch nicht immer und überall als Ersatz zur Verfügung stehen. Andere Nationen warnten früh vor der Erpressbarkeit wegen zu hoher Abhängigkeit von russischem Gas – wir gingen sie ein. Und jetzt verkaufen wir Infrastruktur an China.

Die Wirtschaft lechzt nach Arbeitskräften, während der Staat das gemütliche Sich-Einrichten in transferfinanzierten Inseln erleichtert und sich viele von der Vier-Tage-Woche Selbstverwirklichung erhoffen und dabei vergessen, wie sinnstiftend und beglückend Arbeit sein kann. Vom Gelddrucken und -leihen bis zur Schaffung sogenannter Sondervermögen mit den bekannten Inflationsfolgen – der Staat holt sich zusätzliche Mittel ohne Rücksicht auf Konsequenzen. Und

wann war ein Staat schon mal effizienter und kreativer als die private Wirtschaft? Apropos: Frage nicht, was der Staat für dich tun kann, sondern was du für den Staat und für das Gemeinwohl tun kannst, so formulierte es John F. Kennedy sinngemäß. Bei vielen von uns scheint diese weise Einsicht abhandengekommen zu sein. Dabei weiß jeder erfahrene Mensch, dass wir am meisten für unser eigenes Glück tun, wenn wir uns primär um das Glück anderer kümmern.

Auch die nationale Verteidigung liegt am Boden – und vom Sondervermögen ist noch wenig zu spüren. Der Bau eines mittelmäßigen Flughafens dauert zwölf Jahre länger als erwartet, kostet Milliarden mehr als geplant und bietet nach dieser Tragödie als Visitenkarte des Landes nichts vom Charme und der Kreativität unserer Hauptstadt. Und wann kam die letzte große Vision von weltweiter Bedeutung aus Deutschland? Wann das letzte neue, weltweit wichtige Unternehmen? Unsere Start-up-Kultur hat zwar große Fortschritte gemacht, liegt aber weit abgeschlagen hinter den USA und China.

Wir reden übers Gendern, während China mit gigantischen Mitteln und viel Geschick eine neue Seidenstraße baut und nicht nur Afrika erobert. Und die Zukunft in Indien, Saudi-Arabien und Indonesien gestaltet wird. Die Qualität unserer Schulen – das heißt unsere Exzellenz im Umgang mit unserem größten Kapital – sinkt im internationalen Vergleich. Das Gebot der Menschlichkeit vereinen mit kluger Integrationspolitik und der Rücksicht auf Überforderung – wo gibt es überzeugende Ansätze für eine realistische Flüchtlingspolitik? Mit Blick auf Afrika erleben wir hinsichtlich zu erwartender Fluchtbewegungen erst den Anfang.

Wo stehen wir noch mal hinsichtlich Künstlicher Intelligenz, digitaler Innovationen, Geschwindigkeit unserer Netze oder Lückenlosigkeit des Handyempfanges? Wir haben uns gebetsmühlenartiges Beschwören der Notwendigkeit schnellen Handelns und Investierens angewöhnt, um unsere Verzweiflung zu übertünchen. Kann irgendjemand noch die Phrase vom Bürokratieabbau hören? Oder über Deutsche-Bahn-Witze lachen?

DR. FLORIAN LANGENSCHEIDT

»Denn um die Welt zu ändern, brauche ich viel Zuversicht, dass das geht. Optimismus eben.«

Und wenn jetzt natürlich der Hinweis auf die EU und unsere Partner kommt: Bei wie vielen Themen haben wir so etwas wie eine gemeinsame Linie und können schnell, klug und einstimmig entscheiden und handeln? Und bei wie vielen sind wir blockiert wegen des Einstimmigkeitsprinzips? Es macht erpressbar und verletzlich angesichts der leicht realisierbaren Einflussnahme von außen.

Ich höre schon auf. Ich kann mich selbst nicht ausstehen, wenn ich so etwas schreibe. Bin ich doch bekannt als unerschütterlicher Optimist, der die dahinterstehende Einstellung als wichtigste erneuerbare Energie erachtet. Der Reden darüber hält und Bücher schreibt – schauen wir mal ins Wörterbuch des Optimisten: „Wenn ich wüsste, dass morgen die Welt unterginge, würde ich heute noch ein Apfelbäumchen pflanzen": Martin Luthers berühmter Satz umreißt diese Grundeinstellung auf das Schönste.

Es ist wie beim Fotografieren: Mit falschen Einstellungen kann ich das vollkommenste Motiv ruinieren. Und die meisten Menschen bemühen sich um eine schöne Sicht auf die Dinge, wenn sie fotografieren. Man motiviert die Fotografierten zum Lachen, man komponiert schöne Bildausschnitte, fotografiert lieber das Naturwunder als die Müllhalde. Damit soll das Negative in der Welt weiß Gott nicht verdrängt oder verleugnet werden. Nur bringt es niemanden weiter, sich darauf zu fokussieren. Entweder ist es nicht zu ändern oder wir haben Chancen zur Verbesserung – aber dann ist der Optimist sicherlich der mit der größeren Energie und Hoffnung. Denn um die Welt zu ändern, brauche ich viel Zuversicht, dass das geht. Optimismus eben.

Es war Willy Brandt, dem wir den Kniefall in Warschau und die Entspannungspolitik verdanken, der anmerkte: „Zur Summe meines Lebens gehört im Übrigen, dass es Ausweglosigkeit nicht gibt." Und Immanuel Kant notierte lange davor: „Der Himmel hat den Menschen als Gegengewicht zu den vielen Mühseligkeiten des

Lebens drei Dinge gegeben: die Hoffnung, den Schlaf und das Lachen." Manche Menschen fragen, wie man angesichts der Not und des Elends in dieser Welt Optimismus entwickeln kann. Ich frage eher: Wie kann man existieren ohne? Hätte ich nicht das Gefühl, etwas zum Positiven ändern zu können, wie könnte ich leben in der Ungerechtigkeit? „Die Hoffnung ist der Regenbogen über den herabstürzenden Bach des Lebens", formulierte Nietzsche.

Optimismus und Hoffnung sind der Treibstoff für den Motor unserer Existenz. Sie treiben uns voran, lassen uns glauben und kämpfen. Ohne sie würde es dunkel werden in der Welt und wirklich Grund zu Pessimismus geben. Mit ihnen – das ist wie eine self-fulfilling prophecy – gibt es Grund zum Hoffen. Wir kennen das aus dem Alltag: Wer ständig glaubt, dass alles schiefgeht, dem geht alles schief. Wer furchtsam an große Aufgaben herangeht, hat schon halb verloren. Positives Denken hingegen zieht das Gelingen an und rechtfertigt sich dadurch rückwirkend. „Die Hoffnungslosigkeit ist schon die vorweggenommene Niederlage", meinte Karl Jaspers.

Kein Unternehmen würde existieren, gäbe es nicht Unternehmer*innen, die optimistisch an die Möglichkeit des Erfolges ihres Produktes glaubten. Und gäbe es keine Unternehmen, es gäbe keine Arbeitsplätze, keine Wirtschaft, keine Rente, kein Bürger- oder Kindergeld.

Wie gesagt: Wir können nicht ohne. Politisch, philosophisch, wirtschaftlich, seelisch. Ohne Optimismus bricht alles in sich zusammen. „Alle Hoffnungen sind naiv, aber wir leben von ihnen", sagte Primo Levi.

Dabei ist der Optimist nicht einer, der aus dem 9. Stock eines Hauses springt und sich beim 3. sagt, er lebe ja noch. Nein, er sieht die Realität in all ihrer Komplexität und macht einfach das Beste daraus. Und weiß, dass ihn eine positive Herangehensweise zu einem glücklicheren, gesünderen und gewinnenderen Wesen werden lässt. Optimist*innen „gedeihen", Pessimist*innen „welken dahin", beobachtet die US-Psychologin Barbara Fredrickson. Optimismus baut den Grund, auf dem er steht. Hoffnung gebiert Veränderung und rechtfertigt sich dadurch selbst – das Gegenteil des Teufelskreises.

Da das Leben voll von Angelhaken und Fallstricken ist, kann nur der handeln, der optimistisch daran glaubt, dass sein Ziel schon irgendwie erreichbar ist. Jeder andere wird die Flinte schnell ins Korn werfen. „Ein Pessimist sieht eine Schwierigkeit in jeder Gelegenheit, ein Optimist sieht eine Gelegenheit in jeder Schwierigkeit", sagte Winston Churchill dazu. Und Eckart von Hirschhausen etwas salopper: „Shit happens. Die Frage ist nur, ob ich die Taube bin oder das Denkmal." Der Optimist atmet auf, wenn er das Licht am Ende des Tunnels sieht; der Pessimist erkennt darin den entgegenkommenden Zug.

Also packen wir es an. Der Berg vor uns ist hoch. Aber wer hat im Vertrag mit dem Leben gelesen, dass es einfach ist? Wir müssen den Turnaround nur wollen und uns als Team Deutschland fühlen. Du bist Deutschland!

DR. FLORIAN LANGENSCHEIDT

»Gäbe es keine Unternehmen, es gäbe keine Arbeitsplätze, keine Wirtschaft, keine Rente, kein Bürger- oder Kindergeld.«

Und wer war seit Jahrzehnten die Lokomotive für Wachstum, Wohlstand und Innovation und hat all das erwirtschaftet, das momentan so großzügig verteilt wird? Die Industrie, die Privatwirtschaft und insbesondere der Mittelstand.

Daher dieses Buch und die breit angelegte Kampagne „Best of German Industry". Die hier vorgestellten Unternehmen haben Spitzenpositionen im weltweiten Wettbewerb. Sie sind häufig Weltmarktführer (und oft Hidden Champions) made in Germany. Hier geht man los, anstatt ewig zu diskutieren. Hier fokussiert man sich auf die Chancen und lernt aus seinen Fehlern. Hier regieren nicht Bedenkenträger*innen, sondern verantwortungsvolle, innovative und risikobereite Unternehmer*innen. Sie sind für mich Held*innen der Jetztzeit. Ihnen wollen wir eine Bühne bauen, da sie sich aus vielen Gründen ungern exponieren. Wir brauchen in Zeiten wie diese Vorbilder. Damit Deutschland nicht absteigt, sondern aufblüht und noch stärker wird.

Dr. Florian Langenscheidt wurde 1955 in Berlin geboren. Er studierte Germanistik, Journalismus und Philosophie in München und promovierte mit einer Doktorarbeit über Werbung. Nach Kompaktseminaren über Verlagswesen und Medien in Cambridge und zweijähriger publizistischer Tätigkeit in New York machte er den MBA am INSEAD in Fontainebleau bei Paris.

Viele Jahre hatte Dr. Florian Langenscheidt führende Positionen in der Langenscheidt Verlagsgruppe inne, zum Beispiel war er von 1988 bis 2001 Vorstandsmitglied bei Duden und Brockhaus. Er schrieb Bücher, zahlreiche Zeitungs- und Zeitschriftenartikel und Kolumnen zu Sprache, Medien und Wirtschaft (unter anderem für die FAZ, DIE ZEIT, SZ, Max, Capital und FOCUS) und ist Herausgeber des „Deutschen Markenlexikons" sowie des „Lexikons der deutschen Familienunternehmen". Von 1988 bis 2001 hatte er einen Lehrauftrag an der Ludwig-Maximilians-Universität in München.

Dr. Florian Langenscheidt hält mehrere Beiratsmandate, unterstützt mit Rat und Kapital junge Firmen und ist Gründer sowie Kuratoriumsvorsitzender von Children for a better world. Darüber hinaus engagiert er sich als Stiftungsrat der Deutschen Kinder- und Jugendstiftung und als Kuratoriumsmitglied des Deutschen Museums sowie der Deutschen Akademie für Sprache und Dichtung. Er ist Gründungsmitglied des BRAND CLUB und Sprecher des Kuratoriums Deutscher Gründerpreis.

DETERMINED, NOT DEFEATED

Dr Florian Langenscheidt

© Patrycia Lukas

From football to athletics, Germany's competitive standing is slowly deteriorating in many areas. We must be mindful of this: if we fail to put all our efforts, ideas and abilities into countering this trend, we will lose the leading position in global rankings to which we have become accustomed. I love our country but I am becoming concerned.

Key German industries are beginning to totter. It's all down to competition from China, rising energy prices and strategic errors. Even the panes of glass used in the renovation of our National Gallery were only available from China. Our energy policy is rudderless and makes no sense. Carbon-free nuclear power, which has operated so safely in Germany, has been irrationally demonized and deactivated. Significant, established forms of energy have been radically reduced while wind, hydro and solar are not yet able to offer ubiquitous, ever-present replacements. Other countries warned us at an early stage that our reliance on Russian gas would make us vulnerable – yet we embraced it. And now, we're selling off our infrastructure to China.

While business is crying out for skilled workers, the state is accommodating those seeking a comfortable life in tax havens, and many employees hope to realise their dreams of a four-day week, having forgotten just how meaningful and fulfilling work can be. From printing and lending money to creating special investment funds in full awareness of the inflationary pressure such measures create, the state is rustling up additional funds without considering the consequences. And

when has a state ever operated more efficiently or shown more creativity than the private sector? As John F. Kennedy said: "Ask not what your country can do for you – ask what you can do for your country." Many of us feel that this sage insight has been lost. And yet, the experienced among us know that we do the most for our own happiness when we concern ourselves primarily with the happiness of others.

Our national defences are in disarray and the special investment fund is yet to yield tangible effects. The construction of a medium-sized airport took twelve years longer than expected, ended up billions over budget and, now that the farce is over, serves as the business card for our country without any of the charm or creativity of our capital city. When was the last major vision of global significance to originate in Germany? When did we last produce a new company of global import? Our start-up culture has taken big strides forward, yet it continues to lag far behind the USA and China.

While we spend our time debating gender politics, China has invested huge sums and demonstrated great skill in building a new Silk Road and winning Africa's favour. Meanwhile, India, Saudi Arabia and Indonesia have been busy shaping the future. The quality of our schools – that is, our excellence in developing our most important asset – is tumbling down the international rankings. Despite the calls to combine humanity with a prudent integration policy and regard for the risks of overextending ourselves, where are the proposals for a realistic refugee policy? And, looking to Africa, it appears that the refugee numbers we are seeing today may only be the beginning.

What are we doing about artificial intelligence? How about digital innovation, network speeds or the spottiness of our mobile phone reception? We have learned to repeat a mantra, an exhortation to act swiftly and invest as a means of suppressing our doubts. Does anybody still buy the political promises to cut red tape? Or laugh at jokes about the Deutsche Bahn?

DR FLORIAN LANGENSCHEIDT

»Ultimately, changing the world requires confidence that such change is possible. It takes optimism.«

And, if we turn our attention to the EU and our European partners, on how many topics do we have anything resembling a shared position? How often are we able to act swiftly, shrewdly and unanimously? How many proposals does the principle of unanimity end up blocking? In the end, it only makes us weak and vulnerable in the face of powerful external influences.

I'll stop there. I can't abide this sort of narrative. I'm known, after all, as an unflinching optimist; someone who believes that a positive attitude is the most impor-

tant renewable energy source we have. I give lectures about this. I write books about it. Let's take a leaf from the optimists' handbook: "If I knew the world would end tomorrow, I would still plant an apple tree today." Martin Luther's famous aphorism is still the most beautiful description of this mindset.

It's like taking a photograph: using the wrong settings can ruin even the most magnificent scene. And, when we take a photograph, most of us strive to provide a positive view of things. We encourage the subjects to smile, strive to create aesthetic compositions and prefer to photograph a natural wonder than a rubbish dump. The aim, of course, is not to repress or deny the negative things in the world. Focusing on the negatives, however, does not help anyone. Either they cannot be changed or there are ways to improve them – and, if there are, it will undoubtedly be the optimists that show the most energy and hope. Ultimately, changing the world requires confidence that such change is possible. It takes optimism.

Willy Brandt, the West German Chancellor we have to thank for his genuflection in Warsaw and the policy of détente, wrote: "The sum total of my life includes the insight that there is no complete hopelessness." Long before him, Immanuel Kant had noted: "Heaven has given human beings three things to balance the odds of life: hope, sleep and laughter." Many people ask how anyone can develop a sense of optimism in the face of the pain and suffering in the world. I ask a different question: How can we exist without optimism? If I didn't believe it was possible to change things for the better, how could I continue to live in a world of injustice? "Hope is the rainbow over the cascading brook of life," Nietzsche wrote.

Optimism and hope are the fuel that powers the motor of our existence. They drive us forward, give us faith and the strength to battle on. Without them, the world would be a dark place and there would truly be cause for pessimism. But with them – and this is, ultimately, a self-fulfilling prophecy – we have reason to hope. We all have experience of this. If you consistently believe that everything will go wrong, it almost certainly will. If you approach major tasks with timidity and fear, the battle is already half lost. By contrast, positive thinking is conducive to success and, in hindsight, is always vindicated. "Hopelessness is simply an anticipation of defeat," wrote Karl Jaspers.

No companies would exist were it not for entrepreneurs who believed optimistically in their products' potential to succeed. And, if there were no companies, there would be no jobs, no business, no pensions, no citizens' basic income, no child benefits.

So, as I said, we simply cannot exist without optimism. Whether political, philosophical, commercial, or psychological, without optimism, everything would fall apart. "All hopes are naïve, but we live on them," said Primo Levi.

Somebody who jumps from the 9th floor of a building and notes that he is still alive as he passes the 3rd floor is not an optimist. No – he is seeing reality in all its complexity and simply making the best of it. He knows that a positive mindset helps to make us happier, healthier and more successful individuals. Optimists thrive while pessimists wither, as the American psychologist Barbara Fredrickson noted. Optimism lays the very foundations upon which it stands. Hope engenders change and vindicates itself; it is the opposite of a vicious cycle.

With life so full of traps and pitfalls, the only route forward is the optimistic belief that, somehow, we can reach our goals. If we lack optimism, we may as well throw in the towel. "The pessimist sees difficulty in every opportunity; an optimist sees opportunity in every difficulty," said Winston Churchill. Eckart von Hirschhausen put it rather more crudely: "Shit happens. The question is whether I'm the pigeon or the statue." The optimist sighs with relief when they see the light at the end of the tunnel; the pessimist sees it as a train barrelling toward them.

So, let's get to it. We have a big climb ahead of us. But where in the contract for this life did it say that things would be easy? All we have to do is choose to turn things around and feel part of Team Germany. You are Germany! And who, for decades, was the engine of growth, affluence and innovation? Who generated the prosperity that is now being so generously distributed? It was industry, the private sector and, in particular, the Mittelstand.

DR FLORIAN LANGENSCHEIDT

»If there were no companies, there would be no jobs, no business, no pensions, no citizens' basic income, no child benefits.«

Hence the motivation behind this book and our multi-pronged "Best of German Industry" campaign. The companies showcased in this book are leaders in the global competitive arena. They are often world market leaders, many are hidden champions, and all are made in Germany. They get to work rather than holding endless discussions. They focus on opportunities and learn from their mistakes. They are led not by sceptics or worriers but by innovative entrepreneurs willing to shoulder responsibility and accept risks. They are, to my mind, modern-day heroes. This book is intended to give them a stage because, for many reasons, these entrepreneurs rarely express themselves publicly. In times like these, we need role models. This way, we can ensure that Germany does not decline and, instead, blossoms and grows even stronger.

Dr Florian Langenscheidt was born in Berlin in 1955. He studied German literature, journalism and philosophy in Munich and gained his doctorate with a thesis on advertising. After completing short courses on publishing and the media in Cambridge and spending two years working in journalism in New York, he obtained his MBA from INSEAD in Fontainebleau, near Paris.

For many years, Dr Florian Langenscheidt held leading positions in the Langenscheidt Publishing Group, including serving on the Management Boards of Duden and Brockhaus from 1988 to 2001. He has written books and countless articles and columns in newspapers and magazines on language, the media and business (including for FAZ, DIE ZEIT, SZ, Max, Capital and FOCUS). He is the publisher of high-profile books showcasing German companies, including "Deutsches Markenlexikon" and "Lexikon der deutschen Familienunternehmen". He also lectured at Ludwig-Maximilians-Universität in Munich from 1988 to 2001.

Dr Florian Langenscheidt serves on a number of Advisory Boards, supports young companies with advice and financing, and is the founder and Chair of the Board of Trustees of Children for a Better World. He also sits on the Council of the German Children and Youth Foundation (DKJS) and is a member of the Boards of Trustees of the Deutsches Museum and the German Academy for Language and Literature. In addition, Langenscheidt is a founding member of BRAND CLUB and spokesperson for the Advisory Board of the German Entrepreneur Award.

STOLZ AUF DAS, WAS WIR SCHAFFEN

Sarna Röser

© Anne Grossmann

Wenn ich heute auf unser Land blicke, auf das, was wir als Gesellschaft und Wirtschaft erreicht haben, in welchem Wohlstand ich als junger Mensch und meine Elterngeneration aufwachsen durften, bin ich stolz auf das Erreichte. Auch wenn wir natürlich zu keinem Zeitpunkt unsere Geschichte vergessen dürfen. Mir ist durchaus bewusst, dass man je nach Herkunft und Milieu von Deutschland sehr unterschiedliche Bilder haben kann. Sicherlich ist hier nicht alles perfekt. Aber sicherlich gibt es mehr Positives als Negatives zu berichten. Ich würde mich freuen, wenn ich noch mehr Menschen davon überzeugen könnte, dass das Glas halb voll und nicht halb leer ist. Und dass wir dann gemeinsam daran arbeiten, das Glas wieder bis zum Rand zu füllen.

Meine Generation hinterfragt gern, und sie entwickelt einen anderen Blick auf die Dinge – auch auf Deutschland. Ich habe dies unlängst in meinem Buch „Ein Plädoyer für die Mehrheit" getan, aus dem ich hier zitiere. Ich sehe – wie fast überall – gewisse Parallelen zum Unternehmertum. Vor einigen Jahren habe ich mir selbst die Frage gestellt, ob ich mir vorstellen kann, in unser Familienunternehmen einzusteigen. Was will ich anders machen? Wie schaffe ich es, das Traditionsunternehmen im Sinne der nächsten Generation fortzuführen? Und wie stelle ich mich als Arbeitgeber auf, um diese junge Generation für uns zu begeistern? Warum stehe ich jeden Tag auf und tue das, was ich tue? Ich muss diese Fragen beantworten können. Denn warum sollten junge Menschen ausgerechnet für unser Unternehmen arbeiten wollen? Um darauf eine Antwort geben zu können, müssen wir uns als Familien- und Traditionsunternehmen neu hinterfragen. Wir müssen neue Antworten finden und diese auch ganz klar kommunizieren.

Betrachten wir Deutschland mit dem gleichen Blick, muss ich mir die Frage stellen: Will ich mich in diesem Land und will ich mich für dieses Land engagieren? Welche Vision haben wir? Und wo wollen wir hin? Sich für dieses Land zu engagieren, bedeutet vor allem, sich für die Menschen zu engagieren, Antworten darauf zu finden und zu geben, wie wir uns zukunftsfähig aufstellen, um unsere Ziele zu erreichen. Für mich ist die Antwort klar: Ich will. Deutschland ist meine Heimat. Deutschland ist das Land, in dem ich gerne lebe. Ich liebe seine Traditionen, das Zuhause-Gefühl und die Ausdrucksstärke unserer Sprache – auch wenn sie aus unternehmerischer Sicht oft ein Hindernis ist. Ich liebe den Facettenreichtum der unterschiedlichen Regionen, unsere Industrie, unsere mittelständischen Betriebe – unser Unternehmertum. Ich liebe sogar unsere kleinen – oftmals größeren – Schwächen. Und ich nehme die dunklen Seiten dieses Landes und seine Geschichte als Verpflichtung an. Gerade von meinen Großeltern habe ich viel von unserer Vergangenheit gehört und gelernt. Wie schnell die Stimmung in einem Land ins Negative kippen kann. Wie schlimm Hass und Krieg sind – und wie wichtig es ist, für Frieden und Freiheit zu kämpfen. Wenn ich die Augen schließe und an Deutschland denke, dann sehe ich vor mir ein mündiges, weltoffenes Land, das Chancengerechtigkeit bietet und solidarisch mit den Schwächeren seiner Bürgerinnen und Bürger ist. Das ist das Land, das ich gestalten möchte. Unternehmertum ist ein entscheidender Hebel dafür.

Viele Menschen vergessen, wie groß der Einfluss von Unternehmen und insbesondere von Familienunternehmen auf ihre Heimat ist. Familienunternehmen spielen in Deutschland eine bedeutende Rolle in der Wirtschaft. Wussten Sie, dass nach Angaben des Instituts für Mittelstandsforschung Bonn im Jahr 2020 rund 90 Prozent aller Unternehmen in Deutschland Familienunternehmen waren? Diese Unternehmen beschäftigen nicht nur rund 60 Prozent der Arbeitnehmerinnen und Arbeitnehmer in unserem Land, sondern tragen auch über 50 Prozent zum Bruttoinlandsprodukt bei. „Deutschlands Familienunternehmen denken im Rhythmus von Generationen und nicht im Takt von Aktionärsversammlungen", heißt es im Vorwort eines opulenten Bildbandes zum Einfluss von Familienunternehmen auf ihre Region. Und es stimmt. Gerade Familienunternehmen haben oft eine besondere Beziehung zu ihrer Heimatregion, da sie in dieser meist über mehrere Generationen ansässig und tief in der lokalen Gemeinschaft verwurzelt sind. Aus diesem Grund tragen Familienunternehmen eine besondere Verantwortung für ihre Heimatregion und die Menschen, die dort leben. Im Großen und im Kleinen. Sie sind die Ersten, die gefragt werden, wenn die A-Jugend neue Trikots braucht, wenn die Freiwillige Feuerwehr einen finanziellen Zuschuss für ein neues Fahrzeug benötigt oder wenn ein Kulturprogramm fürs Seniorenheim gesponsert werden soll. Die Liste der kulturellen, sportlichen, bildungsfördernden, sozialen oder infrastrukturellen Maßnahmen von Traditionsunternehmen in ihrer Region lässt sich wohl endlos fortsetzen. Leider haben die wenigsten Familienunternehmen ihre Investitio-nen quantitativ oder qualitativ dokumentiert. Während Konzerne Corporate-Social-Responsibility-Berichte als Marketinginstrument nutzen, reden Familienunternehmen viel zu selten über ihr Engagement. Eine größere Offenheit im Sinne eines „Tue Gutes und rede darüber" würde aus meiner Sicht hier helfen. Denn sie würde die politische Wahrnehmung der Familienunternehmen noch weiter steigern.

SARNA RÖSER

»Wenn ich die Augen schließe und an Deutschland denke, dann sehe ich vor mir ein mündiges, weltoffenes Land, das Chancengerechtigkeit bietet.«

Aber wer mit offenen Augen durch Deutschland reist, dem kann es eigentlich nicht entgehen: Vor allem abseits gelegene Landstriche profitieren von der Präsenz einzelner engagierter Unternehmen. Denn Deutschlands Unternehmerinnen und Unternehmer sitzen nicht überwiegend in unseren Metropolen, sondern in den Regionen. Diese Unternehmen ziehen von dort nicht freiwillig ins Ausland. Ihre Inhaberinnen und Inhaber verkaufen nicht an Konzerne, denen die örtliche A-Jugend völlig egal ist, wenn sie nicht dazu gezwungen werden. Denn obwohl in vielen Familienunternehmen das Auslandsgeschäft den deutschen Markt längst überholt hat, bleiben die meisten Zentralfunktionen am Firmensitz. Dazu zählen besonders Forschung und Entwicklung (F&E), Kern des Erfolges vieler deutscher Hidden Champions des Mittelstandes. Exemplarisch sei dieses Beispiel genannt: Auf dem Markt für Babynahrung gibt es drei große Namen. Zwei der Namen, Alete und Milupa, wurden von großen Lebensmittelkonzernen geschluckt. Der dritte Name ist Hipp. Es gab viele Stimmen, die gesagt haben, dass auch Hipp als Familienunternehmen nicht überleben wird. Die Konzerne hätten bessere Forschungs- und Entwicklungsabteilungen, das bessere Marketing und den besseren Vertrieb sowieso. Aber Hipp hat als unabhängiges Familienunternehmen überlebt und dominiert den Markt. Die Strategie fasst Stefan Hipp so zusammen: „All unser Denken und Handeln ist langfristig ausgerichtet. Wir werden weiterhin ressourcenschonend wirtschaften und wollen gesund wachsen. Für uns ist wichtig, unsere Werte und Traditionen weiterzuleben und der Welt auch etwas zurückzugeben. So wollen wir bis 2025 als gesamtes Unternehmen klimapositiv sein." Und so wie die Hipps denken viele andere Unternehmen.

Diese regional tief verwurzelten Unternehmen – in vielen Bereichen Exportweltmeister – haben Verbindungen in alle Welt. Wir wirtschaften in einer globalisierten und digitalisierten Welt. Unsere Wettbewerber sitzen nicht mehr nur in Berlin, Frankfurt und München, sondern überall in der Welt. Aber diese Verbindungen in die ganze Welt sind längst nicht mehr nur wirtschaftlicher Art. Auch unsere Mitarbeitenden – und

vor allem unsere potenziellen Mitarbeitenden – kommen aus der ganzen Welt. Die internationalen Verbindungen, die ich hier meine, sind keine Kundenbeziehungen, sondern Nachbarschaften und Freundschaften und oft schon längst familiärer Art: Laut dem Statistischen Bundesamt hatte im Jahr 2021 jeder vierte in

SARNA RÖSER

»Denn Deutschlands Unternehmerinnen und Unternehmer sitzen nicht überwiegend in unseren Metropolen, sondern in den Regionen.«

Deutschland lebende Mensch einen Migrationshintergrund. Das entspricht etwa 22,3 Millionen Menschen. Viele Studien beweisen, dass Unternehmen mit Teams, deren Mitglieder viele unterschiedliche Persönlichkeiten mit unterschiedlicher Sozialisation haben, erfolgreicher wirtschaften. Es sind nämlich genau die unterschiedlichen Perspektiven dieser Menschen, die uns davor schützen, betriebsblind zu werden, und neue Gedanken entfachen. Die integrative Kraft, die Unternehmen in Deutschland entwickeln können, müssen wir nutzen. Durch die Schaffung von Arbeitsplätzen und die Einstellung von Menschen mit den unter-

SARNA RÖSER

»Die integrative Kraft, die Unternehmen in Deutschland entwickeln können, müssen wir nutzen.«

schiedlichsten Hintergründen können Unternehmen ganz bewusst dazu beitragen, unter anderem auch die Integration von Einwanderinnen und Einwanderern zu fördern – in die Unternehmen und in die Gesellschaft. Arbeit bietet nicht nur finanzielle Stabilität, sondern auch soziale Kontakte und die Möglichkeit, die deutsche Sprache und Kultur kennenzulernen. Unternehmen ermöglichen Teilhabe und Aufstieg. Erfolgsgeschichten wie die von Uğur Şahin und Özlem Türeci, die 2008 das biopharmazeutische Unternehmen BioNTech gegründet haben, brauchen wir noch viel mehr. Lassen Sie uns dafür jetzt die Grundlagen schaffen!

Wer Verantwortung übernimmt und gestaltet, der darf auch stolz auf das sein, was er geschaffen hat. Wer Menschen motiviert, ihre Lebenswelt und ihre Zukunft zum Besseren zu verändern, der kann zu Recht stolz sein: auf seine Stadt, auf seine Region und, ja, sogar auf sein Unternehmen. Wer „vor Ort" etwas gestaltet und erschafft, der wird am Ende stolz auf das Ergebnis sein. Der Wille zum Gestalten erwächst aus der Verwurzelung. Denn es muss ja einen Grund haben, wenn sich Industrieunternehmen, unser Mittelstand und Selbstständige in dieser globalisierten Welt dazu entschließen, gerade in Deutschland anzupacken. Ob diese Wurzeln schon seit 100 Jahren in die Tiefe reichen oder ob sie sich gerade erst ihren Weg bahnen, ist dabei zweitrangig – es kommt auf die Stärke des Willens an.

Dieser Text erschien erstmals im Buch der JUNGEN UNTERNEHMER von Sarna Röser „Ein Plädoyer für die Mehrheit" im Juli 2023. Er wurde für diese Publikation redaktionell überarbeitet.

Sarna Röser ist Unternehmerin, Aufsichtsrätin, Beirätin, Business Angel und Bundesvorsitzende des Wirtschaftsverbandes DIE JUNGEN UNTERNEHMER. Das Wirtschaftsmagazin Capital zählt sie zu den Top 40 unter 40 Talenten der deutschen Wirtschaft und das Handelsblatt zu den 100 Frauen, die Deutschland voranbringen. Zudem wurde sie vom Handelsblatt und der Boston Consulting Group als Vordenkerin ausgezeichnet.

Im Juli 2023 wurde sie mit ihrem ersten Buch „Ein Plädoyer für die Mehrheit" zur SPIEGEL-Bestsellerautorin. Im Jahr 2022 erhielt Sarna Röser den Preis Soziale Marktwirtschaft der Konrad-Adenauer-Stiftung.

Seit 2018 ist Sarna Röser Bundesvorsitzende des Wirtschaftsverbandes DIE JUNGEN UNTERNEHMER von DIE FAMILIENUNTERNEHMER e. V. und vertritt in diesem Amt über 1500 junge Familien- und Eigentümerunternehmerinnen und -unternehmer bis 40 Jahre. Kurz: die Next Generation der deutschen Traditionsunternehmen. Zudem steht Sarna Röser für die vierte Generation der Röser Unternehmensgruppe, in der sie designierte Nachfolgerin für die 1923 gegründeten Zementrohr- und Betonwerke Karl Röser & Sohn GmbH, Mitglied der Geschäftsleitung der Röser FAM GmbH & Co. KG sowie Mitgesellschafterin der Beteiligungsgesellschaft FAIR VC GmbH ist. Darüber hinaus ist sie an unterschiedlichsten Start-ups beteiligt.

Im Juli 2020 wurde Sarna Röser als jüngstes Mitglied in den Aufsichtsrat der Fielmann AG gewählt, Deutschlands größter Optikerkette. Des Weiteren ist sie seit 2020 eine der jüngsten Beirätinnen der Deutschen Bank AG sowie seit 2021 als Beirätin der neuen Coding School 42 der Dieter-Schwarz-Stiftung (LIDL/Kaufland) aktiv. Zudem ist Sarna Röser Mitglied im Kuratorium des Deutschen Start-up Verbandes und stellvertretende Vorsitzende der Ludwig-Erhard-Stiftung.

TAKING PRIDE IN OUR ACHIEVEMENTS

Sarna Röser

© Anne Grossmann

Today, when I look at our country, at what we have achieved as a society and as an economy, at the prosperity my generation and my parents' generation enjoyed in our youth, I am proud of our achievements. Of course, we must never forget the events of our country's past. And I am well aware that people from different backgrounds and different regions of Germany have very different views of our country. I am not pretending that everything is perfect. Yet, the positives undoubtedly outweigh the negatives. I would be delighted if I could convince even more people that, here in Germany, our glass is half full, not half empty, and that we should work together to fill it to the brim once again.

My generation challenges assumptions and is developing a different perspective of things – including Germany. I did this at length in my book, "Ein Plädoyer für die Mehrheit" (The Case for the Majority), which I will refer to here. I see certain parallels between my book – and almost everywhere in society – and entrepreneurship. A few years ago, I asked myself whether I could imagine myself joining my family's business. What did I want to do differently? How could I continue our tradition-steeped company in the interests of the next generation? How would I position myself as an employer in an effort to get this young generation interested in our company? And, ultimately, why do I get up every day and do what I do? I needed to be able to answer these questions. Because why should young people want to work for our company over all others? As a family company with a rich tradition, finding answers to these questions meant examining ourselves in detail.

We had to find new answers and communicate them with absolute clarity.

If we apply the same scrutiny to Germany, I have to ask myself certain questions. Do I want to commit myself to this country? Am I prepared to champion it? What is our vision? And what do we want to achieve? Above all, committing to this country means committing to its

SARNA RÖSER

»When I close my eyes and think of Germany, I see a mature, cosmopolitan country that offers equal opportunities.«

people; it means finding and communicating answers to crucial questions, such as how we should position ourselves to achieve our goals for the future. For me, the answer is clear: I want to commit to Germany. Germany is my home. Germany is where I want to live. I love its traditions, its sense of home and the expressive power of our language – even if, from an entrepreneurial perspective, it might seem more like a hindrance. I love the multifaceted nature of the different regions of our country. I love our industry and the Mittelstand. I love our entrepreneurship. I even love our weaknesses – some of which are minor, though many are rather more significant. And I accept the dark side of our country and its history as a covenant. My grandparents spoke at length about our past and taught me a great deal. How rapidly the atmosphere in a country can turn sour. How dangerous hate and war can be. And how important it is to fight for peace and freedom. When I close my eyes and think of Germany, I see before me a mature, cosmopolitan country that offers equal opportunities and stands in solidarity with its neediest citizens. This is the country I want to help shape. Entrepreneurship is a crucial lever in this process.

Many people forget just how much influence companies, and family-owned companies in particular, have on our homeland. Family companies play a vital role in the German economy. Did you know that, according to the Institut für Mittelstandsforschung (IfM) Bonn, around 90% of all companies in Germany in 2020 were family owned? Not only do these companies employ around 60% of our country's total workforce, they also generate over 50% of our gross domestic product. As a glossy coffee-table book on the influence of family companies on their respective regions described in its foreword, "Germany's family-owned companies think in a rhythm that spans generations rather than focusing on shareholder meetings." And it's true. Family companies in particular often have a very special relationship with their home region, often because they have been based there for several generations and have deep roots in local communities. For this reason, family companies often have a very special sense of responsibility to their home region and the people who live there. This

responsibility is borne out in measures both large and small. These companies are the first port of call when the local youth football team needs new jerseys, the volunteer fire brigade is raising funds for a new fire engine, or a retirement home is seeking sponsors to support a cultural programme for its residents. The list of cultural, sporting, educational, social and infrastructural initiatives in which established companies engage in their regions is seemingly endless. Unfortunately, very few family companies keep quantitative or qualitative documentation of these investments. While major corporations use CSR reports as marketing tools, family companies talk far too little about their engagement in this area. In my view, publicising such activities to a wider audience would be helpful, in keeping with a German proverb: "Tue Gutes und rede darüber" – literally, "Do good and talk about it". This approach would further enhance the political perception of family companies.

That said, anyone who pays attention as they travel across Germany will see that every community, especially those in remote regions, benefit from the presence of a handful of committed companies. Ultimately, Germany's entrepreneurs are not predominantly based in our sprawling cities but in the surrounding regions. These companies would prefer not to move abroad. Unless forced, their owners will not sell up to major corporations with no interest in the local youth football team. Although many family-owned companies in Germany now rely on foreign trade more than their domestic business, the majority of core functions are still based at their headquarters. This includes research and development (R&D), which is at the heart of many hidden champions' success in the German Mittelstand. Let's consider an example: three major brands dominate the German baby food market. Two of the names, Alete and Milupa, have been swallowed up by food industry giants. The third name is Hipp. Plenty of people prophesied that Hipp would be unable to survive as a family company. The giants had better R&D departments, they said, plus more effective marketing and sales activities. Yet, Hipp has survived as an independent family enterprise and continues to dominate the market. Stefan Hipp describes his company's strategy as follows: "Our thoughts and actions are always geared towards the long term. We will continue to operate in a resource-conserving manner and aim to achieve healthy growth. What matters to us is that we keep our values and traditions alive and give something back to the planet, too. With this in mind, we hope to make our entire company climate-positive by 2025." And there are plenty of other companies who think like the Hipps.

With their deep regional roots, these companies – which include world export champions in many fields – have connections that span the globe. We are living and operating in a globalised, digitalised world. Our competitors are no longer limited to Berlin, Frankfurt and Munich: they are all around the world. Yet, these globe-spanning connections are not solely economic in nature. Far from it: our employees – and, most importantly, our future employees – come from all around the world. The international connections to which I am referring are not merely customer relationships: they are neighbourly relationships, friendships and, often, familial ties. According to the Federal Statistical Office, one in every four people living in Germany in 2021 was from an immigrant background. This corresponds to around 22.3 million people. Many studies show that companies with diverse teams made up of people with different backgrounds and different experiences are

SARNA RÖSER

»Germany's entrepreneurs are not predominantly based in our sprawling cities but in the surrounding regions.«

more successful in business. It is precisely these different perspectives that a variety of people bring with them that protects us against tunnel vision and sparks new ideas. We have to leverage the integrative power that companies in Germany could cultivate. By creating jobs and employing people from a wide range of backgrounds, companies can make a very deliberate contribution, including by helping immigrants to integrate – into our companies and into wider society. Employment not only provides financial stability, it also creates social contacts and an opportunity to learn the German language and culture. Companies promote social par-

»We have to leverage the integrative power that companies in Germany could cultivate.«

ticipation and advancement. We need more success stories like that of Uğur Şahin and Özlem Türeci, who founded the biopharmaceutical firm BioNTech in 2008. So, let's create the conditions for them!

If you take responsibility and help to shape the future, you can be proud of your achievements. If you motivate other people to transform the world around them and their future for the better, you have every right to take pride: in your city, your region and, yes, even your company. And, if you work "on the ground" to build and create something, you can feel proud of the results. The desire to build something, to shape something, grows stronger when companies put down roots. After all, there must be a reason why, in this globalised world, industrial enterprises, our Mittelstand and self-employed people decide to commit to Germany. Whether these roots have stretched into the soil for 100 years or are only just gaining a foothold is a secondary issue. What matters is the strength of their commitment.

This text was first published in Sarna Röser's "Ein Plädoyer für die Mehrheit" (The Case for the Majority), published with Die Jungen Unternehmer in July 2023. It has been edited and translated for this publication.

Sarna Röser is an entrepreneur, Supervisory Board member, Advisory Board member, business angel and National Chair of DIE JUNGEN UNTERNEHMER, an association representing young entrepreneurs in Germany. The business magazine Capital named Röser in its "Top 40 Under 40" list of rising German business stars, while Handelsblatt included her in a list of 100 women to take Germany forward. Furthermore, she has been described as a thought leader by Handelsblatt and the Boston Consulting Group.

In 2023, Röser became a SPIEGEL best-selling author with her first book, "Ein Plädoyer für die Mehrheit" (The Case for the Majority). In 2022, she was presented with the Social Market Economy award by the Konrad-Adenauer-Stiftung.

Since 2018, Röser has served as National Chair of DIE JUNGEN UNTERNEHMER, which is part of the family business advocacy association DIE FAMILIENUNTERNEHMER e. V. In this role, she represents over 1,500 young leaders under the age of 40 at owner-operated and family-owned companies. In short, she gives a voice to the next generation of tradition-steeped German companies. Sarna Röser is also the fourth family generation involved in the Röser corporate group: she is the designated successor to the leadership of Zementrohr- und Betonwerke Karl Röser & Sohn GmbH, a concrete solutions provider founded in 1923, a member of the Management Board of Röser FAM GmbH & Co. KG and a joint partner in the investment company FAIR VC GmbH. She also holds interests in a wide range of start-ups.

In July 2020, Sarna Röser became the youngest member to be elected to the Supervisory Board of Fielmann AG, Germany's largest opticians chain. The same year, she became one of the youngest members of the Deutsche Bank AG Advisory Board and, in 2021, joined the Advisory Board of 42, a new programming school funded by the Dieter Schwarz Foundation (LIDL/Kaufland). In addition, Sarna Röser sits on the Board of Trustees of the German Startups Association (Startup-Verband) and is Deputy Chair of the Ludwig Erhard Foundation.

BEST OF GERMAN INDUSTRY

ABUS

Geht es um individuelle Sicherheit oder den Schutz vor Diebstahl, ist für Privatpersonen und Unternehmen weltweit das Beste ihre erste Wahl. Ob ein Vorhängeschloss für den Gartenschuppen oder das Boot, ob Fahrradhelme für den Familienausflug oder internationale Radteams, ob Hightech-Schließanlagen für internationale Hotelketten oder Diamantenbörsen: Überall setzt ABUS mit einer Vielzahl von Produkten die Standards und wird rund um den Globus für deren einzigartige Qualität geschätzt.

„Sicher, stabil und zuverlässig" sind seit Anbeginn die wichtigsten Attribute der Marke ABUS. 1924 gründete der Schlossmacher August Bremicker gemeinsam mit einigen seiner Söhne in Volmarstein an der Ruhr die August Bremicker und Söhne KG, kurz: ABUS. In ihrer Kellerschmiede fertigten sie hochwertige Vorhangschlösser aus Blech und Stahl nach dem Motto „Sicherheit braucht Qualität". Das Vorhängeschloss „The Iron Rock" war ein ikonisches Produkt, das den Verwender*innen schon damals das „gute Gefühl der Sicherheit" gab – ein Produktversprechen, für das ABUS bis heute einsteht. Automatisierte industrielle Fertigungsprozesse und insbesondere die Expansion des Exportgeschäfts ließen das Unternehmen schnell prosperieren. Ende der 1930er-Jahre hatte ABUS bereits 300 Mitarbeitende. 1938 starb August Bremicker. Nach Kriegsende leiteten seine Söhne einen umfassenden Neuanfang ein, der bis in die Gegenwart richtungsweisend für den Erfolg des Unternehmens sein sollte. 1969 gründete das familiengeführte Industrieunternehmen die ABUS Hong Kong Ltd. Die Kooperation mit ausländischen Partnern erfolgte unter der Leitung von ABUS Mitarbeitenden, die die Fertigung koordinierten und überwachten. Dieses Dualitätsprinzip bewährte sich und wurde für alle ABUS Auslandsmärkte adaptiert. In den 1970er-Jahren positionierte ABUS sein erweitertes Angebot unter dem Begriff „Mechanische Sicherheit für Haus und Wohnung", hinzu kamen

When it comes to personal security and protecting against theft, the first choice for private individuals and companies around the world is also the best. Whether it's padlocks for tool sheds or boats, bicycle helmets for everything from family outings to international cycling teams, or high-tech locking systems for international hotel chains or diamond exchanges, ABUS sets the standard with a variety of products that are valued around the world for their unique quality.

From the very outset, the ABUS brand has been renowned for its "safe, stable and reliable" products. In 1924, lockmaker August Bremicker and his sons started up their own business in Volmarstein, not far from the Ruhr, by the name of August Bremicker und Söhne KG – or ABUS for short. In their workshop, situated in the cellar of the family home, they produced high-quality padlocks from tin and steel under the motto "Security built on quality". The Iron Rock padlock became an iconic product, giving users a "good feeling of security" – a product claim that ABUS relies on to this day. The company soon prospered thanks to automated industrial manufacturing processes and, in particular, the expansion of its export activities. By the end of the 1930s, ABUS had around 300 employees. August Bremicker died in 1938. Following the Second World War, his sons embarked on a new beginning for the company, setting a course that has guided ABUS to success through to the present day. In 1969, the family-run industrial enterprise founded ABUS Hong Kong Ltd. The company's cooperation with international partners is led by ABUS employees, who coordinate and monitor manufacturing operations. This principle of duality proved successful and was adapted for all foreign markets in which ABUS operated. In the 1970s, ABUS positioned its expanded product range under the slogan "Mechanical security for house and home", also adding bicycle locks, helmets and panniers. Today, ABUS offers and continuously develops an array of

Unternehmensname
ABUS AUGUST BREMICKER SÖHNE KG

Industriezweig
SICHERHEITSTECHNIK

Gründung
1924

Gründer
AUGUST BREMICKER (1860-1938) UND EINIGE SEINER SÖHNE

Produkte
SCHLÖSSER UND BESCHLÄGE, SMART HOME, DIGITALE SICHERHEIT UND ZWEIRADSICHERUNGEN

Mitarbeitende
ÜBER 4000 WELTWEIT

Company name
ABUS AUGUST BREMICKER SÖHNE KG

Industry
SECURITY TECHNOLOGY

Founded
1924

Founder
AUGUST BREMICKER (1860-1938) AND SOME OF HIS SONS

Products
LOCKS AND FITTINGS, SMART HOME SYSTEMS, DIGITAL SECURITY AND BICYCLE LOCKS

Employees
AROUND 4,000 WORLDWIDE

Mit einem Kern aus Wolfram-carbid ist das Bügelschloss Granit Super Extreme 2500 die neue Referenz für hoch-sichere Fahrradschlösser

The Granit Super Extreme 2500 D-lock, which features a tungsten carbide core, is the new benchmark for ultra-secure bicycle locks

Zweiradschlösser sowie Fahrradhelme und -taschen. Heute bietet ABUS in den Bereichen Haus-, Objekt- und mobile Sicherheit eine Vielfalt von Produkten, die fortwährend weiterentwickelt werden: von mechanischen und mechatronischen Zusatzsicherungen zum Schutz von Gebäuden über neu entwickelte Motorradschlösser, Fahrradschlösser und -helme bis hin zu elektronischen Zutrittskontrollsystemen sowie komplexen Smart-Home-Systemen.

ABUS treibt die Entwicklung und Realisation innovativer Sicherheit sowohl für private als auch gewerbliche Nutzer*innen weiter voran. So zählt ABUS TOUCH zu der neuen Generation von Vorhängeschlössern, die bequem per Fingerabdruck von bis zu 20 Personen genutzt werden können. Sie verriegeln und entsperren Kellertüren, Geräteschuppen und vieles andere schlüssellos, einfach und bequem. 9001 IoTect ist ein digitales Schließmodul, zum Beispiel für hochwertige oder sensible Transportgüter, das per App und über das Webinterface „ABUS cMap" verwaltet und gesteuert wird. Das cloudbasierte Online-Portal zeigt alle relevanten Informationen rund um die eingesetzten Schlösser in einem Dashboard und ermöglicht die Vergabe individueller, zeitlich wie räumlich beschränkter Zugriffsrechte.

ABUS bekennt sich mit fünf heimischen Produktionsstätten und Dependancen zum Industriestandort Deutschland. Zur Unternehmensgruppe gehören die ABUS August Bremicker Söhne KG am Gründungsstandort Wetter an der Ruhr, ABUS Security Center GmbH & Co. KG in Affing bei Augsburg und ABUS Pfaffenheim GmbH in Jahnsdorf bei Chemnitz. Das global agierende Industrieunternehmen vertreibt seine Produkte, in einigen Segmenten als Marktführer, weltweit auf allen Kontinenten: mit rund 25 Niederlassungen in Europa, den USA und Lateinamerika sowie in Asien. Weltweit beschäftigt ABUS rund 4000 Mitarbeitende. Das Unternehmen wird in vierter und fünfter Generation von der Familie geleitet. ABUS wurde von namhaften Publikationen und Institutionen vielfach ausgezeichnet: für seine Produkte (DIE WELT, 2023), Innovationen (FOCUS Money, 2020; Capital, 2021; DIE WELT, 2021) und als Arbeitgeber (WirtschaftsWoche, 2020; F.A.Z.-Institut, 2020; STERN, 2021; Statista, 2021; CHIP, 2021).

„Wir wollen das Leben ein Stück sicherer machen." Das war die Maxime der ABUS Gründer August Bremicker und seiner Söhne. Dank ihnen und der nachfolgenden Generationen hat ABUS weltweit mehr als das erreicht und zählt heute „sicher, stabil und zuverlässig" zu den besten Industrieunternehmen Deutschlands.

domestic, commercial and mobile security products: from mechanical and mechatronic locks for building security to newly developed motorbike locks, bicycle locks and helmets to electronic access control systems and complex smart home systems.

ABUS promotes the development and implementation of innovative security solutions for both private and commercial users. The ABUS TOUCH, for example, is part of a new generation of padlocks that can be unlocked by fingerprint and programmed to accept up to 20 fingerprints. These padlocks secure and unlock cellar doors, tool sheds and many other facilities easily and conveniently – without the need for a key. The IoTect 9001 is a digital locking module that can be used for purposes such as transporting valuable or sensitive goods, as the lock is controlled and managed via the web-based ABUS cMap interface. This cloud-based portal displays all relevant information about the user's locks in an online dashboard and enables them to grant individual, time-limited and geographically limited access rights.

ABUS is committed to Germany as a location for industry, with five domestic production sites and branch offices. The corporate group also includes ABUS August Bremicker Söhne KG in Wetter, a town close to the Ruhr and the place the company was founded, ABUS Security Center GmbH & Co. KG in Affing near Augsburg, and ABUS Pfaffenheim GmbH in Jahnsdorf near Chemnitz. As an industrial enterprise with global operations and a market leader in several segments, ABUS sells its products across every continent with around 25 subsidiaries in Europe, the USA, Latin American and Asia. ABUS has around 4,000 employees around the world and is now led by the fourth and fifth generations of the Bremicker family. ABUS has received numerous titles and accolades from prestigious publications and institutions for its products (DIE WELT, 2023), innovations (FOCUS Money, 2020; Capital, 2021; DIE WELT, 2021) and as an employer (WirtschaftsWoche, 2020; F.A.Z.-Institut, 2020; STERN, 2021; Statista, 2021; CHIP, 2021).

"Making life a little safer" – that was the maxim by which ABUS founder August Bremicker and his sons lived and worked. Thanks to their efforts, and those of subsequent generations, ABUS has achieved that and more around the world, becoming a "safe, stable and reliable" member of Germany's industrial elite.

»ABUS steht nicht nur für Produkte, sondern für eine Emotion: das gute Gefühl der Sicherheit.«

Zeitgemäße Lösungen zur Videoüberwachung und mehr – denn für den ganzheitlichen Ansatz in Sachen Unternehmenssicherheit bietet ABUS die Integration von Alarm- und Zutrittsprodukten als technologieübergreifende Lösung

Contemporary solutions for video surveillance and much more besides – because, as part of its holistic approach to commercial security, ABUS integrates alarm and access control systems to create a cross-technology solution

Für den Wochenendausflug, für das tägliche Pendeln, für Profi-Sportler*innen – mit einem umfassenden Sortiment an Fahrradhelmen bietet ABUS für jeden Typ Radfahrer*in das passende Produkt

Whether it's for a weekend trip, the daily commute or professional athletes, ABUS offers the perfect product for every type of cyclist in its extensive range of bicycle helmets

»ABUS provides more than just products, it provides an emotion: the good feeling of security.«

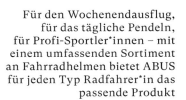

Zahlreiche Sicherheitsmerkmale auf kleinstem Raum: der Türzylinder MagTec verfügt unter anderem über eine patentgeschützte Magnettechnologie, die einen zusätzlichen Schutz vor unberechtigten Schlüsselkopien bietet

Numerous security features in a compact design: the MagTec door cylinder features patented magnet technology that offers additional protection against unauthorised key copying

ACHENBACH

Mit der Kraft einer Lokomotive und der Präzision eines Uhrwerkes produzieren Folienwalzwerke von Achenbach dünnste Aluminiumfolie mit Geschwindigkeiten von mehr als 2000 Meter pro Minute. Die auf höchstem technologischen Niveau gefertigten Anlagen des Weltmarktführers haben in diesem Segment einen Marktanteil von 75 Prozent. Die Folien, die bis zu einer minimalen Stärke von 0,0045 Millimeter (entspricht etwa dem 15tel der Dicke eines menschlichen Haares) gewalzt und anschließend weiterverarbeitet werden, finden zum Beispiel in nachhaltigen Verpackungslösungen für Lebensmittel und Pharmaprodukte oder als Kondensator- und Haushaltsfolie Einsatz. Auch Lithium-Ionen-Batterien für Elektroautos benötigen dünnste Kathodenfolie, die fast ausschließlich auf Achenbach-Walzwerken produziert wird.

Das Familienunternehmen aus Kreuztal-Buschhütten ist führender Spezialist für Walzwerke und Folienschneidmaschinen und liefert maßgeschneiderte Anlagen zur Herstellung und Verarbeitung von Aluminiumfolien und -bändern in die ganze Welt.

1452 errichteten die Gebrüder Busch am Ferndorfbach im heutigen Kreuztal einen wasserradgetriebenen Eisenhammer. Aus verhüttetem Eisen stellten sie schmiedbares Eisen her und waren mit ihrer Gründung namensgebend für den Ort Buschhütten, bis heute Stammsitz des Unternehmens. Nach der Übernahme durch die Gebrüder Achenbach entstand 1846 deren Eisengießerei. Mit einer wahrhaft dynamischen Entwicklung des Unternehmens über Generationen wurde Achenbach durch die Weiterentwicklung des Walzens von Nicht-Eisen-Metallen schließlich zum Spezialisten unter den Walzwerkbauern. In achter Generation ist André E. Barten als Gesellschafter und Vorsitzender der Geschäftsführung für das Familienunternehmen verantwortlich.

With the power of a locomotive and the precision of a watch mechanism, foil rolling mills from Achenbach produce aluminium foil at rates in excess of 2,000 metres per minute. As the world market leader, it relies on state-of-the-art production systems and holds a 75% market share in this segment. The aluminium foils, which can be rolled as thin as 0.0045 millimetres (around one-fifteenth of the width of a human hair) before subsequent processing, are used in applications ranging from sustainable packaging solutions for food and pharmaceutical products to capacitor foil and household tin foil. Lithium-ion batteries for electric cars also require exceptionally thin cathode foils, which are almost exclusively produced by Achenbach rolling mills.

The family business from the Buschhütten district of Kreuztal, near Siegen, is a leading specialist in rolling mills and foil slitting machines. It supplies customised systems for producing and processing aluminium films and strips to customers around the world.

In 1452, the Busch brothers erected a waterwheel-driven hammer mill on the banks of the Ferndorfbach, a river that flows through Kreuztal, where they turned smelted iron into forgeable iron. Their enterprise ultimately gave the town of Buschhütten its name, with the company based there to this day. In 1846, the Achenbach brothers acquired the business and constructed an iron foundry. The company enjoyed truly dynamic growth over several generations: by refining the process of rolling non-ferrous metals, Achenbach became a specialist rolling mill developer. André E. Barten, President and CEO of Achenbach, is the eighth generation to lead the family-owned company.

Today, Achenbach has 550 employees around the world, 500 of whom are based at the company's headquarters in Buschhütten. As a systems supplier, the company

ACHENBACH

Das Achenbach OPTIMILL® Folienwalzwerk zur Herstellung dünnster Aluminiumfolien, unter anderem für die Verpackungsindustrie

The Achenbach OPTIMILL® foil rolling mill for producing ultra-thin aluminium foils, including for the packaging industry

Heute beschäftigt Achenbach weltweit 550 Mitarbeitende, davon 500 am Stammsitz in Buschhütten. Als Systemanbieter konstruiert, fertigt und montiert das Unternehmen von der einzelnen Technologiekomponente bis hin zur schlüsselfertigen Gesamtanlage alles aus einer Hand. Ebenfalls zum Portfolio zählen Systeme zur Abluftreinigung und energieoptimierten Abscheidung, Rückgewinnung und Regeneration von Walzöl sowie eine cloudbasierte Plattform zur digitalen Anlagenvernetzung ganzer Produktionsprozesse. Diese Technologie, mit der sowohl die Produktivität des Herstellungsprozesses als auch die Qualität und der CO_2-Fußabdruck des Produktes anlagenübergreifend überwacht, analysiert und optimiert werden kann, wurde 2019 vom Handelsblatt mit dem Award „Best Industrial Business Solution 4.0" (2. Platz) ausgezeichnet.

Basis allen Handelns ist das Leitbild „Technology for Future Concepts", das fest im Mindset verankert ist: Achenbach hat das Wissen, um die Zukunftsideen seiner Kunden umzusetzen, damit diese in ihrem Markt erfolgreich sind. Technologisches Know-how und gezielte Entwicklungsarbeit – derzeit hält Achenbach etwa 100 Patente – sind dabei entscheidend, um den Herausforderungen der Zukunft, insbesondere dem Anspruch an Nachhaltigkeit zu begegnen. Unterstützt durch Künstliche Intelligenz und IoT-Technologie setzt das Unternehmen Maßstäbe mit zukunftsweisenden Innovationen und Produkten, die eine gleichermaßen profitable wie energieeffiziente und ressourcenschonende Produktion ermöglichen.

Leuchtturmprojekt ist der Campus Buschhütten: In Zusammenarbeit mit verschiedenen Partnern aus Wissenschaft, regionaler Industrie und Start-ups ist in einer früheren Produktionshalle auf dem Firmengelände ein Raum für digitale Transformation geschaffen worden, an dem innovative Produktionstechnologien erforscht und erprobt werden – ein optimales Umfeld für die Aus- und Weiterbildung der Fachkräfte von morgen und Ort der modernen Lehrwerkstatt von Achenbach.

Vorsprünge in der Technologie sind immer Vorsprünge durch Menschen. Neben der hohen Innovationskraft zeichnet sich das Unternehmen auch durch seine gesellschaftliche Verantwortung aus. 2021 durften Geschäftsführung und Betriebsrat den renommierten „Preis Soziale Marktwirtschaft" der Konrad-Adenauer-Stiftung in Berlin entgegennehmen, mit dem Achenbach für seine gelebte Sozialpartnerschaft ausgezeichnet wurde.

Hinter allem steht ein über 570-jähriges, zukunftsorientiertes Familienunternehmen: 100 Prozent unabhängig, eigentümergeführt, innovativ und damit in jeder Epoche technologisch führend sowie durch vielfältiges regionales Engagement im Siegerland tief verwurzelt.

designs, manufactures and assembles everything from individual technological components to whole production plant – all from a single source. Its portfolio also includes systems for exhaust air purification and the energy-optimised separation, recovery and regeneration of rolling oil as well as a cloud-based platform to digitally network machinery throughout entire production processes. In 2019, this technology – which makes it possible to monitor, analyse and optimise production process efficiency and the quality and carbon footprint of finished products – achieved second place in the Handelsblatt "Best Industrial Business Solution 4.0" award.

Everything Achenbach does is based around its vision of creating "technology for future concepts", which is firmly anchored in the company's mindset. Achenbach has the technological knowledge to implement the future ideas of its customers with the aim of supporting them to be successful in their market. In total, Achenbach holds around 100 patents at present, and its combination of technological expertise and targeted development are decisive in meeting the challenges of the future, especially in relation to sustainability. Incorporating artificial intelligence and IoT technologies, the company sets new standards with pioneering innovations and products that facilitate profitable, energy-efficient and resource-conserving production.

Campus Buschhütten is a flagship project for the company: Achenbach has teamed up with various partners from the world of science, as well as industrial firms and start-ups from across the region, to create a space dedicated to the digital transformation at a former production hall on the company's premises. It accommodates research and testing of innovative production technologies – and provides a perfect setting in which to train the specialists of tomorrow as well as a workshop for Achenbach's apprentices.

Technological advances are always the result of human achievement. In addition to its impressive innovative capacity, the company is also characterised by its social responsibility. In 2021, the Management Board and Works Council received the prestigious Social Market Economy award from the Konrad-Adenauer-Stiftung in Berlin, which recognised Achenbach's commitment to the social partnership.

Behind all of this is a more than 570-year-old, future-oriented, family-owned business: 100% independent, owner-operated, innovative and a technological leader in every era, with wide-ranging regional engagement that maintains its deep roots in Siegerland.

»Mit unserem Wissen ermöglichen wir Kunden, ihre Zukunftsideen zu verwirklichen, neue Produkte zu entwickeln und in ihren Märkten erfolgreich zu sein.«

Achenbach OPTIFOIL HeavySlit® Schneidmaschine zur Verarbeitung von Aluminiumbändern und -folien, etwa für Kaffeekapseln, Wärmetauscher und Klimaanlagen

Achenbach OPTIFOIL HeavySlit® slitting machine for processing aluminium strips and foils, such as for coffee capsules, heat exchangers and air-conditioning systems

SLAB – die Smarte Lernfabrik auf dem Campus Buschhütten

The Smart Training Factory (Smarte Lernfabrik Achenbach Buschhütten – SLAB) at Campus Buschhütten

CEO André E. Barten

VISION

»With our knowledge, we enable our customers to realise their future ideas, develop new products and be successful in their markets.«

ALTENDORF GROUP

Die Altendorf Group ist ein weltweit führendes Unternehmen in der Herstellung hochwertiger Formatkreissägen und Kantenanleimmaschinen. Ihre Geschichte begann 1906 mit der Gründung durch Wilhelm Altendorf und der Entwicklung der ersten Format- und Besäumkreissäge, die das bis heute gültige Prinzip der Formatkreissäge „System Altendorf" begründete. Seitdem sorgt die Altendorf Group regelmäßig für wesentliche Innovationen und neue Entwicklungen innerhalb der holzverarbeitenden Handwerksbranche.

Im Laufe der Jahrzehnte hat sich das Unternehmen kontinuierlich weiterentwickelt und ist zum Weltmarktführer im Premiumsegment aufgestiegen. Es zählt zu den Hidden Champions des deutschen Mittelstandes und genießt weltweit hohes Ansehen. Das erfolgreichste Produkt ist die Formatkreissäge F 45, international bekannt als „Die Altendorf" – für viele mittlerweile Synonym für die Produktkategorie Formatkreissägen. Der Name Altendorf steht für höchste Qualität, technologischen Fortschritt und Partnerschaft mit dem Handwerk. Die Ausrichtung aller Aktivitäten und Entwicklungen innerhalb der Altendorf Group liegt auf der Kundenzentriertheit, denn das Unternehmen hat stets die Bedürfnisse, Wünsche und Anforderungen seiner Kunden im Blick. Qualität, Weitsicht und ständige Innovationen machen die Altendorf Group zu einer vertrauensvollen und kompetenten Partnerin des Handwerks – jetzt und in Zukunft.

Innovation ist tief in der DNA des Unternehmens verankert. Die neueste bahnbrechende Entwicklung ist HAND GUARD, ein weltweit einzigartiges Früherkennungssystem mit zwei Kameras zum Schutz von Mensch, Maschine und Material. Diese Technologie wurde mit renommierten Preisen wie dem Deutschen Arbeitsschutzpreis, dem IVSS International Safety Award und dem World Technology Leader Award ausgezeichnet und Altendorf dafür zum „Innovator des

The Altendorf Group is a world market leader in the manufacture of high-quality sliding table saws and edge banding machines. Its history stretches back to 1906 and its foundation by Wilhelm Altendorf. He developed the first sliding table saw and edging circular saw, which established the "Altendorf system" for sliding table saws – a principle that underpins the company's saws to this day. Since then, the Altendorf Group has regularly produced significant innovations and shaped new developments in the manual woodworking industry.

The company has developed continuously over the years, rising to become the world market leader in the premium segment. It is one of the hidden champions of the German Mittelstand and enjoys an excellent reputation around the world. Its most successful product is the F 45 sliding table saw: known internationally simply as "The Altendorf", it has now become a synonym for sliding table saws more widely. The name Altendorf stands for top quality, technological progress and partnership with the skilled trades. The principle of customer centricity guides all activities and developments within the Altendorf Group, as the company always strives to respond to the wishes and requirements of its customers. Quality, foresight and constant innovation make the Altendorf Group a trustworthy and competent partner for the trade – both today and in the future.

Innovation is deeply embedded in the company's DNA. Its latest groundbreaking development is HAND GUARD, a globally unique early detection system with two cameras to protect people, machinery and materials. This technology has won prestigious accolades, including the German Occupational Safety Award, the ISSA International Safety Award, the World Technology Leader Award and the Innovator of the Year Award. Altendorf is proud to be the first and only mechanical engineering company to have developed an AI-assisted

Unternehmensname
ALTENDORF GROUP

Industriezweig
SEKUNDÄRE HOLZVERARBEITUNG

Gründung
1906 IN BERLIN

Gründer
WILHELM ALTENDORF

Produkte
FORMATKREISSÄGEN UND KANTENANLEIMMASCHINEN

Vertrieb
WELTWEITES VERTRIEBSNETZ, TOCHTERGESELLSCHAFTEN IN AUSTRALIEN, CHINA, INDIEN UND USA

Mitarbeitende
400

Company name
ALTENDORF GROUP

Industry
SECONDARY WOODWORKING

Founded
1906 IN BERLIN

Founder
WILHELM ALTENDORF

Products
SLIDING TABLE SAWS AND EDGE BANDING MACHINES

Distribution
WORLDWIDE DISTRIBUTION NETWORK; SUBSIDIARIES IN AUSTRALIA, CHINA, INDIA AND THE USA

Employees
400

HAND GUARD Format-kreissäge mit Sicherheits-assistenzsystem

HAND GUARD sliding table saw with safety assistance system

Jahres" gekürt. Altendorf ist stolz darauf, das erste und einzige Maschinenbauunternehmen zu sein, das mithilfe von Künstlicher Intelligenz in Zusammenarbeit mit Berufsgenossenschaft und IFA ein derartiges zertifiziertes Sicherheitssystem entwickelt hat.

Zwei große Marken, eine starke Gruppe: Seit 2018 gehört auch Hebrock mit seinen hochwertigen Kantenanleimmaschinen zur Altendorf Group. Diese strategische Akquisition stärkt die Position als Komplettanbieter und ermöglicht es, den Kunden umfassendere Lösungen anzubieten. Damit bietet die Altendorf Group zwei wichtige Bearbeitungsbereiche für das plattenverarbeitende Handwerk.

Die Unternehmensgruppe agiert als digitaler Impulsgeber für das Handwerk und als Vorreiter im Bereich der Digitalisierung. Mit der App myALTENDORFGROUP und der Voice-Control-Sprachsteuerung wird die Arbeit der Kunden erleichtert und Maßstäbe in der Branche gesetzt, etwa durch den Chat- oder Videosupport des Altendorf Group Service direkt an der Maschine. Zudem profitieren Anwender*innen von einem direkten Kontakt und zahlreichen Mehrwertleistungen sowie einem professionellen Service und einer zuverlässigen Ersatzteilversorgung.

Mit Tochtergesellschaften in Australien, China, Indien und den USA ist die Altendorf Group global präsent. Und mit insgesamt 400 Mitarbeiter*innen und drei Produktionsstandorten in Minden und Hüllhorst, Deutschland, sowie Qinhuangdao, China, ist die Altendorf Group bestens aufgestellt, um als Innovationstreiberin in der holzverarbeitenden Handwerksbranche weiteres nationales und internationales Wachstum zu realisieren. Diese globale Präsenz und das internationale Renommee sind das Ergebnis harter Arbeit und kontinuierlicher Weiterentwicklung.

Der Erfolg beruht nicht nur auf herausragenden Produkten, sondern auch auf dem Engagement und der Fachkompetenz des Teams. Mit über 100 Jahren Erfahrung bildet das Expertenwissen einen zentralen Pfeiler der Innovationskraft und anhaltenden Marktführerschaft. Die Altendorf Group ist nicht nur ein Unternehmen, sondern vor allem auch eine Gemeinschaft von Menschen, die sich für Exzellenz und Innovation einsetzen. Die Erfolgsgeschichte ist noch lange nicht zu Ende: Die Altendorf Group ist fest entschlossen, auch in Zukunft die höchsten Standards zu setzen und einen wesentlichen Beitrag für die holzverarbeitende Handwerksbranche, weitere Anwendungsbereiche und die Gesellschaft zu leisten.

safety solution in cooperation with the German Employers' Liability Insurance Association (BG) and the German Social Accident Insurance's Institute for Occupational Health and Safety (IFA).

Two great brands, one strong group: Hebrock, which produces high-quality edge banding machines, became part of the Altendorf Group in 2018. This strategic acquisition consolidated Altendorf's position as a full-range supplier and made it possible to offer customers more comprehensive solutions. Consequently, the Altendorf Group covers two important machining areas for the panel processing trade.

The Group acts as a digital innovator for the skilled trades and a pioneer of digitalisation. The myALTENDORFGROUP app and voice control function make customers' work easier and set standards in the industry, such as chat and video support by the Altendorf Group's service specialists, directly at the machine. In addition, users benefit from direct contact, various value-added services, professional customer service and a reliable supply of spare parts.

The Altendorf Group maintains a global presence through subsidiaries in Australia, China, India and the USA. With a total of 400 employees and three production sites – in Minden and Hüllhorst, Germany, and in Qinhuangdao, China – the Altendorf Group is ideally positioned to realise further national and international growth as a driver of innovation in the manual woodworking industry. Its global presence and international reputation are the result of hard work and continuous development.

The company's success is based not only on outstanding products, but also on the commitment and expertise of its team. Drawing on over 100 years of experience, its expert knowledge forms a central pillar of its innovative strength and continued market leadership. The Altendorf Group is not just a company: it is a community of people committed to excellence and innovation. And its success story is far from over: the Altendorf Group is determined to continue setting the highest standards and making a significant contribution to the manual woodworking industry, other areas of application and society as a whole.

»Qualität, Innovation und Kundenzentriertheit sind tief in unserer DNA verankert.«

Blick in die Produktion bei Altendorf

Production activities at Altendorf

Peter Schwenk, CEO der Altendorf Group

Peter Schwenk, CEO of the Altendorf Group

Vit Kafka, CSO der Altendorf Group

Vit Kafka, CSO of the Altendorf Group

PETER SCHWENK, CEO OF THE ALTENDORF GROUP

»Quality, innovation and customer centricity are deeply embedded in our DNA.«

Firmensitz der Altendorf Group in Minden

Headquarters of the Altendorf Group in Minden

ARNO ARNOLD

Das Miteinander ist entscheidend. Weil niemand allein das Ganze beherrschen kann und erst gemeinsam Projekte erfolgreich gelingen, ob bei innovativen Schutzabdeckungen für hochsensible Maschinenteile und Apparate – oder beim Tanz. Zu beidem gehören Leidenschaft, Präzision und Idealismus. Ernst Louis Arnold muss von all dem reichlich besessen haben, als er 1864 im sächsischen Carlsfeld den Grundstein für eines der erfolgreichsten Maschinenzulieferunternehmen des Landes legte: die Arno Arnold GmbH. Sie entwickelt, konstruiert und produziert flexible Abdeckungen, um Menschen während des Fertigungsvorgangs vor Klemm- und Quetschverletzungen zu schützen sowie Maschinen und Apparate während des Arbeitsprozesses vor Spänebefall, Schmutz, Staub, Hitze oder Fetten.

Dass Arnold-Produkte wie Faltenbälge, flexible Teleskopbleche, WMB-Spiralen, Rolloabdeckungen, Gliederschürzen und einbaufertige komplette Maschinenwände heute weltweit im Maschinen- und Apparatebau, in der Medizin-, Automations-, Solar- und Automobiltechnik, ja sogar in der Raumfahrt eingesetzt werden, hängt mit dem argentinischen Tango zusammen. Ende des 19. Jahrhunderts eroberte dieser Gesellschaftstanz im 4/8-Takt die Bars der Großstädte in aller Welt – und mit ihm das Instrument, auf dem er gespielt wurde: das Bandoneon, dessen Faltenbalg die Töne weiterleitet.

Seit 1864 stellten Ernst Louis Arnold und seine Söhne das für den Tango prädestinierte Musikinstrument in feiner Handarbeit her. Bandoneons der Marke „AA" aus Carlsfeld bedienten 95 Prozent des Weltmarkts. Sie galten als Stradivaris unter den Balginstrumenten und sind heute kostbare Raritäten.

Mit der fortschreitenden Industrialisierung entwickelte Arno Arnold die Windlade für das Bandoneon weiter zum Faltenbalg für die industrielle Nutzung und erhielt für diese Erfindung 1930 das erste Patent mit der

Working together is crucial. Nobody can handle everything alone. Ultimately, it is only through cooperation that projects can succeed, whether it's innovative protective covers for highly sensitive machine parts and equipment – or the art of dance. Both rely on passion, precision and idealism. Ernst Louis Arnold must have possessed all three in abundance when, in 1864, he laid the foundations for what would become one of Germany's most successful machine suppliers: Arno Arnold GmbH. Founded in Carlsfeld, Germany, the company develops, designs and produces flexible covers to protect people from clamping and crushing injuries during manufacturing processes – while also protecting machinery and equipment from swarf, dirt, dust, heat and grease during work processes.

The fact that Arnold products such as bellows, flexible telescopic sheets, WMB spiral springs, roll-up covers, apron covers and ready-to-install complete machine walls are used around the world today in machinery and equipment construction, in medical, automation, solar and automotive technology – and, yes, even in space travel – has a lot to do with the Argentine tango. At the end of the 19th century, this ballroom dance with a 4/8 rhythm conquered bars in cities around the globe – and so too did the instrument used to play its music: the bandoneon, which features bellows that carry the musical notes.

From 1864, Ernst Louis Arnold and his sons produced fine, handcrafted models of the instrument that subsequently became inextricably linked with the tango. AA-branded bandoneons from Carlsfeld accounted for 95% of the global market. They were the Stradivarius of bellows-driven instruments and are now rare, valuable items.

As industrialisation continued to advance, Arno Arnold developed the bandoneon's windchest to produce bel-

Unternehmensname
ARNO ARNOLD GMBH

Industriezweig
MASCHINEN-, ANLAGEN- UND APPARATEBAU, MEDIZIN- UND AUTOMATIONSTECHNIK, FAHRZEUG-, TEXTIL- UND SOLARTECHNIK

Gründung
1864 IN CARLSFELD/ERZGEBIRGE

Gründer
ERNST LOUIS ARNOLD

Produkt
FLEXIBLER MASCHINEN- UND APPARATESCHUTZ

Vertrieb
WELTWEIT

Maschinenrückwände als einbaufertige Module. Der flexible Schutz gewährt Sicherheit für das Innere wertvoller Maschinenteile und Apparate

Machine back walls as ready-to-install modules. This flexible protection keeps valuable internal machine components and equipment safe

Company name
ARNO ARNOLD GMBH

Industry
MACHINERY, PLANT AND EQUIPMENT CONSTRUCTION; MEDICAL, AUTOMATION, AUTOMOTIVE, TEXTILE AND SOLAR TECHNOLOGIES

Founded
1864 IN CARLSFELD, ERZGEBIRGE

Founder
ERNST LOUIS ARNOLD

Product
FLEXIBLE MACHINERY AND EQUIPMENT PROTECTION

Distribution
WORLDWIDE

Bezeichnung „Harmonikaförmig gestalteter Balg zur Schutzabdeckung für Führungsbahnen an Werkzeugmaschinen, in Sonderheit an Schlittenführung für Schleifmaschinen".

Der Zweite Weltkrieg und seine Folgen setzten dem Familienunternehmen ein ungewolltes Ende. Arno Arnold kehrte dem sächsischen Carlsfeld den Rücken und nahm 1949 im hessischen Obertshausen den Betrieb wieder auf. In den 1970er-Jahren vollzogen Arno Arnolds Tochter Sigrid Weinmann und ihr Ehemann Günter den endgültigen Wandel vom Musikinstrumentenhandwerk zum Industrieunternehmen. Seither ist der Firma Innovation in die DNA gelegt. Sie beweist fortwährend ihre Innovationskraft durch viele Patent-, Gebrauchsmuster- und Schutzanmeldungen.

Entwickelt, gefertigt und weltweit vertrieben werden Arnold-Produkte in Obertshausen und auch wieder in Carlsfeld sowie in einer Tochterfirma in China. Zusätzlich verkaufen eine Tochter in Italien und Geschäftspartner in den USA und Kanada das Sortiment. Mit der Übernahme der Geschäftsleitung 1984 durch Simone Weinmann-Mang, der Enkelin Arno Arnolds, und ihren Ehemann Wolf Matthias Mang entwickelte sich das Familienunternehmen zum internationalen Experten für kundenspezifische Lösungen im Bereich Schutz- und Sicherheitssysteme. Um sicherzustellen, dass Arnold Schutzabdeckungen im täglichen Einsatz hohen Anforderungen dauerhaft gerecht werden, wurde ein werkseigenes Testzentrum errichtet. Dort werden in aufwendigen Dauertests und Simulationsverfahren Material, Flexibilität, Robustheit und Verfahrgeschwindigkeiten geprüft.

Mit Isabelle Mang und Dr. Benedikt Himbert führt seit 2021 die sechste Generation die Geschäfte. Das junge Paar treibt den Erfolgskurs des traditionsreichen Familienbetriebs weiter voran, vertraut auf die Expertise der Mitarbeitenden und belohnt Fleiß und Loyalität mit fairer Bezahlung, hoher Wertschätzung, vielfältigen Weiterbildungs- und Studienprogrammen und vielen weiteren Benefits.

Persönliche, christliche und unternehmensspezifische Werte verbindet die Geschäftsleitung mit dem Kerngedanken der Nachhaltigkeit. Neben der gesellschaftlichen Verantwortung, die Arno Arnold seit Jahrzehnten mit Bildungsprojekten und sozialem Engagement wahrnimmt, wurden in den vergangenen Jahren der sparsame Umgang mit Ressourcen sowie die konsequente Reduktion von Emissionen in den Fokus gerückt. Diese Klimastrategie berücksichtigt ökonomische, ökologische und soziale Aspekte gleichermaßen und hält das Unternehmen zukunftsfähig.

lows suitable for industrial use. In 1930, it secured its first patent for this invention, described as a "harmonica-shaped bellows for the protective cover of guideways on machine tools, in particular on slide guides for grinding machines".

World War Two and its aftermath put an unwanted end to the family company. Arno Arnold moved away from Carlsfeld, Saxony, and resumed operations in Obertshausen, Hesse, in 1949. In the 1970s, Arno Arnold's daughter Sigrid Weinmann and her husband Günter finally shifted the company's focus away from crafting musical instruments, turning into an industrial enterprise. Innovation has been part of its DNA ever since. It continues to demonstrate its innovative power through numerous applications for patents, utility models and trademarks.

Today, Arnold products are developed, produced and globally distributed from Obertshausen and, once again, Carlsfeld, as well as by a subsidiary in China. In addition, a subsidiary in Italy and business partners in the USA and Canada market the company's product range. When Simone Weinmann-Mang, the granddaughter of Arno Arnold, and her husband Wolf Matthias Mang took the reins in 1984, the family company developed into an international expert in customer-specific solutions in the field of safety and protection systems. The company established an in-house test centre to ensure that Arnold protective covers consistently satisfy stringent requirements in day-to-day use. The facility accommodates sophisticated endurance testing and simulations to examine products' materials, flexibility, robustness and travel speeds.

In 2021, Isabelle Mang and Dr Benedikt Himbert became the sixth generation of the family to join the company's leadership. The young couple have continued the tradition-steeped family company's pursuit of success, trusting in their employees' expertise and rewarding their industry and loyalty with fair pay, high appreciation, wide-ranging professional development and study programs and a range of other benefits.

The management combines personal, Christian and company-specific values with the core idea of sustainability. In addition to social responsibility, which Arno Arnold has practised for decades through educational projects and social engagement, in recent years the company has also focused on promoting sparing use of resources and systematically reducing its emissions. This climate strategy incorporates economic, environmental and social aspects in equal measure and ensures the company is ready for the future.

»Die wichtigsten Innovationen sind die, die das Denken verändern.«

Arno Arnold ist weltweit ein gefragter Ansprechpartner, wenn es darum geht, kundenspezifische Schutzabdeckungen zu entwickeln und zu produzieren – just in time und funktionsgeprüft

Arno Arnold is a sought-after partner around the world for the development and production of customer-specific protective covers – providing just-in-time, function-tested solutions

Die Eheleute Wolf Matthias Mang und Simone Weinmann-Mang leiten das Unternehmen seit 1984. Die sechste Generation ist mit Isabelle Himbert (geb. Mang) und ihrem Mann, Dr. Benedikt Himbert, bereits in Geschäftsführungsverantwortung

Husband-and-wife team Wolf Matthias Mang and Simone Weinmann-Mang have led the company since 1984. Isabelle Himbert (née Mang) and her husband, Dr Benedikt Himbert, have since become the sixth generation of the family to join the company's management

»The most important innovations are the ones that change the way we think.«

Arnold-Schutzabdeckungen haben sich millionenfach in den unterschiedlichsten Anwendungen bewährt

Arnold protective covers have proven their worth millions of times in all manner of applications

BAADER

Ein Blick zurück ins Jahr 1919: Lübecks Straßen sind von Pferdekutschen geprägt, Technologien wie Fernseher oder Computer noch Utopie. Doch auf der pittoresken Lübecker Altstadtinsel legte Rudolph Max Joseph Baader den Grundstein für eine Revolution: Er gründete die Firma Nordischer Maschinenbau, aus der in den folgenden 100 Jahren der Technologieführer BAADER emporwuchs.

Von der ersten automatisierten Fischverarbeitungsanlage und Filetiermaschine – eine Revolution zu der damaligen Zeit, die die Industrie zum Schwärmen brachte und zum Standard wurde – bis zu den heutigen Hightech-Systemen, die im Rhythmus eines elektronischen Herzschlages bis zu 800 Fischfilets pro Minute herstellen: BAADER schafft als Innovationsführer die perfekte Balance zwischen Technologie und Vision.

Die stetige Innovationskraft des Unternehmens blieb auch nach dem Tod des Gründers 1953 erhalten und wurde sogar ausgeweitet. Unter der Leitung von Rudolf G. T. Baader und später von dessen visionärer Tochter Petra entwickelte sich BAADER kontinuierlich weiter und integrierte auch Geflügelverarbeitungsmaschinen durch den Kauf der US-Firma Johnson Food Equipment und der dänischen Gesellschaft Linco Food Systems. Diese strategischen Schritte sicherten BAADER den Platz als weltweitem Marktführer für Fischverarbeitungsanlagen und Spitzenreiter in der Geflügelverarbeitung.

Es ist diese unermüdliche Forschungsleidenschaft und dieser stete Wissensdurst, der das Unternehmen über Generationen auszeichnet. Und der Know-how-Transfer, gepaart mit einer tiefverwurzelten Wertschätzung für Nahrung, Technologie und Menschlichkeit. „Unser Herz schlägt für Food, für Technologie und für Menschen", formuliert es BAADER-CEO Petra Baader treffend.

Let's go back to 1919: Lübeck's streets are filled with horse-drawn carriages, while technologies such as televisions and computers are a utopian dream. Yet here, in Lübeck's picturesque Old Town, an island flanked by branches of a river, Rudolph Max Joseph Baader laid the foundations for a revolution. He founded Nordischer Maschinenbau, a company that, over the course of the following century, grew to become the technology leader BAADER.

From the first automated fish processing line and filleting machine – a revolution at the time, which set the industry into raptures and became the new standard – through to today's high-tech systems that produce up to 800 fish fillets per minute with the consistency of an electronic heartbeat, BAADER strikes the perfect balance between technology and vision as a leader of innovation.

The company's constant innovation continued and even intensified after the death of its founder in 1953. Under the leadership of Rudolf G. T. Baader and, subsequently, his visionary daughter, Petra, BAADER continued to develop and also integrated poultry processing machinery following the acquisition of the US company Johnson Food Equipment and the Danish firm Linco Food Systems. These strategic steps secured BAADER's place as the global market leader for fish processing systems and a leading provider of poultry processing solutions.

It is precisely this tireless passion for research and an unquenchable thirst for knowledge that has characterised the company for generations. These qualities combine with a transfer of expertise and a deep-rooted appreciation for food, technology and humanity. Petra Baader, CEO of BAADER, aptly describes the company's values: "Food, technology and people all have a special place in our heart."

Unternehmensname
BAADER GLOBAL SE

Industriezweig
**LEBENSMITTELTECHNOLOGIE/
MASCHINEN- UND ANLAGENBAU**

Gründer
RUDOLPH MAX JOSEPH BAADER

Hauptfertigungsstätte
LÜBECK

Vertrieb
WELTWEIT

Mitarbeitende
1600

Company name
BAADER GLOBAL SE

Industry
**FOOD TECHNOLOGY/MECHANICAL
AND SYSTEMS ENGINEERING**

Founder
RUDOLPH MAX JOSEPH BAADER

Main production facility
LÜBECK

Distribution
WORLDWIDE

Employees
1,600

BAADER entwickelt komplette
Verarbeitungslösungen für Fisch und
Geflügel – über sämtliche Prozess-
schritte. Hier zu sehen der BAADER-
Geflügel-Deboner Modell 660A14

BAADER develops complete processing solutions for fish and poultry
across all process steps. The machine
shown here is the BAADER 660A14
poultry deboner

Inmitten der digitalen Transformation setzt BAADER Maßstäbe über seinen Maschinenpark hinaus, strebend nach Innovationen entlang der gesamten Nahrungsmittelkette. Ein Ziel hat das Lückecker Unternehmen immer fest im Blick: eine wachsende Weltbevölkerung mit qualitativ hochwertigen, nachhaltigen Lebensmitteln zu versorgen. Tierwohl, Transparenz und die optimale Ressourcennutzung stehen dabei im Mittelpunkt. Mit über einem Jahrhundert Erfahrung und einem pulsierenden Netzwerk von mehr als 1600 passionierten Mitarbeiter*innen in über 100 Ländern steht BAADER für zuverlässige Technologie und Qualität. Stets mit dem Fokus auf Mensch und Nachhaltigkeit, entwirft das Unternehmen Lösungen für die Fisch- und Geflügelverarbeitung, die Betriebskosten senken, CO_2-Fußabdrücke optimieren und den Energieverbrauch minimieren – und dabei 100 Prozent der Proteinquellen nutzen.

Der Hidden Champion ist ein glänzendes Aushängeschild für „made in Germany", weil BAADER nicht nur für das traditionelle deutsche Unternehmertum steht, sondern auch globaler Partner für eine nachhaltige Lebensmittelproduktion ist. 2022 kündigte BAADER die Gründung der Holdinggesellschaft BAADER Global SE an, die den Weg für zukünftiges Wachstum ebnet, ohne die familiären Wurzeln zu vernachlässigen. Denn trotz neuer Strukturen ändert sich die Eigentümerkonstellation nicht: BAADER ist und bleibt ein Familienunternehmen. Mit den Geschäftsführern Robert Focke (Fisch) und Dr. Norbert Engberg (Geflügel und Digitalisierung) an der Spitze, verkörpert die BAADER Global SE sowohl Innovation als auch Beständigkeit. Und die BAADER Global SE bietet laut CFO Torsten Krausen ein passendes Dach für die gesamte Gruppe, unter dem sich die kulturell unterschiedlichen Standorte weltweit mit der Marke verbinden. Darüber hinaus unterstreicht die neue Struktur, dass BAADER ein internationales und wachsendes Unternehmen ist.

Seine Sachverständigkeit nutzt BAADER, Trends entlang der gesamten Lebensmittelwertschöpfungskette zu interpretieren und zu prognostizieren. In enger Zusammenarbeit mit seinen Kunden strebt das Unternehmen nach mehr Effizienz, Rückverfolgbarkeit, Transparenz, Rentabilität und Nachhaltigkeit. Das Ziel: die Nutzung von Lebensmittelressourcen zu maximieren, indem Verarbeitungslösungen angeboten werden, die Rentabilität und Nachhaltigkeit in Einklang bringen. Als typisches Familienunternehmen hat sich dieser Ansatz in den über 100 Jahren seit seiner Gründung konstant bewährt.

In the context of the digital transformation, BAADER sets the standard in its machinery and beyond, striving to generate innovations throughout the entire food value chain. The Lübeck-based company never loses sight of its goal: to provide the world's growing population with high-quality, sustainable food. Animal welfare, transparency and optimal use of resources are all central considerations. With over a century of experience and a vibrant network of over 1,600 passionate employees across 100 countries, BAADER is known for its reliable technology and high quality. With an unwavering focus on people and sustainability, the company produces solutions for the fish and poultry processing sector that cut operating costs, optimise carbon footprints and minimise energy consumption – while making use of 100% of protein sources.

This hidden champion is a shining example of quality machinery made in Germany. Ultimately, BAADER not only continues the German tradition of entrepreneurship but is also a global partner for sustainable food production. In 2022, BAADER announced the establishment of a holding company, BAADER Global SE, thereby paving the way for future growth without abandoning its family roots. Despite the introduction of new structures, the company's ownership remains unchanged: BAADER is – and will remain – a family company. Led by its Managing Directors, Robert Focke (Fish) and Dr Norbert Engberg (Poultry and Digitalisation), Baader Global SE embodies both innovation and consistency. According to its CFO, Torsten Krausen, BAADER Global SE is the ideal umbrella to cover the entire corporate group, uniting culturally distinct locations around the world with the brand. Furthermore, the new corporate structure underscores BAADER's identity as an international, growing enterprise.

BAADER applies its expertise to interpret and forecast trends throughout the food industry's value creation chain. Collaborating closely with its customers, the company strives to improve efficiency, traceability, transparency, profitability and sustainability. Its goal is to extract maximum value from food resources by offering processing solutions that square profitability with sustainability. This approach has consistently proven its worth in the more than 100-year history of this exemplary family company.

PETRA BAADER, CEO BAADER GLOBAL SE

»Bei BAADER
sind wir uns
der Verantwortung
bewusst, ein zu-
verlässiger Partner
für diejenigen
zu sein, die die Welt
ernähren.«

Innovationen – geschaffen von mehr als
1600 BAADER-Mitarbeiter*innen weltweit.
Hier am Produktionsstandort Lübeck

Innovations – created by more than 1,600
BAADER employees worldwide, including
here at its Lübeck production facility

Petra Baader inmitten ihres Teams auf der
Seafood Processing Global 2023 in Barcelona,
der Weltleitmesse für Fischverarbeitung

Petra Baader, flanked by her team, at Seafood
Processing Global 2023 in Barcelona –
the world's leading fish processing trade fair

PETRA BAADER, CEO OF BAADER GLOBAL SE

»At BAADER,
we believe we have
a responsibility
to serve as a reliable
partner to
those who feed
the world.«

CEO Petra Baader leitet
das Unternehmen in der
dritten Generation

CEO Petra Baader
is the third generation
of the family to
lead the company

BASF

„Elektromobilität, moderne Windparks oder die Ernährung der Weltbevölkerung – für all das braucht es unsere Forschung und unsere Innovationen. Mich begeistert immer wieder aufs Neue, wie winzige Moleküle dabei helfen, riesige Aufgaben zu meistern", erklärt Dr. Martin Brudermüller, Vorstandsvorsitzender der BASF SE. „Mit rund 2,3 Milliarden Euro Forschungs- und Entwicklungskosten sind wir das größte forschende Chemieunternehmen der Welt. In all unseren Geschäften entwickeln wir ständig unser Produktportfolio mit unseren Kunden in Richtung Nachhaltigkeit weiter."

Rund 111 500 Mitarbeitende tragen weltweit zum Erfolg der BASF-Gruppe bei. Die Geschäfte sind in den Segmenten Chemicals, Materials, Industrial Solutions, Surface Technologies, Nutrition & Care sowie Agricultural Solutions zusammengefasst. BASF ist in 91 Ländern vertreten. Das Unternehmen betreibt 239 Produktionsstandorte weltweit. BASF liefert Produkte und Dienstleistungen an rund 82 000 Kunden in nahezu alle Länder der Welt – vom globalen Großkunden über mittelständische Unternehmen bis hin zu Endverbraucher*innen.

Am Standort Ludwigshafen wurde 1865 der Grundstein für das Verbundkonzept gelegt, das bis heute eine Stärke von BASF ist. Die intelligente Verknüpfung und Steuerung der Anlagen im Verbund schafft effiziente Wertschöpfungsketten – von Basischemikalien bis zu hochveredelten Produkten wie Lacken oder Pflanzenschutzmitteln. Nebenprodukte aus einer Anlage werden beispielsweise als Rohstoff in anderen Betrieben genutzt. Das spart Rohstoffe und Energie, vermeidet Emissionen, senkt Logistikkosten und nutzt Synergien.

Neben Ludwigshafen betreibt BASF fünf weitere Verbundstandorte in Antwerpen/Belgien, Freeport/Texas, Geismar/Louisiana, Kuantan/Malaysia und Nanjing/China. Ein weiterer Verbundstandort entsteht bis 2030

"E-mobility, modern wind farms and feeding the world's population – all these areas require our research and our innovations. I always get excited by the fact that tiny molecules can help overcome enormous challenges," says Dr Martin Brudermüller, Chairman of the Board of Executive Directors of BASF SE. "With around €2.3 billion in research and development costs, we are the largest researching chemical company in the world. In all of our businesses, we are constantly refining our product portfolio in collaboration with our customers towards sustainability."

Around 111,500 employees contribute to the BASF Group's success worldwide. The business is divided into the Chemicals, Materials, Industrial Solutions, Surface Technologies, Nutrition & Care and Agricultural Solutions segments. BASF is present in 91 countries and operates 239 production sites worldwide. It supplies products and services to around 82,000 customers in almost every country in the world – from major global customers and medium-sized enterprises to end consumers.

The foundation for the Verbund concept was laid in 1865 at the Ludwigshafen site in Germany and is still one of BASF's strengths today. Intelligently linking and steering the Verbund plants creates efficient value chains – from basic chemicals to high value-added solutions such as coatings or crop protection products. By-products from one facility are used as feedstocks elsewhere, for example. This saves on raw materials and energy, avoids emissions, reduces logistics costs and takes advantage of synergies.

In addition to Ludwigshafen, BASF operates five other Verbund sites in Antwerp, Belgium; Freeport, Texas; Geismar, Louisiana; Kuantan, Malaysia; and Nanjing, China. A new Verbund site will be built by 2023 in Zhanjiang, China, to serve the rapidly growing market

Unternehmensname
BASF SE

Industriezweig
CHEMIE

Gründung
1865 IN MANNHEIM

Gründer
FRIEDRICH ENGELHORN

Mitarbeitende
RD. 111 500 WELTWEIT (2022)

Jahresumsatz
87,3 MRD. EURO (2022)

Company name
BASF SE

Industry
CHEMICALS

Founding
1865, MANNHEIM

Founder
FRIEDRICH ENGELHORN

Employees
AROUND 111,500 WORLDWIDE (2022)

Annual sales
€87.3 BILLION (2022)

BASF forscht weltweit an innovativen Kathodenmaterialien für hochleistungsfähige Lithium-Ionen-Batterien, die die Elektromobilität weiter voranbringen

Globally, BASF is conducting research on innovative cathode materials for high-performance lithium-ion batteries that make electromobility a reality

in Zhanjiang in China, um den dort stark wachsenden Markt zu bedienen. Von Beginn an ist der Standort als Vorreiter für Nachhaltigkeit geplant. Das Ziel: 100 Prozent Grünstrom vom ersten Tag an. Damit ist BASF Pionier in der chemischen Industrie.

Derzeit durchläuft das Unternehmen einen tiefgreifenden Transformationsprozess. Zum wiederholten Mal in der über 150-jährigen Geschichte verändert sich BASF. Diesmal in Richtung Klimaneutralität und Kreislaufwirtschaft. BASF arbeitet intensiv daran, seinen CO_2-Fußabdruck deutlich zu reduzieren. Das Ziel: Netto-Null-Emissionen bis 2050. Die Verbundstruktur ist und bleibt dafür zentral. Allein am größten Standort in Ludwigshafen sind für die grüne Transformation langfristig Investitionen von rund 2 Milliarden Euro pro Jahr eingeplant. Ludwigshafen soll der Vorzeigestandort einer klimaneutralen Chemieproduktion in Europa werden – nicht zuletzt, weil BASF hier das breiteste Portfolio an Produkten herstellt und der Verbundstandort zahlreiche Möglichkeiten eröffnet, um neue Technologien in bestehende Strukturen einzufügen und zu erproben. Die Nähe zur Forschung ist dabei ein entscheidender Vorteil.

Mehr und dringender denn je braucht es derzeit neue Wege und Lösungen. Der Klimawandel schreitet voran, natürliche Ressourcen werden knapper. Chemie ist hierbei von zentraler Bedeutung. Nur ein Beispiel von vielen: klimafreundliche Mobilität. Ab 2035 dürfen in Europa keine Autos und Kleintransporter mehr neu zugelassen werden, die noch Kohlendioxid ausstoßen. Die Alternative sind Elektroautos. Ihre Leistungsfähigkeit hängt überwiegend von der Leistungsfähigkeit der Batterie ab. Und das ist alles Chemie. Denn Batterien von Elektroautos sind nichts anderes als kleine chemische Reaktoren. Batteriematerialien von BASF sorgen dafür, dass diese Reaktoren die bestmögliche Leistung liefern.

„Wir wollen in der Chemieindustrie vorangehen und den Wandel verantwortungsvoll gestalten – mit ehrgeizigen Zielen und einem konkreten Fahrplan: So stellen wir unsere Energie- und Rohstoffversorgung schrittweise von fossilen auf erneuerbare Quellen um. Wir passen unsere Verbundstruktur als Basis für eine ressourceneffiziente, sichere und zuverlässige Produktion an die neuen Gegebenheiten an. Wir entwickeln neue, wegweisende Verfahren zur CO_2-freien und CO_2-armen Herstellung unserer Produkte. Wir beschleunigen unsere Innovationsprozesse und vertiefen die Zusammenarbeit mit Kunden, Lieferanten und weiteren Partnern, um noch leistungsfähigere Produkte zu entwickeln, die zugleich einen niedrigeren CO_2-Fußabdruck haben", fasst Brudermüller zusammen.

there. From the very beginning, the site has been planned as a pioneering example of sustainability. The goal is to use 100 per cent green electricity from day one. This makes BASF a trailblazer in the chemical industry.

BASF is currently undergoing a far-reaching transformation process. Once again in its more than 150-year history, BASF is changing. This time, it is moving toward climate neutrality and the circular economy. BASF is working intensively to significantly reduce its carbon footprint. The goal: net zero emissions by 2050. The Verbund structure is and remains central to this. At the largest site in Ludwigshafen alone, long-term investments of around €2 billion per year are planned for the green transformation. Ludwigshafen is to become the model site for climate-neutral chemical production in Europe – not least because this is where BASF manufactures the broadest portfolio of products and the Verbund site offers numerous opportunities to incorporate and test new technologies in existing structures. The proximity to R&D is a decisive advantage here.

More and more urgently than ever, new directions and solutions are needed. The climate is changing, and natural resources are becoming scarcer. Chemistry plays a key role here. Climate-smart mobility is just one example of many. From 2035, all new CO_2-emitting cars and vans may no longer be sold in Europe. The alternative is electric vehicles. Their performance depends mainly on the performance of the battery – and that's all chemistry. After all, electric car batteries are nothing more than small chemical reactors. Battery materials from BASF help to ensure that these reactors deliver the best possible performance.

"We want to lead the way in the chemical industry and responsibly shape the change – with ambitious targets and a concrete roadmap. This is why we are gradually switching our energy and raw materials supplies from fossil to renewable sources. We are adapting our Verbund structure to the new circumstances as the basis for resource-efficient, safe and reliable production. We are developing new, pioneering carbon-free and low-carbon production processes for our products. We are accelerating our innovation processes and deepening cooperation with customers, suppliers and other partners to develop high-performance products with a lower carbon footprint," summarises Brudermüller.

»Chemie für eine nachhaltige Zukunft, dafür steht BASF.«

In einem Forschungstechnikum am Standort Ludwigshafen betreibt BASF hochautomatisierte Versuchsanlagen

BASF operates highly automated experimental facilities in a research centre at its Ludwigshafen site, Germany

BASF stellt die Energieversorgung schrittweise auf erneuerbare Quellen um. Ein Beispiel: der Solarpark in Schwarzheide

BASF is gradually converting its energy supply to renewable sources. One example of this is the solar park in Schwarzheide, Germany

»At BASF, we create chemistry for a sustainable future.«

Das Stammwerk von BASF in Ludwigshafen am Rhein ist der größte von einem Unternehmen betriebene Chemiekomplex der Welt

BASF's Ludwigshafen Verbund site is the largest chemical complex in the world operated by a single company

BÖTTCHER

Seit fast 300 Jahren am Markt und weltweit die Nummer eins in der Technologie elastomerbeschichteter Walzen – das ist die Böttcher-Gruppe. In 38 Ländern geben täglich 2000 Mitarbeitende ihr Bestes, um unterschiedlichste Branchen zu betreuen. Ob für die Herstellung und Verarbeitung von Metallen, Kunst- und Zellstoffen oder von Textilien und Holz: Walzen von Böttcher sind aus vielen Industrieprozessen nicht mehr wegzudenken. Genauso ist das Unternehmen in der Welt neuer Industrien wie der Wind- und Solarenergie zu Hause. Böttcher-Walzen tragen auf, dosieren, verteilen, tauchen ein, lenken um, ziehen ab, drücken, schälen, prägen oder quetschen ab. Zudem unterstützen die langlebigen und energiesparenden Walzenbeschichtungen die Entwicklung neuer, umweltfreundlicher Verpackungsdruckmaterialien.

Auf dem Fundament eines über Generationen inhabergeführten Familienunternehmens ruhend, aber nie stillstehend: Das ist es, was Böttcher zu einem modernen, krisenfesten Unternehmen macht, zu einem echten Hidden Champion. Böttcher ist Weltmarktführer bei der Beschichtung rotationssymmetrischer Körper (Walzen, Sleeves) in industriellen Anwendungen. In Europa, Nordamerika und Asien nehmen die regionalen Böttcher-Organisationen ebenfalls Spitzenpositionen ein. In der Druckbranche ist das Unternehmen globaler Technologieführer: Circa 70 Prozent aller weltweit gebauten Druckmaschinen werden mit Walzenbeschichtungen von Böttcher erstausgerüstet. Neben Walzenbeschichtungen beliefert das Unternehmen seine Kunden aus den unterschiedlichsten Branchen mit Verbrauchsmitteln wie Waschmitteln, Drucktüchern, Lackplatten, Feuchtmittelzusätzen und anderen Druckhilfsmitteln. Einen ähnlich hohen Stellenwert hat das Unternehmen in der Metall-, Kunststoff- und Holzindustrie. Böttcher betreut rund um den Globus mehr als 50 000 Kunden und ist Entwicklungspartner von weltweit mehr als 400 Maschinenbauern.

With a history stretching back almost 300 years, the Böttcher Group is now the world market leader in the field of elastomer-coated rollers. Every day, its 2,000 employees in 38 countries give their all to support customers in various sectors. Designed to produce and process everything from metals, plastics and cellulose to textiles and wood, rollers manufactured by Böttcher are an indispensable part of many industrial processes. The company is also well established in new industries, such as wind energy and solar energy. Böttcher rollers apply, dispense, distribute, immerse, redirect, separate, print, peel, imprint and squeeze. In addition, its durable, energy-saving roller coatings support the development of new, environmentally friendly printed materials for packing.

As an owner-operated family company stretching back generations, Böttcher is built on solid foundations – but never stands still. This is what makes it a modern, resilient company, a true hidden champion. Böttcher is the world market leader in coatings for rotationally symmetrical bodies (i.e. rollers and sleeves) in industrial applications. Böttcher's regional organisations in Europe, North America and Asia are also leaders in their markets. The company is a global technology leader in the printing industry. In fact, around 70% of all printing machines produced around the world are manufactured with Böttcher roller coatings. In addition to roller coatings, the company supplies its customers in wide-ranging sectors with consumables such as detergents, printing blankets, coating plates, fountain solution additives and other printing aids. It also enjoys similar prominence in the metals, plastics and wood industries. Böttcher serves more than 50,000 customers around the globe and is a development partner to more than 400 machine manufacturers worldwide.

An important building block in this success is the company's strong focus on its in-house development exper-

Since 1725

Unternehmensname
FELIX BÖTTCHER GMBH & CO. KG

Industriezweig
ELASTOMERBESCHICHTETE WALZEN UND SLEEVES

Gründung
1725

Vertrieb
WELTWEIT, IN 123 LÄNDERN AUF ALLEN KONTINENTEN

Mitarbeitende
2000 WELTWEIT

Jahresumsatz
252 MIO. EURO WELTWEIT (2020)

Company name
FELIX BÖTTCHER GMBH & CO. KG

Industry
ELASTOMER-COATED ROLLERS AND SLEEVES

Founded
1725

Distribution
WORLDWIDE, IN 123 COUNTRIES ACROSS ALL CONTINENTS

Employees
2,000 WORLDWIDE

Annual sales
€252 MILLION WORLDWIDE (2020)

Böttcher fertigt Austausch-walzen für weltweit führende Druckmaschinenhersteller

Böttcher produces replacement rollers for world-leading printing machine manufacturers

Ein wichtiger Baustein für diesen Erfolg ist unter anderem der starke Fokus auf die eigene Entwicklungskompetenz sowie das firmeneigene Mischwerk im rheinland-pfälzischen Gelsdorf. Die 80 Entwickler*innen bei Böttcher entwickeln und testen Werkstoffe, die den hohen Ansprüchen an den messbaren Nutzen für seine Kunden genügen. Da die Herstellung von Druckwalzenwerkstoffen eine Königsdisziplin innerhalb der Kautschukindustrie ist, betreibt das Kölner Unternehmen ein eigenes Mischwerk. So garantiert es die hohe und gleichbleibende Qualität seiner Werkstoffe – egal, wo auf der Welt es sie verarbeitet. Böttcher beliefert auch Industrien wie die Pharmabranche: Die Verschlüsse von Insulinampullen garantieren ein Höchstmaß an Reinheit und Konstanz.

Den Grundstein für den Global Player legten zwei Firmen unabhängig voneinander: die 1725 in Köln von Jacobus Loosen gegründete Gerberei und der rund 150 Jahre später entstandene Leipziger Betrieb von Felix Böttcher für die Produktion von Gelatinewalzen. 1910 fusionierten die beiden mittelständischen Unternehmen, und 1952 wurden erstmals elastomere Walzenbeschichtungen eingesetzt. Heute ist Böttcher Technologie- und Marktführer auf allen Kontinenten in 123 Ländern, davon in 38 Ländern mit eigenen Mitarbeitenden, und betreibt 27 Produktionsstätten in 19 Ländern.

Bei Böttcher sind ökonomische Leistungsstärke, gesellschaftliche Verantwortung und der rücksichtsvolle Umgang mit der Natur untrennbar miteinander verbunden. Nachhaltigkeit ist dabei ein integraler Bestandteil der Unternehmenspolitik. Ein ganzheitlicher Ansatz ermöglicht es dem Unternehmen weltweit, bereits während der Entwicklung von neuen Produkten, bei der Beschaffung, bei der Produktion und im Rahmen des Vertriebes Verantwortung im Sinne zukünftiger Generationen zu übernehmen. Ziel ist es, dass Böttcher-Produkte in der Anwendung einen Beitrag zu mehr Nachhaltigkeit leisten. Zusätzlich entwickelt der Technologieführer zielgerichtet Produkte, die die Energie- und Mobilitätswende unterstützen. „Bewahre das Gute aus der Tradition und schaffe das Neue aus der eigenen Stärke" – mit diesem Leitmotiv schreibt Böttcher seit mehr als 295 Jahren Erfolgsgeschichte.

tise and its compounding plant in Gelsdorf, Rhineland-Palatinate. Böttcher's 80 R&D specialists develop and test materials that satisfy its customers' high demands by delivering measurable benefits. Manufacturing printing roller materials is an elite discipline in the rubber industry, so Cologne-based Böttcher operates its own compounding plant. This way, it can guarantee that its materials are of consistently high quality – no matter where they are processed around the world. Böttcher also serves industries such as the pharmaceutical sector, where its closures for insulin vials guarantee first-rate hygiene and consistency.

Now a global player, Böttcher can trace its foundations back to two companies: a tannery founded in Cologne in 1725 by Jacobus Loosen and a Leipzig-based enterprise specialising in gelatine roller production, which was founded by Felix Böttcher around 150 years later. The two medium-sized enterprises merged in 1910, with the first elastomer roller coatings launched in 1952. Today, Böttcher is a technology and market leader on every continent with activities in 123 countries. It has employees in 38 countries and operates 27 production sites in 19 countries.

Economic performance, social responsibility and a considered approach to the environment are inextricably linked at Böttcher. Sustainability is an integral part of its corporate policy. The company's holistic approach enables it to fulfil its responsibilities to future generations around the world in its development, procurement, production and distribution activities. Its aim is for Böttcher products to contribute to improved sustainability when in use. The technology leader also concentrates on developing products to support the energy and mobility transitions. "Retain the good things from tradition and create the new from our own strength": this ideal has enabled Böttcher to write a success story spanning over 295 years.

FRANZ-GEORG HEGGEMANN, CEO

»Unser Ziel als Weltmarkt- und Technologieführer ist es, immer höhere Standards zu setzen und zu halten.«

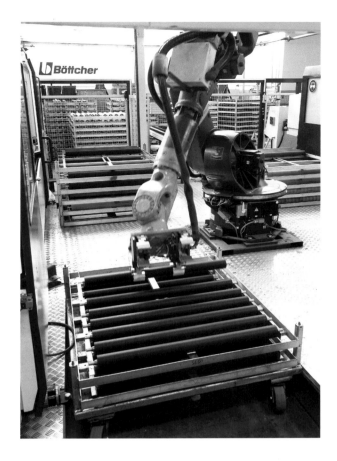

Robotergestützte Produktion in der Serienfertigung

Robot-assisted series manufacturing

Hohe und gleichbleibende Qualität: Gummimischung aus dem eigenen Mischwerk im rheinland-pfälzischen Gelsdorf

Consistent high quality: a rubber compound from the company's compounding plant in Gelsdorf, Rhineland-Palatinate

Geschäftsführer Franz-Georg Heggemann

CEO Franz-Georg Heggemann

FRANZ-GEORG HEGGEMANN, CEO

»As the global market leader and a technology leader, our goal is to set and meet increasingly high standards.«

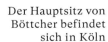

Der Hauptsitz von Böttcher befindet sich in Köln

Böttcher's headquarters are in Cologne

BOGE

Heute Hersteller von Premiumkompressoren für Industrieanwendungen, früher Anbieter von Motorrädern, Spezialwerkzeugen und Türschließern – BOGE Kompressoren blickt mit über 115 Jahren auf eine ereignisreiche Firmengeschichte zurück. Das bereits über vier Generationen familiengeführte Unternehmen wurde 1907 von Otto Boge gegründet, der zusammen mit seinem Bruder Türschließer herstellte. Nach dem Ersten Weltkrieg machte sich Otto Boge mit Spezialwerkzeugen für die noch junge Autoindustrie und mit Motorrädern rasch einen Namen. Kolbenkompressoren waren ab 1925 im Programm. Schließlich wurde BOGE zum Experten für Kompressoren und Druckluftanlagen und ist auf diesem Gebiet dank seiner Kernkompetenz – der eigenen Fertigung der Verdichterstufen – einer der weltweit führenden Anbieter. Dabei ist BOGE als Familienunternehmen fest in Ostwestfalen verwurzelt.

Das Portfolio von BOGE umfasst Schrauben- und Kolbenkompressoren in ölgeschmierter und ölfreier Ausführung, Scroll- und Turbokompressoren sowie zusätzliche Komponenten zur Druckluftaufbereitung, Steuerung und Wärmerückgewinnung. Der Druckluftexperte bietet vielfältige Branchenlösungen in zum Teil anspruchsvollen Einsatzbereichen wie der Medizintechnik, der PET-Industrie und der Oberflächenbeschichtung. Auch Spezialgas-Generatoren gehören zum Portfolio. Dabei geht der Premiumhersteller individuell auf die unterschiedlichen Kundenbedürfnisse ein und hat den Anspruch, stets die beste Lösung für jede Anforderung zu bieten. Die Druckluftproduktion erfüllt höchste Qualitätsstandards und ist daher auch für besonders sensible Anwendungsbereiche in der Lebensmittelproduktion, im Gesundheitsbereich und in der pharmazeutischen Industrie geeignet.

Der Experte für Druckluftsysteme ist in über 120 Ländern vertreten und generiert weltweit Umsätze. Dabei wird der Vertrieb über den eigenen Außendienst,

Starting out as a producer of motorcycles, specialist tools and door closers before becoming a manufacturer of premium industrial compressors, BOGE Kompressoren can look back on an eventful 115-year history. Already passed down through four generations, the family-run company was founded in 1907 by Otto Boge, who manufactured door closers with his brother. Following the First World War, Boge made a name for himself by producing specialist tools for the fledgling automotive industry and manufacturing motorcycles. In 1925, the company launched its first piston compressors. Ultimately, BOGE became a specialist in compressors and compressed air systems. Thanks to its core expertise – manufacturing compressor air-ends – it has become a leading supplier in this field. Nevertheless, BOGE remains a family company with deep roots in East Westphalia.

The BOGE portfolio includes screw compressors and piston compressors, which are available in oil-free and oil-lubricated versions, scroll compressors, turbo compressors and additional components for compressed air treatment, heat recovery and control. The compressed air specialist offers a range of industry solutions, including in challenging fields such as medical technology, the PET industry and surface treatment. Its portfolio also includes special gas generators. The premium manufacturer tailors its services to different customer needs and aspires to offer the best solution for every requirement. Its compressed air systems satisfy the highest quality standards, which makes them suitable for use in highly sensitive areas such as food production, healthcare and the pharmaceutical industry.

A specialist in compressed air systems, BOGE is represented in 120 countries and generates sales around the world. It distributes its products through its own field sales network, international subsidiaries and certified retailers. By relying on these high-performing struc-

Unternehmensname
**BOGE KOMPRESSOREN
OTTO BOGE GMBH & CO. KG**

Industriezweig
MASCHINENBAU

Gründung
1907 IN BIELEFELD

Hauptfertigungsstätte
BIELEFELD

Vertrieb
**WELTWEIT ÜBER
TOCHTERUNTERNEHMEN
UND HÄNDLER**

Mitarbeitende
800

Company name
**BOGE KOMPRESSOREN
OTTO BOGE GMBH & CO. KG**

Industry
MECHANICAL ENGINEERING

Founded
1907 IN BIELEFELD

Main manufacturing facility
BIELEFELD

Distribution
**WORLDWIDE THROUGH
SUBSIDIARIES AND RETAILERS**

Employees
800

Energiesparend, wartungs-
freundlich und leise: BOGE
Schraubenkompressor S 75-4 LF

Energy-saving, easy to maintain
and quiet in operation: the BOGE
S 75-4 LF screw compressor

internationale Tochtergesellschaften und zertifizierte Händler organisiert. Mit diesen leistungsfähigen Strukturen erfüllt BOGE die hohen Ansprüche hinsichtlich Produkt- und Servicequalität. Produziert wird in Deutschland und China. Der größte Produktionsstandort mit rund 430 Mitarbeitenden befindet sich in Bielefeld am Hauptsitz des Unternehmens, ein weiteres Werk mit 40 Mitarbeitenden ist im sächsischen Großenhain beheimatet. Das Werk in China liegt in Shanghai und beschäftigt 60 Mitarbeitende.

Der Druckluftexperte ist aber kein reiner Kompressorlieferant. BOGE agiert gleichfalls als Turnkey-Anbieter und übernimmt auch den kompletten Anlagenbau: von der Konzeptionierung bis zur Inbetriebnahme. Zudem hält das Unternehmen einen umfassenden Aftersales-Service bereit. Mit einem großflächigen Händlernetz deckt BOGE die Wartung und Inspektion sowie technische Kundenberatung ab. Um eine hohe Servicequalität dauerhaft zu garantieren, werden Mitarbeitende regelmäßig in der Druckluft-Akademie geschult. Kunden können auf einen umfangreichen und schnellen Premium-Service vertrauen – eine persönliche Ansprechperson steht immer bereit. Dabei setzt der Druckluftexperte auch auf digitale Tools. So beweist BOGE connect beispielsweise, dass sich die Effizienzwerte bei der Inbetriebnahme und im Service steigern sowie die Betriebskosten langfristig senken lassen. Anwender haben ihre Betriebsdaten ständig im Blick. Auffälligkeiten können damit sofort erkannt und Störungen frühzeitig behoben werden.

Die Bielefelder legen besonderes Augenmerk auf hohe Effizienz und Nachhaltigkeit ihrer Produkte. Dabei setzt das Unternehmen auf Technologien, die die freiwerdende Energie bei der Kompressoren-Nutzung für den Anwender gewinnbringend verwerten, zum Beispiel in Form von Wärmeenergie. Statt als Umgebungswärme verloren zu gehen, kommt diese bei der Beheizung von Lager- und Betriebsbereichen oder beim Erwärmen von Wasser oder Ölen zum Einsatz. So lassen sich bis zu 94 Prozent der eingesetzten Energie nutzen. Konkrete Anwendungsgebiete sind unter anderem die Aufbereitung von Trink-, Brauch-, Heizungs- und Prozesswasser. Letzteres wird für industrielle Waschvorgänge verwendet, beispielsweise in Recyclingunternehmen. Auf diese Weise unterstützt BOGE seine Kunden dabei, ihren CO_2-Fußabdruck zu reduzieren. Das Unternehmen sieht sich für die kommenden Anforderungen bestens gewappnet. Die Wachstumsstrategie für die Zukunft liegt in der Entwicklung neuer, digitaler Geschäftsmodelle.

tures, BOGE fulfils high standards for product and service quality. It has manufacturing operations in Germany and China. Its largest manufacturing facility, which has around 430 employees, is at the company's headquarters in Bielefeld, while a further factory with 40 employees is located in Großenhain, Saxony. Its factory in China is situated in Shanghai and has 60 employees.

The compressed air expert does far more, however, than simply produce compressors. BOGE is also a turnkey provider and offers all aspects of plant construction, from concept creation through to commissioning. In addition, the company provides a comprehensive after-sales service. BOGE offers maintenance, inspection and technical support through its extensive retailer network. In addition, its employees undergo regular training at the BOGE Compressed Air Academy to ensure consistently high service quality. Customers can rely on a comprehensive, swift, premium service, with a personal contact available at all times. At the same time, the compressed air specialist also relies on digital tools. For example, its BOGE connect tool monitors and displays improvements in efficiency indicators following commissioning and servicing, along with lasting reductions in operating costs. It also ensures that users always have an overview of their operating data. This way, users can identify abnormalities straight away and rectify faults in a timely manner.

The Bielefeld-based company places particular emphasis on the efficiency and sustainability of its products. It also implements technologies that capture the energy released when its compressors are in use and make it available to the user, such as in the form of heat energy. This means that, rather than simply being lost as ambient heat, it can be used for heating in warehouses and production areas or to heat water and oil. Consequently, BOGE systems use up to 94% of the total input energy. Specific applications for BOGE systems include the treatment of drinking water, service water, heating water and process water. The latter is used in industrial washing processes, such as in recycling companies. BOGE thereby helps its customers to reduce their carbon footprint. The company believes it is ideally equipped to face the challenges that lie ahead. Its growth strategy for the future is based on the development of new, digital business models.

OLAF HOPPE, CEO VON BOGE

»Getreu unserem Motto möchten wir in der Nische wachsen und auch in 100 Jahren noch ein Familienunternehmen mit internationaler Relevanz sein.«

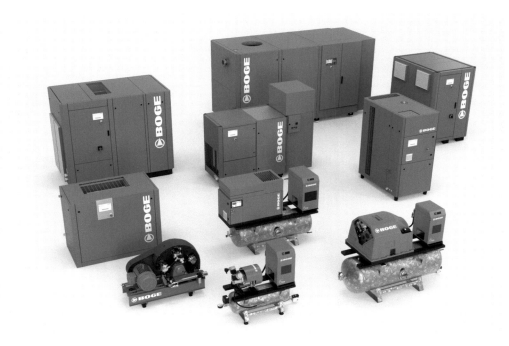

Zum breiten Produktportfolio gehören Schrauben- und Kolbenkompressoren, Scroll- und Turbokompressoren sowie Druckluftzubehör

Its wide-ranging product portfolio includes screw compressors, piston compressors, scroll compressors, turbo compressors and accessories for compressed air systems

BOGE produziert unter anderem im sächsischen Großenhain

BOGE also has a manufacturing facility in Großenhain, Saxony

OLAF HOPPE, CEO OF BOGE

»Staying true to our motto, we hope to grow in our niche so that, in 100 years' time, we are still an internationally relevant family company.«

Der Hauptsitz von BOGE befindet sich in Bielefeld

BOGE's headquarters are in Bielefeld

Die Geschäftsführer Olaf Hoppe (rechts) und Michael Rommelmann

Managing Directors Olaf Hoppe (right) and Michael Rommelmann

BUMAT

Alles, was sich dreht, zieht Aufmerksamkeit auf sich – und offenbart unterschiedliche Blickachsen. Diese Faszination nutzen Wirtschaftsunternehmen, Kulturschaffende und private Bauherr*innen, um ihre Produkte, Exponate oder Lieblingsstücke in Szene zu setzen: Mit dem Effekt des Drehens entsteht Dynamik auf kleinstem Raum.

Der Spezialist fürs Drehen sitzt im baden-württembergischen Hockenheim. Bumat ist Weltmarktführer für elektrisch angetriebene Drehscheiben und bietet den weltweit größten Bestand an Miet-Drehscheiben. Es gibt viele Anwendungsbereiche in den unterschiedlichsten Branchen. Dazu zählen die Automuseen von Porsche und Mercedes-Benz in Stuttgart, das IKEA-Logistikzentrum in Wien, eine Privatvilla in Teheran, das Deutsche Fußballmuseum in Dortmund, eine Gucci-Modenschau in Mailand, aber auch die Oper in Tokyo und das Deutsche Zentrum für Luft- und Raumfahrt.

Das Unternehmen versteht sich als Maschinenbauspezialist, der Indoor- und Outdoor-Drehscheiben aus Aluminium, Stahl oder Edelstahl am Firmensitz in Hockenheim entwickelt, konstruiert, produziert und rund um den Globus selbst in Betrieb nimmt. Auf Wunsch sind die Drehteller gemäß einer vorgegebenen Choreografie programmierbar, positionierbar und Smart-Home integrierbar. Bumat Technologien und Know-how werden außerdem in aller Welt geschätzt von privaten Automobilsammler*innen, Yacht-Eigner*innen, Architekt*innen und Interior Designer*innen.

Ein neuer Trend ist die Ausstattung von „Man Caves" in Privatresidenzen: Auf der Ebene des privaten Gym drehen sich die Raritäten der eigenen Autosammlung.

60 Prozent des Umsatzes werden mit Kunden außerhalb Deutschlands erzielt. Die Bumat Servicetechniker*innen montieren in der ganzen Welt.

Everything that rotates attracts attention – and opens up different perspectives. Companies, creatives and private customers exploit this fascination to cast a spotlight on their products, exhibits and showpiece items. Rotation creates a sense of dynamism in even the smallest of spaces.

The specialist for rotating systems is based in Hockenheim, Baden-Württemberg. Bumat is the global market leader for electrically driven turntables and offers the world's largest range of rental turntables. Its products are used in various applications across a wide range of industries. These include the Porsche and Mercedes-Benz museums in Stuttgart, the IKEA Logistics Centre in Vienna, a private villa in Tehran, the German Football Museum in Dortmund, a Gucci fashion show in Milan, an opera hall in Tokyo and the German Aerospace Centre.

The company positions itself as a mechanical engineering specialist that develops, designs and produces indoor and outdoor turntables from aluminium, steel and stainless steel at its headquarters in Hockenheim before commissioning them around the world. Its revolving platforms can be programmed in line with a specific choreography, positioned as desired and integrated into smart home systems. Bumat technology and expertise are cherished around the world by private car collectors, yacht owners, architects and interior designers.

A new trend has emerged in which these turntables are installed in "man caves" in private residences, allowing customers to display their prized specimens from their car collection alongside their private gym.

The company generates 60% of its revenue from customers outside Germany. Bumat service engineers travel around the world to assemble the systems.

The Turntable Company

Unternehmensname
BUMAT BEWEGUNGSSYSTEME GMBH

Industriezweig
MASCHINENBAU

Gründung
1948

Gründer
JOSEF BURGMEIER

Produkte
DREHSCHEIBEN UND KINETISCHE SONDERKONSTRUKTIONEN

Hauptfertigungsstätte
HOCKENHEIM

Mitarbeitende
25

Company name
BUMAT BEWEGUNGSSYSTEME GMBH

Industry
MECHANICAL ENGINEERING

Founded
1948

Founder
JOSEF BURGMEIER

Products
TURNTABLES, REVOLVING PLATFORMS AND SPECIAL KINETIC CONSTRUCTIONS

Main production facility
HOCKENHEIM

Employees
25

Die Drehscheiben von Bumat setzen die neuen Modelle der Automobilhersteller wirkungsvoll in Szene – ob auf Messen, in Showrooms oder Museen

Turntables from Bumat provide impactful staging for automotive manufacturers' latest models – at trade fairs, in showrooms and in museums

Seine Innovationsführerschaft zeigt Bumat bei seinen Spezialdrehscheiben. Für Kundenwünsche, die bis dahin nur als Skizze oder Idee existieren, schafft das Ingenieurteam innovative und individuelle Lösungen – zum Beispiel einen drehenden Baum auf dem Unicampus in Zug-Rotkreuz in der Schweiz, der sich innerhalb von 24 Stunden einmal um die eigene Achse dreht. Oder eine Drehscheibe mit 33 Metern Durchmesser, auf der sich eine Tribüne mit 1200 Zuschauer*innen dreht.

In den vergangenen Jahren kristallisierte sich ein neuer Einsatzbereich im hochwertigen Innenausbau heraus. So entwickelte das Familienunternehmen drehende Sitzmöbel wie Sunlounger, Sofas und Betten für den Einsatz auf Super-Yachten und in Privathäusern.

Im Gegensatz hierzu setzen die Schwerlastdrehscheiben von Bumat andere Akzente: Im Mercedes-Benz Werk in Düsseldorf hilft ein Bumat Schwerlast-Drehring mit 26 Metern Durchmesser dabei, den Produktionsprozess des Mercedes-Benz Sprinter zu optimieren. Und am neu errichteten IKEA-Standort in Wien dient eine 12 Meter große Bumat Lkw-Drehscheibe als Rangierhilfe zur Logistikoptimierung. Einzelhandelsunternehmen wie Aldi und Lidl, aber auch die holländische Nationalbank zählen bei dem Produktsegment „Schwerlastdrehscheiben" zur geschätzten Kundschaft.

Die wohl spektakulärste Anwendung von Bumat kann man seit 2013 in einem Privathaus in Teheran bestaunen. Eine kinetische Sonderkonstruktion lässt dort ganze Räume drehen, was auf einer alten persischen Bautradition basiert. Klimabedingt haben dort viele Häuser einen Wohnraum für den Sommer und einen für den Winter. Auf drei Etagen gibt es eine sich drehende „Raum-im-Raum"-Konstruktion, die sich je nach Wetter um 90 Grad nach außen beziehungsweise innen drehen lässt. Innerhalb von nur zwei Minuten kann man das Haus so von der Sommerresidenz zum Winterdomizil umgestalten.

Bei Bumat ist also die ganze Welt eine (Dreh-)Scheibe. Seit 1948.

Bumat also demonstrates its innovation leadership through its special constructions. If customers only have a sketch or a rough idea of their desired system, Bumat's engineering team craft innovative, bespoke solutions – such as a rotating tree on the university campus in Rotkreuz, in the canton of Zug, Switzerland, which rotates on its own axis once every 24 hours. Another example is a rotating platform with a 33-metre diameter upon which a 1,200-seater terrace rotates.

In recent years, a new area of application has emerged for Bumat's products: high-end interior design. The family company has developed a range of rotating furniture, including sun loungers, sofas and beds for super yachts and private homes.

In contrast to this, Bumat's heavy-duty turntables have very different applications: at the Mercedes-Benz factory in Düsseldorf, a Bumat heavy-duty turntable with a 26-metre diameter helps to optimise the production process of the Mercedes-Benz Sprinter. And, at IKEA's newly built facility in Vienna, a 12-metre Bumat truck turntable assists with manoeuvring operations, thereby optimising logistics processes. Retail companies such as Aldi and Lidl are among the valued customers in Bumat's heavy-duty turntable segment, alongside others including the Dutch Central Bank.

Arguably the most spectacular use of Bumat's products to date is a private home in Tehran, completed in 2013. A special kinetic construction allows entire rooms to rotate. This concept is based on an ancient Persian architectural tradition in which people use one living room in summer and a different one in winter. Three storeys of the Tehran home feature a "room-in-room" design that allows the entire space to rotate by 90° to face either inside or outside depending on the weather. This entire building can be transformed from a summer home to a winter hideaway within just two minutes.

For Bumat, all the world's a (rotating) stage – and has been since 1948.

»Wir drehen jedes Ding. Seit 1948.«

20 Meter große Drehscheibe für die Gucci-Modenshow in Mailand 2020

A 20-metre turntable for the Gucci fashion show in Milan, 2020

Ein besonders komfortabler Einsatzbereich für die Drehscheiben von Bumat: Sunlounger für Super-Yachten

A comfortable application for Bumat's turntables – rotating sun loungers for super yachts

Spektakuläre Projekte: Bumat hat sich auch im Bereich der kinetischen Architektur einen Namen gemacht und für diese Privatvilla in Teheran rotierende Räume konstruiert, produziert und montiert

Spectacular projects: Bumat has made a name for itself in the field of kinetic architecture, including by designing, producing and installing rotating rooms for this private villa in Tehran

Lkw-Schwerlastdrehscheiben von Bumat kommen auch in Logistikzentren zum Einsatz – wie hier bei IKEA in Wien

Bumat truck turntables are used in logistics centres – as shown here at IKEA's facility in Vienna

»We make the world go round. Since 1948.«

CLAAS

Wer im Sommer über Land fährt, der begegnet zwangsläufig saatengrünen Mähdreschern der Marke CLAAS. Das Familienunternehmen aus dem ostwestfälischen Harsewinkel gehörte vor mehr als 70 Jahren zu den ersten europäischen Landtechnikunternehmen, die den Trend zum Ernte-Selbstfahrer erkannten. Heute ist CLAAS europäischer Marktführer bei Mähdreschern, vertreibt seine mehr als 40 Modelle aber weltweit. Beim Feldhäcksler, dem JAGUAR, ist CLAAS Weltmarktführer. „Unser Erfolgsrezept sind hocheffiziente Maschinen, gepaart mit niedrigen Verschleiß- und Wartungskosten, dem professionellsten Service sowie dem schnellsten Ersatzteilwesen der Branche und einer außerordentlichen Wertstabilität", fasst CEO Jan-Hendrik Mohr zusammen. Mohr führt seit April 2023 das 12 000 Mitarbeitende zählende Unternehmen, das er nach fast 40-jähriger Tätigkeit in verschiedenen Entwicklungs- und Managementbereichen quasi in- und auswendig kennt.

1913 gegründet, ist CLAAS heute der einzige familiengeführte Landtechnikhersteller unter den weltweiten Top 5. Familiäre Werte prägen das Unternehmen – und trotz des weltweiten Trends zu immer größeren Agrarbetrieben und immer leistungsstärkerer Technik vergisst CLAAS bäuerliche Familienbetriebe nicht: Zu den neuesten Produkten gehört der EVION, ein Mähdrescher für kleinere landwirtschaftliche Strukturen, der im Sommer 2023 unter dem Motto „Familie zählt" eingeführt wurde.

Im starken Kontrast dazu stehen riesige Agrarbetriebe in Nordamerika, Südamerika oder Australien, die CLAAS mit Erntetechnik wie dem LEXION Mähdrescher und dem JAGUAR Feldhäcksler schon lange erfolgreich beliefert. Bei Traktoren – einem Produktbereich, der erst 1997 mit dem Systemtraktor XERION und 2003 mit Übernahme der Traktorensparte von Renault ins Unternehmen kam – ist man in vielen Marktregionen noch

If you ever find yourself driving across Germany in summertime, there's one thing you can be sure of: a host of seed-green CLAAS combine harvesters will be working the fields. Over 70 years ago, the family business from Harsewinkel in East Westphalia became one of the first European agricultural machinery firms to identify the trend towards self-propelled harvesters. Today, CLAAS is the European market leader for combine harvesters, but sells more than 40 models worldwide. And, when it comes to forage harvesters, CLAAS is the global market leader with its JAGUAR line. "Our recipe for success combines high-efficiency machines with low wear and maintenance costs, the most professional customer service and the fastest spare parts supplies in the industry, along with outstanding value retention," explains Jan-Hendrik Mohr, CEO of CLAAS. Mohr has headed up the company, which has a workforce of 12,000 employees, since April 2023. After working in various development and management-related positions for almost 40 years, he knows the company inside out.

Founded in 1913, CLAAS is the only family-owned company among the top five global agricultural machinery manufacturers. Family values shape the company – and, despite worldwide trends towards bigger agricultural enterprises and increasingly powerful technology, CLAAS has still not forgotten about family-run farms. Its most recent products include the EVION, a combine harvester for smaller-scale agricultural undertakings, which was launched in the summer of 2023 with the slogan "family matters".

In stark contrast to such farms are the vast agricultural enterprises in North America, South America and Australia, which CLAAS has successfully served for a long time with harvesting technology such as the LEXION combine harvester and the JAGUAR forage harvester. When it comes to tractors – a product area that CLAAS first tapped into with the launch of the XERION system

Unternehmensname
CLAAS KGAA MBH

Industriezweig
LANDTECHNIK

Gründung
1913

Hauptfertigungsstätte
HARSEWINKEL

Mitarbeitende
12 000

Jahresumsatz
4,9 MRD. EURO

Company name
CLAAS KGAA MBH

Industry
AGRICULTURAL MACHINERY

Founded
1913

Main manufacturing facility
HARSEWINKEL

Employees
12,000

Annual sales
€4.9 BILLION

CLAAS ist weltweiter Marktführer bei selbstfahrenden Feldhäckslern, aber noch bekannter für seine Mähdrescher. Damit ist das Familienunternehmen Marktführer in Europa

CLAAS is the world market leader for self-propelled forage harvesters. However, it is even better known for its combine harvesters – an area in which the family company remains the European market leader

neu auf dem Spielfeld. Mit besonderem Fokus auf Nordamerika als Absatzmarkt wurde daher ein neues, 653 PS starkes Traktor-Flaggschiff entwickelt. Der XERION 12.650 TERRA TRAC wiegt bis zu 32 Tonnen, arbeitet aber dennoch bodenschonend. Der Clou: im eigenen Haus bei CLAAS Industrietechnik in Paderborn entwickelte und gebaute Raupenlaufwerke für optimale Kraftübertragung bei minimalem Bodendruck. 25 Jahre Erfahrung kann CLAAS vorweisen – eine Kompetenz, die auch externe Abnehmer schätzen.

Im internationalen Wettbewerbsumfeld muss CLAAS heute mehr denn je den Spagat zwischen Tradition und Innovation meistern. Zu den Top-Zukunftstechnologien der Branche gehört neben nachhaltigen Antrieben vor allem Autonomie. CLAAS setzt dabei nicht nur auf eigene Innovationskraft, sondern auch auf Kooperationen. So wurde in das niederländische Start-up AgXeed investiert, das autonome AgBots entwickelt und vermarktet. Mit einem weiteren Investor hat man 2023 das weltweit erste Konsortium für die herstellerübergreifende Weiterentwicklung von Automatisierung und Autonomie in der Landtechnik gegründet.

Am Fundament dafür wird bereits seit mehr als 30 Jahren gebaut. 1991 brachte CLAAS als First Mover erste Produkte und Technologien für die satellitenbasierte „Smart Farming"-Präzisionslandwirtschaft auf den Markt. Digitale Welt und Maschinen verschmelzen nun immer mehr zu einem Ökosystem: Aus Traktoren und Erntemaschinen werden smarte Maschinen, die vernetzt und mithilfe einer komplexen Onboard-Intelligenz Daten sammeln und austauschen und ihre eigene Effizienz und Produktivität optimieren.

Effizienz zählt auch in der Produktion: Mit immer individuelleren Kundenwünschen nimmt die Variantenvielfalt bei den Produkten zu – eine Herausforderung im Produktionsmanagement bei so komplexen Maschinen wie einem Mähdrescher, der aus mehr als 50 000 Teilen und Komponenten besteht. Fertigung nach dem neuesten Stand der Technik ist daher ein Muss: Allein seit 2019 wurden mehr als 120 Millionen Euro in das Traktorenwerk in Le Mans, in die Mähdreschermontage in Harsewinkel und in das Werk für Futtererntetechnik in Bad Saulgau investiert. Angenehme Nebeneffekte: Die Arbeitsplätze in der Produktion sind heller und komfortabler, schwere Arbeiten übernehmen fahrerlose Transportsysteme (FTS) und Cobots. Darüber hinaus spart die neue Mähdreschermontage in Harsewinkel allein rund 750 Tonnen CO_2 pro Jahr ein. Weitere 2500 Tonnen CO_2-Einsparung wird durch Erstbetankung aller Neumaschinen aus den Werken Harsewinkel und Le Mans mit nachhaltigen hydrierten Pflanzenölen (HVO) erzielt.

tractor in 1997 and the acquisition of Renault's tractor division in 2003 – the company remains a new player in many regions. CLAAS therefore developed a new 653 hp flagship tractor, focusing in particular on driving sales in the North American market. The XERION 12.650 TERRA TRAC weighs up to 32 tonnes but remains soil-friendly in operation. Its show-stopping feature is the crawler track assembly: developed and manufactured in-house at CLAAS Industrietechnik in Paderborn, it delivers optimal power transmission with minimal soil compaction. CLAAS can now draw on 25 years of experience in this area – expertise that customers value highly.

Today, in the arena of international competition, CLAAS is forced more than ever to manage the balancing act between tradition and innovation. In addition to sustainable drive systems, the key future technologies in the agricultural machinery sector also include autonomy. CLAAS relies not only on its own innovative power but also on collaborations with others. It has invested, for example, in the Dutch start-up AgXeed, which develops and markets autonomous AgBots. Together with another investor, CLAAS founded the world's first consortium for the cross-manufacturer development of automation and autonomy in agricultural machinery in 2023.

The foundations for this venture were laid over 30 years ago. In 1991, CLAAS became a first mover by introducing products and technologies for satellite-based "smart farming" precision agriculture. The digital and mechanical worlds are increasingly merging to form a single ecosystem. Tractors and harvesting machinery are becoming smart, networked machines with complex on-board intelligence systems to collect and exchange data and optimise efficiency and productivity.

Efficiency also counts in production: as customer requests become increasingly individual, the range of product variants continues to grow – which presents a challenge for production management with machines as complex as combine harvesters, which feature over 50,000 components. With this in mind, state-of-the-art manufacturing is a must. Since 2019 alone, CLAAS has invested over €120 million in its tractor factory in Le Mans, its combine harvester assembly plant in Harsewinkel and its forage harvesting technology plant in Bad Saulgau. Positive side effects of this investment include brighter, more pleasant workplaces on production sites, with strenuous manual tasks performed by driverless transport systems and cobots. In addition, the new combine harvester assembly line in Harsewinkel saves around 750 tonnes of CO_2 per year. A further 2,500 tonnes of CO_2 are saved by ensuring all new machinery leaving the Harsewinkel and Le Mans plants are filled with sustainable hydrotreated vegetable oil (HVO).

»Wir machen Landwirte zu den besten in ihrem Feld.«

Seit 2019 investierte CLAAS mehr als 120 Millionen Euro in eine modernisierte und stärker automatisierte Produktion, den Großteil davon im Traktorenwerk im französischen Le Mans und am Stammsitz Harsewinkel

Since 2019, CLAAS has invested over €120 million in modernised, increasingly automated production systems, with the majority of this investment focused on its French tractor plant in Le Mans and its headquarters in Harsewinkel

CLAAS sieht sich als führend in der Landtechnikbranche bei bodenschonenden Antriebstechnologien für Landmaschinen, wie hier beim JAGUAR TERRA TRAC

CLAAS considers itself a leader in the agricultural machinery sector when it comes to soil-friendly drive technologies for agricultural machinery, such as the JAGUAR TERRA TRAC shown here

Jan-Hendrik Mohr, CEO von CLAAS

Jan-Hendrik Mohr, CEO of CLAAS

»We make farmers the best in their field.«

D+H

Frische Luft ist das Element von D+H – denn darum dreht sich alles, wofür das Unternehmen einsteht. Seine Geschichte begann 1968 mit einem der ersten elektromotorischen Rauchabzüge. Durch viel Leidenschaft, Pioniergeist und Innovationsfreude ist die ursprüngliche Garagenfirma zu einem der weltweit führenden Lösungsanbieter für intelligente Rauchabzugssysteme und Lüftungslösungen gewachsen. Die Fensterantriebe und Steuerungen von D+H sorgen in Gebäuden weltweit für eine sichere und gesunde Atmosphäre.

Innerhalb von fünf Jahrzehnten hat sich die D+H Gruppe zu einer starken Marke und zum Innovationstreiber entwickelt. Und vereint dabei den familiären Charakter der regional verankerten Firmenkultur mit den wachsenden Ansprüchen und Herausforderungen einer internationalen Gruppe mit weltweit zehn Tochterunternehmen. In einem globalen Partnernetzwerk arbeiten über 500 Mitarbeitende gemeinsam daran, Gebäude in aller Welt durch D+H Technologien und Fachexpertise sicherer und behaglicher zu machen.

Die familiengeführte und unabhängige D+H Mechatronic AG mit Sitz im Nordosten der Metropolregion Hamburg ist Unternehmenszentrale und Produktionsstandort zugleich. Die hier hervorgebrachten Produktentwicklungen bestimmen seit Firmengründung das Marktgeschehen. In zwei Werken werden diese mit großer Fertigungstiefe produziert und umfangreich geprüft und getestet. Ein zertifiziertes Qualitätsmanagementsystem sichert, wofür die Marke D+H seit jeher am Markt steht: höchste Qualität.

Ob maschinelle Entrauchung oder natürliche Lüftung: Mit hochpräzisen Fensterantrieben und intelligenten Steuerungstechnologien sorgt D+H weltweit für ein gesundes Raumklima und Komfort sowie für ausreichend Luft zum Atmen im Brandfall. Von internationalen Flughäfen über große Einkaufszentren, architek-

Fresh air is the domain of D+H: it is at the heart of everything the company stands for. The company's story began in 1968 with the production of one of the first smoke vents operated by an electric motor. A wealth of passion, pioneering spirit and innovation transformed what began as a home-based microenterprise into one of the world's leading providers of intelligent smoke vent systems and ventilation solutions. Window drives and control panels produced by D+H create a safe, healthy atmosphere in buildings around the world.

Over the course of five decades, the D+H Group has developed into a strong brand and a driver of innovation. It combines the familiar character of a company firmly rooted in its home region with the growing aspirations and challenges inherent in an international group with ten subsidiaries worldwide. In its global partner network, 500 employees work to make buildings around the globe safer and more comfortable with the help of D+H technologies and expertise.

Based in the north-east of the Hamburg metropolitan region, the independent, family-owned D+H Mechatronic AG serves as the Group's headquarters and a production site. Since the company's foundation, this site has pioneered product developments that have shaped the market situation. D+H manufactures its products with a high degree of vertical integration and conducts extensive testing at two factories. A certified quality management system safeguards a crucial aspect that has always been central to the D+H brand: outstanding quality.

Whether in relation to mechanical smoke extraction or natural ventilation, D+H produces ultra-precise window drives and intelligent control technologies that provide a healthy, comfortable indoor climate while also ensuring a sufficient air supply in the event of fire.

BUILDING ATMOSPHERE

Unternehmensname
D+H MECHATRONIC AG

Industriezweig
ELEKTROTECHNIK

Gründung
1968

Produkt
**RAUCHABZUG UND
NATÜRLICHE LÜFTUNG**

Hauptfertigungsstätte
AMMERSBEK BEI HAMBURG

Mitarbeitende
ÜBER 500 WELTWEIT

Company name
D+H MECHATRONIC AG

Industry
ELECTRICAL ENGINEERING

Founded
1968

Product
**SMOKE VENTS AND
NATURAL VENTILATION**

Main manufacturing facility
AMMERSBEK, NEAR HAMBURG

Employees
OVER 500 WORLDWIDE

D+H Bestseller und
mittlerweile Branchenikone:
der orangefarbene
Rauchabzugstaster

The orange smoke vent
button – a D+H bestseller that
has become an industry icon

tonisch anspruchsvolle Museen bis hin zu komplexen Bürogebäuden und Sportstadien – die D+H Gruppe bringt intelligente und zertifizierte Systemlösungen für modernste Gebäudeautomation an jede Fassade und an jedes Dach. Architekt*innen, Fachplaner*innen, Metall- und Fassadenbauer*innen und Profilsystemhäuser wissen: Wo D+H draufsteht, ist auch das Plus an Qualität „made in Germany" drin.

Die D+H Mechatronic AG ist Muttergesellschaft der D+H Gruppe und agiert von Beginn an als unabhängiges Familienunternehmen. Die Geschäftsleitung haben die Gründungsväter Henner Dingfelder und Helmut Kern erfolgreich an ihre Söhne Dirk Dingfelder und Christoph Kern weitergegeben. Seit 2023 ergänzen die langjährigen Mitarbeiter Maik Schmees und Mirko Matenia den Vorstand. Die Vorstände engagieren sich seit Jahrzehnten aktiv in Präsidien und anderen Führungsgremien der wichtigsten Fachverbände, Innungen und Kammern, wie zum Beispiel dem Hamburger Gesamtverband des Handwerks und dem Verband der Elektro- und Digitalindustrie (ZVEI).

Regionale Verbundenheit bedeutet für D+H nicht nur das feste Bekenntnis zum Fertigungsstandort Ammersbek, sondern auch die Förderung des gesamten Unternehmensumfeldes. Trotz der Internationalisierung des Marktes und eines Auslandsumsatzes von mittlerweile über 60 Prozent, bietet D+H am Hauptsitz in Ammersbek mit mehr als 250 Stellen nach wie vor die meisten Arbeitsplätze in der Gemeinde. Dazu kommen jährlich rund zehn Ausbildungsplätze.

D+H Produkte und Lösungen wurden bereits vielfach ausgezeichnet. 2017 erhielt die D+H Gruppe den „German Brand Award" in der Kategorie „Industry Excellence in Branding – Buildings & Elements". Auch auf der VDMA-Bestenliste ist D+H als „Best of German Engineering" vertreten. Für sein Talentmanagement wurde D+H 2015 mit dem 1. Platz beim Deutschen Bildungspreis ausgezeichnet.

Als Frischluftversorger und Lebensretter produziert D+H nicht nur intelligente Systemlösungen, die in Gebäuden Fenster öffnen und schließen. Bei D+H geht es um weit mehr als um Technologien für Rauchabzug und natürliche Lüftung. Lösungen von D+H bringen Gebäude zum Atmen. Und damit Schutz und Sicherheit sowie Komfort und Wohlbefinden zu den Menschen. So wurde daraus das Markenversprechen: BUILDING ATMOSPHERE.

From international airports to major shopping centres, and from architecturally ambitious museums to complex office buildings and sports stadia, the D+H Group supplies intelligent, certified system solutions for state-of-the-art building automation in every façade and every roof. Architects, technical planners, metalworkers, façade builders and profile system companies know that the D+H brand is an indicator of high-quality products made in Germany.

D+H Mechatronic AG is the parent company of the D+H Group and has always been an independent family enterprise. The founding fathers, Henner Dingfelder and Helmut Kern, have successfully passed on responsibility for company management to their sons, Dirk Dingfelder and Christoph Kern. Two long-serving employees, Maik Schmees and Mirko Matenia, joined the Executive Board in 2023. Its members have been actively involved in the steering committees and other leadership bodies of leading professional associations, guilds and chambers, including the Hamburg Skilled Crafts Association (HGH) and the German Electro and Digital Industry Association (ZVEI).

For D+H, regional ties mean more than a firm commitment to its Ammersbek manufacturing facility: they also extend to supporting the wider community. Despite the internationalisation of its market, with foreign sales now accounting for over 60% of total turnover, D+H remains the largest employer in Ammersbek, providing 250 jobs for people living nearby. It also offers around ten apprenticeship places every year.

D+H products and solutions have already won numerous awards. In 2017, the D+H Group received the German Brand Award in the "Industry Excellence in Branding – Buildings & Elements" category. D+H also appears on the VDMA's "Best of German Engineering" list. In 2015, D+H secured first place in the German Education Award in recognition of its talent management activities.

Dedicated to supplying fresh air and saving lives, D+H provides intelligent system solutions that open and close windows in buildings. However, D+H does far more than produce technologies that vent smoke and provide natural ventilation: D+H solutions enable buildings to breathe. In doing so, they keep people safe and support their comfort and well-being. This is crystallised in its brand promise: BUILDING ATMOSPHERE.

DIRK DINGFELDER, VORSTANDSVORSITZENDER

»Wir finden
Lösungen
für grundlegende
Bedürfnisse:
Wenn es um sichere
und gesunde Atmo-
sphäre in Gebäuden
geht, sind wir in
unserem Element.«

Produktion made in Germany:
digitale Prozesse und präzise Handarbeit

Made in Germany:
Digital processes and precise
manual labour

Vielfältige Fenster-
antriebe von D+H bringen
Gebäude auf der ganzen
Welt zum Atmen

Wide-ranging window
drives from D+H enable
buildings around the
world to breathe

Hauptsitz und Produk-
tionsstandort der D+H
Gruppe ist Ammersbek
bei Hamburg

The D+H Group's head-
quarters and production
site is situated in Ammersbek, near Hamburg

DIRK DINGFELDER, CEO

»We find solutions
for basic needs.
When it comes to
creating a safe,
healthy atmosphere
in buildings, we're
in our element.«

Der D+H Vorstand (von links):
Maik Schmees (Technik),
Dirk Dingfelder (Vorsitz),
Christoph Kern (Vertrieb) und
Mirko Matenia (Finanzen)

The D+H Executive Board
(from left):
Maik Schmees (Technology),
Dirk Dingfelder (Chair),
Christoph Kern (Sales) and
Mirko Matenia (Finance)

DOLEZYCH

Dolezych ist der Marktführer in Sachen Seil-, Hebe-, Anschlag- und Ladungssicherungstechnik. Das 1935 von Franz Dolezych gegründete Familienunternehmen vertrieb zunächst Drahtseile für Industrie, Schifffahrt und Bergbau und entwickelte sich durch beständige Innovation und Erweiterung der Expertise zum Komplettanbieter in seiner Branche. Mit rund 120 Patenten und Gebrauchsmustern bietet Dolezych alle Fachprodukte zum Heben und Transportieren von Lasten, einen umfangreichen Prüfservice vor Ort beim Kunden oder im hauseigenen Prüfungslabor und ein breites Seminarangebot.

Die Geschäftsführer Udo und Tim Dolezych (zweite und dritte Generation) verantworten das operative Geschäft des weltweit an acht Standorten agierenden Unternehmens mit Hauptsitz in Dortmund. Dolezych verfügt über eigene Auslandsniederlassungen und arbeitet mit mehr als 100 internationalen und nationalen Händlern zusammen. Nicht zuletzt sind die 250 Mitarbeitenden am Hauptsitz sowie über 400 weitere Mitarbeitende weltweit der Garant für die hohe Produktqualität und die Spitzenposition am Markt. Dolezych bildet bereits seit Jahrzehnten in verschiedenen Ausbildungsberufen aus und kümmert sich um die Weiterbildung aller Mitarbeitenden. Ob als Azubis, Studierende oder Profis – das Unternehmen bietet zahlreiche Möglichkeiten, sich einzubringen, getreu der Unternehmensmission: „Jeden Tag eine neue Lösung".

Auch Dolezych selbst musste sich nach dem Zweiten Weltkrieg neu erschaffen: 1949 begann der Wiederaufbau, 1951 erfolgte der Umzug an den heutigen Standort am Dortmunder Hafen. Als verstärkt synthetische Fasern auf den Markt kamen, ergriff das Unternehmen die Chance und entwickelte textile Hebemittel und Zurrgurte, die Ende der 1970er-Jahre ins Portfolio eingeführt wurden. Maßgeschneiderte Sicherheit für jeden Fahrzeugtyp gibt es in Form der DoKEP®-Ladungs-

Dolezych is the market leader for rope, lifting, slinging and load securing technology. Founded in 1935 by Franz Dolezych, the family company initially sold wire rope for industrial, maritime and mining applications. By consistently innovating and expanding its expertise, Dolezych became a full-range supplier in its industry. With around 120 patents and utility models, Dolezych offers all specialist products needed to lift and transport loads, an extensive testing service – available either at customers' premises or in its in-house lab – and a wide range of seminars.

Its managing directors, Udo and Tim Dolezych (second and third generation respectively) oversee operational activities for the company, which has eight locations around the world and its headquarters in Dortmund. Dolezych has its own international subsidiaries and cooperates with over 100 international and national retailers. The 250 employees at its headquarters and over 400 further employees around the world act as a guarantee of high product quality and the company's leading market position. Dolezych has provided training in various professions for decades and strives to promote the professional development of all its employees. From apprentices to students and professionals, the company offers numerous opportunities for employees to play an active part, in keeping with the company mission: "A new solution every day."

Dolezych was forced to reinvent itself after the Second World War. The company began its reconstruction in 1949 and relocated to its current site in Dortmund Port following in 1951. As synthetic fibres began to penetrate the market, Dolezych seized the opportunity and developed textile lifting equipment and lashing straps, which it integrated into its portfolio in the late 1970s. Its DoKEP® load securing nets provide customised safety for every type of vehicle. The company has also developed the Dolezych-Simple-Method© for swift cal-

Unternehmensname
DOLEZYCH GMBH & CO. KG

Industriezweig
SEIL-, HEBE- UND LADUNGSSICHERUNGSTECHNIK

Gründung
1935 IN DORTMUND

Produkt
TEXTILE KETTE DONOVA®

Hauptfertigungsstätte
DORTMUND

Mitarbeitende
ÜBER 650 WELTWEIT

Company name
DOLEZYCH GMBH & CO. KG

Industry
ROPE, LIFTING AND LOAD SECURING TECHNOLOGY

Founded
1935 IN DORTMUND

Product
DONOVA® TEXTILE CHAIN

Main manufacturing facility
DORTMUND

Employees
OVER 650 WORLDWIDE

Textile Hebemittel können auch U-Boote heben

Textile lifting equipment can even lift submarines

sicherungsnetze. Eine Eigenentwicklung ist die soge- nannte Dolezych-Einfach-Methode©, um schnell die korrekte Ladungssicherung zu berechnen. In jüngerer Zeit konnte Dolezych die Weltneuheit DoNova® präsen- tieren, die sich bald im Einsatz erfolgreich unter Beweis stellte: Textile Ketten sind genauso leistungsfähig wie Stahlketten und sichern und heben selbst schwerste Lasten. Mit bis zu 80 Prozent weniger Gewicht wird so ein ergonomisches Arbeiten ermöglicht. Ebenso inno- vativ sind der Ratschlastspanner DoRa mit Aus- und Überdrehsicherung sowie der zertifizierte Tension- Controller für den Pkw- und Lkw-Transport.

Expertise in der Branche spricht sich herum, und so war Dolezych gleich zweimal an Kunstprojekten von Christo und Jeanne-Claude beteiligt: bei der Verhüllung des Berliner Reichstages 1995 und des Arc de Triomphe in Paris im Herbst 2021. Ihren Sachverstand und ihr Engagement bringen die beiden Geschäftsführer auch gerne in Fachverbänden und bei regionalen Wirt- schaftsverbänden ein. Tim Dolezych macht sich für das junge Unternehmertum stark, Vater Udo Dolezych ist unter anderem Ehrenpräsident der IHK zu Dortmund und Stifter des Schulpreises Wirtschaftswissen. Zudem ist es für beide selbstverständlich, Standards zukunfts- fähig weiterzuentwickeln und sich in der deutschen, europäischen und internationalen Normung zu enga- gieren. Dolezych steht dazu in engem Austausch mit Partnerorganisationen wie dem „Deutschen Institut für Normung" (DIN), dem „European Committee for Stan- dardization" (CEN), der amerikanischen „Web Sling & Tie Down Association" (WSTDA) sowie den „Associated Wire Rope Fabricators" (AWRF).

Die Erfüllung von Spezialwünschen und die Abwick- lung außergewöhnlicher Projekte erfordert eine ein- wandfrei funktionierende Struktur, die das zertifi- zierte Qualitätsmanagement (DIN EN ISO 9001) von Dolezych garantiert. Auch das Umweltmanagement des Unternehmens ist zertifiziert (DIN EN ISO 14001) und beinhaltet etwa die Abfallvermeidung und den sparsamen Umgang mit Ressourcen. Nicht zuletzt wur- de der Firmenfuhrpark auf E-Autos umgestellt, und das Unternehmen spart durch eine eigene Photovoltaik- anlage CO_2 ein.

Zur optimalen Ausführung von Sicherungsmaßnah- men umfasst das Schulungsangebot von Dolezych die praktische Demonstration von Produkten und Metho- den, das Erlernen des sachgerechten Umgangs mit die- sen und die Sensibilisierung für die entsprechenden Vorschriften. Die Ladungssicherheit auf der ganzen Welt populär zu machen, ist die Antriebsfeder für die Geschäftsführung und zugleich die Unternehmens- vision: „Wir machen die Welt sicherer und einfacher."

culation of suitable load securing systems. Recently, Dolezych presented a world first: the DoNova®, which soon demonstrated its benefits in practice. Textile chains are just as effective as steel chains and are capa- ble of lifting and securing even the heaviest loads. And, as they weigh up to 80% less than the steel version, they also facilitate ergonomic working. Equally innovative solutions include the DoRa ratchet load bindings with a limit stop and overwinding stop, plus the certified TensionController for car and truck transport.

Word of its expertise spread quickly in the industry, with Dolezych involved in two art projects led by Chris- to and Jeanne-Claude: 'Wrapped Reichstag' in Berlin in 1995 and 'Arc de Triomphe, Wrapped' in Paris in the autumn of 2021. The two managing directors are also happy to share their expertise and commitment in industry associations and regional trade associations. Tim Dolezych is an outspoken champion of young entrepreneurship, while his father Udo Dolezych is Honorary President of the Chamber of Commerce and Industry (IHK) for Dortmund and a benefactor of Schulpreis Wirtschaftswissen, a schools science com- petition. The duo also believe it is essential to advance standards, ensuring they are fit for the future, and therefore engage in German, European and interna- tional standardisation processes. Dolezych also coordi- nates closely with parter organisations including the German Institute for Standardization (DIN), the Euro- pean Committee for Standardization (CEN), the US- based Web Sling & Tie Down Association (WSTDA) and the Associated Wire Rope Fabricators (AWRF).

Fulfilling special requests and handling exceptional projects requires flawless, functional internal struc- tures, which Dolezych guarantees through its certified quality management system (DIN EN ISO 9001). The company's environmental management system is also certified (DIN EN ISO 14001) and covers topics includ- ing waste prevention and sparing use of resources. Dolezych has also procured electric cars for its vehicle fleet and reduces its CO_2 emissions through its own photovoltaic installation.

In order to ensure that its safety and load securing measures are implemented as effectively as possible, Dolezych offers training sessions that include practical demonstrations of its products and methods, teaching professionals to apply them correctly, and raising awareness of relevant regulations. As the company strives to popularise load securing solutions around the world, its management – and the company as a whole – is guided by a shared vision: "We make the world safer and simpler."

»Wir machen die Welt sicherer und einfacher.«

Ein Hingucker: Mehr als 2600 Dolezych-Zurrgurte hielten 25 000 Quadrat-meter Stoff, mit dem das Team des Künstler-ehepaars Christo und Jeanne-Claude den Pariser Triumphbogen verhüllte

Eye-catching: More than 2,600 Dolezych lashing straps held 25,000 square metres of material with which the team of artist couple Christo and Jeanne-Claude team wrapped the Arc de Triomphe in Paris

Die textile Kette DoNova® besteht aus Kettengliedern, die aus mehreren Lagen Gurtband mit der Hochleistungsfaser Dyneema® gefertigt sind

The DoNova® textile chain consists of chain links comprising several layers of webbing made from Dyneema® high-performance fibre

Die Geschäftsführer Tim und Udo Dolezych

Managing Directors Tim and Udo Dolezych

»We make the world safer and simpler.«

E3/DC

Die Transformation der Energieversorgung stellt hohe Ansprüche an deren Zukunftsfähigkeit, Sicherheit, CO_2-Bilanz und Unabhängigkeit. Eine zunehmend wichtige Option ist die autarke Eigenversorgung von Gebäuden mit regenerativer Energie aus Photovoltaikanlagen. E3/DC bietet durchdachte Systemlösungen für die besonders effiziente, CO_2-freie DC-Speicherung von Solarstrom und die intelligente Steuerung der Energieflüsse in Wohnhäusern und Gewerbeimmobilien sowie Ladetechnik für E-Fahrzeuge. Im Markennamen steht E3 für einsparend, erneuerbar und effektiv, DC für effiziente Gleichstromtechnik.

Herzstücke der Eigenversorgung sind die Hauskraftwerke von E3/DC, mit denen völlige energetische Autarkie möglich ist. Sie sind Zwischenspeicher für den Strom aus Photovoltaikanlagen oder der Kraft-Wärme-Kopplung und zugleich Schaltzentralen zur Verteilung des gespeicherten Stroms, unabhängig von fossilen Energieträgern. Die E3/DC-Systeme nach dem All In One-Prinzip – mit Wechselrichter, flexiblem und erweiterbarem Batteriesystem sowie einem Energiemanagement – gibt es in mehreren Leistungsklassen und Varianten: vom kombinierten Hauskraftwerk S10 SE bis zum S20 X PRO, das mit seiner beispiellosen Leistungsfähigkeit ausgelegt ist für Objekte mit sehr großen Dächern und hohem Strombedarf. Die E3/DC-Wallbox erweitert die Stromspeicher, sodass E-Autos mit Solarstrom vom eigenen Dach betrieben werden können. In naher Zukunft fungiert das Elektroauto zudem als bidirektionaler Batteriespeicher, zum Beispiel als Notstromversorgung. Alle Komponenten der äußerst effizienten und wirtschaftlichen E3/DC-Hauskraftwerke kommen aus einer Hand, made in Germany. Software-Updates per Fernwartung und das Batteriemonitoring sichern den verlässlichen Betrieb der E3/DC-Systeme. Durch die dreiphasige Ersatzstromversorgung sind bei einem Netzausfall komplette Gebäude abgesichert.

The transformation of the energy supply system presents extensive requirements regarding its future viability, security, carbon footprint and independence. Fitting buildings with autonomous supply systems is an increasingly important option, with renewable energy provided by photovoltaic installations. E3/DC offers sophisticated system solutions that enable ultra-efficient, zero-carbon DC storage of solar electricity and facilitate intelligent control over energy flows in residential and commercial properties. It also provides charging technology for electric vehicles. In the company's name, E3 stands for "einsparend, erneuerbar" and "effektiv" (saving, renewable and effective), while DC refers to the company's efficient direct current technology.

Central to self-sufficient domestic supply systems are the E3/DC home power stations, which provide complete energy independence. They temporarily store the electricity generated by photovoltaic or cogeneration systems and also serve as control centres regulating the distribution of stored electricity – entirely independent of fossil fuels. E3/DC systems follow the all-in-one principle – and comprise an inverter, a flexible, expandable battery system and an energy management system – and come in a variety of power classes and types: from the S10 SE combined home power station to the S20 X PRO, which is designed to deliver peerless performance when installed on buildings with very large roofs and high electricity requirements. The E3/DC wallbox supplements the battery storage system and enables homeowners to charge their EVs with solar power from their own roofs. In the near future, electric cars will also act as bidirectional battery storage systems, such as for an emergency power supply. All components of the exceptionally efficient and economical E3/DC home power stations are made in Germany and supplied from a single source. Software updates implemented via remote maintenance and battery monitoring functions ensure that E3/DC systems operate

ENERGY STORAGE
E3/DC

Unternehmensname
E3/DC BY HAGERENERGY GMBH

Industriezweig
PV-SPEICHERSYSTEME

Gründung
2010

Produkt
HAUSKRAFTWERKE

Vertrieb
DEUTSCHLAND, ÖSTERREICH, SCHWEIZ

Mitarbeitende
300

Company name
E3/DC BY HAGERENERGY GMBH

Industry
PV STORAGE SYSTEMS

Founded
2010

Product
HOME POWER STATIONS

Distribution
GERMANY, AUSTRIA, SWITZERLAND

Employees
300

Das meistverkaufte Hauskraftwerk S10 X: der Standard in der solaren Eigenversorgung

The top-selling S10 X home power station: setting the standard in self-generated solar power

E3/DC entstand 2010 durch eine Ausgliederung der Wilhelm Karmann GmbH für Automobil- und Karosseriebau in Osnabrück. Mit dem Know-how aus der Energiespeicherentwicklung für Automobile avancierte das von Geschäftsführer Dr. Andreas Piepenbrink gegründete Unternehmen erfolgreich zum Entwickler intelligenter Stromspeicherlösungen. Seither setzt E3/DC immer wieder Standards in der unabhängigen energetischen Eigenversorgung.

E3/DC ist Deutschlands Marktführer in der dreiphasigen Ersatzstromversorgung und verfügt als einziger Integrator von Wechselrichter-, Speicher- und Ladetechnik über eine herausragende technische Bandbreite. In seinem Marktsegment bietet nur E3/DC perfekt aufeinander abgestimmte, multifunktionale Systemkomponenten in höchster Qualität. Auch im deutschen Speichermarkt zählt das Unternehmen quantitativ zur Spitzengruppe und setzt hier die seit 25 Jahren in Automobilen bewährte Lithium-Ionen-Technologie höchster Qualität ein. E3/DC ist mit 300 Mitarbeitenden an vier deutschen Standorten vertreten. Alle Produkte werden in Osnabrück und Göttingen entwickelt und in Wetter (Ruhr) gefertigt. Zertifizierte Vertriebspartner in Deutschland, Österreich und der Schweiz übernehmen die Konfiguration und Installation der kompletten Systeme sowie der Photovoltaikanlagen. E3/DC ist eine Marke der HagerEnergy GmbH, einer Business Unit der Hager Group, die als deutsches Familienunternehmen weltweit im Bereich Elektroinstallation tätig ist.

E3/DC ist Träger von Gütesiegeln wie TOP Brand PV Speicher und TOP Brand Wallbox (EuPD Research) sowie Marke des Jahrhunderts und wurde ausgezeichnet mit dem German Brand Award, dem German Design Award und dem Solar Prosumer Award (EuPD Research). Zu den vielbeachteten Innovationen von E3/DC zählen die TriLINK®-Technologie zur dreiphasigen Leistungssteuerung des Hauskraftwerks auch im Gleichstrombereich sowie Lösungen für intelligente Sektorenkopplung (Wärme und solare E-Mobilität) und für bidirektionales Laden. Die Entwicklungsarbeit ist fokussiert auf Fortschritte in der Leistungselektronik, beim bidirektionalen Laden und bei besonders leistungsstarken Gewerbespeichern. Kontinuierlich vorangetrieben werden weitere Maßnahmen zur Erreichung der projektierten Klimaschutz- und Transformationsziele in der Energieversorgung. Seit jeher richtet E3/DC alle Produkte und Neuentwicklungen konsequent aus auf eine möglichst vollständige, selbstbestimmte Energiewende in Gebäuden – zukunftssicher, CO_2-neutral und unabhängig von den Strompreisen des freien Marktes.

reliably. The three-phase emergency power supply also protects entire buildings against blackouts.

E3/DC was born in 2010 as a spin-off from Wilhelm Karmann GmbH, an automotive engineering and body manufacturing company in Osnabrück. It was founded by Dr Andreas Piepenbrink, who was a Managing Director at Karmann at the time. The company applied its existing expertise in the development of energy storage systems from the automotive industry, pivoting to become a successful developer of intelligent energy storage devices. Since then, E3/DC has repeatedly set new standards in independent, autonomous energy supply solutions.

E3/DC is the German market leader for three-phase emergency power solutions and offers outstanding technical breadth as the only company to integrate inverter, storage and charging technology. In its market segment, E3/DC is the only provider of perfectly matched, multifunctional system components of the highest quality. It is also among the leading suppliers by volume in the German energy storage market, applying high-quality lithium-ion technology that has proven its worth in the automotive industry for 25 years. E3/DC has 300 employees across four locations in Germany. All of its products are developed in Osnabrück and Göttingen and manufactured in Wetter (Ruhr). Certified distribution partners in Germany, Austria and Switzerland configure and install complete systems and photovoltaic systems. E3/DC is a brand of HagerEnergy GmbH, which is a business unit of the Hager Group, a German family company with electrical installation operations around the world.

E3/DC has been awarded quality certifications including TOP Brand PV Storage and TOP Brand Wallbox (EuPD Research) as well as Brand of the Century – and has also received the German Brand Award, the German Design Award and the Solar Prosumer Award (EuPD Research). The much-noted innovations developed by E3/DC include TriLINK® technology, a three-phase output management system for home power stations that also functions with direct current, as well as intelligent solutions for sector coupling (heating and solar e-mobility) and bidirectional charging. Its development work focuses on making progress in power electronics, bidirectional charging and ultra-high-output commercial storage. The company is also pressing ahead with activities to achieve planned climate protection and transformation targets in relation to power supply. From the very outset, E3/DC has developed products and innovations with a systematic focus on driving the most comprehensive, self-directed energy transition possible in buildings – one that is future-proof, carbon neutral and independent of free-market electricity prices.

»Das Hauskraft-
werk steht für die
Unabhängigkeit
von fossiler Energie
und für die
Nutzung CO_2-
freien Stroms rund
um die Uhr.«

Die inhouse entwickelte
Leistungselektronik
macht die Qualität der
Produkte aus

The power electronics
developed in-house
are a key factor in the
products' high quality

Die Fertigung der
E3/DC-Hauskraftwerke in
Wetter (Ruhr) in NRW

E3/DC home power
stations in production
in Wetter (Ruhr),
North Rhine-Westphalia

»The home power
station gives you
independence from
fossil fuels as well
as carbon-free
electricity around
the clock.«

Die E3/DC-Firmenzentrale
in Osnabrück

E3/DC headquarters
in Osnabrück

EWS

Mit ihrer Dachmarke EWS zählt die EWS Weigele GmbH & Co. KG zu den Weltmarktführern im Industriezweig Werkzeugmaschinenbau. EWS entwickelt, fertigt und vertreibt hochpräzise Werkzeugsysteme für CNC-Dreh-Fräs- und Bearbeitungszentren. Zu den Kunden rund um den Globus zählen Unternehmen aus den Wirtschaftssparten Maschinenbau und Automobilindustrie sowie Luft- und Raumfahrt. EWS betreibt Produktionsstätten an drei Standorten: in Uhingen, Deutschland, in Ramsey, Minnesota/USA, und Changwon, Südkorea. EWS Produkte werden weltweit vertrieben und insbesondere von Unternehmen nachgefragt, die Verfahren der Zerspanungstechnik in ihrer Fertigung anwenden. Internationales Renommee hat sich der Werkzeugmaschinenbauer erworben mit seinem hochspezialisierten Know-how und einer Reihe wichtiger Innovationen. So gilt zum Beispiel das EWS.Varia Schnellwechselsystem als optimale Lösung für die Rüstzeitoptimierung von Fertigungszentren und wurde 2006 mit dem Innovationspreis des Landes Baden-Württemberg ausgezeichnet. Auch mit der Entwicklung einer neuen Sensorik für Werkzeugsysteme hat EWS Standards gesetzt und 2017 den Innovationspreis des Landkreises Göppingen erhalten.

Unter der Maxime „Precision meets Motion" subsumiert der global agierende Werkzeugmaschinenbauer wichtige Attribute für alle EWS Produkte und Lösungen: Bewegung, Schnelligkeit und Präzision. Doch erst das Zusammenwirken mit der in Form und Funktion einzigartigen Ausführung auf höchstem Qualitätsniveau gewährleistet, dass EWS den spezifischen Anforderungen der Kunden und Märkte weltweit stets optimal gerecht wird. Ebenso maßgeblich für den Unternehmenserfolg und den Ausbau des technologischen Vorsprungs sind die große Expertise und das Engagement der Mitarbeitenden. Die Produktion unterliegt zudem ständigen Qualitätskontrollen, deren Prozesse in Zusammenarbeit mit externen Instituten

EWS Weigele GmbH & Co. KG is among the global market leaders in the machine tool engineering industry through its umbrella brand EWS. EWS develops, fabricates and distributes ultra-precise tool systems for CNC turning, milling and machining centres. Its customers around the world include companies in the mechanical engineering, automotive and aerospace industries. EWS has production facilities at three locations: Uhingen, Germany; Ramsey, Minnesota, USA; and Changwon, South Korea. EWS products are sold around the world, with particularly strong demand from companies that rely on machining processes in their manufacturing activities. The machine tool manufacturer has achieved international renown thanks to its highly specialised expertise and a host of key innovations. The EWS.Varia quick-change system, for example, is an ideal solution to optimise set-up times at manufacturing facilities and received the Baden-Württemberg Innovation Award in 2006. EWS has also set standards in the development of new sensor technology for tool systems, for which it won the Göppingen Innovation Award in 2017.

The global machine tool manufacturer's maxim – "precision meets motion" – neatly expresses the three key attributes of all EWS products and solutions: motion, speed and precision. However, it is the combination of premium-quality design and unique form and function that ensures EWS is always able to effectively satisfy the specific requirements of customers and markets around the world. The expertise and dedication of the company's employees are also crucial to its success and its efforts to consolidate its technological advantage. The manufacturer's production activities are subject to constant quality checks, which rely on processes developed in cooperation with external institutes. Extensive investments also ensure that EWS production lines are future-proofed.

Tool Technologies

Unternehmensname
EWS WEIGELE GMBH & CO. KG

Industriezweig
WERKZEUGMASCHINENBAU

Gründung
1960 IN KÖNGEN BEI STUTTGART

Hauptfertigungsstätte
DEUTSCHLAND

Mitarbeitende
RD. 400 WELTWEIT, DAVON 200 IN DEUTSCHLAND

Jahresumsatz
CA. 55 MIO. EURO WELTWEIT, DAVON CA. 35 MIO. EURO IN DEUTSCHLAND (2022)

Company name
EWS WEIGELE GMBH & CO. KG

Industry
MACHINE TOOL ENGINEERING

Founded
1960 IN KÖNGEN, NEAR STUTTGART

Main production facility
GERMANY

Employees
APPROX. 400 WORLDWIDE, INCLUDING 200 IN GERMANY

Annual sales
APPROX. €55 MILLION WORLDWIDE, INCLUDING APPROX. €35 MILLION IN GERMANY (2022)

Die EWS.TechLine ist ausgestattet mit den neuesten Technologien aus dem Hause EWS

The EWS.TechLine is equipped with the latest technology developed by EWS

entwickelt werden. Überdies gewährleisten umfangreiche Investitionen die Zukunftssicherheit der EWS Fertigungslinien.

Bei EWS hat die digitale Transformation bereits große Fortschritte initiiert und ist von zentraler Bedeutung für die erfolgreiche Forschung und Entwicklung. Die neu geschaffene EWS Plattform ist technologiegetrieben und ermöglicht Anwender*innen, in Sekundenschnelle einen digitalen Zwilling zu erstellen und direkt für die Prozesssimulation einzusetzen. Weitere EWS Innovationen sind auf Schnittstellenlogiken basierende Maschinen-Ausrüstungsassistenten sowie eine neu entwickelte Sensorik, die einen hohen Stellenwert für die Implementierung chancenreicher Geschäftsmodelle hat.

EWS wurde 1960 von Ernst Weigele gemeinsam mit seinen Söhnen Gerhard und Karl gegründet. Nach den Anfängen als Zulieferer für hydraulische Komponenten entwickelte sich das Unternehmen mit Werkzeugaufnahmen für die ersten NC-Drehmaschinen zum prosperierenden Werkzeugmaschinenbauer. Mit dem Einstieg in die Geschäftsführung der beiden Söhne von Gerhard Weigele – Frank und Matthias Weigele – hat sich EWS zu einem weltweit agierenden mittelständischen Industrieunternehmen im Familienbesitz entwickelt. Seit 2021 führt Matthias Weigele die Geschäfte der Familienholding mit Tochterunternehmen als alleiniger Geschäftsführer.

EWS forciert seine Aktivitäten auf dem Fachkräftemarkt und unterstützt diese seit Längerem durch attraktive Maßnahmen im Unternehmen. Aus einer Reihe dualer Studiengänge sowie Ausbildungsgängen in den Bereichen Industriemechanik, Fachinformatik, Metalltechnik, Zerspanungsmechanik, Groß- und Außenhandel sowie für Industriekaufleute übernimmt EWS kontinuierlich Nachwuchsfachkräfte. Allen Mitarbeitenden werden eine wertschätzende Arbeitsatmosphäre, individuelle Weiterbildungsmöglichkeiten und gute Entwicklungschancen sowie eine hohe Arbeitsplatzsicherheit geboten. Sie haben Anspruch auf monetäre und qualitative Benefits, zum Beispiel durch ein breit angelegtes Gesundheitsmanagement. Dieses bietet hausinterne Firmenfitnesskurse, ergonomische Arbeitsplätze, freie Besuche bei Heilpraktiker*innen und Physiotherapeut*innen und Zuschüsse zum Training im Fitnessstudio. Das Unternehmen ist Bildungspartner verschiedener Schulen in seiner Heimatregion und garantiert die Grundversorgung des von ihm ins Leben gerufenen Projektes Heart4Children.de in Uganda.

EWS ist stets fokussiert auf das Maximum des technisch Machbaren für seine Kunden und legt weiterhin ein besonderes Augenmerk auf die Verantwortung für seine Mitarbeitenden und die Gesellschaft.

The digital transformation has already instigated significant advances at EWS and is crucial for successful research and development. The newly created EWS platform is driven by technology and enables users to create digital twins in a matter of seconds before using them directly in process simulations. Other EWS innovations include machine tooling assistants based on interface logic models and a newly developed sensor technology that has significant implications for the implementation of promising business models.

EWS was founded in 1960 by Ernst Weigele together with his sons, Gerhard and Karl. From its origins as a supplier of hydraulic components, the company evolved to provide tool mounts for the first NC lathes and later became a prosperous machine tool manufacturer. By the time Frank and Matthias Weigele – the two sons of Gerhard Weigele – joined the company's management team, EWS had become a family-owned, medium-sized industrial enterprise with global operations. In 2021, Matthias Weigele became the sole Managing Director of the family holding company and its subsidiaries.

EWS is pressing ahead with its activities to recruit skilled professionals, including through a range of attractive employee packages. The company is also continuously training talented young professionals through a series of dual work-study programs and apprenticeships in the fields of industrial mechanics, informatics, metal technology, machining, wholesale trade, foreign trade and for industrial business assistants. It offers all employees an atmosphere of appreciation, tailored professional development programmes and excellent progression opportunities as well as a high level of workplace safety. Furthermore, employees receive a variety of financial and non-financial benefits, such as an extensive health management programme. This includes internal fitness courses, ergonomic workstations, free visits to natural health professionals and physiotherapists, and subsidised gym memberships. EWS has also partnered with a number of schools in its home region and guarantees core funding for Heart4Children.de – a project the company initiated in Uganda.

EWS always extracts the maximum value for its customers within the confines of technical feasibility, placing particular emphasis on its responsibility to its employees and to society.

MATTHIAS WEIGELE, GESCHÄFTSFÜHRER

»Es ist nicht die Komplexität einer Innovation, sondern der Nutzen.«

EWS.Varia VX – das Schnellwechsel-system zur Rüstzeitoptimierung

EWS.Varia VX – the quick-change system for optimised set-up times

EWS Stammsitz mit Produktion und Technologiezentrum in Uhingen

EWS headquarters in Uhingen, including the Production and Technology Centre

MATTHIAS WEIGELE, MANAGING DIRECTOR

»It isn't the complexity of an innovation that counts but the value it provides.«

Matthias Weigele, Geschäftsführer des Familienunternehmens in dritter Generation, mit der vierten Generation

Matthias Weigele, Managing Director of the family company in the third generation, pictured with the fourth generation

FREUDENBERG-GRUPPE

Freudenberg ist ein globales Technologieunternehmen, das agil und beweglich ist und einen wissenschaftlich begründeten Fortschrittsanspruch hat. Die Produkte und Services des Konzerns sind technisch führend, das Portfolio ist vielfältig: Dichtungen, schwingungstechnische Komponenten, Batterien und Brennstoffzellen, technische Textilien, Filter, Reinigungstechnologien und -produkte, Spezialchemie und medizintechnische Produkte kommen in Tausenden Anwendungen in rund 40 Märkten zum Einsatz – meist nicht sichtbar, aber immer unverzichtbar. Dank Freudenberg ist die Luft in Räumen sauberer, heilen Wunden schneller und sind E-Autos sicherer. Dies sind nur drei Beispiele für die große Vielfalt und den Mehrwert der Freudenberg-Produkte.

Und ständig kommen Innovationen hinzu. Das Unternehmen erzielte im Jahr 2022 rund ein Drittel seines Umsatzes mit Produkten, die jünger als vier Jahre sind. Damit das so bleibt, investiert die Freudenberg-Gruppe kräftig – in Forschung und Entwicklung, Maschinen und Anlagen sowie Zukunftstechnologien. Im Jahr 2022 flossen allein rund 580 Millionen Euro in Forschungs- und Entwicklungsaktivitäten.

Neu zu denken und den Wandel zu gestalten, hat bei der Freudenberg-Gruppe Tradition. Im Jahr 1849 gründete Carl Johann Freudenberg in Weinheim eine Gerberei, ein Jahr später entwickelte diese mit dem Lackleder ihre erste Innovation. Im Lauf der Jahrzehnte erweiterte das Unternehmen sein Know-how und Angebot. 1929 produzierte Freudenberg die ersten Lederdichtungen, 1936 wurden sie erstmals aus Elastomeren hergestellt. Ende der 1940er-Jahre entwickelte das Unternehmen Vliesstoffeinlagen für die Textilindustrie – aus einem Nebenprodukt entstand im Jahr 1948 eine Innovation, die noch heute viele Verbraucher*innen schätzen: die Vileda-Reinigungstücher.

Freudenberg is a global technology group that is agile, flexible and has a scientifically based standard of progress. Its offers a wide-ranging portfolio of leading technological products and services: its seals, vibration-control components, batteries and fuel cells, technical textiles, filters, cleaning technologies and products, special chemicals and medical devices are used in thousands of applications in around 40 markets – usually not visible, but always indispensable. Thanks to Freudenberg, the air in rooms is cleaner, wounds heal faster and electric cars are safer. These are just three examples of the wide variety of Freudenberg's products and the added value they provide – with further innovations constantly being developed.

In 2022, products released in the last four years accounted for around one third of the group's sales. The Freudenberg Group invests heavily to preserve this innovative power – in research and development, machinery and plant, and in the technologies of the future. This includes investing €580 million in research and development in 2022 alone.

The Freudenberg Group has a rich tradition of fresh thinking and shaping change. In 1849, Carl Johann Freudenberg established a tannery in Weinheim. The following year, the company delivered its first innovation: patent leather. Over the decades that followed, the company expanded its expertise and its portfolio. In 1929, Freudenberg produced the first leather seals, with elastomer seals manufactured for the first time in 1936. In the late 1940s, the company developed non-woven interlinings for the textile industry. And, in 1948, a secondary product was transformed into an innovation that many consumers value to this day: Vileda cleaning cloths.

At the turn of the millennium, Freudenberg moved into the fields of medical technology and battery and fuel

FREUDENBERG
INNOVATING TOGETHER

Unternehmensname
FREUDENBERG-GRUPPE

Inhaberfamilie
**CA. 360 NACHKOMMEN
IN DER SIEBTEN GENERATION**

Produkte und Lösungen
**DICHTUNGEN, SCHWINGUNGS-
TECHNIK, BATTERIEN,
BRENNSTOFFZELLEN, TECHNISCHE
TEXTILIEN, FILTER, REINIGUNGS-
UND MEDIZINTECHNISCHE
PRODUKTE, SPEZIALCHEMIE**

Vertrieb
WELTWEIT IN CA. 60 LÄNDERN

Mitarbeitende
51 462 (STAND 31.12.2022)

Jahresumsatz
11,8 MRD. EURO (STAND 31.12.2022)

Company name
FREUDENBERG GROUP

Owner family
**APPROX. 360 DESCENDANTS,
NOW IN SEVENTH GENERATION**

Products and solutions
**SEALS, VIBRATION-CONTROL
TECHNOLOGY, BATTERIES, FUEL
CELLS, TECHNICAL TEXTILES,
FILTERS, CLEANING TECHNOLOGIES,
MEDICAL DEVICES, SPECIAL
CHEMICALS**

Distribution
**WORLDWIDE IN APPROX.
60 COUNTRIES**

Employees
51,462 (31/12/2022)

Annual sales
€11.8 BILLION (31/12/2022)

Das Freudenberg-Portfolio ist vielfältig. Der Konzern ist unter anderem Spezialist in der Luft- und Wasserfiltration. Hier ein Blick in die Filterproduktion in Kaiserslautern

The Freudenberg Group has a wide-ranging portfolio and specialises in fields such as air and water filtration. This image shows its filter production facility in Kaiserslautern

Im neuen Jahrtausend stieg Freudenberg unter anderem in die Medizintechnik sowie in die Batterie- und Brennstoffzellentechnologie ein und baut diese Bereiche seitdem stetig weiter aus. Ein Beispiel ist die Entwicklung eines Brennstoffzellen-Batterie-Antriebssystems mit einem Kooperationspartner. Diese emissionsfreien Brennstoffzellen werden herkömmliche Dieselantriebe in Bussen und Lkw ersetzen sowie in maritimen Anwendungen zum Einsatz kommen.

Das Erbe von Carl Johann Freudenberg wirkt bis heute weiter. Inzwischen ist der Konzern in siebter Generation in Familienbesitz – und gehört rund 360 Nachkommen des Firmengründers. Diese stabile Eigentümerstruktur und die damit mögliche langfristige Orientierung sind eine der Stärken der Unternehmensgruppe. Eine andere ist das unternehmerische Handeln auf allen Ebenen. Das operative Geschäft liegt in der Hand von selbstständigen Gesellschaften, deren Geschäftsführungen eigenverantwortlich agieren. Die einzelnen Unternehmen sind zu Geschäftsgruppen zusammengefasst.

Der Vorstand des Gesamtkonzerns konzentriert sich darauf, die Strategie der Freudenberg-Gruppe zu entwickeln, große Investitionen zu beschließen und strategische Richtlinien zu setzen. Im Vorstand sind derzeit Dr. Mohsen Sohi (CEO), Dr. Tilman Krauch (CTO), Dr. Ralf Krieger (CFO) und Esther Maria Loidl (CHRO). Sie werden wiederum vom Aufsichtsrat der Freudenberg-Gruppe bestellt, in dem mindestens sieben der aktuell 13 Mitglieder aus der Familie stammen müssen. An der Spitze des Gremiums steht Martin Wentzler.

Die Freudenberg-Gruppe beschäftigt rund 51 500 Mitarbeitende, die im vergangenen Jahr einen Umsatz von rund 11,8 Milliarden Euro erwirtschaftet haben. Der Konzern wächst profitabel und verfügt über eine starke Bilanz. Besonders hervorzuheben ist die komfortable Eigenkapitalquote von 54 Prozent.

Doch der Freudenberg-Gruppe sind nicht nur Märkte und Zahlen wichtig: Das Unternehmen übernimmt auch Verantwortung für Menschen und die Umwelt. Dazu gehört, dass der Konzern die Energiewende vorantreibt – mit seinen Produkten und dem Anspruch, bis 2045 ein klimaneutrales Unternehmen zu sein. Außerdem fördert Freudenberg Vielfalt innerhalb der Belegschaft und steht für eine Unternehmenskultur, in der alle Mitarbeitenden ihre Stärken einbringen können.

Freudenberg unterstützt auch außerhalb des Unternehmens vielfach dort, wo Hilfe gebraucht wird, etwa mit Sofortspenden für notleidende Menschen in der Ukraine und in Syrien. Oder mit einem weltweiten Programm zur Förderung von Bildung und Umweltschutz.

cell technology – and has expanded these segments continuously ever since. One example is its work to develop an integrated fuel cell/battery drive system with a cooperation partner. These emission-free fuel cells are designed to replace conventional diesel drive systems in buses, trucks and maritime applications.

Carl Johann Freudenberg's legacy lives on to this day. The group is now in its seventh generation of family ownership, shared between roughly 360 descendants of its founder. This stable ownership structure, and the long-term approach it enables, are one of the group's strengths. Another is its entrepreneurial approach at every level. Operational business is in the hands of independent companies, whose management conducts business under their own responsibility. These individual companies are, in turn, organised into business groups.

The corporate group's Board of Management concentrates on developing the overall strategy for the Freudenberg Group, deciding on major investments and setting strategic guidelines. The Board of Management currently comprises Dr Mohsen Sohi (CEO), Dr Tilman Krauch (CTO), Dr Ralf Krieger (CFO) and Esther Maria Loidl (CHRO). Its members are appointed by the Freudenberg Group's Supervisory Board, of which at least seven of the current 13 members must be part of the owning family. Martin Wentzler is the Chairman of the Supervisory Board.

The Freudenberg Group has around 51,500 employees, who together achieved sales of around €11.8 billion last year. The Group is growing profitably and has a strong balance sheet. One aspect particularly worthy of note is its healthy equity ratio of 54%.

However, the Freudenberg Group is focused not only on markets and figures, but also on taking responsibility for people and the environment. This includes advancing the energy transition – through its products and the aspiration of becoming a climate-neutral company by 2045. Freudenberg also promotes diversity in its workforce and fosters a corporate culture in which all employees can apply their strengths.

In addition, Freudenberg has also provided support outside the company on numerous occasions, such as by making donations to people in need in Ukraine and Syria and through a global programme to support education and environmental protection.

»Freudenberg bietet kreative technische Lösungen in exzellenter Qualität. Die Basis dafür sind eine große Materialkompetenz und Innovationskraft.«

Freudenberg treibt die Energiewende voran – im eigenen Unternehmen und mit seinen Produkten. Hier bewegt ein Freudenberg-Mitarbeiter eine Aluminiumfolienrolle – ein Bestandteil von Lithium-Ionen-Batterien – in eine Stanzmaschine

Freudenberg is advancing the energy transition, both within the company and through its products. In this image, a Freudenberg employee is moving a roll of aluminium foil – a material used in lithium-ion batteries – into a punching machine

Im Jahr 1948 entwickelte Freudenberg eine Innovation, die noch heute viele Verbraucher*innen schätzen: die Vileda-Reinigungstücher. Die Anzeige für das Fenstertuch stammt aus dem Jahr 1950

In 1948, Freudenberg developed an innovation that many consumers still value to this day: Vileda cleaning cloths. This advertisement for window cloths dates back to 1950

»Freudenberg offers creative technical solutions in excellent quality, based on extensive materials expertise and innovative power.«

Der Vorstand der Freudenberg-Gruppe (von links): Dr. Tilman Krauch, Dr. Mohsen Sohi, Esther Maria Loidl und Dr. Ralf Krieger

The Freudenberg Group Board of Management (from left): Dr Tilman Krauch, Dr Mohsen Sohi, Esther Maria Loidl and Dr Ralf Krieger

HARTING TECHNOLOGIEGRUPPE

Die HARTING Technologiegruppe ist ein Weltmarktführer in der industriellen Verbindungstechnik. Die Connectivity-Lösungen des Unternehmens werden in zahlreichen Industriebranchen zur Übertragung von Daten, Signalen und Strom genutzt, unter anderem in den Wirtschaftszweigen Automatisierung, Elektromobilität, Erneuerbare Energien, Maschinenbau und Transportation. Neben einem komplexen Portfolio von Steckverbindern, den Schnittstellen in der Elektrotechnik, bietet HARTING ein vielfältiges Leistungsspektrum. Dazu zählen die Konfektion, Modifikation, Neu-Entwicklung und Fertigung kundenspezifischer Lösungen und Komponenten ebenso wie Installationskonzepte, globale Anschlusstechnik, Sondermaschinen und Spritzgussformen. Die HARTING Technologiegruppe produziert zudem Ladetechnik für Elektrofahrzeuge und elektromagnetische Aktuatoren für den automotiven und industriellen Serieneinsatz.

Wilhelm und Marie Harting gründeten 1945 die „Wilhelm Harting Mechanische Werkstätten" in Minden und initiierten damit die Erfolgsgeschichte des heutigen Global Players. Sie fertigten zunächst Geräte für den alltäglichen Bedarf wie Sparlampen, Waffeleisen, Kochplatten und Bügeleisen. Noch vor Beginn des wirtschaftlichen Aufschwungs sahen sie den steigenden Bedarf an technischen Produkten für die Industrie voraus und entwickelten gemeinsam mit Mitarbeitenden erste Ideen. Schließlich konstruierten sie einen robusten, anwenderfreundlichen Steckverbinder, langlebig und flexibel einsetzbar. Der Han® setzte in den 1950er-Jahren weltweit den Standard und wurde zum Synonym für Industrie-Steckverbinder. Seit den 1990er-Jahren ist das Han-Modular®-Programm die Benchmark für modulare Steckverbindungen. Das Kerngeschäft mit Steckverbindern ist bis heute die Erfolgsbasis des Technologieführers, der rund 2800 anhängige Patente und Gebrauchsmuster hält (Stand 2023).

The HARTING Technology Group is a global market leader in industrial connection technology. Its connectivity solutions are used to transmit data, signals and power in numerous industrial sectors, including in the fields of automation, electromobility, renewable energy, mechanical engineering and transportation. In addition to a sophisticated portfolio of connectors – crucial interfaces for electrical technologies – HARTING offers a wide-ranging service spectrum. These include designing, developing, modifying and manufacturing customer-specific solutions and components as well as installation concepts, global networking technology, special machinery and injection-moulded parts. The HARTING Technology Group also produces charging technology for electric vehicles and electromagnetic actuators for series application in automotive and industrial production.

In 1945, Wilhelm and Marie Harting founded Wilhelm Harting Mechanische Werkstätten in the town of Minden, thereby launching a success story that would lead to the company becoming a global player today. To begin with, the company produced devices to meet everyday needs, such as energy-saving bulbs, irons, hotplates and waffle irons. Even before the German economy began to boom, they identified the growing demand for technical products for industrial applications, working with their employees to develop their first ideas. Eventually, they designed a robust, user-friendly connector that was both durable and versatile. The Han® set standards around the world in the 1950s and became a synonym for industrial connectors. Since the 1990s, the Han-Modular® range has served as the benchmark for modular connectors. Its core business of manufacturing connectors remains the basis of the technology leader's success to this day. HARTING has around 2,800 pending patents and utility models (as of 2023).

Unternehmensname
HARTING TECHNOLOGIEGRUPPE

Industriezweig
ELEKTROTECHNIK- UND ELEKTRONIK-INDUSTRIE

Gründung
1945 IN MINDEN, WESTFALEN

Produkt
INDUSTRIELLE VERBINDUNGSTECHNIK

Mitarbeitende
RD. 6500

Jahresumsatz
1,059 MRD. EURO WELTWEIT

Company name
HARTING TECHNOLOGY GROUP

Industry
ELECTRICAL ENGINEERING AND ELECTRONICS

Founded
1945 IN MINDEN, WESTPHALIA

Product
INDUSTRIAL CONNECTION TECHNOLOGY

Employees
APPROX. 6,500

Annual sales
€1.059 BILLION WORLDWIDE

Pushing Performance
Since 1945

Der SmEC (Smart Electrical Connector) ist eine intelligente Schnittstelle, die mit übergeordneten Systemen kommuniziert und mit ihrem Digitalen Zwilling Mehrwerte in der Entwicklung, dem Betrieb und der Wartung von Maschinen und Anlagen bietet

The SmEC (Smart Electrical Connector) is an intelligent interface that communicates with higher-level systems and, with its digital twin, offers added value in the development, operation and maintenance of machinery and plant

1962 verstarb Wilhelm Harting, und seine Ehefrau Marie Harting leitete das Unternehmen alleine. Ende der 1960er-Jahre übernahmen auch die Söhne Dietmar und Jürgen Harting (verstorben 1973) unternehmerische Verantwortung. Margrit Harting, Dietmar Hartings Ehefrau, die 1987 in das Unternehmen eintrat, ist Vorstand und Gesellschafterin. Mit CEO Philip Harting und CFO Maresa Harting-Hertz führt nunmehr die dritte Generation die HARTING Technologiegruppe. Vier familienfremde Vorstände komplettieren die Führungsebene des unabhängigen Unternehmens, das zu 100 Prozent im Besitz der Familie Harting ist. Die HARTING Technologiegruppe mit Sitz im ostwestfälischen Espelkamp verfügt über 14 Produktionsstätten und 44 Vertriebsgesellschaften auf allen Kontinenten. Distributionszentren in Europa, Asien und Amerika sichern eine leistungsstarke, zertifizierte Lieferkette.

HARTING übernahm von jeher Verantwortung für Mensch und Umwelt und wurde mehrfach für seine Corporate Social Responsibility ausgezeichnet. Nachhaltigkeit ist ein integraler Bestandteil aller Tätigkeiten und Prozesse im Unternehmen – von der Kommunikation über Logistik und Finanzen bis zur Entwicklung, Beschaffung und Produktion. Die HARTING Technologiegruppe ist Teil der weltweiten Wertegemeinschaft von Unternehmen, die aus Überzeugung zur Entwicklung nachhaltiger Technologien beitragen. Mit seinen industriellen Connectivity-Lösungen forciert HARTING die Vernetzung in allen Bereichen der digitalen Transformation – so etwa intelligente Steckverbinder und deren Digitale Zwillinge. Durch innovative Funktionen werden sie zu einem entscheidenden Baustein für die effiziente und ressourcenschonende Nutzung von Energie. Der Digitale Zwilling trägt dazu bei, dass die Connectivity und die damit verbundenen Prozesse einer digitalen Umgebung überwacht, analysiert, gesteuert und optimiert werden können.

Der Klimaschutz und die Schonung der Ressourcen haben für HARTING hohe Priorität. Schon seit 1975 wird das Galvanik-Spülwasser wiederverwertet und seit 1992 arbeiten alle Produktionsstätten FCKW-frei. Durch die zunehmende Umstellung auf regenerative Energiequellen sowie vier Biomethan-Blockheizkraftwerke wurde die Energieeffizienz um 20 Prozent gesteigert. Seit 2011 werden im Schnitt jährlich 18 500 Tonnen CO_2-Äquivalente eingespart: durch „grüne", auch selbst produzierte Energie, durch Photovoltaikanlagen und energieeffiziente Produktionsprozesse. Geprägt von langfristigem, unternehmerischem Denken und mit Blick auf zukünftige Generationen steht die HARTING Technologiegruppe dafür ein, ökonomischen Erfolg und ökologische Verantwortung immer besser miteinander zu vereinbaren.

After Wilhelm Harting died in 1962, his wife Marie led the company on her own. In the late 1960s, the founding couple's sons Jürgen Harting (who died in 1973) and Dietmar Harting took on responsibility for the company. Margrit Harting, Dietmar Harting's wife, joined the company in 1987 and is now Member of the Board and Partner. With Philip Harting (CEO) and Maresa Harting-Hertz (CFO), the HARTING Technology Group is now led by the third generation of the Harting family. Four board members from outside the owning family complete the management team of this independent company, which is still fully owned by the Harting family. The HARTING Technology Group is based in Espelkamp in East Westphalia and has 14 production sites and 44 sales companies across every continent. Furthermore, its distribution sites in Europe, Asia and the Americas ensure a highly efficient, certified supply chain.

HARTING has always shouldered responsibility for people and the planet, and has received numerous awards in recognition of its corporate social responsibility. Sustainability is an integral part of all of the company's activities and processes – from communications to logistics, and from finance to development, procurement and production. The HARTING Technology Group is part of a global community of companies that share fundamental values and staunchly support the development of sustainable technologies. With its industrial connectivity solutions, HARTING is driving forward connectivity in every area of the digital transformation, including through intelligent connectors and their digital twins. Thanks to their innovative functions, these solutions are making a decisive contribution to the push for efficient, resource-conserving energy use. Digital twins are making it possible to monitor, analyse, control and optimise connectivity and the associated processes in a digital environment.

Climate protection and resource conservation are top priorities for HARTING. It has reused electroplating rinse water since 1975, with all production sites operating CFC-free since 1992. Furthermore, its increasing shift to renewable energy sources and the installation of four biomethane cogeneration units has also improved the company's energy efficiency by 20%. Since 2011, the company has saved an average of 18,500 tonnes of CO_2 equivalent per year by turning to "green" energy, some of it self-generated, installing photovoltaic systems and implementing energy-efficient production processes. Characterised by long-term, entrepreneurial thinking and with an eye on future generations, the HARTING Technology Group is committed to more harmoniously reconciling economic success and environmental responsibility.

»Grün ist unser Denken, und Grün ist unser Handeln.«

Blick in die Fertigungsstätte der HARTING Technologiegruppe in Espelkamp

Inside the HARTING Technology Group's production site in Espelkamp

Produktbilder zur Geräteanschlusstechnik

Images of device connectivity products

»Green is how we think, and green is how we act.«

Die leitenden Familienmitglieder: Philip Harting, Margrit Harting, Maresa Harting-Hertz und Dietmar Harting (von links)

Family members at the top of the company (from left): Philip Harting, Margrit Harting, Maresa Harting-Hertz and Dietmar Harting

HELD

Auf einer Anlage Hightech-Materialien etwa für Brenn-stoffzellen, Elektrolyseure oder die 5G-Technologie und den Leichtbau fertigen – dies und vieles mehr kann die isobare Doppelbandpressen-Anlage von HELD. In diesem Segment ist das 1949 gegründete Unternehmen Weltmarktführer und ausgezeichnet für seine besonderen Innovationsleistungen. In vierter Generation familiengeführt, fertigt HELD ausschließlich am Firmensitz in Trossingen, Baden-Württemberg, und beliefert von hier aus Kunden in aller Welt.

Isobare Doppelbandpressen sind die idealen Anlagen für eine kontinuierliche Herstellung von Bahnen- und Plattenmaterial wie Folien, Gewebe, Vliese, Granulate oder Pulver und erlauben diverse Bearbeitungsvarianten wie Verpressen, Laminieren, Kompaktieren, Konsolidieren und Glätten. Unternehmen etlicher Industriebranchen präferieren für den Verbund verschiedener Werkstoffe zur Herstellung von Halbzeugen die HELD Doppelbandpressen. Genutzt werden die Anlagen von der Energiewirtschaft, zum Beispiel für Energiespeicher und Wasserstofftechnologien, im Elektroniksektor unter anderem für Drohnen und Flächenheizungen, in den Wirtschaftszweigen Automotive, Luft- und Raumfahrt, zum Beispiel für Leichtbauteile, sowie von der Möbelindustrie für Dekorlaminat. Technisches Alleinstellungsmerkmal ist die einzigartige Kombination aus hohem isobarem Druck und hoher Temperatur im kontinuierlichen Herstellungsprozess, die den Industriekunden im Vergleich zu anderen Verfahren erhebliche Vorteile in puncto Produktqualität und Wirtschaftlichkeit sichert. In Europa werden die Kunden direkt von HELD betreut, in Übersee kooperiert das Vertriebsteam zusätzlich mit etablierten Händlernetzwerken. Aufbau und Service vor Ort übernehmen Expert*innen des Maschinenbauers.

Die Entwicklung der Doppelbandpresse mit einem Anlagenwert von mehreren Millionen Euro fand auf

Producing high-tech materials for use in fuel cells, electrolysers, 5G technology and lightweight construction – the isobaric double belt presses from HELD can do all of this and more. Founded in 1949, the company is now a global market leader in this segment and has been recognised for its outstanding, innovative services. Now led by the fourth generation of the owning family, HELD exclusively manufactures its systems at its headquarters in Trossingen, Baden-Württemberg, and ships them to customers around the world.

Isobaric double belt presses are the ideal systems for continuous production of sheet and plate materials such as films, fibres, fabrics, granulates and powders. They facilitate a wide range of processing methods, such as pressing, laminating, compacting, consolidation and smoothing. Companies in all manner of industries choose HELD double belt presses to combine different materials for pre-product manufacturing. These systems are used in the energy industry, including for energy storage systems and hydrogen-based technologies, in the electronics industry for drones and panel heating systems, to produce lightweight components in the automotive and aerospace industries, and in the production of decorative veneers for the furniture industry. The technical characteristic that sets HELD systems apart is their unique combination of high isobaric pressure and high temperature in a continuous production process, which offers industry clients proven advantages in terms of product quality and cost efficiency compared to other techniques. HELD supports its customers in Europe directly and cooperates with established retailer networks to serve customers overseas. The machine builder's in-house experts take care of on-site assembly and servicing.

The story behind the development of a double belt press worth several million euro is an unconventional one. In 1949, Adolf Held established a polishing workshop for

Unternehmensname
HELD TECHNOLOGIE GMBH

Industriezweig
MASCHINENBAU

Gründung
1949 IN TROSSINGEN

Gründer
ADOLF HELD

Vertrieb
EUROPA, NORD- UND SÜDAMERIKA, ASIEN

Jahresumsatz
21,3 MIO. EURO (2022)

Doppelbandpressen-Anlage mit dem Herzstück – der Presse – in der Mitte sowie vor- und nach-gelagerten Abwickel- und Aufwickel-einheiten für das Materialhandling

A double belt press with the centre-piece – the press – in the centre, along with upstream and downstream unwinding and winding units for material handling

Company name
HELD TECHNOLOGIE GMBH

Industry
MECHANICAL ENGINEERING

Founded
1949 IN TROSSINGEN

Founder
ADOLF HELD

Distribution
EUROPE, NORTH AND SOUTH AMERICA, ASIA

Annual sales
€21.3 MILLION (2022)

unkonventionelle Weise statt: 1949 gründete Adolf Held eine Polierwerkstatt für Uhrengehäuse und setzte Maschinen und Vorrichtungen ein, die sein Sohn Kurt Held konstruierte. 1963 wurde der Fokus auf die Herstellung von Montagemaschinen zur Küchenmöbelproduktion gelegt. Der Durchbruch gelang 1975 mit der Markteinführung der weltweit ersten isobaren Doppelbandpresse. Die Ingenieurskunst und der Pioniergeist ihres Erfinders spiegeln sich in der heutigen Innovations-DNA der Firma wider, die zugleich das internationale Renommee von HELD als einem führenden Unternehmen des Sondermaschinenbaus begründet: Mit anhaltender Innovationsfreude fertigt HELD kundenspezifische Lösungen und setzt fortwährend Branchenstandards. Dazu zählen unter anderem Doppelbandpressen mit bis zu 400 Grad Celsius Heiztemperatur und gleichzeitig bis zu 80 Bar isobarem Flächendruck, die Einführung der schnellsten Anlage zur Herstellung von Möbellaminat (CPL) mit einer Produktionsgeschwindigkeit von 48 Metern pro Minute und die weltweit erste Presse zur formatfreien Produktion von Hochdruck-Möbellaminat (HPL) mit einer Stärke von 1,2 Millimetern. 2024 stellt HELD eine digitalisierte und automatisierte Maschinengeneration vor, die den technologischen Vorsprung des Unternehmens ausbauen und festigen wird. Allein für „Hailey", eine Showroom-Maschine dieser neuen Generation, auf der Kunden im HELD Technologiepark auch Materialien testen und fertigen können, werden 100 innovative Ideen appliziert. Durch den Einsatz Künstlicher Intelligenz und individueller Softwarelösungen werden HELD Anlagen zukünftig zum integralen Bestandteil digitaler Produktionsstätten.

Der Anteil nachhaltiger Lösungen steigt stetig. HELD optimiert seine Klimabilanz durch Wärmerückgewinnung sowie durch Energieeinspeisungen eines Gas-Blockheizkraftwerks und der Photovoltaikanlagen. Der Strom, den HELD darüber hinaus bezieht, wird zu 100 Prozent aus Wasserkraft erzeugt. Dem Fachkräftemangel wirkt das Unternehmen mit zahlreichen Maßnahmen entgegen, darunter vielfältige Ausbildungsgänge, duales Studium, Weiterbildungsangebote und Zusatzleistungen für Mitarbeitende sowie eine gute Work-Life-Balance. Zur Förderung hochqualifizierter Nachwuchskräfte unterstützt HELD als Partner die Duale Hochschule Baden-Württemberg (DHBW). Das Unternehmen ist Mitglied von Organisationen und Netzwerken wie dem Verband der Maschinen- und Anlagenbauer (VDMA) oder dem Cluster Brennstoffzelle BW und erhielt 2022 das Prädikat „Ehrenamtsfreundlicher Arbeitgeber" und 2023 das „TOP 100 Innovator"-Siegel.

Seit jeher entstehen bei HELD aus ingeniösem Schaffen kundenorientierte Innovationen – stets unter dem Credo „turning ideas into solutions".

clock cases, using machinery and equipment built by his son, Kurt Held. In 1963, the company's focus shifted to the manufacture of assembly machinery for the kitchen furniture industry. However, it was in 1975 that the company achieved its breakthrough by launching the world's first isobaric double belt press. The engineering skill and pioneering spirit of the company's founder is reflected to this day in its innovative DNA, which underpins HELD's international reputation as a leading manufacturer of specialist machinery. With its unwavering passion for innovation, HELD produces customer-specific solutions and continues to set industry standards. These include double belt presses with heating temperatures of up to 400°C and isobaric surface pressures of up to 80 bar, the introduction of the fastest system for decorative laminate (CPL) production with an output of 48 metres per minute, and the world's first press for format-free production of high-pressure decorative laminate (HPL) with a thickness of 1.2 millimetres. In 2024, HELD will launch a digitalised, automated generation of machinery, which will consolidate and extend the company's technological advantage. In fact, the company has integrated 100 innovative ideas into one machine alone: Hailey, a next-generation showroom machine at the HELD Technology Park, allows customers to test and produce materials. Through the use of artificial intelligence and customised software solutions, HELD machinery will become an integral element of digital manufacturing facilities in the future.

The proportion of sustainable solutions is constantly rising. HELD optimises its climate footprint through heat recovery systems and by generating its own energy with a gas-fired cogeneration plant and photovoltaic systems. HELD sources 100% of its additional electricity requirements from hydropower. The company has introduced a number of measures to counteract the current shortage of skilled workers, including training courses, dual work-study programmes, professional development services, employee benefits and measures to promote a healthy work-life balance. HELD has partnered with the Baden-Württemberg Cooperative State University (DHBW) in Stuttgart in an effort to support highly qualified career entrants. It is also a member of several organisations and networks, such as the German Mechanical and Plant Engineering Association (VDMA) and the Fuel Cell BW Cluster. HELD was awarded the title of "Volunteering-Friendly Employer" in 2022 and received the "TOP 100 Innovator" seal in 2023.

From the outset, HELD has demonstrated ingenuity to produce customer-oriented innovations, always in line with its motto: "Turning ideas into solutions."

»Viele Dinge werden als unmöglich angesehen. Aber wir machen sie möglich.«

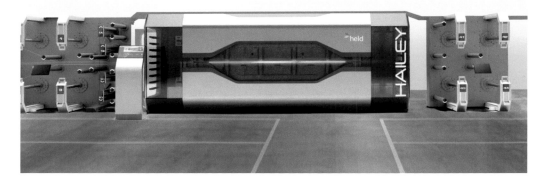

Entwurf der neuen automatisierten und digitalisierten Maschinengeneration

A design for the new automated, digitalised generation of machinery

Das Firmengelände von HELD mit Turm und Büroräumen, Maschinenbau- und zwei Technologie- parks für Versuche, Muster- und Serien- fertigungen

The HELD premises, featuring the tower and office spaces, a mechanical engineering area and two technology parks for testing, sampling and series manufacturing

Die Geschäftsleitung – Till Held (links) und Matthias Fisel – vor der Doppelbandpresse im eigenen Technologie-Park in Trossingen

The company's management team – Till Held (left) and Matthias Fisel – in front of the double belt press at the HELD Technology Park in Trossingen

MATTHIAS FISEL

»Many things are considered impossible. We make them possible.«

HENKEL

Mit Marken wie Loctite, Schwarzkopf und Persil sind die Produkte von Henkel aus dem Alltag von Millionen von Menschen weltweit nicht wegzudenken. Das Familienunternehmen aus Düsseldorf ist mit seinen beiden Unternehmensbereichen Adhesive Technologies und Consumer Brands sowohl im Industrie- als auch im Konsumentengeschäft tätig. Adhesive Technologies ist globaler Marktführer für Klebstoffe, Dichtstoffe und Funktionsbeschichtungen. Mit Consumer Brands ist Henkel insbesondere mit Wasch- und Reinigungsmitteln sowie Haarpflege weltweit in vielen Märkten und Kategorien führend.

Am 26. September 1876 gründete der 28-jährige Kaufmann Fritz Henkel mit zwei Geschäftspartnern in Aachen die Firma Henkel & Cie. Ihr erstes Produkt „Universal-Waschmittel" hatte noch nicht den gewünschten Erfolg. Daher entwickelten sie ihre Waschmittel weiter und brachten bereits zwei Jahre später „Henkel's Bleich-Soda" auf den Markt – das erste Erfolgsprodukt. Zu Beginn des 20. Jahrhunderts gelang der große Durchbruch: Persil, das erste selbsttätige Waschmittel, begründete ab 1907 nicht nur das Wachstum des Unternehmens, sondern trug auch zum gesellschaftlichen Fortschritt bei. Es erleichterte das aufwendige Waschen per Hand und revolutionierte so den Alltag vieler Menschen. Heute ist Persil weltweit in rund 60 Ländern erhältlich.

Henkel ist eine Kommanditgesellschaft auf Aktien (KGaA). Die Henkel Management AG ist alleinige persönlich haftende Gesellschafterin und wird durch einen fünfköpfigen Vorstand geführt, dem Carsten Knobel seit Januar 2020 als Vorstandsvorsitzender vorsteht. Die Familie Henkel ist in den Aufsichtsgremien des Konzerns vertreten: Dr. Simone Bagel-Trah, seit 2009 Vorsitzende des Aufsichtsrats und des Gesellschafterausschusses, repräsentiert die fünfte Generation der Familie. „Mein Ururgroßvater Fritz Henkel war ein

With brands including Loctite, Schwarzkopf and Persil, Henkel's products are a vital part of everyday life for millions of people around the world. The family-owned company from Düsseldorf has two business units – Adhesive Technologies and Consumer Brands – and markets its products to industrial customers and consumers. The Adhesive Technologies business unit is the global leader in the market for adhesives, sealants and functional coatings. With Consumer Brands, the company holds leading positions especially in hair care and laundry and home care in many markets and categories around the world.

On 26 September 1876, a 28-year-old clerk called Fritz Henkel and two business partners founded Henkel & Cie in Aachen. However, their first product, a laundry detergent, failed to deliver the desired success. The partners decided to refine their detergent and, two years later, Henkel released Henkel's Bleich-Soda – the company's first successful product. Then, in the early 20th century, Henkel achieved its big breakthrough with Persil, the first self-acting laundry detergent. Not only did Persil lay the foundations for the company's growth from 1907 onwards, it also contributed to social progress. It reduced the effort involved in washing clothes by hand, fundamentally transforming daily life for vast numbers of people. Today, Persil is available in around 60 countries around the world.

Henkel is a public partly limited partnership (Kommanditgesellschaft auf Aktien – KGaA). Henkel Management AG is the sole personally liable shareholder and is led by a five-strong Management Board, which Carsten Knobel has headed up as CEO since January 2020. The Henkel family is represented on the corporate group's supervisory board: Dr Simone Bagel-Trah, Chairwoman of the Supervisory Board and the Shareholders' Committee since 2009, represents the fifth generation of the family. "My great-great-grandfather, Fritz

Unternehmensname
HENKEL AG & CO. KGAA

Industriezweig
INDUSTRIE- UND KONSUMGÜTER

Gründung
1876 IN AACHEN

Gründer
FRITZ HENKEL

Mitarbeitende
ÜBER 50 000 WELTWEIT

Jahresumsatz
MEHR ALS 22 MRD. EURO WELTWEIT

Company name
HENKEL AG & CO. KGAA

Industry
INDUSTRIAL AND CONSUMER GOODS

Founded
1876 IN AACHEN

Founder
FRITZ HENKEL

Employees
OVER 50,000 WORLDWIDE

Annual sales
OVER €22 BILLION WORLDWIDE

Innovationen sind seit jeher der Schlüssel für den Erfolg von Henkel. An Forschungs- und Entwicklungsstandorten arbeiten weltweit rund 2700 Wissenschaftler*innen

Innovation has always been the key to Henkel's success. Around 2,700 scientists work at the company's research and development sites around the world

echter Unternehmer. Er hat neue Wege ausprobiert. Er war mutig und im Herzen ein Pionier. Er revolutionierte den Alltag der Menschen – aber nicht nur für seine Kunden. Er sorgte sich auch um die Henkelaner, die Gesellschaft und die Umwelt. Lange bevor Nachhaltigkeit so relevant wurde wie heute, dachte er darüber nach, was seine Entscheidungen und Handlungen für zukünftige Generationen bedeuten. Dieser Geist ist bis heute ein fester Bestandteil der Henkel-DNA und in jeder Generation der Familie Henkel zu finden", sagt Dr. Simone Bagel-Trah. Und noch heute sind die Mitarbeitenden bereit, neue Wege zu gehen und auf Innovationen zu setzen, um einen nachhaltigen Mehrwert für Kunden und Verbraucher*innen in aller Welt zu schaffen. Innovationen waren und sind der Schlüssel für den langfristigen Erfolg von Henkel. Henkel betreibt weltweit Forschungs- und Entwicklungsstandorte, an denen rund 2700 Naturwissenschaftler*innen, Materialwissenschaftler*innen, Ingenieur*innen und Techniker*innen arbeiten. Gemeinsam mit ihren Kolleg*innen aus der Produktentwicklung, dem Marketing, der Produktion und der Verpackungsentwicklung stellen sie sicher, dass die neuen Ideen den Bedürfnissen der Kunden und Verbraucher*innen gerecht werden.

Der Purpose bzw. Unternehmenszweck „Pioneers at heart for the good of generations" ist das zentrale Leitbild von Henkel. Er ist die Basis für die strategische Agenda des Unternehmens, das auf ganzheitliches Wachstum setzt. Henkels strategische Prioritäten umfassen ein aktives Portfoliomanagement, klare Wettbewerbsvorteile in den Bereichen Innovation, Nachhaltigkeit und Digitalisierung sowie zukunftsfähige Geschäftsprozesse. Sie bauen auf einer starken Unternehmenskultur auf, in der enge Zusammenarbeit und Gestaltungsspielräume für die Mitarbeitenden im Mittelpunkt stehen. Denn bei Henkel weiß man: Die Voraussetzung für den Unternehmenserfolg sind motivierte und engagierte Teams. Henkel bietet seinen Beschäftigten viele Weiterbildungsmöglichkeiten, flexible Arbeitsmodelle, Betriebskindertagesstätten und eine betriebliche Altersversorgung. Schon seit 1912, lange bevor solche Angebote zum guten Ton gehörten, berät Henkel seine Mitarbeitenden mit einer eigenen Abteilung „Soziale Dienste". Schließlich war schon Fritz Henkel der Meinung: „Das Beste, das durch mein Werk gemacht wurde, ist nicht meinen Gedanken entsprungen, sondern meinen Mitarbeitern im gegenseitigen Zusammenarbeiten."

Am 20. März 2023 feierte Henkel den 175. Geburtstag seines Firmengründers Fritz Henkel. Seine Werte, sein Pioniergeist und sein Verantwortungsbewusstsein prägen die Unternehmenskultur bis heute.

Henkel, was a true entrepreneur. He forged new paths. He was courageous; a pioneer at heart. He revolutionised people's day-to-day lives – and not only for his customers: he also looked after the Henkelaners, society and the environment. Long before sustainability became as relevant as it is today, he considered the consequences of his decisions and actions on future generations. This spirit remains an integral part of the Henkel DNA to this day and lives on in every generation of the Henkel family," says Dr Simone Bagel-Trah. Even today, its employees are willing to forge new paths and embrace innovation in order to deliver sustainable added value for customers and consumers all around the world. Innovations have been and remain the key to Henkel's long-term success. Henkel operates research and development facilities around the world, where it employs around 2,700 natural scientists, materials scientists, engineers and technicians. Together with their colleagues in product development, marketing, production and packaging development, they ensure that new ideas meet the needs of customers and consumers.

Henkel's purpose "Pioneers at heart for the good of generations" is its guiding north star. It is an integral part of the company's strategic agenda for purposeful growth. The main elements of Henkel's strategic framework are an active portfolio management, competitive edge in the areas of innovation, sustainability and digitalisation as well as future-ready operating models, underpinned by a strong foundation of a collaborative culture and empowered people. Henkel is acutely aware that motivated, engaged teams are vital for the company to continue its success into the future. Its employee offering includes a range of professional development opportunities, flexible working models, company childcare facilities and an occupational pension scheme. Even back in 1912, long before such services became commonplace, Henkel established a dedicated Social Services department to advise his employees. Ultimately, Fritz Henkel believed: "The best that was achieved through my work, did not arise from my thoughts, but from my employees in mutual cooperation."

On 20 March 2023, Henkel celebrated the 175th anniversary of the birth of its founder, Fritz Henkel. His values, pioneering spirit and sense of responsibility continue to shape the company's culture to this day.

DR. SIMONE BAGEL-TRAH ZUM WERT
„FAMILIENUNTERNEHMEN" BEI HENKEL

»Wir gestalten unsere Zukunft mit ausgeprägtem Unternehmergeist auf der Grundlage unserer Tradition als Familienunternehmen.«

Mit Marken, Innovationen und Technologien hält Henkel führende Marktpositionen weltweit

With its brands, innovations and technologies, Henkel holds leading market positions worldwide

Dr. Simone Bagel-Trah, Vorsitzende des Aufsichtsrats und des Gesellschafterausschusses von Henkel

Dr Simone Bagel-Trah, Chairwoman of the Supervisory Board and the Shareholders' Committee at Henkel

Der Unternehmenszweck „Pioneers at heart for the good of generations" ist das zentrale Leitbild von Henkel

The company's purpose "Pioneers at heart for the good of generations" is its guiding north star

DR SIMONE BAGEL-TRAH ON THE VALUE OF HENKEL BEING A FAMILY COMPANY:

»We are shaping our future with a strong entrepreneurial spirit based on our tradition as a family business.«

Mit seinen Werten, seinem Pioniergeist und Verantwortungsbewusstsein prägt Fritz Henkel die Unternehmenskultur bis heute

With his values, pioneering spirit and sense of responsibility, Fritz Henkel still has a strong influence on the company culture today

HENNECKE

Polyurethane, kurz PUR, sind Kunststoffe und Kunstharze zur Herstellung von Schaumstoffen, Lacken, Dichtstoffen, Klebstoffen und vielem mehr. Zahllose Varianten bieten der verarbeitenden Industrie fast unbegrenzte Möglichkeiten, unter anderem als Möbel- und Autositzpolster, als Matratzenschaum, zur Dämmung von Gebäuden und Kühlgeräten, in Wärme- und Kältespeichern.

Die Hennecke GROUP entwickelt und produziert führende Maschinen- und Anlagentechnik zur Herstellung und Verarbeitung von Polyurethan. Eine wichtige Rolle spielt dabei das nordrheinwestfälische Stammhaus in Sankt Augustin, welches seit mehr als 75 Jahren Maschinen- und Anlagentechnik sowie Prozesstechnologie zur Polyurethan-Verarbeitung entwickelt.

Bereits 1945 setzte der Gründer Karl Hennecke erste Ideen in die Praxis um, unter anderem für Kaschiermaschinen und Textilwaschanlagen. Er entwickelte eigene Verfahrenstechniken und gründete die Maschinenfabrik Karl Hennecke in Sankt Augustin. Schon früh erkannte er dabei das Potenzial von Polyurethan und erfand das weltweit erste System zur Hochdruckvermischung der PUR-Komponenten Polyol und Isocyanat.

Der Pionier des Polyurethan-Maschinenbaus setzte damit den heutigen globalen Standard. Das Unternehmen festigte seine Position als Technologieführer der Branche mit zahlreichen weiteren Innovationen. Insgesamt wurden über 120 Schutzrechte angemeldet, derzeit hält Hennecke 17 aktive Patente. Das geballte Know-how fließt stetig in Neuentwicklungen ein, oft in enger Kooperation mit Kunden, die von den Qualitäts- und Effizienzsteigerungen in der Verarbeitung und Anwendung technologisch wie wirtschaftlich profitieren.

Polyurethanes (PU) are a group of plastics and synthetic resins used in the manufacture of foams, lacquers, sealants, adhesives and many other products. Countless polyurethane variants offer the processing industry near-unlimited possibilities, including furniture and vehicle upholstery, mattress foam, insulation in buildings and cooling devices, and in heat reservoirs and cold-storage systems.

The Hennecke GROUP develops and produces leading machine and systems technology for polyurethane production and processing. Its headquarters in Sankt Augustin, North Rhine-Westphalia – where Hennecke has been developing machine and system technology as well as process technology for polyurethane processing for more than 75 years – plays an important role in its work to this day.

In 1945, the company's founder, Karl Hennecke, put his initial ideas into practice, including for laminators and textile washing machinery. He developed his own process technologies and founded Maschinenfabrik Karl Hennecke in the town of Sankt Augustin. Even at an early stage, he recognised the potential of polyurethane and invented the world's first system capable of mixing polyol and isocyanate, two components of PU, at high pressures.

In doing so, the pioneer of polyurethane machine construction set a global standard that endures to this day. Over time, the company consolidated its position as a technology leader in the industry with a number of further innovations. In total, Hennecke has registered over 120 trademarks and currently holds 17 active patents. The company continuously channels its accumulated expertise into new developments, often in close cooperation with its customers, who benefit in technological and commercial terms from enhanced quality and efficiency in processing and application.

Hennecke
Polyurethane Technology

Unternehmensname
HENNECKE GMBH

Industriezweig
MASCHINEN- UND ANLAGENBAU

Gründung
1945 IN SANKT AUGUSTIN

Gründer
KARL HENNECKE

Hauptfertigungsstätte
SANKT AUGUSTIN, DEUTSCHLAND

Mitarbeitende
700 MITARBEITENDE WELTWEIT, DAVON 385 AM HAUPTSITZ IN DEUTSCHLAND

Company name
HENNECKE GMBH

Industry
MECHANICAL AND SYSTEMS ENGINEERING

Founded
1945 IN SANKT AUGUSTIN

Founder
KARL HENNECKE

Main production facility
SANKT AUGUSTIN, GERMANY

Employees
700 WORLDWIDE, INCL. 385 AT ITS HEADQUARTER IN GERMANY

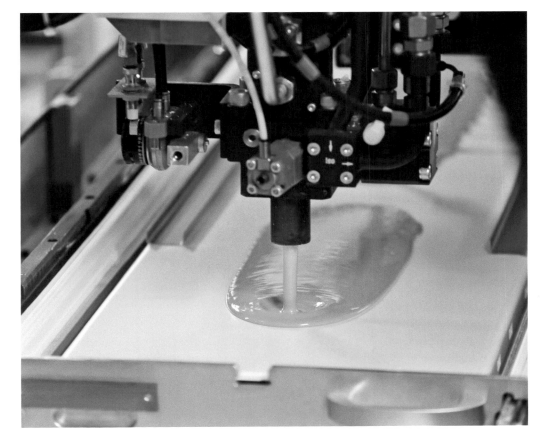

A+++ dank PUR:
Anlagentechnik zur
rohstoffeffizienten
Isolierung von Kühlmöbeln

A+++ thanks to PU:
System technology for
resource-efficient insulation
of refrigeration appliances

Intensive Forschungs- und Entwicklungsarbeit bildet bei Hennecke die Basis für fortschrittliche Systeme mit hohem ökonomischem und ökologischem Nutzen. Unter dem Handelsnamen Hennecke Polyurethane Technology werden State-of-the-Art-Hoch- und Niederdruck-Dosiermaschinen, dazu passende Mischköpfe, Block- und Formschaum-Anlagen sowie Anlagen für technische Isolierungen und PUR-Sprühanwendungen gefertigt. Die Hennecke Roll Forming Technology mit Sitz in Kreuztal (NRW) entwickelt, konstruiert und fertigt hochwertige Profilieranlagen. Dazu zählen Rollformanlagen für isolierende Dach- und Wand-Sandwichelemente, Rollformer und Pressen zur Fertigung von Sektionaltorelementen sowie Querteilanlagen und Hochleistungs-Trapezblech-Profilieranlagen.

Neben den deutschen Standorten gibt es drei weitere Hennecke-Kompetenzzentren in Verano Brianza, Italien, Pittsburgh, USA, und Jiaxing, China, sowie acht weitere Gesellschaften in zentralen Absatzmärkten. Zudem agiert Hennecke mit einem weltumspannenden Netzwerk von Vertriebs- und Service-Vertretungen in mehr als 100 Ländern.

Hennecke-Maschinen und -Anlagen genießen auf der ganzen Welt ein hohes Prestige aufgrund ihrer Präzision, Zuverlässigkeit und Langlebigkeit. Die hohe Dosiergenauigkeit und Rohstoffeffizienz gewährleistet insbesondere bei kontinuierlichen Herstellungsprozessen einen schnellen Return of Investment. Hauptabnehmer weltweit sind die Wirtschaftszweige Transport, Möbel, Bauwirtschaft, Elektronik, Energie, das Gesundheitswesen, die Agrarwirtschaft und diverse weitere.

Hennecke ist einer der größten Ausbildungsbetriebe seiner Region, kooperiert mit regionalen Bildungseinrichtungen und ist Gründungs- und Fördermitglied der Hochschule Bonn-Rhein-Sieg. Mit seiner überdurchschnittlichen Ausbildungsquote bietet das Unternehmen vielen jungen Talenten eine berufliche Zukunft.

Das Unternehmen hat sich weltweit zum Ziel gesetzt, Wachstum und Maßnahmen für eine nachhaltigere und sozial gerechtere Zukunft erfolgreich zu vereinen und wird dabei von einem externen Unternehmen auditiert. Getreu seinem Credo „FASCINATION PUR" schafft Hennecke stets neue, zukunftsweisende Komplettlösungen in der Polyurethan-Herstellung und -Verarbeitung zur wirtschaftlichen und immer umweltfreundlicheren Realisierung von Produkten, die das Leben komfortabler, gesünder und angenehmer machen.

Intensive research and development forms the basis of Hennecke's advanced systems, generating significant economic and environmental benefits. Under the trade name Hennecke Polyurethane Technology, the company manufactures state-of-the-art high-pressure and low-pressure metering machines along with corresponding mixheads, slabstock and moulded foam systems as well as production lines for technical insulation and PU spray applications. Hennecke Roll Forming Technology, which is based in Kreuztal (North Rhine-Westphalia), develops, designs and manufactures high-quality roll forming systems. These include roll forming systems for insulating roof and wall sandwich panels, roll forming machines and presses to produce sectional door panels as well as cut-to-length systems and high-performance trapezoidal sheet roll forming plant.

In addition to its three sites in Germany, Hennecke also has three centres of excellence in Verano Brianza, Italy, Pittsburgh, USA, and Jiaxing, China, as well as eight companies in core sales markets. Hennecke also has a global network of sales and service representatives in over 100 countries.

Hennecke machinery and systems are held in high regard around the world due to their precision, reliability and durability. Their high metering precision and resource efficiency ensures a rapid return on investment, especially when used in continuous manufacturing processes. Its main customers around the world are the transport, furniture, construction, electronics, energy, healthcare and agriculture industries, among many others.

Hennecke is one of the largest training providers in its region. It cooperates with regional educational institutions and is a founding member and supporter of Hochschule Bonn-Rhein-Sieg, a university of applied sciences also located nearby. With its above-average training ratio, the company offers a professional future for many talented young people.

Hennecke has set itself the goal of working worldwide to successfully combine growth with measures for a more sustainable, socially just future – and has its efforts in this regard audited by an external firm. Staying true to its motto, "FASCINATION PU", Hennecke is constantly creating new and pioneering complete solutions for polyurethane production and processing. Its aim is to facilitate the cost-effective and increasingly environmentally friendly manufacturing of products that make people's lives more comfortable, healthy and enjoyable.

THOMAS WILDT, CEO HENNECKE GROUP

»Bei effizienten und nachhaltigen Komplettlösungen für die Verarbeitung von Polyurethan ist Hennecke seit jeher Innovationsführer.«

Das Herzstück unzähliger Verarbeitungsanlagen weltweit: Hochdruck-Dosiermaschinen für die Verarbeitung von Polyurethan

The linchpin in countless processing plants worldwide: High-pressure metering machines for polyurethane processing

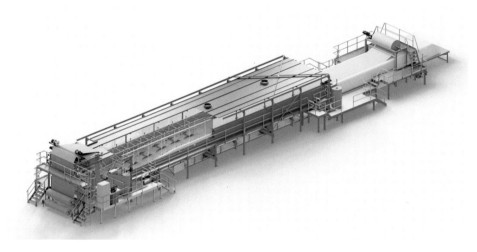

Weltmarktführer im Bereich der kontinuierlichen Herstellung von Komfortschäumen für die Möbelindustrie und technische Anwendungen: Hennecke-Blockschaumanlage vom Typ MULTIFLEX

A global market leader in the continuous production of comfort foam for the furniture industry and technical applications: Hennecke's MULTIFLEX slabstock foam production line

THOMAS WILDT, CEO OF THE HENNECKE GROUP

»When it comes to efficient and sustainable complete solutions for polyurethane processing, Hennecke has always been an innovation leader.«

Der Unternehmenshauptsitz in Sankt Augustin bei Bonn

The company's headquarters in Sankt Augustin, near Bonn

HERAEUS

Der Technologiekonzern Heraeus gehört zu den Top Ten der deutschen Familienunternehmen. Aus der Verbindung von Materialkompetenz mit Technologie- und Applikations-Know-how schafft das Unternehmen in seinen verschiedenen Geschäften und Märkten hochwertige Lösungen für seine Kunden, die deren Wettbewerbsfähigkeit nachhaltig stärken.

Heraeus bündelt seine Aktivitäten in den Business-Plattformen Metalle und Recycling, Gesundheit, Halbleiter und Elektronik sowie industrielle Anwendungen. Das Produkt- und Lösungsangebot reicht von Komponenten bis zu abgestimmten Materialsystemen. Sie finden Verwendung in vielfältigen Industrien, darunter Chemie, Elektronik, Erneuerbare Energien, Umwelttechnik, Automobil, Stahl, Medizintechnik und Telekommunikation.

Seinen Anfang nahm die Familienunternehmung 1660 als Apotheke. 1694 wurde das erste Edelmetallprodukt geliefert. 1851 entwickelte sich daraus ein Industrieunternehmen, als der Apotheker und Chemiker Wilhelm Carl Heraeus mithilfe der Knallgasflamme Platin zum Schmelzen brachte – und somit den Grundstein zur industriellen Nutzung des Edelmetalls legte.

Im Geschäftsjahr 2022 erzielte das Unternehmen mit rund 17 200 Mitarbeitenden an mehr als 100 Standorten in 40 Ländern einen Gesamtumsatz von 29,1 Milliarden Euro. Mit Heraeus CEO Jan Rinnert steht ein Mitglied der Gesellschafterfamilie an der Spitze der Geschäftsführung: „Die heutige Zeit stellt Unternehmen vor vielfältige Herausforderungen und bietet einzigartige Chancen. Mit rund 20 eigenständigen, diversifizierten Geschäftseinheiten ist Heraeus hervorragend positioniert. So sind wir einerseits in der Lage, von wichtigen Megatrends der Zukunft zu profitieren, und können andererseits die langfristige, erfolgreiche Entwicklung des Familienunternehmens gewährleisten." Die einzel-

The technology company Heraeus is among the top ten German family enterprises. By combining materials expertise with specialist technology and applications know-how, the company creates high-quality solutions that support lasting improvements in its customers' competitiveness across various segments and markets.

Heraeus concentrates its activities into a series of business platforms, namely metals and recycling, healthcare, semiconductors and electronics, and industrials. Its portfolio of products and solutions ranges from individual components to customised material systems. Their applications span a wide range of industries, including the chemicals industry, electronics, renewable energy, environmental engineering, the automotive industry, the steel industry, medical technology and telecommunications.

The family company was established in 1660, originally as a pharmacy. The company launched its first product made from precious metal in 1694. In 1851, the business developed into an industrial enterprise when Wilhelm Carl Heraeus, a pharmacist and chemist, used an oxyhydrogen gas blower to melt platinum – thereby laying the foundations for the metal's industrial use.

In the 2022 business year, the company had roughly 17,200 employees at over 100 sites in 40 countries and recorded total sales of €29.1 billion. Jan Rinnert, a member of the shareholder family, leads the company's management as Heraeus CEO. "The world today presents companies with manifold challenges and offers unique opportunities," he says. "With around 20 independent, diversified business units, Heraeus is ideally positioned. On the one hand, we can profit from the central megatrends of the future; on the other hand, we can secure the long-term, successful development of our family business." The individual Heraeus business units operate with a high degree of entrepreneurial

Heraeus

Unternehmensname
HERAEUS HOLDING GMBH

Industriezweig
TECHNOLOGIEKONZERN

Gründung
1851

Produkte
EDELMETALLE UND RECYCLING, GESUNDHEIT, HALBLEITER UND ELEKTRONIK SOWIE INDUSTRIELLE ANWENDUNGEN

Mitarbeitende
17 200 WELTWEIT

Jahresumsatz
29,1 MRD. EURO (2022)

Company name
HERAEUS HOLDING GMBH

Industry
TECHNOLOGY COMPANY

Founded
1851

Products
METALS AND RECYCLING, HEALTHCARE, SEMICONDUCTORS AND ELECTRONICS, INDUSTRIALS

Employees
17,200 WORLDWIDE

Annual sales
€29.1 BILLION (2022)

Heraeus ist der weltweit größte Anbieter von industriellen Edelmetall-dienstleistungen

Heraeus is the world's leading provider of industrial precious metals services

nen Geschäfte von Heraeus agieren dabei mit einem hohen Grad an unternehmerischer Freiheit. „Durch gezielte, marktspezifische Strategien können sich unsere Unternehmen stärker auf Marktveränderungen und sich entwickelnde Kundenbedürfnisse einstellen", erklärt Jan Rinnert.

Allen Geschäftseinheiten gemeinsam ist das Ziel, auf ihren jeweiligen Märkten eine führende Rolle einzunehmen. Darüber hinaus legt Heraeus in seinen Geschäften einen klaren Fokus auf Kundenorientierung, Innovation und Exzellenz sowie motivierte und engagierte Mitarbeiterinnen und Mitarbeiter.

Knapp sechs Prozent des Gesamtumsatzes ohne Edelmetalle investierte Heraeus 2022 in Forschung und Entwicklung, um die einzelnen Geschäfte zu stärken sowie neue Technologiefelder und Märkte zu erschließen, zum Beispiel amorphe Werkstoffe und grünen Wasserstoff. „Innovation ist das Herz unserer Arbeit bei Heraeus. Ohne die ständige Entwicklung neuer Produkte und Lösungen für unsere Kunden wäre Heraeus nicht das, was es heute ist – ein weltweit führender Technologiekonzern", sagt Jan Rinnert. Dazu kooperiert Heraeus auch mit externen Partnern, wie anderen Unternehmen, Forschungsnetzwerken und Universitäten. Mit einem eigenen, 2019 ins Leben gerufenen Accelerator-Programm stärkt Heraeus die Zusammenarbeit mit externen Start-ups.

Seine bestehenden Geschäfte ergänzt Heraeus immer wieder um Kompetenzen und Technologien durch Zukäufe von außen. So stieg die Heraeus Gruppe Anfang 2023 beim Berliner KI-Start-up Smart Steel Technologies (SST) ein. SST bietet auf Künstlicher Intelligenz (KI) basierende Softwarelösungen an, die Prozesse in der Stahlindustrie optimieren. Ein Jahr zuvor erwarb Heraeus eine Mehrheitsbeteiligung an revalyu, einem weltweit führenden Recyclingunternehmen von PET-Flaschen. 2021 erweiterte die Heraeus Gruppe ihre Medizintechnik-Expertise durch die Akquisition des US-Unternehmens Norwood Medical, eines Herstellers von medizinischen Instrumenten, Geräten und Komponenten. Mit der Gründung eines Joint Ventures mit BASF in China für Edelmetallrecycling aus Autokatalysatoren unterstreicht Heraeus seine weltweit führende Position in der Edelmetallindustrie.

„Die hohe Motivation und das herausragende Engagement unserer Mitarbeiterinnen und Mitarbeiter weltweit tragen maßgeblich zum Erfolg von Heraeus bei", betont Jan Rinnert. Die Unternehmensgruppe hat den Anspruch, ihre Mitarbeitenden langfristig zu binden und zu fördern. Heraeus setzt hierzu auf moderne Arbeitskonzepte, interne Award- und Konferenzformate sowie auf ein globales Führungsmodell, das auf Vorbildfunktion basiert.

freedom. "By implementing targeted, market-specific strategies, our companies can adapt better to market changes and changing customer needs," Rinnert adds.

All business units are united by the goal of taking a leading role in their respective markets. Furthermore, Heraeus concentrates squarely on the aspects of customer orientation, innovation and excellence, and also strives to ensure its employees are motivated and engaged.

In 2022, Heraeus invested almost 6% of its total sales (excluding precious metals) in research and development in order to consolidate its individual business platforms and open up new markets and fields of technology, such as amorphous materials and green hydrogen. "Innovation is the heart of our work at Heraeus," says Rinnert. "Heraeus would not be what it is today – a world-leading technology company – were it not for the constant development of new products and solutions for our customers." As part of this work, Heraeus cooperates with external partners, including other companies, research networks and universities. In 2019, it launched the Heraeus Accelerator programme to strengthen its cooperation with external start-ups.

In addition, Heraeus supplements its existing business units with expertise and technologies through frequent acquisitions. In early 2023, for example, the Heraeus Group acquired a stake in Smart Steel Technologies (SST), an AI start-up in Berlin. SST offers AI-based software solutions that optimise processes in the steel industry. The year before, Heraeus acquired a controlling interest in revalyu, a world leader in PET bottle recycling. In 2021, the Heraeus Group developed its expertise in the field of medical technology by acquiring the US-based company Norwood Medical, which manufactures medical instruments, devices and components. Furthermore, Heraeus has launched a joint venture with BASF in China to recycle precious metals from automotive catalytic converters, underscoring its world-leading position in the precious metals industry.

"The strong motivation and outstanding commitment shown by our employees around the world are a vital contribution to the success of Heraeus," emphasises Rinnert. The corporate group strives to retain its employees for the long term and support their development. To this end, Heraeus has implemented modern working concepts, internal award and conference formats and a global management model based on leading by example.

JAN RINNERT, HERAEUS CEO

»Innovation ist das Herz unserer Arbeit.«

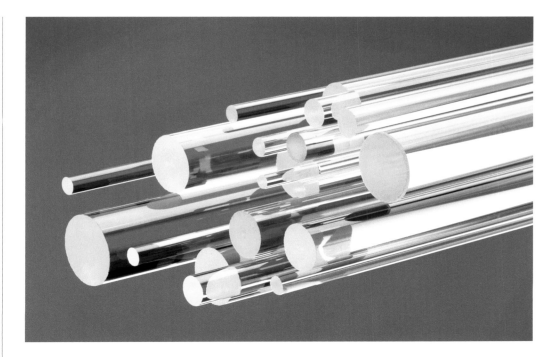

Hochreines Quarzglas von Heraeus – aus dem Hightech-Werkstoff werden unter anderem Glasfasern für schnelles Internet hergestellt

Ultra-pure quartz glass from Heraeus – a high-tech material for applications including the production of fibre optics for high-speed internet

Heraeus beschäftigt rund 17 200 Mitarbeitende an über 100 Standorten weltweit

Heraeus has around 17,200 employees at over 100 locations worldwide

Heraeus CEO Jan Rinnert

JAN RINNERT, HERAEUS CEO

»Innovation is the heart of our work.«

IFM

In Zeiten der Digitalisierung produzieren Maschinen und Anlagen unendlich viele Daten. Die Kunst besteht nun darin, die tatsächlich relevanten Informationen aufzubereiten und über alle Ebenen hinweg zur Verfügung zu stellen. Das Herzstück einer solchen, nachhaltigen Automatisierung bilden Hard- und Software: Dabei fungieren die langlebigen, intelligenten Sensoren sozusagen als Sinnesorgane, während Steuerungen, Software und Systeme wie ein Nervensystem funktionieren, das die Signale miteinander vergleicht, kombiniert und filtert. Dieses Zusammenspiel sorgt innerhalb einer digitalen Fabrik für die Optimierung der gesamten Wertschöpfungskette, trägt bei zur deutlichen Reduzierung des Ressourcenverbrauchs und zu steigender Nachhaltigkeit in der Industrie 4.0. Schlagworte sind hier unter anderem Real Time Maintenance (RTM) oder Predictive Maintenance.

Die „Ingenieurgemeinschaft für Messtechnik" ifm beschritt von Anfang an einen erfolgreichen Weg, um Automatisierungstechnik grundsätzlich zu verbessern. Vor über 50 Jahren begannen der Elektroingenieur Robert Buck und der Vertriebler Gerd Marhofer in der Buck'schen Küche im baden-württembergischen Tettnang, eigene Sensoren und Schaltungen zu entwickeln. Sie waren angetrieben von der Vision, Dinge „besser zu machen": besser in der Zusammenarbeit mit der Belegschaft und auch besser in der Zusammenarbeit mit den Kunden.

Das Startkapital der Firma bestand im Wesentlichen aus Bleistift und Papier, zwei Köpfen voller Ideen und einigen Prototypen, um Schaltungen zu erproben. Aus der Zweckgemeinschaft der Gründer, die beide in einer elsässischen Firma arbeiteten, in der sie Anlagen in Walz- und Stahlwerken in Betrieb nahmen, entwickelte sich eine freundschaftliche Partnerschaft – und aus ifm wurde ein weltumspannendes Unternehmen.

In the age of digitalisation, machinery and systems generate endless quantities of data. The skill lies in preparing information that is actually relevant and making it available across all levels. Hardware and software solutions are at the heart of this sustainable automation: durable, intelligent sensors effectively serve as sensory organs, while control units, software and systems act like a nervous system by comparing, combining and filtering signals. In a digital factory, this synergy achieves optimisations throughout the entire value chain, contributes to significant reductions in resource consumption and facilitates increased sustainability in Industry 4.0. Key terms in this context include real-time maintenance (RTM) and predictive maintenance.

From the outset, ifm – which stands for Ingenieurgemeinschaft für Messtechnik (literally: Engineering Association for Measurement Technology) – forged a successful path in its efforts to fundamentally improve automation technology. More than 50 years ago, electrical engineer Robert Buck and salesman Gerd Marhofer began developing their own sensors and circuits in Buck's kitchen in Tettnang, Baden-Württemberg. They were driven by a vision: "making things better" through cooperation with both their workforce and their customers.

The company's start-up capital primarily comprised pencils and paper, two minds brimming with ideas and a handful of prototypes for testing circuits. The founders worked at the same company in Alsace, where they were tasked with commissioning systems in rolling mills and steelworks. Their partnership of convenience evolved into a friendly partnership – and ifm became a global enterprise.

The company's first product, the inductive proximity sensor, was a world first and achieved success. Robert Buck invented further products and soon compiled a

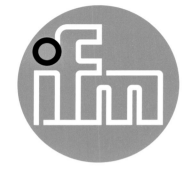

Unternehmensname
IFM-UNTERNEHMENSGRUPPE

Industriezweig
AUTOMATISIERUNGSTECHNIK

Gründung
1969 IN ESSEN

Gründer
**ROBERT BUCK UND
GERD MARHOFER**

Vertrieb
IN ÜBER 165 LÄNDERN

Mitarbeitende
8750

Jahresumsatz
1,366 MRD. EURO

Company name
IFM GROUP

Industry
AUTOMATION TECHNOLOGY

Founded
1969 IN ESSEN

Founders
**ROBERT BUCK AND
GERD MARHOFER**

Distribution
IN OVER 165 COUNTRIES

Employees
8,750

Annual sales
€1.366 BILLION

Millionen ifm-Sensoren sind täglich weltweit in unterschiedlichsten Anlagen und Maschinen im Einsatz. Die Kommunikations- und Steuerungssysteme bilden die Grundlage für einen reibungslosen Prozessablauf

Millions of ifm sensors are in use around the world every day in all manner of systems and machinery. Its communication and control systems lay the foundations for smooth processes

Schon das erste Produkt, der induktive Näherungssensor, war eine erfolgreiche Weltneuheit. Robert Buck erfand weitere Produkte und stellte bald ein kleines Portfolio aus vier verschiedenen Artikeln zusammen. 1976 gründet ifm die ersten internationalen Niederlassungen in Frankreich und Japan.

Heute gehört ifm zu den weltweit führenden Unternehmen der Automatisierungs- und Digitalisierungsbranche. In über 165 Ländern werden mehr als 155 000 Kunden aus Maschinenbau und Industrie durch selbstständige Vertriebsgesellschaften oder Handelsvertretungen betreut. Für sie entwickelt und vertreibt ifm Lösungen für die Automatisierung von Produktionsprozessen – mit Sensoren, Steuerungen, Systemen und Software. Der Vertrieb spielt dabei eine entscheidende Rolle, folgerichtig arbeiten rund 1900 der etwa 8750 Beschäftigten in diesem Bereich. Auch die Forschungs- und Entwicklungsabteilung ist mit derzeit rund 1390 Mitarbeitenden gut besetzt. Die Kooperation mit Forschungseinrichtungen, Universitäten und jungen Unternehmen prägt den innovativen Geist von ifm: Über 1170 aktive Patente und 100 Patentanmeldungen im Jahr 2022 sind das Ergebnis. Gemäß dem Firmenmotto „ifm – close to you!" halten die Mitarbeitenden engen Kontakt zu den Kunden; sie kennen alle speziellen Marktanforderungen und landestypischen Eigenschaften. So vereint ifm die Flexibilität eines mittelständischen Familienunternehmens mit der Innovationskraft einer internationalen Firmengruppe.

Das Unternehmen soll auch weiterhin in Familienhand bleiben. Bereits 2001 übergaben die Gründer den Staffelstab an ihre Söhne. Seitdem leiten Martin Buck und Michael Marhofer als Vorsitzende des Vorstandes sowie Gesellschafter die Geschicke von ifm. In den vergangenen Jahren konnten sie den Firmenumsatz kontinuierlich bis auf 1,366 Milliarden Euro (2022) steigern.

Schlüssel des Erfolgs sind von jeher die Menschen bei ifm. Eine Vielzahl von Auszeichnungen – von der Benennung zur „Fabrik des Jahres 2020", der Gold-Zertifizierung der Deutschen Gesellschaft für Nachhaltiges Bauen (DGNB), der Prämierung von Kunden wie dem „Bosch Global Supplier Award", dem „Tetra Pak Gold Supplier Award 2021" bis hin zum „Top-Arbeitgeber für Ingenieure" – sprechen eine deutliche Sprache.

Derzeit und auch künftig steht das Unternehmen vor der Aufgabe, die Herausforderungen und Erfordernisse auf dem Weg in eine nachhaltige Industrie 4.0 zu meistern. Die Schwerpunkte liegen auf dem Datenhandling, der Vorverarbeitung und Auswertung. ifm investiert daher weiter in den Softwarebereich. Als Wegbereiter für Industrie-4.0-Lösungen lässt ifm so die nachhaltige „Smart Factory" Wirklichkeit werden.

small portfolio of four different items. In 1976, ifm founded its first international subsidiaries in France and Japan.

Today, ifm is one of the world's leading companies in the automation and digitalisation sector. It serves more than 155,000 customers in the fields of mechanical engineering and industry in over 165 countries through independent sales companies and trade representations. ifm develops and distributes automation solutions for production processes, from sensors and control units to systems and software. Its sales activities play a decisive role in serving its customers, with around 1,900 of its 8,750 employees in sales-related roles. Its R&D division is also well staffed, with around 1,390 employees in this area at present. Cooperation with research institutes, universities and start-ups fosters a spirit of innovation at ifm, resulting in over 1,170 active patents and 100 patent applications filed in 2022. In keeping with the company's motto, "ifm – close to you!", its employees maintain close contact with its customers, which ensures they remain familiar with all market-specific requirements and country-specific qualities. This way, ifm combines the flexibility of a medium-sized, family-owned company with the innovative power of an international corporate group.

The company is set to stay in family hands in the future. In 2001, the founders passed the baton on to their sons. Since then, Martin Buck and Michael Marhofer have controlled the fate of ifm as Chairmen of the Board and co-CEOs. In recent years, they have overseen a continuous increase in the company's sales, which reached €1.366 billion in 2022.

The key to the success of ifm has always been its people. A number of accolades – from being named "Factory of the Year 2020" and receiving Gold certification from the German Sustainable Building Council (DGNB) to customer awards including the Bosch Global Supplier Award, the Tetra Pak Gold Supplier Award 2021 and the title of "Top Employer for Engineers" – provide emphatic proof of this.

Today, and in the future, the company must face and tackle the challenges and requirements of the path to creating a sustainable Industry 4.0. Key focus areas include data handling, pre-processing and evaluation, so ifm is continuing to invest heavily in software. As a pioneer of Industry 4.0 solutions, ifm is making the sustainable smart factory a reality.

»ifm fordert und fördert umweltbewusste Entscheidungen und Verhaltensweisen.«

Smart Factory: Die Idee der digitalen Fabrik hat ifm bereits am eigenen Standort am Bodensee verwirklicht. Dafür wurde die Unternehmensgruppe mit dem Titel „Fabrik des Jahres 2020" ausgezeichnet

Smart Factory: ifm has already realised its vision of a digital factory at its site by Lake Constance. The company received the "Factory of the Year 2020" title in recognition of this achievement

Eine Doppelspitze als Führungsteam: Martin Buck (links) und Michael Marhofer leiten das Familienunternehmen in zweiter Generation

The leadership duo: Martin Buck (left) and Michael Marhofer head up the second-generation family-run company

»ifm demands and promotes ecologically conscious decisions and conduct.«

In Tettnang befindet sich der Hauptproduktionsstandort der ifm-Unternehmensgruppe mit vier weiteren Standorten in der Bodenseeregion

The ifm group has its primary production site in Tettnang, with four further sites around Lake Constance

JUNGHEINRICH

Der weltweit agierende Intralogistik-Lösungsanbieter Jungheinrich kann 2023 bereits sein 70-jähriges Jubiläum feiern – dank des weitsichtigen Gründers, Dr. Friedrich Jungheinrich, und einer stetig auf Innovation ausgerichteten Unternehmenspolitik ist er auch bestens für die Zukunft aufgestellt. Jungheinrich ist ein börsennotierter Konzern mit dem Charakter eines Familienunternehmens und bietet seinen Kunden Lösungen für die Herausforderungen der Industrie 4.0 an. Ein umfangreiches Portfolio an Flurförderzeugen, Lager- und Materialflusstechnik, Automatiksystemen und Software machen Jungheinrich zu einem Global Player, der im weltweiten Markt unter den Top 3 ist. Die Produkte von Jungheinrich sind in Logistik, Handel und Industrie großflächig im Einsatz. Schon von Anbeginn wurden energieeffiziente Maschinen entwickelt, wie Elektro-Deichsel-Hubwagen und Elektro-Gabelstapler, und später rund um die Lithium-Ionen-Technologie eine brancheneinmalige Energiekompetenz aufgebaut. Das Unternehmen hält mit Stand Ende des Jahres 2022 insgesamt 2010 angemeldete und erteilte Patente.

Eine solche Entwicklung erfordert motivierte und engagierte Mitarbeitende, die Jungheinrich beispielsweise durch Kooperationen mit Hochschulen von sich überzeugen kann. Für Schulung, Training und Weiterbildung sorgt die hauseigene „Jungheinrich Academy". Darüber hinaus gibt es Betriebssportangebote, Programme zur Förderung der Work-Life-Balance und eine betriebliche Altersvorsorge. 20 000 Mitarbeitende weltweit sind Teil des Firmenerfolges, davon 8000 in Deutschland. Das Familienunternehmen verfügt weltweit über zwölf Produktionsstätten, davon befinden sich sechs Werke in Deutschland an den Standorten Norderstedt, Lüneburg, Moosburg, Degernpoint, Landsberg und Dresden. Service- und Vertriebsgesellschaften gibt es in 42 Ländern. Die heutige Organisationsform ist eine Aktiengesellschaft – der Börsengang erfolgte 1990 unter der damaligen Finanzvorständin Karin Martin.

In 2023, the global intralogistics solution provider Jungheinrich is celebrating its 70th anniversary. Thanks to its visionary founder, Dr Friedrich Jungheinrich, and its unwavering pursuit of innovations, the company is in an excellent position for the future. Jungheinrich is a listed company with the character of a family business and offers its customers solutions to the challenges of Industry 4.0. Its extensive portfolio of forklifts, storage technology, material flow technology, automated solutions and software make Jungheinrich a global player among the top three in the world market. Jungheinrich's products are commonplace in logistics, commerce and industrial settings. From the outset, the company has developed energy-efficient machinery, such as electric pedestrian pallet trucks and electric forklifts, and later developed expertise in lithium-ion technology that is unmatched in its industry. At the end of 2022, the company had a total of 2,010 pending and issued patents.

Development on this scale requires motivated, dedicated employees, so Jungheinrich engages in collaborations with universities to make an impression on talented minds. In addition, the in-house Jungheinrich Academy provides appropriate training and development services. Jungheinrich also offers company sports programmes, initiatives to promote a healthy work-life balance and company pension plans. The company's success is fuelled by 20,000 employees around the world, 8,000 of whom are based in Germany. The family business has 12 production facilities around the world, six of which are in Germany – in Norderstedt, Lüneburg, Moosburg, Degernpoint, Landsberg and Dresden. It also has service and sales companies in 42 countries worldwide. Today, Jungheinrich is a stock corporation (Aktiengesellschaft – AG), having completed its IPO in 1990 under its former CFO, Karin Martin.

Jungheinrich was the first manufacturer in its industry to launch a series vehicle with lithium-ion technology

Unternehmensname
JUNGHEINRICH AG

Industriezweig
MASCHINENBAU/INTRALOGISTIK

Gründung
1953 IN HAMBURG

Gründer
DR. FRIEDRICH JUNGHEINRICH

Mitarbeitende
20 000 WELTWEIT

Jahresumsatz
4,76 MRD. EURO (2022)

Kompakt und agil: Dank der integrierten Lithium-Ionen-Batterie sind POWERLiNE-Fahrzeuge besonders für den Einsatz in engen Gängen und Warenumschlagsituationen geeignet

Compact and agile: thanks to their integrated lithium-ion battery, POWERLiNE vehicles are ideally suited to use in narrow aisles and transshipment scenarios

Company name
JUNGHEINRICH AG

Industry
MECHANICAL ENGINEERING/ INTRALOGISTICS

Founded
1953 IN HAMBURG

Founder
DR FRIEDRICH JUNGHEINRICH

Employees
20,000 WORLDWIDE

Annual sales
€4.76 BILLION (2022)

Jungheinrich brachte als weltweit erster Hersteller der Branche ein Serienfahrzeug mit Lithium-Ionen-Technologie auf den Markt und gilt seither als Vorreiter in dieser Technologie. Folgerichtig baut das Unternehmen seit März 2023 keine Fahrzeuge mit Verbrenner mehr und setzt komplett auf Elektrofahrzeuge. Zudem konnte 2022 eine Innovation für die besonders kompakte Lagerung und Kommissionierung von Kleinteilen und Stückgut vorgestellt werden: das Behälterkompaktlager PowerCube. Auf der Fachmesse für Intralogistiklösungen und Prozessmanagement LogiMAT 2023 präsentierte Jungheinrich eine Mobile-Robot-Lösung, die dank des Zusammenspiels von Autonomous Mobile Robot, Leitsystem und Toolchain leicht zu integrieren ist und sowohl Performance als auch Effizienz steigert.

Das Unternehmen strebt CO_2-Neutralität in allen Bereichen der Lieferkette an und fördert interne wie externe Projekte, die dem weltweiten Klimawandel entgegenwirken. Die ehrgeizige Unternehmensstrategie 2025+ verfolgt das Ziel, nachhaltig Werte für alle Stakeholder*innen zu schaffen. Zur Minimierung des Rohstoff- und Materialverbrauchs richtet Jungheinrich seine Standorte, Prozesse und Produkte nach den Prinzipien der Kreislaufwirtschaft aus. Bis 2025 soll es beispielsweise keine Deponieabfälle in den deutschen Werken mehr geben. Ein Schwerpunkt der Nachhaltigkeitsstrategie ist eine transparente Lieferkette und nachhaltige Beschaffung. Bis 2025 sollen 80 Prozent des weltweit relevanten Einkaufsvolumens „Sustainable Spend" sein. Mit seinen Klimaschutzzielen, der nachhaltigen Produktion und den innovativen Industrieprodukten will das Unternehmen als „Sustainability Enabler" zur Transformation der Intralogistik beitragen und unterstützt seine Kunden dabei, ihre Klimaziele zu erreichen.

Zudem wird Jungheinrich seiner gesellschaftlichen Verantwortung durch zahlreiche Initiativen auf lokaler Ebene in verschiedenen Ländern gerecht, bei denen die biologische Vielfalt unterstützt wird, unter anderem bei Aufforstungsprojekten in Brasilien und Chile. Außerdem gibt es langfristige Kooperationen, beispielsweise mit dem Deutschen Medikamenten-Hilfswerk action medeor. Zur Förderung des wissenschaftlichen Nachwuchses wurde 2004 die Dr. Friedrich Jungheinrich-Stiftung gegründet. Im Fokus der Stiftungsarbeit stehen die Fächer Elektrotechnik, Logistik, Maschinenbau sowie der MINT-Bereich. Studierende erhalten Bachelor-, Master- oder Promotionsstipendien sowie Unterstützung durch Mentor*innen und Zugang zum Exzellenznetzwerk der Stiftung.

and has been a pioneer of this technology ever since. In keeping with this approach, the company discontinued production of vehicles with internal combustion engines in March 2023 to focus its attention on electric vehicles. In addition, the company launched an innovation in 2022 that facilitates ultra-compact storage and picking of small parts and piece goods: the PowerCube compact container warehouse. Jungheinrich also showcased a mobile robot solution at LogiMAT – the trade fair for intralogistics solutions and process management – in 2023. The autonomous mobile robot (AMR) combines with a newly developed control system and toolchain, which makes it easy to integrate and enhances both performance and efficiency.

The company has targeted carbon neutrality throughout its supply chain and promotes both internal and external projects to counter climate change around the world. Its ambitious 2025+ Strategy aims to create sustainable value for all stakeholders. In an effort to minimise its consumption of materials, Jungheinrich designs and organises its locations, processes and products in line with the principles of the circular economy. For example, the company aims to eliminate landfill waste at its German factories by 2025. Its sustainability strategy also focuses on creating transparency in its supply chain and implementing sustainable procurement practices. This includes the aim of ensuring 80% of its global relevant purchasing volume is "sustainable spend" by 2025. Through its climate protection targets, sustainable production operations and innovative industrial products, Jungheinrich is striving to become a "sustainability enabler", driving the transformation of intralogistics and helping its customers achieve their climate targets.

Furthermore, Jungheinrich lives up to its social responsibility through numerous local initiatives to promote biodiversity in various countries, including reforestation projects in Brazil and Chile. It also maintains long-term charitable partnerships, including with the German medical aid organisation action medeor. In 2004, the company established the Dr Friedrich Jungheinrich Foundation to support junior scientists. The foundation's work concentrates on electrical engineering, logistics, mechanical engineering and other STEM subjects. It awards grants to students on Bachelor's, Master's and doctoral programmes, offers mentoring and provides access to its Excellence Network.

DR. LARS BRZOSKA,
VORSITZENDER DES VORSTANDES

»Nachhaltig Werte schaffen – das ist unser Ziel bei Jungheinrich.«

Blick in die Produktion des Jungheinrich-Werkes in Moosburg: Arbeit am Elektro-Front-Gegengewichtsstapler (EFG)

The Jungheinrich factory in Moosburg: an employee works on an electric counterbalance forklift truck

Bahnbrechender Antrieb: Die elektrisch angetriebene „Ameise" ersetzte schnell den Handhubwagen

A groundbreaking innovation: the Ameise – an electric forklift truck with a name that means "ant" – swiftly replaced manual pallet trucks

DR LARS BRZOSKA,
CHAIR OF THE BOARD OF MANAGEMENT

»Sustainably creating value – that's our goal at Jungheinrich.«

Die Konzernzentrale befindet sich in Hamburg-Wandsbek, wo Jungheinrich Anfang 2016 einen Neubau bezogen hat

The company headquarters in the Wandsbek district of Hamburg, where Jungheinrich moved into new premises in 2016

KÄRCHER

Auf einem der bekanntesten Plätze von Paris, der Place de la Concorde, hat im Frühjahr 2022 eine aufsehenerregende Aktion stattgefunden: Der 3300 Jahre alte Obelisk von Luxor wurde anlässlich des 200. Jahrestags der Entzifferung altägyptischer Hieroglyphen restauriert – und schonend gereinigt. Diese Aufgabe übernahm in Kooperation mit dem französischen Kulturministerium der Weltmarktführer in der Reinigungstechnik: Kärcher. Und zwar kostenlos im Rahmen seines Kultursponsorings.

In dem Familienunternehmen arbeiten mehr als 15 300 Menschen in 80 Ländern mit dem Ziel, die Welt ein Stück sauberer zu machen. Und das geht weit über das Reinigen hinaus, es geht um Pflege und Werterhalt in vielerlei Hinsicht.

Alles begann mit der Idee eines leidenschaftlichen Tüftlers: Getrieben vom Erfindergeist und überdies technikbegeistert, entwickelte der Ingenieur Alfred Kärcher neuartige Heißluftbläser und gründete 1935 das nach ihm benannte Unternehmen. Der Durchbruch gelang Alfred Kärcher 1950 in der Reinigungstechnik mit dem ersten europäischen Heißwasser-Hochdruckreiniger. Von 1955 bis in die 1970er-Jahre bot Kärcher vor allem Dampferzeuger für die Industrie und Bauwirtschaft an.

Dass das Unternehmen heute so berühmt ist, geht auch wesentlich auf Irene Kärcher zurück. Nach dem Tod ihres Ehemannes Alfred Kärcher im Jahr 1959 übernahm sie die Geschäfte und trieb die Internationalisierung voran: 1962 wurde die erste Auslandsgesellschaft in Frankreich gegründet, gefolgt von Standorten in Österreich und der Schweiz. 1984 erschien schließlich der erste Hochdruckreiniger für die private Nutzung. Bis heute ist diese Gerätekategorie wie keine andere mit dem Unternehmen verbunden. Das Verb „kärchern" gehört im Deutschen längst zum Sprachgebrauch, und

The Place de la Concorde, one of the most iconic locations in Paris, was the site of a spectacular project in 2022: the restoration of the 3,300-year-old Luxor Obelisk. It marked the 200th anniversary of the decryption of ancient Egyptian hieroglyphs – and included diligent, delicate cleaning. This task, carried out in cooperation with the French Ministry of Culture, was assigned to the world market leader for cleaning technology: Kärcher. What's more, Kärcher completed the project free of charge as part of its commitment to cultural sponsorship.

The family company has more than 15,300 employees in 80 countries, all striving to make the world a little cleaner. Kärcher's activities also extend far beyond cleaning alone and, in many respects, include maintenance and value preservation.

It all began with an idea thought up by a passionate inventor: driven by ingenuity and a love of technology, the engineer Alfred Kärcher developed an innovative hot-air blower and founded a company bearing his name in 1935. Alfred Kärcher broke into the field of cleaning technology in 1950 with the first European hot-water high-pressure cleaner. From 1955 through to the 1970s, Kärcher primarily produced steam generators for industry and the construction sector.

The company's current renown can be attributed in large part to Irene Kärcher. Following the death of her husband Alfred Kärcher in 1959, she took on the business and advanced its internationalisation. In 1962, the company established its first international subsidiary in France, which was followed by sites in Austria and Switzerland. Finally, in 1984, Kärcher released the first high-pressure cleaner for domestic use. The company is now associated more strongly with this device category than any other. In fact, the verb "kärchern" – literally, to Kärcher – has long since established itself in German,

KÄRCHER

Unternehmensname	**ALFRED KÄRCHER SE & CO. KG**
Industriezweig	**REINIGUNGSTECHNIK**
Gründung	**1935**
Gründer	**ALFRED KÄRCHER**
Vertrieb	**WELTWEIT IN ALLE LÄNDER, DAVON IN 80 LÄNDERN DIREKT**
Mitarbeitende	**15 330 WELTWEIT (2022)**
Jahresumsatz	**3,16 MRD. EURO (2022)**

Company name
ALFRED KÄRCHER SE & CO. KG

Industry
CLEANING TECHNOLOGY

Founded
1935

Founder
ALFRED KÄRCHER

Distribution
IN ALL COUNTRIES WORLDWIDE, INCLUDING IN 80 COUNTRIES DIRECTLY

Employees
15,330 WORLDWIDE

Annual sales
€3.16 BILLION (2022)

Der Hochdruckreiniger steht bis heute wie kein anderes Produkt für das Unternehmen Kärcher

Today, the Kärcher brand is known above all for its high-pressure cleaners

selbst im Französischen steht „le karcher" als Synonym für Hochdruckreiniger.

Heute ist Kärcher Weltmarktführer in der Reinigungstechnik mit einem Umsatz von 3,16 Milliarden Euro im Jahr 2022. Das global agierende Familienunternehmen bietet weltweit innovative Lösungen rund um Reinigung und Pflege an – mit mehr als 3000 Produkten, darunter Hoch- und Höchstdruckreiniger, Sauger und Dampfreiniger, Luftreiniger, Kehr- und Scheuersaugmaschinen, Kfz-Waschanlagen, Reinigungsmittel, Trockeneis-Strahlgeräte, Trink- und Abwasseraufbereitungsanlagen, Wasserspender sowie Pumpen- und Bewässerungssysteme für Haus und Garten. Sie umfassen aufeinander abgestimmte Produkte und Zubehöre sowie Beratung, Service und zahlreiche digitale Anwendungen. Die Produkte sind gefragt: Auf der ganzen Welt besteht ein gesteigertes Bewusstsein für Hygiene und Sauberkeit.

Innovationen sind für Kärcher wesentlicher Bestandteil der Firmenkultur. Aktuell hält das Unternehmen 670 aktive Patente. Mehr als 1000 Mitarbeitende forschen an neuen Geräten und entwickelten zuletzt einen Reinigungsroboter für Gewerbe und Industrie mit leistungsstarker Software und Sensorik, der völlig selbstständig agiert und mit 3-D- und Ultraschallsensoren seine Umgebung im 360-Grad-Winkel nach Hindernissen abmessen kann.

Neben dem ausgeprägten Erfindergeist gehört ökologisch nachhaltiges und sozial verantwortliches Handeln zum Selbstverständnis bei Kärcher. Bis 2025 will das Unternehmen den Recyclingkunststoffanteil in den Geräten auf bis zu 50 Prozent anheben und bis 2030 seinen CO_2-Ausstoß um 42 Prozent gegenüber dem Jahr 2020 reduzieren. 2021 gelangen bereits 18 Prozent, 2022 weitere 5 Prozent. Im Rahmen seines Corporate Citizenship unterstützt Kärcher SOS-Kinderdörfer weltweit finanziell und stattet sie mit Reinigungsgeräten aus. Gemeinsam mit dem Global Nature Fund baut Kärcher Grünfilter- und Trinkwasseranlagen in Ländern des globalen Südens und kooperiert mit der Umweltorganisation One Earth – One Ocean zur Reduktion und Wiederverwendung von Ozeanplastik.

Schaffensdrang und Erfindergeist – das Erfolgsrezept von Alfred Kärcher prägt das von ihm gegründete Unternehmen bis heute. Das gilt auch für die Werte, die dem Gründer stets am Herzen lagen und der einst sagte: „Es sind die Menschen unserer Firma, die einen Erfolg erst möglich machen." Entsprechend wurden alle Mitarbeitenden weltweit einbezogen, um gemeinsam den Unternehmenspurpose zu entwickeln: „Renew to sustain. Together we make a powerful impact towards a clean world."

while "le karcher" has become a common term for high-pressure cleaners in French.

Today, Kärcher is the world market leader in cleaning technology, with sales of €3.16 billion in 2022. As a family company with global operations, Kärcher offers its innovative cleaning and maintenance solutions around the world – with more than 3,000 products ranging from high-pressure and ultra-high-pressure cleaning systems to vacuum cleaners, steam vacuum cleaners, air purifiers, sweepers, scrubber driers, car washing systems, detergents, dry ice blasters, drinking water and wastewater treatment systems, water dispensers, pumps and watering systems for the home and garden. Its portfolio comprises perfectly matched products and accessories as well as consultancy, customer services and numerous digital applications. increased awareness of hygiene and cleanliness around the world has stimulated demand for Kärcher's products.

Innovation is an important element of Kärcher's culture. At present, the company has 670 active patents. It also has more than 1,000 employees focused on research and recently developed a cleaning robot for commercial and industrial applications. It features high-performance software and sensors, is capable of entirely independent operation and uses 3D and ultrasound sensors to gauge its surroundings and identify obstacles through 360°.

In addition to its distinctive ingenuity, Kärcher also demonstrates environmental sustainability and social responsibility as a matter of course. By 2025, the company aims to increase the proportion of recycled plastic in its devices to 50% and reduce its CO_2 emissions by 42% by 2030 compared to 2020. It reduced its emissions by 18% in 2021, with a further 5% reduction in 2022. As part of its commitment to corporate citizenship, Kärcher supports SOS Children's Villages around the world and provides them with cleaning equipment. Together with the Global Nature Fund, Kärcher is building green filter and drinking water systems in countries in the Global South. In addition, it collaborates with the environmental organisation One Earth – One Ocean to reduce and recycle ocean plastic.

Creative drive and ingenuity – Alfred Kärcher's recipe for success – continues to shape the company he founded to this day. The same applies to the values that the founder held dear. As Alfred Kärcher once said: "It is the people in our company that make success possible." In keeping with this ideal, Kärcher actively integrates all its employees around the world in an effort to advance the company's purpose: "Renew to sustain. Together we make a powerful impact towards a clean world."

»Renew to sustain. Together we make a powerful impact towards a clean world.«

In der Produktion in Winnenden werden Scheuersaugmaschinen für die Bodenreinigung an hochmodernen Fertigungslinien montiert

Scrubber driers for floor cleaning are manufactured on ultra-modern assembly lines at the Winnenden production site

Der Sauger T 11/1 Re!Plast besteht zu 60 Prozent aus recyceltem Kunststoff

The T 11/1 Re!Plast vacuum cleaner is made from up to 60% recycled plastic

COMPANY PURPOSE

»Renew to sustain. Together we make a powerful impact towards a clean world.«

Alfred Kärcher entwickelte 1950 den ersten europäischen Heißwasser-Hochdruckreiniger DS 350

In 1950, Alfred Kärcher developed the DS 350 – Europe's first hot-water high-pressure cleaner

KÖRBER

Körber hat ein Händchen für Technologie. Sieht sich als Heimat für Unternehmer*innen und als Ideenschmiede gleichermaßen – als Ort, an dem Nachhaltigkeit Wirklichkeit wird. Bei Körber werden Innovationen geschaffen. Lösungen entwickelt. Wird die Zukunft gestaltet, Tag für Tag. Dabei rankt sich um die Gründung des international führenden Technologiekonzerns mit heute 13 000 Mitarbeitenden an mehr als 100 Standorten weltweit ein Mythos: Die Geschichte beginnt ein Jahr nach Ende des Zweiten Weltkriegs mit einer kleinen Werkstatt im Souterrain eines Industriegebäudes im Hamburger Stadtteil Bergedorf. Dort repariert Kurt A. Körber schrottreife Zigarettenmaschinen. Der Legende nach soll er am 14. Juli 1946 von einer Telefonzelle am Bahnhof Dammtor aus sein erstes Verkaufsgespräch geführt haben – die Geburtsstunde der Hauni Maschinenfabrik. Hauni steht für „Hanseatische Universelle" und war die Keimzelle für das, was den Konzern heute ausmacht: ein globaler Technologiekonzern, der eine breite Palette von Branchen über vier Geschäftsfelder bedient.

Maschinen und Lösungen für sichere und effiziente Prozesse bei der Herstellung, Inspektion und Verpackung pharmazeutischer Produkte sowie zur Rückverfolgbarkeit von Arzneimitteln bietet das Geschäftsfeld „Pharma", während das Geschäftsfeld „Supply Chain" seine Kund*innen dabei unterstützt, die Komplexität der Lieferkette zu beherrschen. Körbers „Layer Picker" etwa ist heute Branchenstandard für die Depalettierung und Pallet-to-Pallet-Kommissionierung. Das vollautomatische Robotersystem baut Lagen schnell und exakt auseinander und wieder neu zusammen und ersetzt so das vormals gängige manuelle Kommissionieren.

Im Geschäftsfeld „Technologies" entwickelt Körber maßgeschneiderte Lösungen für Maschinen und Anlagen, Software, Messgeräte und Aromen sowie Serviceangebote mit Schwerpunkt in der Genussmittelindust-

When it comes to technology, Körber has the Midas touch. It regards itself as a home for entrepreneurs and a think tank in equal measure; a place where sustainability becomes reality. Körber creates innovations. It develops solutions. It shapes the future, day by day. The internationally leading technology group, which now has 13,000 employees at more than one hundred sites worldwide, has an intriguing backstory. It began a year after the end of World War Two, with a small workshop in the basement of an industrial building in the Bergedorf district of Hamburg. In this underground workshop, Kurt A. Körber repaired cigarette machines that otherwise appeared fit for scrap. As the legend goes, on 14 July 1946, he conducted his first business negotiation from a telephone box at Dammtor railway station – and it was there that Hauni Maschinenfabrik was born. Hauni stands for "Hanseatische Universelle" and provided the nucleus for the company today: a global technology group serving a broad range of industries in four business areas.

Its business area Pharma provides machinery and solutions that facilitate safe and efficient processes in the production, inspection and packaging of pharmaceutical products and also ensure traceability. Meanwhile, its business area Supply Chain helps customers to master the complexity of supply chains. Körber's Layer Picker, for example, is now the industry standard for de-palletising and pallet-to-pallet handling. This fully automatic robotic system can disassemble and reassemble layers quickly and precisely, thereby replacing conventional, manual picking and packing processes.

In its business area Technologies, Körber develops customised solutions for machinery and equipment, software, measuring instruments, flavours and service offerings, focusing on the food and beverage industry. The group strives to help accelerate progress towards a carbon-free world, including by developing the Körber

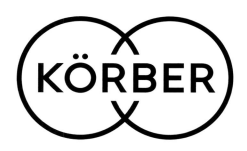

Unternehmensname
KÖRBER AG

Industriezweig
TECHNOLOGIE/GESCHÄFTSFELDER DIGITAL, PHARMA, SUPPLY CHAIN, TECHNOLOGIES

Gründung
1946 IN HAMBURG

Gründer
KURT A. KÖRBER

Produkte
MASCHINEN, ANLAGEN, SOFTWARE UND KI-GESTÜTZTE LÖSUNGEN FÜR DIE INDUSTRIELLE FERTIGUNG

Mitarbeitende
13 000 WELTWEIT

Jahresumsatz
2,5 MRD. EURO (2022)

Company name
KÖRBER AG

Industry
TECHNOLOGY/BUSINESS AREAS: DIGITAL, PHARMA, SUPPLY CHAIN, TECHNOLOGIES

Founded
1946 IN HAMBURG

Founder
KURT A. KÖRBER

Products
MACHINERY, EQUIPMENT, SOFTWARE AND AI-ASSISTED SOLUTIONS FOR INDUSTRIAL MANUFACTURING

Employees
13,000 WORLDWIDE

Annual sales
€ 2.5 BILLION (2022)

Robotergestütztes Lagermanagement für die Intralogistik: Der Layer Picker kann Paletten lagenweise auseinandernehmen und zusammenfügen – etwa zu sogenannten Rainbow-Paletten

Robot-assisted warehouse management for intralogistics: Körber's Layer Picker can disassemble and assemble pallets in layers, creating so-called rainbow pallets

rie. Der Konzern möchte dazu beitragen, dass die Transformation in eine CO_2-freie Welt voranschreitet, etwa mit der Entwicklung des „Cell Maker", der Batteriezellen zum Beispiel für die Automobilindustrie produziert.

In seinem jüngsten Geschäftsfeld „Digital" forciert Körber die digitale Weiterentwicklung des gesamten Konzerns und entwickelt eigene Ventures für die Steigerung von Effizienz und Nachhaltigkeit in der industriellen Fertigung. Mit vaibe, InspectifAI und FactoryPal hat das Geschäftsfeld bereits drei erfolgreiche Start-ups gegründet.

Mit einer überdurchschnittlich hohen Forschungs- und Entwicklungsquote von 7,3 Prozent unterstreicht Körber seinen Anspruch, Technologieführer zu sein. Dank seiner Buy-and-Build-Strategie und einer umfassenden digitalen Transformation avancierte Körber vom klassischen Maschinenbauer zum international erfolgreichen Anbieter eines integrierten Technologie-Stacks mit Hardware, Software und Künstlicher Intelligenz für alle Industrien, die der Konzern bedient. Über Akquisitionen und Partnerschaften erweitert der Konzern sein Portfolio fortlaufend – technologisch, regional sowie auf die Industriezweige seiner Kund*innen abgestimmt. Hier setzt das Unternehmen auf Ökosysteme für möglichst umfassende Lösungspakete und größtmöglichen Mehrwert entlang der Wertschöpfungsketten seiner Kund*innen.

Vom aktuellen Mangel an Fachkräften bleibt auch Körber nicht verschont – und wirkt ihm mit eigens konzipierten Karriere-Events mit Vorträgen, Trainings für Einsteiger*innen und Führungskräfte, Expert*innen-Talkrunden und spannenden Jobangeboten entgegen. Dass die Initiativen fruchten, beweist unter anderem das Ergebnis des „Career Day": 5000 Bewerbungen gingen in der Folge im Konzern ein. Das Unternehmen blickt aber auch nach innen und begünstigt die Weiterentwicklung seiner Mitarbeitenden, etwa durch ein Mentoring-Programm, eine zielgerichtete Nachwuchskräfteförderung und regelmäßige Leadership Camps.

Im Laufe seiner Geschichte hat der Körber-Konzern bewiesen, dass er den Wandel als Chance begreift und sich kontinuierlich weiterentwickelt. So hat sich der Konzern zum Ziel gesetzt, bis 2025 klimaneutral zu produzieren. Mit seiner offenen Haltung gegenüber den sich verändernden Bedürfnissen der Wirtschaft bleibt der Technologiekonzern ein Schlüsselakteur in der globalen Unternehmenslandschaft – und obendrein beispielhaft gesellschaftlich engagiert: Neben lokalen Maßnahmen unterstützt Körber jährlich gemeinnützige Organisationen mit Geldspenden, die das Alter des Konzerns mit 1000 multiplizieren.

Cell Maker, which produces battery cells for the automotive industry among other applications.

In its newest business area Digital, Körber is driving the digital development of the entire group and developing in-house ventures to enhance the efficiency and sustainability of industrial manufacturing. This business area has already produced three successful start-ups: vaibe, InspectifAI and FactoryPal.

Körber's above-average research and development intensity of 7.3% underlines its aspiration to be a technology leader. Thanks to its buy-and-build strategy and a comprehensive digital transformation, Körber evolved from a conventional machine builder into an internationally successful provider of an integrated technology stack with hardware, software and artificial intelligence solutions for all industries served by the group. It is also continuously expanding its portfolio through acquisitions and partnerships – in technological terms, in relevant regions and based on the industries in which its customers operate. Körber aims to create ecosystems in order to provide the most comprehensive solution packages possible and generate maximum added value along its customers' value chains.

While Körber has not escaped the impact of the current shortage of skilled professionals, it has countered this trend by holding its own specifically curated career events, featuring talks, training sessions for career entrants and managers, expert panel discussions and exciting job offers. These initiatives have certainly borne fruit, as evidenced by the 5,000 applications it received following its Career Day event. However, the company also provides ample internal development opportunities for its employees, such as a mentoring programme, a targeted initiative to support talented young employees and regular leadership camps.

Throughout its history, the Körber Group has shown its ability to seize change as an opportunity and continuously develop. It has, for example, set itself the target of making its production operations climate-neutral by 2025. Through its open-minded approach to the changing needs of the economy, the technology group remains a key player in the global business landscape. And, when it comes to social engagement, Körber serves as a role model: in addition to local initiatives, Körber makes donations to charitable organisations, with the annual sum totalling the company's age multiplied by 1,000.

»Unser Streben nach Spitzenleistungen treibt Innovationen. Unsere Vision: Marktführerschaft durch Technologieführerschaft.«

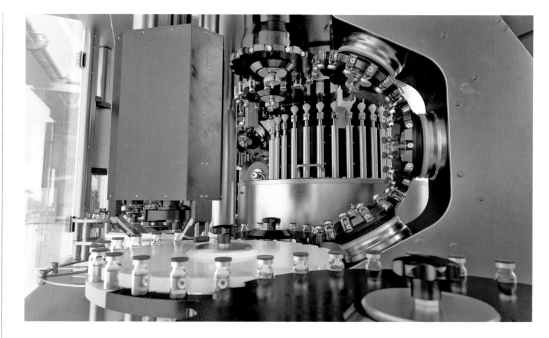

Höchstleistung:
Die Inspektionsmaschine
Switch 350 inspiziert bis
zu 350 Behälter pro Minute
für Spritzen und Vials

Maximum performance:
The Switch 350 inspection
machine examines up to
350 containers per minute
for syringes and vials

Schon den Gründer
Kurt A. Körber zeichnete
ein Erfindergeist aus,
der sich bis heute hält

The company's founder,
Kurt A. Körber, demonstrated
an inventive spirit
that endures to this day

Seit 2012 Vorstandsmitglied, seit 2016
Vorstandsvorsitzender
des Körber-Konzerns:
Stephan Seifert

Stephan Seifert became
a member of the Executive
Board in 2012 and has
been Chairman of
the Executive Board of
Körber AG since 2016

»Our aspiration for elite performance drives innovation. Our vision? Market leadership through technology leadership.«

Die Innovationskraft des
Konzerns zeigt sich auch in der
überdurchschnittlich hohen
Forschungs- und Entwicklungsquote von 7,3 Prozent

The Körber Group's innovative
power is also evidenced by
its above-average research and
development intensity of 7.3%

KSB GROUP

Höhere Effizienz – das war das Ziel, als Johannes Klein 1871 seinen „Kesselspeiseautomaten" konzipierte: einen Apparat, der den Dampf von Dampfmaschinen auffängt und ihn als Wasser zurück in den Kessel fließen lässt. Zusammen mit den Geschäftsleuten Friedrich Schanzlin und Jakob Becker legte Klein damit den Grundstein für die heutige KSB-Gruppe, die ihren Hauptsitz nach wie vor am Gründungsstandort im rheinland-pfälzischen Frankenthal hält. Seit mehr als 150 Jahren sind Effizienz, Zuverlässigkeit und Nachhaltigkeit die Treiber des international führenden und deutschlandweit größten Herstellers von Pumpen und Armaturen. Das Produktportfolio und die Servicedienstleistungen setzen rund um den Globus Maßstäbe.

„People. Passion. Performance.": Unter diesem Motto bietet KSB umfassende Lösungen für die Herausforderungen von morgen und beschäftigt dazu knapp 16 000 Mitarbeitende in Entwicklung, Produktion, Vertrieb und Service weltweit. Ausgestattet mit reicher Expertise, teilen sie alle die Leidenschaft für gelebte Ingenieurskunst – was unter anderem bedeutet, mit eigener Forschungsarbeit beständig Innovationen zu schaffen. Schon früh konzentrierte sich KSB auf die Entwicklung innovativer Technologien im Bereich der Fluidtechnik. Das Unternehmen wuchs stetig, baute sein Produktsortiment aus und konnte als Pionier in der Branche zahlreiche technologische Durchbrüche wie die Normpumpe oder den Synchron-Reluktanzmotor vermelden.

Mit über 100 Gesellschaften in 67 Ländern ist KSB ein Global Player, der Kunden in verschiedenen Industriezweigen bedient. Ob in der Wasser- und Abwasserwirtschaft, in der allgemeinen Industrie, in der Verfahrens-, Kraftwerks- und Gebäudetechnik, in der (Petro-)Chemie, im Energiesektor oder im Bergbau: Die Pumpen, Armaturen und elektronischen oder digitalen Begleitsysteme von KSB bieten auf jedem Markt die passende

Greater efficiency – that was Johannes Klein's goal in 1871 when he designed his "boiler feed apparatus". His invention trapped the steam generated by steam engines and fed it back into the boiler as water. Together with entrepreneurs Friedrich Schanzlin and Jakob Becker, Klein laid the foundations for today's KSB Group – which is still headquartered in Frankenthal, Rhineland-Palatinate, where it was founded. For more than 150 years, efficiency, reliability and sustainability have been the driving forces behind the company, which has become an international leader and Germany's largest manufacturer of pumps and valves. Its product portfolio and services continually set new benchmarks in projects around the globe.

"People. Passion. Performance." Staying true to this motto, KSB offers comprehensive solutions to the challenges of tomorrow and employs almost 16,000 people in development, production, sales and service roles worldwide. Armed with extensive expertise, they all share a passion for the applied art of engineering – which means, among other things, constant innovation made possible by in-house research. KSB concentrated on developing innovative technologies for fluid transfer applications at an early stage. The company grew steadily, expanded its product range and established itself as a pioneer in the sector through numerous technological breakthroughs, including the standardised pump and the synchronous reluctance motor.

With over 100 subsidiaries in 67 countries, KSB is now a global player and serves customers in various sectors of industry. From water and wastewater management to general industry, process engineering, power plant engineering, building technology, the (petro)chemical industry, the energy sector and the mining industry, the pumps and valves produced by KSB along with their electronic and digital monitoring systems provide the perfect solution for every market. The state-of-the-

Unternehmensname	**KSB SE & CO. KGAA**
Industriezweig	**MASCHINENBAU**
Gründung	**1871 IN FRANKENTHAL**
Produkte	**PUMPEN UND ARMATUREN**
Mitarbeitende	**16 000 WELTWEIT**
Jahresumsatz	**2,573 MRD. EURO (2022)**

Bis heute die meistgebaute Industriepumpe der Welt: Etanorm, die Mutter aller Normpumpen

The world's best-selling industrial pump to date: Etanorm, the mother of all standardised pumps

Company name	**KSB SE & CO. KGAA**
Industry	**MECHANICAL ENGINEERING**
Founded	**1871 IN FRANKENTHAL**
Products	**PUMPS AND VALVES**
Employees	**16,000 WORLDWIDE**
Annual sales	**€2.573 BILLION (2022)**

Lösung. Modernste Fertigungstechniken erfüllen selbst die individuellsten Ansprüche und Wünsche der KSB-Kunden. So können mithilfe additiver Produktionsmethoden, besser bekannt als 3-D-Druck, komplexe Bauteile und Kleinserien hergestellt werden, die im Gussverfahren nicht oder nur schwer und kostenintensiv zu produzieren sind. Selbst für Pumpen und Armaturen, die nicht von KSB hergestellt wurden, kann das Unternehmen über 3-D-Druck Ersatzteile liefern.

Für den effizienten Betrieb und eine vorausschauende Wartung seiner Produkte setzt KSB auf die Vorteile modernster Vernetzungstechnologie. Digitale Systeme überwachen die Anlagen der Kunden online und gewährleisten so deren Einsatz mit einem Minimum an ungeplanten Standzeiten. Ohnehin steht bei KSB die Zukunft im Zeichen der Innovation und Digitalisierung. Das Unternehmen investiert in neue Technologien wie Industrie 4.0, Künstliche Intelligenz und smarte Lösungen, um die Effizienz und Zuverlässigkeit seines Sortiments beständig weiter zu verbessern. KSB entwickelt Produkte, die Energie einsparen, Ressourcen schonen, Umweltauswirkungen minimieren und Kunden darin unterstützen, ihren CO_2-Fußabdruck zu reduzieren und die eigene Nachhaltigkeitsagenda voranzutreiben.

KSB hat frühzeitig erkannt, dass nachhaltiges Handeln für den langfristigen Erfolg und die Akzeptanz in der Gesellschaft unerlässlich ist, und orientiert sich an den weltweit anerkannten Standards wie dem Deutschen Corporate Governance Kodex und dem UN Global Compact mit seinen 17 Nachhaltigkeitszielen. Neue Werke werden komplett unter ökologischen Gesichtspunkten geplant und Bestandsbauten nach nachhaltigen Maßgaben saniert.

Das Unternehmen bringt regelmäßig Projekte und Initiativen zur Förderung von Bildung, Gesundheit und der Gemeinschaft auf den Weg. KSB unterstützt mehr als 100 soziale und ökologische Projekte weltweit, fördert junge Menschen, engagiert sich für die Versorgung mit Trinkwasser und schützt die Umwelt. So greift das Unternehmen seit 2012 einer französischen Hilfsorganisation bei der Erschließung neuer Wasserquellen in der Sahara für das Wüstenvolk der Tuareg unter die Arme. Über eine Stiftung finanziert KSB darüber hinaus Forschungsvorhaben, Stipendien für den wissenschaftlichen Nachwuchs und Bildungsprojekte.

art manufacturing techniques applied by KSB satisfy even the most unique requirements and requests from its customers. For example, additive manufacturing methods – more commonly known as 3D printing – make it possible to produce complex components and small batch series that are tricky and cost-intensive if not impossible to produce using casting techniques. In fact, KSB is now able to supply 3D-printed replacement parts for pumps and valves made by other manufacturers.

KSB draws on the advantages of state-of-the-art networking technology to facilitate efficient operation and predictive maintenance of its products. Digital systems monitor customers' systems online, thereby ensuring they can operate with unplanned downtime kept to a minimum. The future of KSB is undoubtedly set to be linked strongly to innovation and digitalisation. The company is investing in new technology in fields such as Industry 4.0, artificial intelligence and smart solutions in pursuit of further, enduring improvements in the efficiency and reliability of its products. KSB is developing products that save energy, conserve resources, minimise environmental impacts and help customers to reduce their carbon footprint and advance their sustainability initiatives.

KSB identified early on that acting sustainably is essential for long-term commercial success and societal acceptance. In light of this, the company oriented itself towards standards including the German Corporate Governance Code and the UN Global Compact with its 17 Sustainable Development Goals. Environmental considerations are fully integrated in plans for new production sites and existing buildings have been renovated to improve their sustainability.

The company regularly launches projects and initiatives to support education, promote health and foster communities. KSB supports over 100 social and environmental projects around the world, promotes youth initiatives, provides drinking water supplies and protects the environment. Since 2012, for example, the company has lent its support to a French aid organisation in its efforts to provide new water sources for the Tuareg people in the Sahara Desert. Furthermore, the KSB Group's foundation finances research projects, offers scholarships to talented young scientists and supports educational initiatives.

DR. STEPHAN TIMMERMANN,
SPRECHER DER GESCHÄFTSLEITUNG

»Verantwortliches Handeln bedeutet, die Balance zwischen Wachstum und gesellschaftlicher Verantwortung sicherzustellen.«

Frauen in der Produktion und in technischen Berufen sind heute kein seltener Anblick bei KSB

Nowadays, women are not a rarity at KSB production sites or in technical roles

Seit 1871 das Zentrum aller Aktivitäten: der KSB-Hauptsitz in der Johann-Klein-Straße 9 in Frankenthal

The centre of all activities since 1871: KSB headquarters at Johann-Klein-Strasse 9 in Frankenthal

DR STEPHAN TIMMERMANN,
CHAIRMAN OF THE BOARD OF MANAGEMENT

»Acting responsibly means striking a balance between profitable growth and corporate social responsibility.«

Geschäftsführende Direktoren (von links): Dr. Matthias Schmitz (CFO), Dr. Stephan Bross (CTO), Dr. Stephan Timmermann (CEO) und Ralf Kannefass (CSO)

Managing Directors (from left): Dr Matthias Schmitz (CFO), Dr Stephan Bross (CTO), Dr Stephan Timmermann (CEO) and Ralf Kannefass (CSO)

LAPP

Kabelverbindungen von Maschinen und Anlagen sind wie Adern und Nervenbahnen im menschlichen Organismus: Erst die Verbindungen zwischen den Organen von Mensch oder Maschine erwecken alles zum Leben. Der Transrapid, Roboterstraßen in Shanghai oder die Metro von Delhi. Gigantische Windanlagen, Kreuzfahrtschiffe, aber auch die Infrastruktur von Flughäfen auf allen Kontinenten. Ohne die Kabelverbindungen von LAPP stünde alles still. Visionen und Erfindungen von Ingenieur*innen und Konstrukteur*innen, die das Leben von Millionen Menschen erleichtern, wären nicht umsetzbar. Immer wenn Energie und Daten fließen, werden Kabelverbindungen gebraucht. Daher das LAPP Motto „We keep your industry alive" oder kurz „alive by LAPP".

Die bahnbrechende Entwicklung, die der Erfinder Oskar Lapp 1957 präsentierte, war die ÖLFLEX®, die erste industriell gefertigte Anschluss- und Steuerleitung. Heute kennt jede*r die farblich gekennzeichneten biegsamen Kabeladern, die auch Lai*innen den Anschluss von Leuchten erleichtern: Die gelb-grüne Ader kommt an den Schutzkontakt, die blaue und die schwarze Ader in die beiden anderen Anschlüsse. Nach diesem Prinzip fertigte LAPP bald Kabelstränge mit bis zu 130 farbigen Adern.

Oskar Lapp ließ sich seine Idee patentieren – und das ist nur eines von über 300 Patenten, das die Gruppe hält. LAPP verbindet zuverlässig seit über sechs Jahrzehnten. Das Unternehmen wird in der dritten Generation geführt, heute wie damals von starken Persönlichkeiten, die ihrer Aufgabe mit Kompetenz und Leidenschaft nachgehen.

Kundenorientierung prägt das Leitbild des Hauses. Nur so gelang es LAPP, sich langfristig am Weltmarkt durchzusetzen. „Man muss flexibel sein, so wie unsere Kabel", kommentierte Ursula Ida Lapp einmal.

Cable connections in machinery and systems are like the blood vessels and nerve pathways in the human body. Ultimately, whether human or machine, it is the links between organs that bring everything to life. From the Shanghai Transrapid maglev train and the Delhi Metro to gigantic wind turbines, cruise ships and airport infrastructure across every continent, everything would come to a standstill without cable connections from LAPP. Engineers and designers would simply not be able to realise their visions and inventions – solutions that make life easier for millions of people. Wherever energy and data flow, cable connections are essential. This fact underpins the LAPP motto "We keep your industry alive", also shortened to "alive by LAPP".

In 1957, the inventor Oskar Lapp presented a groundbreaking innovation: ÖLFLEX®, the first industrially manufactured connection and control cable. Today, everyone knows the colour-coded, flexible wires that make it easier for even ordinary people to connect lights. The green-and-yellow wire connects to the earth contact, while the blue and black wires connect to the other two contacts. Following this principle, LAPP soon developed wiring harnesses with up to 130 colour-coded wires.

Oskar Lapp patented his idea – which is today one of over 300 patents held by the LAPP Group. LAPP has facilitated reliable connections for over six decades. The company is now in third-generation family ownership, still led by strong-willed individuals who perform their duties with expertise and passion.

LAPP is characterised by its customer focus, which has been essential to its long-term success in the global market. As Ursula Ida Lapp once said: "We have to be flexible, just like our cables."

The oil-resistant and flexible control cable immediately achieved success under the apt product name ÖLFLEX®.

Unternehmensname
LAPP

Industriezweig
VERBINDUNGS- UND ELEKTROTECHNIK

Gründung
1959 IN STUTTGART

Gründer
URSULA IDA UND OSKAR LAPP

Mitarbeitende
5055

Jahresumsatz
1,86 MRD. EURO

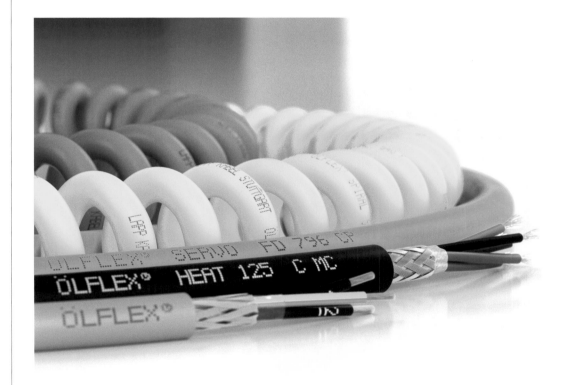

Company name
LAPP

Industry
CONNECTION TECHNOLOGY AND ELECTRICAL ENGINEERING

Founded
1959 IN STUTTGART

Founders
URSULA IDA AND OSKAR LAPP

Employees
5,055

Annual sales
€1.86 BILLION

Der Name ÖLFLEX® ist international zum Synonym für Anschluss- und Steuerleitungen geworden

The name ÖLFLEX® has become a synonym for connection and control cables around the world

Unter der treffenden Bezeichnung ÖLFLEX® verbreitete sich die ebenso ölbeständige wie flexible Steuerleitung umgehend. Inzwischen sind über 40 000 Katalogprodukte aus der Verbindungstechnologie bei LAPP erhältlich. Damit leistet das Unternehmen einen wichtigen wirtschaftlichen und gesellschaftlichen Beitrag, denn wo wären wir ohne eine zuverlässige Energie- und Datenversorgung in allen chemischen, thermischen, mechanischen und weiteren Einsatzgebieten?

LAPP schreitet auch mit der Digitalisierung voran. So gilt es, die Maschinen sowie das Lösungsportfolio für Kunden gemäß den steigenden Anforderungen des IIoT – Industrial Internet of Things – weiterzuentwickeln. Die innovative Gleichstromtechnik ist eine Schlüsseltechnologie für die Energiewende. LAPP bietet als weltweit erster Hersteller ein umfassendes Portfolio von Gleichstromlösungen an.

Die Unternehmensgruppe fertigt an 19 internationalen Standorten und verfügt über 41 eigene Vertriebsgesellschaften. Zudem kooperiert LAPP mit rund 100 Auslandsvertretungen: ein globales, tragfähiges Netzwerk, das auch bei so exklusiven Aufträgen wie der Verkabelung der Bühnentechnik der Rolling Stones oder des Moskauer Bolschoi Theaters zum Zug kam. Egal, ob Afrika oder Australien, LAPP Kunden sollen innerhalb kürzester Zeit, gegebenenfalls auch just-in-time, ihre georderten Komponenten erhalten.

Oskar Lapp war ein Pionier, dessen Ehrgeiz und Fleiß bis heute im Unternehmen fortwirkt. Ursula Ida Lapp hat als mutige und weitsichtige Unternehmerin das Unternehmen aufgebaut. Andreas Lapp und sein Bruder Siegbert E. Lapp haben das Unternehmen international expandiert und zu einer globalen Größe im Markt geformt. Heute wird die Unternehmensgruppe in dritter Generation von Matthias Lapp geführt, dem Vorstandsvorsitzenden der LAPP Holding SE und der CEO LA EMEA.

Die Wirtschafts- und Arbeitswelt ändern sich und LAPP vertraut auf die jungen Köpfe, um die Unternehmensgruppe durch diesen Wandel zu führen. Die Basis des Erfolgs des Familienunternehmens sind die kompromisslose Kundenorientierung, die Stärkung der Innovationskraft, der Fokus auf Marktanforderungen und Services. In Verbindung mit einem umfangreichen Kulturwandel wird das Unternehmen noch schneller und agiler. LAPP stellt sich damit für die Zukunft auf und bleibt gleichzeitig seinen Wurzeln, seinen Werten und seiner Identität als Familienunternehmen treu.

Today, the LAPP product catalogue includes over 40,000 pieces of connection technology. The company thereby makes an important contribution to the economy and to society. After all, where would we be without reliable energy and data supplies in all areas of industry, from chemical and thermal to mechanical and other applications?

LAPP is also following the advance of digitalisation. In this context, it is important to develop machinery and the company's portfolio of solutions in line with the rising requirements of the Industrial Internet of Things (IIoT). Innovative direct current technology is a key technology for the energy transition. LAPP is the world's first manufacturer to offer a comprehensive portfolio of direct current solutions.

The corporate group manufactures its products at 19 international production sites and has 41 sales companies. Furthermore, LAPP cooperates with around 100 sales partners, creating a robust global network that has been involved in exclusive projects including stage cabling for the Rolling Stones and the Bolshoi Theatre in Moscow. Whether in Africa or Australia, LAPP aims to ensure customers receive their orders as quickly as possible, including for just-in-time manufacturing.

Oskar Lapp was a pioneer; his ambition and industry continue to influence the company to this day. Ursula Ida Lapp has overseen the company's growth as a courageous, foresighted entrepreneur. Andreas Lapp and his brother, Siegbert E. Lapp, have advanced the company's international expansion, turning it into a global player. Today, Matthias Lapp is Chairman of the Board of LAPP Holding SE and CEO LA EMEA, having become the third generation of the Lapp family to lead the company.

The world of business and work is changing, so LAPP relies on young minds to guide the corporate group through this transformation. The family company's success is built on an uncompromising customer orientation, investments in its innovative power, a focus on market requirements and tailoring its services accordingly. Besides implementing extensive cultural changes, the company is further increasing its speed and agility. In the process, LAPP is positioning itself for the future while also staying true to its roots, its values and its identity as a family company.

MATTHIAS LAPP

»Die Erfolgs-
geschichte von
LAPP macht mich
stolz. Gemeinsam
mit unserem
weltweiten Team
werden wir
das Unternehmen
weiter in eine
erfolgreiche
Zukunft führen.«

We keep
your industry
alive

LAPP erweckt die Industrie mit
Leben, seine Verbindungslösungen
und Services stellen weltweit Energie-
und Datenübertragungen sicher

LAPP brings industry to life,
providing cable solutions and
services that safeguard energy and
data transfers around the world

Mit einer herausragenden Produktqualität und der weltweit hohen
Verfügbarkeit ist LAPP ein verlässlicher globaler Partner

Thanks to its outstanding product
quality and high product availability
worldwide, LAPP is a dependable
global partner

MATTHIAS LAPP

»I'm proud of the
LAPP success story.
Together with our
global team, we'll
continue to guide
the company into a
successful future.«

Matthias Lapp führt
das weltweit aktive
Familienunter-
nehmen in der dritten
Generation

Matthias Lapp is
the third generation
to lead this global
family company

LEITZ

Leitz ist Weltmarktführer und produzierender Dienstleister für Präzisionswerkzeuge und Werkzeugsysteme zur spanenden Bearbeitung von Holz, Holzwerkstoffen sowie modernsten Werkstoffen. Leitz und die rechtlich selbstständigen Schwesterkonzerne Boehlerit und Bilz bilden die global agierende Brucklacher Gruppe. Der Hartmetallpionier Boehlerit ist einer der weltweit führenden Hersteller für Lösungen zum Verschleißschutz sowie von Zerspanungswerkzeugen zur Bearbeitung von Metall und Verbundwerkstoffen. Bilz ist der internationale Spezialist für präzises Spannen, definiertes Bewegen sowie das manuelle Schnellwechseln von Präzisionswerkzeugen.

Die einzigartige Leistungsstärke der Unternehmensgruppe beruht auf konsequent genutzten Synergien sowie ihrer eng abgestimmten Forschung und Entwicklung. Dank der vertikalen Integration der Schwesterkonzerne erhalten Kunden innovative Produkte und Services sowie im Verbund optimierte Lösungen.

Die Brucklacher Gruppe ist ein auf allen Kontinenten vertretener Global Player, der das Kundenspektrum vom Handwerk bis zu hochspezialisierten Industrien bedient. Die Gruppe verfügt über 16 Produktionsstandorte in Deutschland, Österreich, Italien, Brasilien, China, der Türkei und Indien, eigene Vertriebs- und Servicegesellschaften in 38 Ländern mit 137 Standorten sowie ein globales Partnernetzwerk.

Als Technologieführer setzt Leitz kontinuierlich Branchentrends. Das Unternehmen steht unter anderem für Innovationen wie Diamantschneidstoffe und neuartige Beschichtungen in der Holz- und Holzwerkstoffbearbeitung, lärmreduzierte Werkzeugsysteme sowie Werkzeuge mit integriertem Speicherchip. Bilz hat der induktiven Spanntechnik für Werkzeuge durch seine richtungsweisenden Schrumpfgeräte zum weltweiten Durchbruch verholfen. Boehlerit ist seit Jahrzehnten

Leitz is the world market-leading manufacturing service provider for precision tools and tooling systems for the machining of wood, wood-derived materials and state-of-the-art materials. Leitz and its legally independent sister companies, Boehlerit and Bilz, make up the globally active Brucklacher Group. The carbide pioneer Boehlerit is one of the world's leading producers of solutions for wear protection and cutting tools for processing metals and composite materials. Bilz is the international specialist for precise clamping, defined movement and manual quick-change of precision tools.

The corporate group's unique strength lies in its systematic exploitation of synergies and close links between research and development. Thanks to the vertical integration of these sister companies, customers benefit from innovative products and services as well as solutions optimised through links between the companies.

The Brucklacher Group is a global player represented across all continents, serving a spectrum of customers from skilled manual crafts to highly specialised industries. It has 16 production sites in Germany, Austria, Italy, Brazil, China, Turkey and India, along with its own sales and service companies with 137 locations in 38 countries and a global partner network.

As a technology leader, Leitz continuously sets industry trends. The company is known for its innovations, such as its diamond cutting materials and novel coatings in the processing of wood and wood-derived materials, noise-reducing tooling systems and tools with integrated memory chips. Bilz has helped inductive clamping technology for tools to make a global breakthrough with its pioneering shrink fit devices. Boehlerit has been a leading carbide specialist for decades as well as a pioneer of nanostructured CVD hard substance

Unternehmensname
LEITZ GMBH & CO. KG

Industriezweig
**MASCHINENBAU,
SPARTE PRÄZISIONSWERKZEUGE**

Gründung
1876 IN OBERKOCHEN

Produkte
**PRÄZISIONSWERKZEUGE,
WERKZEUGSYSTEME,
HARTMETALLELEMENTE,
SPANNSYSTEME**

Mitarbeitende
ÜBER 4000 WELTWEIT

Jahresumsatz
450 MIO. EURO (2022)

Als dienstleistender
Vollsortimenter bietet
Leitz nachhaltige
Lösungen mit Weitblick

As a full-range service
provider, Leitz offers
sustainable solutions
with a vision

Company name
LEITZ GMBH & CO. KG

Industry
**MECHANICAL ENGINEERING,
PRECISION TOOLS**

Founded
1876 IN OBERKOCHEN

Products
**PRECISION TOOLS, TOOLING
SYSTEMS, CARBIDE ELEMENTS,
CLAMPING SYSTEMS**

Employees
OVER 4,000 WORLDWIDE

Annual sales
€450 MILLION (2022)

als führender Hartmetall-Spezialist sowie als Pionier der nanostrukturierten CVD-Hartstoffbeschichtung anerkannt. 113 Patente belegen die Innovationskraft der Gruppenkonzerne.

In Zeiten von Industrie 4.0 und vernetzten Fertigungen übernehmen intelligente Werkzeuge eine zentrale Rolle als Informationsträger. Diese Digitalisierung, die starke Kundenorientierung und der weitere Ausbau des weltweiten Produktions-, Vertriebs- und Servicenetzwerks stärken langfristig das Wachstum der Gruppe.

Durch die hohe Ausbildungsquote von zehn Prozent und ein breites Weiterbildungsprogramm nehmen die Unternehmen der Gruppe ihre Verantwortung gegenüber den Belegschaften und künftigen Generationen wahr. Dabei sichern die strategische Personalentwicklung sowie die weltweite Talentförderung den Vorsprung des Weltmarktführers nachhaltig ab.

Für ihre Innovationen, die Produktqualität und das Produktdesign sowie als Arbeitgeber erhielten Leitz, Boehlerit und Bilz national und international zahlreiche renommierte Auszeichnungen.

Umweltschutz und Ressourcenschonung haben in der Brucklacher Gruppe seit Jahrzehnten hohe Priorität. So werden beispielsweise Kundenwerkzeuge aus Hartmetall am Ende des Produktlebenszyklus zur Herstellung neuer Rohelemente zurückgenommen und aufbereitet. Auch durch die Reduzierung des Material- und Energieverbrauchs sowie von Lärm und Staub bei der Werkzeuganwendung wird die Ökobilanz stetig optimiert.

Mit der globalen Initiative WeCare werden in dem Familienunternehmen die teils seit Jahrzehnten bestehenden Aktivitäten in den Bereichen Gesellschaft, Soziales und Kultur sowie Arten-, Natur- und Umweltschutz gebündelt. In den von Dr. Cornelia Brucklacher initiierten weltweit jährlich stattfindenden WeCare Aktionswochen wurden 2023 von 1900 Mitarbeitenden bereits 153 Projekte realisiert. Durch das gemeinsame Handeln vor Ort und durch die finanzielle Unterstützung seitens der Unternehmen wird damit ein weiteres Zeichen der gesellschaftlichen Verantwortung gesetzt. Daneben steht die Unternehmensgruppe seit 1991 als Veranstalter des jährlich stattfindenden internationalen Musikfestivals Jazz Lights für ein Mehr an Attraktivität in ihrer Region.

Leitz wurde 1876 in Oberkochen gegründet. Heute ist Dr. Cornelia Brucklacher in fünfter Generation Gesellschafterin und Vorsitzende der Aufsichtsgremien des traditionsreichen Familienunternehmens. Wie auch die Generationen vor ihr steht sie für die Brucklacher Gruppe, deren Werte und Kultur – als Innovations- und Weltmarktführer – von langfristigem Denken und nachhaltigem Handeln geprägt sind.

coating. The corporate group's innovative power is evidenced by its 113 patents.

In this age of Industry 4.0 and networked manufacturing facilities, intelligent tools have taken on a central role as information carriers. This digitalisation, a strong customer focus and the continued expansion of its global production, sales and service network consolidate the group's long-term growth.

The group lives up to its responsibility to its employees and to future generations through its high training ratio of 10% and an extensive range of professional development opportunities. Furthermore, strategic personnel development and global talent promotion give the global market leader a lasting competitive edge.

Leitz, Boehlerit and Bilz have received numerous awards, both nationally and internationally, for their innovations, product quality, product design and as an employer.

Environmental protection and resource conservation have been top priorities in the Brucklacher Group for decades. For example, it takes customers' carbide tools back at the end of the product life cycle and processes them to extract raw materials for reuse. It also optimises the overall life cycle assessment by reducing material and energy use and minimising the noise and dust the tools produce in use.

The family company combines its activities in the fields of society, social and cultural affairs as well as species, nature and environmental conservation, some of which have been underway for decades, in its global WeCare initiative. During the 2023 WeCare campaign week – an annual initiative launched by Dr Cornelia Brucklacher – 1,900 employees brought 153 projects to fruition. The employees' combined efforts on the ground and financial support from the company provided another example of the group's commitment to social responsibility. Furthermore, the group has organised Jazz Lights, an annual, international music festival, since 1991, boosting the region's appeal.

Leitz was founded in Oberkochen in 1876. Today, Dr Cornelia Brucklacher is a fifth-generation shareholder and Chairwoman of the Advisory Board of this tradition-steeped family company. Just like the generations before her, she is committed to the Brucklacher Group, with its values and culture – as an innovation leader and global market leader – still shaped by a long-term mindset and sustainable actions.

DR. CORNELIA BRUCKLACHER, GESELLSCHAFTERIN UND VORSITZENDE DER AUFSICHTSGREMIEN

»Wir formen eine lebenswerte Zukunft.«

Die Leitz Zukunftswerkstatt symbolisiert die hohe Qualifikation und stetige Weiterbildung

The Leitz Future Workshop symbolises the company's commitment to excellent qualifications and constant professional development

Die global agierende Brucklacher Gruppe wird durch die drei rechtlich selbstständigen Schwesterkonzerne Leitz, Boehlerit und Bilz gebildet

The globally active Brucklacher Group comprises three legally independent sister companies: Leitz, Boehlerit and Bilz

Die globale Initiative WeCare steht für die gesellschaftliche Verantwortung des Familienunternehmens

The global WeCare initiative symbolises the family company's commitment to social responsibility

Dr. Cornelia Brucklacher, Gesellschafterin und Vorsitzende der Aufsichtsgremien, führt die Brucklacher Gruppe strategisch in der fünften Generation

Dr Cornelia Brucklacher, shareholder and Chairwoman of the Advisory Board, is the fifth generation of the family to strategically guide the Brucklacher Group

DR CORNELIA BRUCKLACHER, SHAREHOLDER AND CHAIRWOMAN OF THE ADVISORY BOARD

»We are forming a liveable future.«

MÄDLER

Im ausgehenden 19. Jahrhundert erlebte Deutschland die Hochphase der Industrialisierung und wurde nach Großbritannien und den USA die drittgrößte Industrienation der Welt. Wie andere namhafte Pioniere dieser Zeit wagte auch Bruno Mädler, Sohn eines Leipziger Kofferfabrikanten, den Schritt in die Selbstständigkeit. 1882 gründete er in Berlin einen Handelsbetrieb, der Baubeschläge, Nieten, Schrauben und Muttern verkaufte, und legte damit den Grundstein für ein Industrieunternehmen mit großer Historie. Das Unternehmen entwickelte sich äußerst dynamisch, und die Zahl der Kund*innen, Produkte und Mitarbeitenden stieg rasant an. Schon in den 1930er-Jahren war MÄDLER mit rund 300 Beschäftigten eines der führenden Werkzeug- und Maschinenbau-Unternehmen Deutschlands. Zu den späteren Kriegsfolgen zählten leider die Zerstörung des Berliner Stammhauses und der Verlust des Handelsunternehmens in Ost-Berlin. 1959 entstand in Stuttgart eine neue MÄDLER Niederlassung. Lieferengpässe und hohe Qualitätsansprüche forcierten Pläne für eine eigene Produktion, die 1968 vorerst über eine Beteiligung realisiert wurde. 1984 schließlich nahm der erste eigene Fertigungsbetrieb seine Arbeit auf, die Verzahnungstechnik Mädler GmbH.

Heute ist MÄDLER ein global agierendes Unternehmen der Industriesparte Maschinenbau/Antriebstechnik und einer der weltweit führenden Hersteller und Händler in seinem Segment – mit über 140 Jahren Erfahrung und mehr als 32 000 Kund*innen. Die Fertigung und der Vertrieb von mechanischen Antriebselementen für ein breites Branchenspektrum mit großer Anwendungsvielfalt bilden das Kerngeschäft. In weiteren Geschäftsbereichen wurden die Fertigung und der Handel mit Normteilen, Bedienteilen und Befestigungsteilen kontinuierlich ausgebaut. Mit insgesamt über 35 000 Artikeln bietet das Unternehmen seinen Anwender*innen ein extrem vielfältiges Sortiment aus einer Hand. Weitere überzeugende Argumente für MÄDLER sind die

Germany experienced rapid industrialisation in the late 19th century, becoming the world's third-largest industrial power behind the United Kingdom and the USA. Like other renowned pioneers of that era, Bruno Mädler, the son of a suitcase manufacturer from Leipzig, decided to found his own company. In 1882, he founded a commercial undertaking in Berlin selling construction hardware, nuts, bolts and rivets – and laid the foundations for an industrial enterprise that would achieve considerable success. The company enjoyed dynamic early growth, rapidly expanding its customer base, product range and workforce. By the 1930s, MÄDLER had already become one of the leading toolmaking and mechanical engineering firms in Germany with around 300 employees. Unfortunately, the Second World War led to the destruction of the company's Berlin headquarters and the loss of its trading company in East Berlin. In 1959, a new MÄDLER subsidiary was established in Stuttgart. Supply shortages and stringent quality requirements forced MÄDLER to draw up plans to manufacture its own products, initially by acquiring a stake in another company in 1968. The company opened its first in-house manufacturing facility in 1984 under the name Verzahnungstechnik Mädler GmbH.

Today, MÄDLER is a global player in mechanical engineering and drive technology, having become a world-leading manufacturer and retailer in its segment – with over 140 years' experience and more than 32,000 customers. Its core business lies in manufacturing and distributing mechanical drive components for a variety of applications across a wide range of industries. The company has continuously expanded its operations in other fields by manufacturing and distributing standard parts, operating elements and fastening elements. With over 35,000 products in total, the company offers its customers an extremely wide assortment from a single source. Other convincing arguments in

Unternehmensname
MÄDLER GMBH

Industriezweig
ANTRIEBSTECHNIK/ MASCHINENBAU

Gründung
1882 IN BERLIN

Gründer
BRUNO MÄDLER

Vertrieb
WELTWEIT

Jahresumsatz
80 MIO. EURO WELTWEIT

Mit über 35 000 Artikeln bedient MÄDLER die Kund*innen mit beinahe allen Antriebselementen, die aktuell auf dem Markt gefordert werden

With over 35,000 products, MÄDLER offers its customers almost all drive components available on the market today

Company name
MÄDLER GMBH

Industry
DRIVE TECHNOLOGY/ENGINEERING

Founded
1882 IN BERLIN

Founder
BRUNO MÄDLER

Distribution
WORLDWIDE

Annual sales
€80 MILLION WORLDWIDE

Fertigung an deutschen Standorten, eine vielfältige Bevorratung mit hohen Stückzahlen sowie der flexible Service mit schnellen Lieferungen und sofortiger Abholung.

In Deutschland ist MÄDLER an drei Standorten mit 100 Beschäftigten vertreten. Die Zentrale und eine Produktionsstätte haben in Stuttgart ihren Sitz. In Düsseldorf und Stapelfeld nahe Hamburg sind Dependancen für Produktion und Vertrieb angesiedelt. International verfügt MÄDLER über Produktions- und Vertriebsstandorte in Feuerthalen (Schweiz), Wien (Österreich), Debrecen (Ungarn), Bradenton (USA) und Shenzhen (China) und kooperiert rund um den Globus mit 36 Repräsentanzen. Der Firmenverbund beschäftigt insgesamt 150 Mitarbeitende.

Mit fortschrittlichsten Technologien und CNC-gesteuerten Werkzeugmaschinen fertigt MÄDLER eine große Auswahl von Werkstücken: ob als Einzelanfertigungen nach Zeichnung oder Muster, in größeren Serien oder als einbaufertige Baugruppen. Die maßgeschneiderten, sofort einsetzbaren Antriebselemente erfüllen höchste Ansprüche und Qualitätsanforderungen. Neben zahlreichen weit verbreiteten Produktionsverfahren bietet MÄDLER auch stark nachgefragte, aber kaum noch verfügbare Fertigungstechniken wie das Rollen und Wirbeln von Trapezgewindespindeln an.

Als Teil seiner unternehmerischen Verantwortung, auch gegenüber nachfolgenden Generationen, fördert MÄDLER die Entwicklung nachhaltiger Produkte und ressourcenschonender Maßnahmen. Signifikante Beiträge leistet MÄDLER bereits durch die Nutzung der beim Produktionsprozess frei werdenden Energie, mit einem Mehrweg-System zur Reduzierung von Verpackungsmaterialien und dem Recycling der bei der Produktion abfallenden Rohstoffe.

MÄDLER folgt weiterhin seiner wachstumsorientierten Agenda. Am Industriestandort Deutschland wird massiv in die Fertigung investiert. Unter anderem implementiert das Unternehmen stetig neu entwickelte Maschinen, die den wachsenden Bedarf an Sonderteilen und die steigende Nachfrage nach Individualisierung der Antriebselemente noch effizienter und schneller abdecken. International werden sowohl die Erschließung neuer Absatzmärkte als auch die Expansionsaktivitäten intensiviert. Die hohen Investitionen in neueste Technologien, die Weiterentwicklung der ressourceneffizienten Produktion und ein fortschrittliches Arbeitsumfeld sollen auch die Attraktivität als Arbeitgeber für Fachkräfte weltweit weiter steigern. Expertise und Ambitionen des Unternehmens bringt das MÄDLER Motto auf den Punkt: „Wir sorgen für Antrieb".

favour of MÄDLER include its German-based manufacturing operations, its wide-ranging and extensive product inventory and its flexible services, including rapid delivery and immediate collection.

MÄDLER employs 100 people across three locations in Germany. Its headquarters and one of its production facilities are in Stuttgart. It has production and distribution sites in Düsseldorf and Stapelfeld, near Hamburg. Internationally, MÄDLER has production and distribution facilities in Feuerthalen (Switzerland), Vienna (Austria), Debrecen (Hungary), Bradenton (USA) and Shenzhen (China) and cooperates with 36 branch offices around the world. The corporate group employees 150 people in total.

MÄDLER relies on state-of-the-art technologies and CNC machining to manufacture a wide range of work pieces – from one-off, custom-made components according to drawings or templates to larger series and prefinished assemblies. Its customised drive components, which can be used straight away, fulfil the highest standards and quality requirements. In addition to various widely used production processes, MÄDLER also offers manufacturing techniques that are highly sought after but rarely available, such as rolling and whirling of trapezoidal threaded spindles.

As part of its entrepreneurial responsibility, including to subsequent generations, MÄDLER promotes the development of sustainable products and measures that conserve resources. Indeed, MÄDLER already makes a significant contribution by recovering energy that would otherwise be wasted in the production process, operating a packaging return system to reduce material consumption and recycling waste material generated in its production operations.

Furthermore, MÄDLER continues to pursue a growth-focused agenda. It has made massive investments in Germany as a location for industry. For example, the company is constantly implementing newly developed machinery in order to respond more swiftly and efficiently to the rising demand for special components and drive component customisation. Internationally, MÄDLER is working to open up new markets and intensify its expansion activities. The company's significant investments in state-of-the-art technologies, resource-efficient production operations and a progressive working environment are part of its efforts to enhance its appeal as an employer to specialists around the world. The company's expertise and ambitions are concisely captured by the MÄDLER motto: "We keep things moving."

STEFFEN KROTZ, GESCHÄFTSFÜHRUNG
DER MÄDLER GRUPPE

»Unser Ziel ist es, maßgefertigte Antriebselemente in hoher Qualität für uns und für nachfolgende Generationen einbaufertig und nachhaltig zu produzieren.«

MÄDLER bietet Sonderfertigungen nach Zeichnung oder Muster, Einzel-anfertigungen in größerer Serie bis zu einbaufertigen Baugruppen

MÄDLER offers custom builds made according to drawings or templates as well as large-series custom parts and ready-to-install assemblies

Die Niederlassung in Stuttgart bildet zusammen mit den neu gebauten Fertigungs- und Lager-hallen das Herzstück der MÄDLER Gruppe

The Stuttgart site, including the newly built production halls and warehouses, are the beating heart of the MÄDLER Group

STEFFEN KROTZ, MANAGING DIRECTOR
OF THE MÄDLER GROUP

»Our goal is to produce custom-ised, high-quality drive components that are ready to install and are sustainable for us and for subsequent generations.«

Der Gründer Bruno Mädler und Mitarbeiter in den Anfängen des Unternehmens um 1900

Founder Bruno Mädler with employees in the early days of the company, circa 1900

MAYR

Seit vielen Jahrzehnten sichern Kupplungen und Bremsen von mayr® Antriebstechnik tagtäglich die Bewegungen in Maschinen rund um den Globus. Diese Aufgabe erlaubt keine Abstriche bei der Qualität. Denn Sicherheitsbremsen und Kupplungen sind Komponenten, die im Notfall Leben retten. Maschinen – das sind einerseits die klassischen Produktionsanlagen oder Fertigungsstraßen. Aber nicht nur. Die Sicherheit von Maschinen betrifft uns alle – und das ganz konkret in unserem Alltag. Wie selbstverständlich benutzen die meisten von uns fast täglich einen Aufzug – im Büro, beim Einkaufen, im Parkhaus. Was passiert, wenn die Bremsen nicht funktionieren, will sich niemand vorstellen. Im Theater, Konzert oder Stadion müssen wir keine Angst haben, dass über unseren Köpfen Bühnentechnik, Scheinwerfer oder fliegende Kameras plötzlich abstürzen. Der Baukran auf dem Grundstück des Nachbarn wird auch bei Wind und Sturm nicht umstürzen und der Roboterarm des operationsunterstützenden Roboters bei der Augen-OP nicht absinken. Warum nicht?

Weil die Qualität der Maschinen in Bezug auf ihre Funktion und Anwendung bei uns heute selbstverständlich ist und sein muss. Sicherheit duldet keine Kompromisse.

Sicherheit, Zuverlässigkeit und Innovation: Das sind die Leitgedanken des renommierten Familienunternehmens. Sie liegen seinem Qualitätsanspruch zugrunde. Kompromisslose Qualität beginnt bei mayr® Antriebstechnik mit einem „überlegenen Produkt". Bei dessen Herstellung ziehen alle Mitarbeitenden an einem Strang. Sie können dabei auf das umfassende Know-how und die vielen Jahrzehnte Erfahrung des international führenden Unternehmens zurückgreifen. Als Komponentenhersteller verfolgt mayr® Antriebstechnik den technologischen Fortschritt des Marktes aufmerksam und bietet proaktiv neue Lösungen an.

For decades, couplings and brakes from mayr® power transmission have safeguarded the movements of machinery around the globe. In this critical task, there is no room to compromise on quality: safety brakes and couplings are components that save lives in an emergency. When we speak about machinery, we might think of conventional manufacturing facilities and production lines. But that's not all machinery is. In truth, the safety of machinery affects us all in very tangible ways in our day-to-day lives. Most of us, for example, use a lift every day as a matter of course, whether at the office, out shopping or in a multi-storey car park. Nobody wants to imagine what would happen if the brakes were to fail. When we are in a theatre, a concert venue or a stadium, we need not worry about stage machinery, spotlights or suspended cameras crashing down on our heads. The construction crane on our neighbour's property will not come crashing down, even in windy, stormy conditions, and the robotic arm assisting a surgeon will not drop in the middle of an eye operation. Why?

Because, today, high machinery quality in terms of its function and application is self-evident – as it should be. Safety does not tolerate compromise.

Safety, reliability and innovation: these are the guiding principles of this renowned family-owned company. They underpin its commitment to quality. For mayr® power transmission, uncompromising quality starts with a superior product. Its manufacturing activities rely on all employees pulling in the same direction. They can draw on their internationally leading company's extensive expertise and decades of experience. As a component manufacturer, mayr® power transmission closely monitors technological progress on the market and proactively offers new solutions. Today, this means that its couplings and brakes are starting to speak, in a way, by becoming smart, networked solutions. They

Ihr zuverlässiger Partner

Unternehmensname
MAYR® ANTRIEBSTECHNIK

Industriezweig
MASCHINENBAU

Gründung
1897

Produkte
**SICHERHEITSBREMSEN,
SICHERHEITSKUPPLUNGEN,
WELLENKUPPLUNGEN**

Vertrieb
WELTWEIT

Mitarbeitende
1350 WELTWEIT

Innovation aus Mauerstetten: Mit der ROBA®-servostop® Baureihe hat mayr® Antriebstechnik Federdruckbremsen für Servomotoren entwickelt, die speziell an die hohen Anforderungen der Robotik angepasst sind

An innovation made in Mauerstetten: The ROBA®-servostop® series from mayr® power transmission offers spring-applied safety brakes for servomotors specifically tailored to the stringent requirements of robotics applications

Company name
MAYR® POWER TRANSMISSION

Industry
MECHANICAL ENGINEERING

Founded
1897

Products
**SAFETY BRAKES, SAFETY
COUPLINGS, SHAFT COUPLINGS**

Distribution
WORLDWIDE

Employees
1,350 WORLDWIDE

Das bedeutet heute, dass die Kupplungen und Bremsen sozusagen zu sprechen beginnen, dass sie smart und vernetzt werden. Sie liefern Daten und ermöglichen damit intelligente Sicherheit – für die smarte Produktion und vorausschauende Maschinenwartung.

mayr®-Qualität bedeutet Qualität „made in Germany" weltweit. Nicht nur in Mauerstetten, wo die Mehrheit der weltweit rund 1350 Beschäftigten arbeitet, sondern auch in den Werken und Tochtergesellschaften. International betreibt mayr® Antriebstechnik zwei weitere Werke in Polen und China und plant aktuell eine Niederlassung in Indien. Mit Tochtergesellschaften in den USA, in Frankreich, Großbritannien, Italien, Singapur, Japan und in der Schweiz sowie rund 40 weiteren Ländervertretungen ist das Unternehmen global präsent. mayr®-Qualität bedeutet also gleiche Qualität unabhängig vom Standort.

Das Besondere an mayr® Antriebstechnik ist die Ausrichtung als Familienunternehmen. Geschäftsführer Ferdinand Mayr leitet das Unternehmen mittlerweile in fünfter Generation. Dieses Engagement durch die Familie schafft Konstanz und Zuverlässigkeit. Tradition und Innovation sind dabei die tragenden Säulen, die seit Generationen die Stabilität garantieren. In einer Welt, die immer schnelllebiger und unsicherer wird, bedeutet dies Zuverlässigkeit und langfristige Sicherheit – auch in Krisenzeiten. So hat mayr® Antriebstechnik in den vergangenen Jahren kräftig in den Stammsitz Mauerstetten investiert und damit die Voraussetzungen und den Gestaltungsraum für eine erfolgreiche Zukunft geschaffen. Das Familienunternehmen, das im Jahr 2022 sein 125-jähriges Jubiläum feierte, untermauert auf diese Weise seine Stabilitätspolitik und das Bekenntnis zum Standort im Allgäu, zum Produktionsstandort Deutschland.

Nachhaltiges Wirtschaften, inklusive nachhaltiger Lieferketten, prägt die Firmenphilosophie von Anfang an. Und auch Klimaschutz ist dem Unternehmen wichtig, das seit 2020 klimaneutral ist. Der Betrieb setzt dafür auf einen breiten Katalog an Maßnahmen – von eigener Stromerzeugung über die Minimierung des Papierverbrauches bis hin zum Zukauf von Klimazertifikaten. Damit gehört das Unternehmen zu den ersten der Branche, das seine Emissionen nach dem Kyoto-Protokoll freiwillig kompensiert.

provide data and thereby facilitate intelligent safety – for smart production and predictive machine maintenance.

mayr® is known around the world as an indicator of high-quality products made in Germany. This is true in Mauerstetten, where the majority of the company's 1,350 employees are based, but also in its other factories and subsidiaries. mayr® power transmission has two further factories, in Poland and China, and is currently planning to establish a subsidiary in India. It already maintains a global presence through subsidiaries in the USA, France, the United Kingdom, Italy, Singapore, Japan and Switzerland, alongside a further 40 national distributors. The mayr® brand is also committed to ensuring consistent quality across all its locations.

What is special about mayr® power transmission is its direction as a family company. Ferdinand Mayr, Managing Director, is the fifth generation of the family to lead the company. The family's commitment to the company provides consistency and reliability. Tradition and innovation are the pillars that have ensured the company's stability for generations. In an increasingly fast-paced, uncertain world, this means reliability and long-term security – even in times of crisis. Consequently, mayr® power transmission has invested heavily in its Mauerstetten headquarters in recent years, laying stable foundations and creating the scope to build a successful future. The family company, which celebrated its 125-year anniversary in 2022, thereby underpins its policy of stability as well as its commitment to its site in Allgäu and to Germany as a business location.

Sustainable business, including sustainable supply chains, has shaped the company's philosophy from the outset. Climate protection is another priority for the company, which achieved climate neutrality in 2020. It introduced an array of measures to achieve this, from generating its own electricity and minimising its paper consumption to purchasing climate credits. In doing so, the company became one of the first in its industry to voluntarily offset for its emissions in accordance with the Kyoto Protocol.

Das Kommunikationszentrum mayr.com ist das repräsentative Zentrum des Unternehmens: ein Ort der Begegnung und des direkten Austauschs von Mensch zu Mensch

The mayr.com Communications Centre is the prestigious heart of the company – a place where people can meet and exchange views directly, person to person

Mit Optimismus in die Zukunft: Ferdinand Mayr, CEO von Mayr-Antriebstechnik (zweiter von links), im Kreise seines 2023 neu aufgestellten Leitungsteams

Embracing the future with optimism: Ferdinand Mayr, CEO of mayr® power transmission (second left), with the new management team assembled in 2023

Firmengelände von mayr® Antriebstechnik in Mauerstetten

Headquarters of mayr® power transmission in Mauerstetten

FERDINAND MAYR, GESCHÄFTSFÜHRER

»Wir stehen für Konstanz und Zuverlässigkeit und haben gleichzeitig eine klare Vision für die Zukunft.«

FERDINAND MAYR, MANAGING DIRECTOR

»We stand for consistency and reliability, while also offering a clear vision for the future.«

MEWA

Im Rundum-Service versorgt Mewa kleine Betriebe und große Unternehmen mit Putztüchern, Berufskleidung, Schutzkleidung, Fuß- und Ölauffangmatten. Das nachhaltige Mehrwegprinzip entlastet Betriebe, spart Ressourcen und schont die Umwelt.

Die Erfolgsgeschichte des Dienstleisters begann bereits vor mehr als 100 Jahren. Mit wachsender Produktivität in der Industrie stieg damals der Bedarf an Putztüchern. Doch nach ihrem Gebrauch landeten die schmutzigen Lappen im Abfall. Da hatte der sächsische Unternehmer Hermann Gebauer eine innovative Idee: Dreckige Putztücher sollten nicht weggeworfen, sondern gewaschen und wiederverwendet werden. Er gründete 1908 die Mechanische Weberei Altstadt – kurz Mewa – und bot Tücher im Mehrwegsystem an. Dieses nachhaltige Prinzip hat sich bewährt und erscheint heute relevanter denn je.

Inzwischen wäscht das Unternehmen jährlich mehr als eine Milliarde Putztücher, die für die Reinigung von Maschinen und Anlagen genutzt werden. Auch gehören Berufs- und Schutzkleidung sowie Matten und biologische Teilereiniger zur Angebotspalette. Der Service umfasst das Bereitstellen, Holen, Waschen, Warten und Wiederanliefern sowie die Pflege aller Produkte bis hin zur Wartung von Schutzkleidung. Auf diesen Service vertrauen derzeit rund 200 000 Vertragskunden aus Industrie, Handel, Handwerk und Gastronomie. Europaweit tragen über 1,1 Millionen Beschäftigte Berufskleidung von Mewa. Damit gehört das Unternehmen zu den Marktführern der Branche.

Dabei setzt Mewa auf umweltverträgliche Produktionsprozesse und einen sorgsamen Umgang mit Ressourcen. Sämtliche Unternehmensbereiche sind auf Nachhaltigkeit ausgerichtet. Bereits seit 1997 sind alle Standorte gemäß der internationalen Umweltmanagementnorm ISO 14001 zertifiziert, seit 2016 ergänzt durch die Norm

Mewa's full service provides companies from small businesses to large enterprises with cleaning cloths, workwear, protective clothing, foot mats and oil-trapping mats. Its sustainable principle of reusing products relieves the burden on companies, saves resources and protects the environment.

The service provider's success story dates back over 100 years. As industrial productivity increased, so too did demand for cleaning cloths. After use, however, the soiled cloths were sent to landfill. This gave entrepreneur Hermann Gebauer from Saxony an innovative idea: instead of simply throwing dirty cleaning cloths away, they could be washed and reused. In 1908, he founded Mechanische Weberei Altstadt – Mewa for short – and offered a reusable cleaning cloth system. This sustainable principle has proven its worth and today appears more relevant than ever.

The company now washes over a billion cloths for cleaning machinery and equipment every year. Its product range also features workwear, protective clothing, mats and biological parts cleaners. Mewa's service includes providing, collecting, washing, maintaining, resupplying and caring for all its products as well as repairing protective clothing. At present, around 200,000 commercial customers from the fields of industry, retail, skilled trades and catering place their trust in this service. Over 1.1 million employees across Europe rely on Mewa workwear. These figures make the company one of the market leaders in its sector.

Mewa relies on environmentally friendly production processes and ensures careful use of resources. All of its business units are geared towards sustainability. All Mewa sites have been certified in accordance with the ISO 14001 international energy management standard since 1997 and with the ISO 50001 energy management standard since 2016. In the company's washing opera-

Unternehmensname
MEWA TEXTIL-SERVICE AG & CO. MANAGEMENT OHG

Industriezweig
TEXTIL-SERVICE

Gründer
HERMANN GEBAUER

Hauptfertigungsstätten
DEUTSCHLAND, ÖSTERREICH, ITALIEN, BELGIEN, FRANKREICH

Vertrieb
IN 21 EUROPÄISCHEN LÄNDERN

Mitarbeitende
5700 EUROPAWEIT

Company name
MEWA TEXTIL-SERVICE AG & CO. MANAGEMENT OHG

Industry
TEXTILE SERVICES

Founder
HERMANN GEBAUER

Main manufacturing facilities
GERMANY, AUSTRIA, ITALY, BELGIUM, FRANCE

Distribution
IN 21 EUROPEAN COUNTRIES

Employees
5,700 ACROSS EUROPE

Mewa wäscht jährlich über eine Milliarde Mehrweg-Putztücher, die für die Reinigung von Maschinen und Anlagen in Industrie und Handwerk genutzt werden

Each year, Mewa washes over a billion reusable cleaning cloths that are used to clean machinery and equipment in trades and industry

ISO 50001 für Energiemanagement. In den waschenden Betrieben sorgen speziell entwickelte Anlagen und Prozesse dafür, dass der Einsatz von Wasser, Energie und Tensiden so gering wie möglich ausfällt. Beispielsweise reduziert eine spezielle Kaskadentechnik den Frischwasserverbrauch im Vergleich zu herkömmlichen Waschverfahren auf die Hälfte. Die Einsparung fossiler Rohstoffe wird durch Wärmerückgewinnungssysteme und die thermische Verwertung der aus den Putztüchern ausgewaschenen Schmutzstoffe ermöglicht. Zur Nachhaltigkeitsstrategie gehört ebenfalls eine ressourcenorientierte Produktentwicklung sowie eine umweltschonende Distribution: Mit nachhaltigen Mobilitätskonzepten wie dem Einsatz von Elektro-Hubs und Lastenrädern in Großstädten wie Berlin und Hamburg werden neue Wege im City-Service eingeschlagen.

Mewa hat in Europa 47 Standorte und bietet Unternehmen in 21 Ländern eine einheitlich hohe Qualität – egal ob es sich um Produkte, Services oder Umweltstandards handelt. Hier profitieren Kunden vom Know-how eines internationalen Branchenführers. Gleichzeitig bewahrt jeder Standort sein individuelles Profil – geprägt von der Region, den Menschen und deren Mentalität. Die persönliche Betreuung vor Ort ist der Kern des Geschäftes. Denn im Unterschied zu einem Unternehmen, das Produkte nur verkauft, bleibt ein Dienstleister dauerhaft in der Kundenbeziehung und in der Verantwortung.

Mit 5700 Mitarbeitenden europaweit versteht sich Mewa als Chancengeber für Fach- und Nachwuchskräfte. In den Bereichen Gewerbe und Technik, Dienstleistung sowie im kaufmännischen Sektor bietet das Unternehmen jungen Menschen, die frisch von der Schule kommen, Berufsausbildungen an. In Kooperation mit Hochschulen werden berufsbegleitende Studiengänge angeboten. Fach- und Führungskräfte können sich in speziellen Programmen weiterqualifizieren. Wer für das Serviceunternehmen arbeitet, kann generell ein umfassendes Weiterbildungsangebot nutzen, denn die individuelle Kompetenz, Qualifikation und Motivation – auch bei einem Neu- oder Quereinstieg in den Beruf – stehen im Vordergrund. Diese gilt es zu fördern, im Team zusammenzubringen und damit das Unternehmen als Gemeinschaft zu stärken.

tions, specially developed systems and processes keep water, energy and detergents usage as low as possible. For example, a special cascade technique cuts freshwater consumption by half compared to conventional washing methods. In addition, fossil fuel consumption is reduced through heat-recovery systems and thermal utilisation of the contaminants washed out of cleaning cloths. Mewa's sustainability strategy also includes resource-oriented product development and environmentally friendly distribution. Sustainable transport concepts, such as the use of electro hubs and cargo bikes in large cities like Berlin and Hamburg, are breaking new ground in inner-city services.

Mewa has 47 locations in Europe and offers companies consistently high quality in 21 countries – in terms of its products, services and environmental standards. Its customers benefit from the expertise of an international industry leader. At the same time, each location has a unique identity, shaped by the local region, its people and their mindset. Personal, face-to-face service is at the heart of Mewa's approach. This is because, unlike companies that simply sell their products, a service provider must constantly maintain ongoing customer relationships and shoulder responsibility.

With 5,700 employees across Europe, Mewa considers itself a provider of opportunities for professionals and career entrants. The company offers young people who have recently completed their school education vocational training in industrial, technical, service-related and commercial roles. It also cooperates with universities to offer a range of dual work-study programmes. Employees and management staff can also gain further qualifications through special programmes. All employees have access to an extensive range of professional development courses because fostering individual expertise, qualifications and motivation – including among new and lateral entrants – is a particular priority. Mewa aims to provide support in these areas, bring them together within its team and thereby strengthen the sense of community within the company.

BERNHARD NIKLEWITZ, CEO MEWA TEXTIL-SERVICE

»Wir sind ein
werteorientiertes
Unternehmen.
Wir denken
nicht in Quartals-
abschlüssen,
sondern richten
uns generationen-
übergreifend aus.«

Beratung, Pflege, Aufbereitung und
Logistik: Mewa bietet Unternehmen
jeder Branche passende Berufskleidung im Rundum-Service an

Consultancy, maintenance,
preparation and logistics:
Mewa offers suitable workwear to
companies in every industry
through its full service model

Funktionserhaltende
Waschprozesse:
In Zusammenarbeit mit
dem Fraunhofer Institut
entwickelte Mewa eine
automatisierte Prüfanlage
für Warnkleidung

Function-preserving
washing processes:
Mewa collaborated with a
Fraunhofer Institute to
develop an automated
testing system for high-
visibility clothing

BERNHARD NIKLEWITZ,
CEO OF MEWA TEXTIL-SERVICE

»We are a value-
oriented company.
We don't think in
quarterly accounts;
instead, we follow a
cross-generational
approach.«

Mewa verfolgt eine Nachhaltigkeitsstrategie, die sich über sämtliche
Prozesse im Unternehmen erstreckt –
auch Logistik und Mobilität werden
berücksichtigt

Mewa pursues a sustainability
strategy that spans all processes
in a company – including logistics
and transport

ONI-WÄRMETRAFO

Angesichts der aktuellen Weltsituation müssen Anstrengungen in Richtung nachhaltige und effiziente Nutzung von Primärenergien mit größter Intensität vorangetrieben werden! Lieferwege für Primärenergieträger wie Erdgas und Erdöl werden enger, Energie-kosten steigen drastisch und die Umweltproblematik wird sich zumindest in den nächsten Jahren nicht abschwächen. Daraus erklärt sich eine bisher nie dagewesene Nachfrage nach unserem breit gefächerten Produkt- und Leistungsspektrum in Richtung effiziente und nachhaltige Energieverwendung sowie nach unserem einzigartigen System-Know-how.

Dass viele Unternehmen in ihren Systemen und Anlagen schon seit Jahrzehnten weniger Energie verbrauchen als früher, haben sie Wolfgang Oehm zu verdanken. Er gründete 1983 in Lindlar, Nordrhein-Westfalen, die Firma ONI-Wärmetrafo GmbH, die als Pionier in Sachen Entwicklung und Bau energiesparender Systemlösungen für Industriebetriebe gilt. Mit der Entwicklung des weltweit ersten Wärmerückgewinnungssystems für Kunststoffmaschinen im Jahr 1982 schrieb Oehm Geschichte. Heute ist ONI ein weltweit führendes Unternehmen in der Planung und dem Bau effizienzoptimierter Anlagen und Systeme. Das Unternehmen entwickelt und baut Anlagen für die Bereiche Kühl- und Kältetechnik, Wärmerückgewinnung, Klima-, Lüftungs- und Reinraumtechnik, Druckluftsysteme, Blockheizkraftwerke mit erforderlicher Peripherie sowie seit 2018 Kühlwasser-Behandlungssysteme, die ohne den Einsatz von Biozid auskommen. Zukunftsorientiert ausgerichtet setzt ONI verstärkt auf nachhaltige Kältetechnologien, etwa mit natürlichen Kältemitteln, oder auf hocheffiziente Wärmepumpentechnik.

ONI beliefert bereits mehr als 6200 Industriekunden in mehr als 70 Ländern der Welt, vom kleinen, mittelständischen Unternehmen bis zum großen, global agierenden Konzern. Die Kunden kommen aus den

Given the current global situation, it is vital that we further intensify our efforts to promote the sustainable, efficient use of primary energy sources. Supplies of primary energy sources such as natural gas and crude oil are becoming increasingly constrained, energy prices are soaring and the environmental issues we face are not likely to improve within the next few years at least. These factors are creating unprecedented demand for wide-ranging products and services in relation to efficient, sustainable energy use and outstanding systems expertise.

Many companies with industrial facilities have reduced their energy consumption over recent decades – and have Wolfgang Oehm to thank. In 1983, he founded ONI-Wärmetrafo GmbH in Lindlar, North Rhine-Westphalia, which became a pioneer in the development and construction of energy-saving system solutions for industrial enterprises. Oehm had already made history the year before by developing the first heat-recovery system for plastics machines. Today, ONI is a world leader in the planning and construction of energy-optimised industrial systems. It develops and builds systems for use in cooling and refrigeration technology, heat recovery, compressed air systems, cogeneration plants with the necessary peripheral equipment, air-conditioning, ventilation and cleanroom technology – and, as of 2018, cooling water treatment systems that do not rely on biocides. With its clear focus on the future, ONI is increasingly turning to sustainable cooling technologies, such as natural coolants and high-efficiency heat pump technology.

ONI already supplies its solutions to more than 6,200 industrial customers in over 70 countries, from small and medium-sized enterprises to major global corporations. Its customers operate in various sectors, from plastics and metal processing to the automotive industry, the chemicals industry, the food industry and

Wir nutzen Energie sinnvoll

Unternehmensname
ONI-WÄRMETRAFO GMBH

Industriezweig
INDUSTRIEANLAGENBAU

Gründung
1983

Gründer
WOLFGANG OEHM

Produkte
ENERGIESPARENDE UND PROZESSOPTIMIERENDE ANLAGENSYSTEME

Hauptfertigungsstätten
LINDLAR, GROSSRÖHRSDORF, KUNSHAN (CHINA)

Jahresumsatz
86,5 MIO. EURO (2022)

Company name
ONI-WÄRMETRAFO GMBH

Industry
INDUSTRIAL PLANT ENGINEERING AND CONSTRUCTION

Founded
1983

Founder
WOLFGANG OEHM

Products
ENERGY-SAVING AND PROCESS-OPTIMISING SYSTEMS

Main production sites
LINDLAR, GROSSRÖHRSDORF (BOTH GERMANY), KUNSHAN (CHINA)

Annual sales
€86.5 MILLION (2022)

Neueste Wärmepumpentechnologie mit nachhaltigem Kältemittel R515B sorgt für eine hohe Effizienz in der Kühlwasser-erzeugung. Die dabei entstehende Abwärme mit 75 Grad Celsius steht als kostenlose Heizwärme zur Verfügung

State-of-the-art heat pump technology with the sustainable R515B coolant ensures highly efficient cooling water generation. The resulting waste heat, at a temperature of 75°C, represents a free source of heat

verschiedensten Branchen. Die Bandbreite reicht von der Kunststoff- und Metallverarbeitung über die Automobilindustrie sowie die Chemie- und Lebensmittelbranche bis zur Medizintechnik. ONI hält Patente zu Wärmerückgewinnungssystemen und zur Energieoptimierung an Maschinen und Anlagen, des Weiteren sind Patente zu einem komplexen Wasserbehandlungssystem ohne Biozid-Einsatz und zu einem Stromsparsystem für Pumpen in Kühlwassersystemen angemeldet. Seit etwa 15 Jahren wird die Lieferung von Anlagen durch ein umfassendes Service- und Dienstleistungspaket ergänzt. Dazu gehört beispielsweise eine permanente Fernüberwachung der Anlagensicherheit und -effizienz weltweit. Zudem bietet ONI ein ungewöhnliches Finanzierungsmodell an: „Spar 100, zahl 50" meint, dass die Kunden mit der einen Hälfte der eingesparten Energiekosten die Energiesparmaßnahme bezahlen und ihnen die andere Hälfte direkt als zusätzliche Liquidität zugutekommt. Darüber hinaus bietet ONI einen kostenlosen Erstberatungsservice und die Unterstützung bei der Beantragung von Fördermitteln.

Wolfgang Oehm versteht Unternehmertum als eine ganzheitliche Verantwortung. Dazu gehört auch eine täglich gelebte ethische und soziale Verantwortung gegenüber seinen Mitarbeitenden, Mitmenschen und Organisationen des Gemeinwohls. So werden wesentliche Gewinnanteile an Mitarbeitende, karitative Einrichtungen, Kindergärten und eine große Anzahl von Vereinen ausgeschüttet. Um nur ein Beispiel herauszugreifen: Mit einem Aufwand von mehr als 1,1 Millionen Euro wurden für mehr als 50 Asylsuchende Sprachkurse organisiert, 10 Asylsuchende davon wurden erfolgreich ausgebildet und in ein festes Arbeitsverhältnis übernommen. Der Unternehmenserfolg ist für Oehm Verpflichtung, neue Arbeits- und Ausbildungsplätze in Deutschland zu schaffen. Die Ausbildungsquote ist überdurchschnittlich hoch und alle Auszubildenden wurden bisher übernommen. Insgesamt beschäftigt die Unternehmensgruppe an den drei Standorten Lindlar, Großröhrsdorf und Kunshan 490 Mitarbeitende. Die gesamte Belegschaft erwirtschaftete im Jahr 2022 einen Jahresumsatz von 86,5 Millionen Euro.

ONI ist ein inhabergeführtes Familienunternehmen und wird von Wolfgang Oehm zusammen mit drei Geschäftsführern geleitet. Wolfgang Oehm wurde für seine unternehmerische Leistung und sein außergewöhnliches soziales Engagement mehrfach ausgezeichnet, unter anderem 2016 mit dem Verdienstkreuz 1. Klasse des Verdienstordens der Bundesrepublik Deutschland und für sein Lebenswerk 2019 durch die Oskar-Patzelt-Stiftung und 2021 durch die Handwerkskammer zu Köln mit der Goldenen Münze.

medical engineering. ONI holds patents for heat-recovery systems and energy optimisations for machinery and installations, with further patent applications submitted for a complex water-treatment system that does not rely on biocides as well as a power-saving system for pumps in cooling water systems. Around 15 years ago, ONI introduced an extensive service package to supplement its portfolio of technical systems. It includes continuous remote monitoring of system safety and efficiency around the world. In addition, ONI offers an unconventional financing model: in its "Save 100, Pay 50" scheme, customers use half of their energy cost savings to pay for the energy-saving measure, while the other half provides additional liquidity. Furthermore, ONI provides free initial consultations and assistance with funding applications.

Wolfgang Oehm believes that entrepreneurship entails comprehensive responsibility. This includes actively demonstrating ethical and social responsibility each and every day – to his employees, to his fellow citizens and to organisations working in support of the common good. The company therefore distributes a considerable share of its profits to its employees, charitable organisations, preschools and an array of clubs and associations. To give just one example, the company invested over €1.1 million to organise language courses for more than 50 asylum seekers, 10 of whom successfully completed their training and received permanent employment contracts. For Oehm, the company's success incurs an obligation to create new jobs and trainee positions in Germany. It has an above-average training ratio and has hired all its trainees to date. In total, the corporate group has 490 employees across three sites in Lindlar, Großröhrsdorf and Kunshan. The entire workforce achieved annual sales of €86.5 million in 2022.

ONI is an owner-operated family business led by Wolfgang Oehm along with three managing directors. Wolfgang Oehm has received numerous accolades for his entrepreneurial achievements and extraordinary social engagement, including the Officer's Cross of the Order of Merit of the Federal Republic of Germany in 2016, as well as honours from the Oskar Patzelt Foundation in 2019 and the Gold Medallion from the Cologne Chambers of Commerce in recognition of his life's work.

»Wir müssen
besser und
schneller als unsere
Wettbewerber sein,
um uns weiterhin
so erfolgreich zu
entwickeln.«

In einer Fertigungshalle am Standort Lindlar,
die in Richtung Energieoptimierung, nachhaltige
Energieverwendung und physiologische
Arbeitsplatzgestaltung optimiert wurde, werden
unter anderem Container-Kühlanlagen für den
weltweiten Einsatz gebaut

A production hall at the ONI's Lindlar site, which
has been optimised in respect of energy efficiency,
sustainable energy use and ergonomic workplace
design. Activities at the facility include constructing
container-based cooling systems for global use

Wolfgang Oehm und Mona Neubaur,
Wirtschaftsministerin und stellvertretende NRW-Ministerpräsidentin,
vor einem dynamisch arbeitenden
Temperiersystem der ONI Temperier-
technik Rhytemper® GmbH

Wolfgang Oehm and Mona Neubaur,
State Minister for the Economy
and Deputy Minister-President of
North Rhine-Westphalia, in front of a
dynamic temperature control system
manufactured by ONI Temperier-
technik Rhytemper® GmbH

»We must be better
and faster than
our competitors if
we are to continue
our success into
the future.«

Installation einer großen, modular
aufgebauten Container-Kühlanlage
auf einer Plattform in 20 Meter
Höhe. Hier wird das Modul 2 der
Containeranlage aufgesetzt

Installation of a large, modular,
container-based cooling system on
a platform at a height of 20 m.
The image shows Module 2 of
the container-based system being
moved into place

OTTOBOCK

1919 gründete Otto Bock die „Orthopädische Industrie GmbH" in Berlin. Was folgte, veränderte die Branche der Orthopädietechnik grundlegend. Bis dahin wurden Prothesen ausschließlich in Handarbeit hergestellt. Otto Bock erkannte, dass die Zehntausenden Kriegsversehrten, die der Erste Weltkrieg hinterlassen hatte, so kaum zu versorgen waren. Seine damals revolutionäre Idee: Er unterteilte die Prothesen in Komponenten und ermöglichte die Serienproduktion einzelner Passteile. Auch nach dem Umzug der Firma ins thüringische Königsee bewahrte sich der Unternehmer seinen Pioniergeist. So setzte Otto Bock bereits in den 1930er-Jahren erstmals leichte Aluminiumteile in der Prothetik ein. Nach dem erneuten Weltkrieg stand das erfolgreiche Unternehmen aber plötzlich vor dem Nichts: Das gesamte Privatvermögen der Familie und die Fabrik in Königsee wurden von der sowjetischen Besatzungsmacht enteignet.

Den Neubeginn schaffte das Unternehmen im niedersächsischen Duderstadt, nahe der innerdeutschen Grenze. Max Näder, der Schwiegersohn Otto Bocks, baute die bisherige Zweigstelle zum neuen Hauptsitz der „Otto Bock Orthopädische Industrie KG" auf. Schnell bewies die nächste Generation an der Spitze der Firma unternehmerischen Weitblick: Als Alternative zum knappen Rohstoff Holz setzte Max Näder Polyurethan-Kunststoffe in der Beinprothetik ein. Schon 1965 folgte der nächste Meilenstein: Ottobock brachte myoelektrisch – also durch schwache elektrische Impulse – gesteuerte Armprothesen auf den Markt. Erstmals konnten Anwender*innen sowohl leichte und zerbrechliche als auch schwere Gegenstände greifen.

1990 trat mit Prof. Hans Georg Näder der heutige Eigentümer und Vorsitzende des Verwaltungsrats in das Unternehmen ein. In den folgenden Jahrzehnten baute er das globale Netzwerk aus, forcierte Marketing und Vertrieb. Wie sein Vater und Großvater treibt Hans

In 1919, Otto Bock founded Orthopädische Industrie GmbH in Berlin. In the years that followed, the company fundamentally transformed the orthopaedic technology industry. Before then, prosthetics had been produced exclusively by hand. Otto Bock realized that this approach would not sufficiently support the tens of thousands of veterans who returned from the First World War with disabilities. His idea, which was revolutionary at the time, involved dividing prosthetics into individual components to facilitate series production. The company relocated to Königsee, a town in Thuringia, where it retained its pioneering spirit. In the 1930s, for example, Otto Bock implemented lightweight aluminium components in prosthetics for the first time. However, following the Second World War, the previously successful company was suddenly left with nothing when all of the family's private assets and the Königsee production facility were expropriated by the occupying Soviet forces.

The company started afresh in Duderstadt, a city in Lower Saxony not far from the border with East Germany. Max Näder, Otto Bock's son-in-law, expanded what had previously been a branch office to become the new headquarters of Otto Bock Orthopädische Industrie KG. As part of a new generation at the top of the company, Näder soon demonstrated his entrepreneurial vision, replacing scarcely available wood with polyurethane plastics in the company's prosthetic legs. The next milestone followed in 1965 when Ottobock launched myoelectric prosthetic arms, controlled by weak electrical signals. This enabled the prosthetics' users to grip light, fragile objects as well as heavier items.

Prof. Hans Georg Näder, the company's current owner and Chairman of the Management Board, joined the company in 1990. In the decades since, he has expanded the company's global network and advanced its sales and marketing activities. Just like his father and grand-

ottobock.

Unternehmensname
OTTOBOCK SE & CO. KGAA

Industriezweig
HEALTHTECH

Gründung
1919 IN BERLIN

Gründer
OTTO BOCK

Produkte
PROTHESEN, ORTHESEN, MANUELLE UND ELEKTRISCHE ROLLSTÜHLE, EXOSKELETTE

Vertrieb
IN MEHR ALS 135 LÄNDERN

Mitarbeitende
9000 WELTWEIT

Company name
OTTOBOCK SE & CO. KGAA

Industry
HEALTH TECH

Founded
1919 IN BERLIN

Founder
OTTO BOCK

Products
PROSTHETICS, ORTHOTICS, MANUAL AND ELECTRIC WHEELCHAIRS, EXOSKELETONS

Distribution
IN MORE THAN 135 COUNTRIES

Employees
9,000 WORLDWIDE

Seit über 100 Jahren verhilft Ottobock Menschen zu mehr Unabhängigkeit und Bewegungsfreiheit

Ottobock has helped people to gain more independence and freedom of movement for over 100 years

Georg Näder Forschung und Entwicklung als Basis für zukunftsweisende Innovationen voran. Doch auch Tradition und Heimatverbundenheit bleiben entscheidende Werte bei Ottobock. 1992 kaufte Familie Näder den Stammsitz in Königsee zurück, wo das Unternehmen seitdem Rollstühle produziert.

Heute ist Ottobock Weltmarktführer in „wearable human bionics" – tragbarer menschlicher Bionik, die Teile des Körpers erweitert oder ersetzt. Dazu gehören neben Prothesen Lösungen im Bereich Orthetik, NeuroMobility, Patient Care und Exoskelette. Angetrieben vom Wunsch, die Lebensqualität der Anwender*innen zu verbessern, entwickelt das Unternehmen alltagstaugliche Hightech-Produkte, inspiriert vom menschlichen Körper. Mit dem weltweit ersten mikroprozessorgesteuerten Kniegelenk – dem C-Leg – hebt Ottobock den Standard in der Prothetik auf ein neues Level. 25 Jahre nach der Einführung setzt die neueste Generation des C-Leg weiterhin Maßstäbe. Ebenfalls eine Weltneuheit ist der Exopulse Mollii Suit. Der Neuromodulationsanzug verbessert die Versorgung von Menschen mit neurologischen Erkrankungen fundamental. Er stimuliert gezielt bestimmte Körperstellen mit niedrigfrequenten elektrischen Impulsen, um etwa Spastiken und damit verbundene Schmerzen zu reduzieren. Seit 2018 überträgt Ottobock die Expertise in der Biomechanik auf Exoskelette. Diese am Körper getragenen Stützstrukturen entlasten das Muskel-Skelett-System bei körperlich anspruchsvollen Tätigkeiten, wie beispielsweise Überkopfarbeit.

Das global agierende Traditionsunternehmen hat Produktions- und Vertriebsstandorte in 60 Ländern und unterhält mehr als 400 eigene Patientenversorgungszentren. Die über 9000 Mitarbeitenden erwirtschafteten im Jahr 2022 einen Umsatz von 1,3 Milliarden Euro. Bereits seit 1988 ist Ottobock Partner der Paralympics und bietet allen Athlet*innen während der Spiele einen kostenlosen technischen Support an. Der gesellschaftlichen Verantwortung eines Global Players ist sich Ottobock natürlich bewusst: Seit 2015 ist das Unternehmen Mitglied im UN Global Compact – der weltweit größten und wichtigsten Initiative für nachhaltige und verantwortungsvolle Unternehmensführung. Daneben setzt sich die Ottobock Global Foundation für die Versorgung von Kindern in Kriegs- und Krisengebieten mit Prothesen und Rollstühlen ein.

Mit Julia und Georgia Näder, den Töchtern des Eigentümers, ist die vierte Generation der Gründerfamilie bereits in das Unternehmen eingebunden. So wird sich Ottobock auch in Zukunft immer wieder neu erfinden – und doch bleiben, was es schon seit über 100 Jahren ist: The human empowerment company.

father, Hans Georg Näder promotes research and development as the basis of pioneering innovations. Nevertheless, preserving tradition and maintaining strong ties to its roots remain key values for Ottobock. In 1992, the Näder family repurchased the company's original headquarters in Königsee, which has since served as its wheelchair production facility.

Today, Ottobock is a global market leader in wearable human bionics – prosthetics that enhance or replace parts of the human body. These include prosthetic solutions in the areas of orthotics, neuromobility, patient care and exoskeletons. Driven by the determination to improve users' quality of life, the company develops high-tech products suitable for everyday use, drawing inspiration from the human body. Ottobock again raised the bar for prosthetics when it launched the C-Leg – the world's first microprocessor-controlled knee joint. Today, 25 years after the original model was launched, the latest generation of the C-Leg continues to set the standard. The Exopulse Mollii Suit is another world first: this neuromodulation suit has radically improved the care available to people with neurological conditions. It uses low-frequency electrical impulses to provide targeted stimulation of certain parts of the body in order to reduce spasms and relieve associated pain. Since 2018, Ottobock has applied its expertise in the field of biomechanics to exoskeletons. These support structures, which are worn on the body, relieve the strain on the musculoskeletal system when performing physically strenuous activities such as overhead work.

A global company with a rich tradition, Ottobock has production and sales sites in 60 countries and operates more than 400 patient care centres. With more than 9,000 employees around the world, the company recorded a turnover of €1.3 billion in 2022. Furthermore, Ottobock has been a partner of the Paralympic Games since 1988, offering free technical support to all athletes during the event. Ottobock is acutely aware of its social responsibility as a global player. In 2015, the company signed up to the UN Global Compact – the world's largest and most important initiative in support of sustainable, responsible business management. In addition, the Ottobock Global Foundation works to provide prosthetics and wheelchairs to improve healthcare for children in regions affected by war and conflict.

With Julia and Georgia Näder, the current owner's daughters, the fourth generation of the founding family is already actively involved in the company's operations. Ottobock will continue to reinvent itself time and again in the future while remaining what it has been for over 100 years: the human empowerment company.

»Innovation für mehr Lebensqualität – das ist unser Purpose, seit mehr als 100 Jahren.«

Überkopfarbeit neu definiert: Das Exoskelett Ottobock Shoulder unterstützt als natürliche Erweiterung des Körpers bei anstrengenden Tätigkeiten oberhalb der Schulter

Overhead work – redefined: the Ottobock Shoulder exoskeleton acts as a natural extension of the body, providing support when performing strenuous activities above shoulder height

Aktiv trotz Zerebralparese: Dank des innovativen Neuromodulationsanzugs Exopulse Mollii Suit und dem Gehtrainer Walker kann der kleine Justus sich selbstständig und sicher bewegen

Mobile despite cerebral palsy: Thanks to the innovative Exopulse Mollii Suit and an assistive walker, little Justus is able to walk safely and independently

»Innovating to improve quality of life – that is our raison d'être, as it has been for over 100 years.«

Prof. Hans Georg Näder, Eigentümer und Verwaltungsratsvorsitzender, ist der Enkel des Unternehmensgründers Otto Bock

Prof. Hans Georg Näder, owner and Chairman of the Management Board, is the grandson of company founder Otto Bock

PILZ

Deutschland erlebte in der Nachkriegszeit ein anhaltendes Wirtschaftswunder: mit Vollbeschäftigung, einem Exportboom und weltweiter Begeisterung für Produkte „made in Germany". An diesem Aufstieg partizipierte auch Pilz, der globale Anbieter von Produkten, Systemen und Dienstleistungen für die Automatisierungstechnik. Wie die soziale Marktwirtschaft feierte das Unternehmen 2023 sein 75-jähriges Bestehen.

1948, gleich zu Beginn des Wiederaufbaus, gründeten Hermann Pilz und seine Frau Herta mit Mut und Kreativität eine Glasbläserei. Für Kliniken, Hochschulen und chemische Betriebe fertigten sie medizinischtechnische Messinstrumente, auf den Zehntelmillimeter exakt auskalibriert. Bald erweiterten sie die Produktpalette um industriell genutzte Quecksilberschaltgeräte. Damit begann die Erfolgsgeschichte als Entwickler und Hersteller für Industrieschaltgeräte.

Sohn Peter Pilz erkannte die Zeichen der Zeit: Der Elektronik gehört die Zukunft. Er arbeitete ab den 1960er-Jahren im elterlichen Betrieb mit und erweiterte das Produktportfolio. 1968 übernahm Peter Pilz die Unternehmensführung. Er leitete mit den ersten drei Tochtergesellschaften auch die Internationalisierung ein. In den 70er-Jahren entwickelte sich das Unternehmen dynamisch weiter. Pilz setzte Standards und wurde vom Pionier zu einem der führenden Industrieelektronik-Gerätehersteller.

Nach dem plötzlichen Tod von Peter Pilz im Jahr 1975 übernahm seine Frau Renate Pilz, bis dahin Hausfrau und Mutter zweier Kinder, die Unternehmensführung. Sie arbeitete sich in Technik und Betriebsführung ein und gründete in den folgenden Jahrzehnten weitere 33 internationale Tochtergesellschaften in Europa, Nord- und Südamerika und Asien. 1987 entwickelte Pilz ein bahnbrechendes Sicherheitsprodukt: PNOZ war das weltweit erste Not-Aus-Schaltgerät für den

In the years following the Second World War, Germany experienced a prolonged economic miracle: full employment, an export boom and global enthusiasm for products "made in Germany". One company that contributed to the country's economic resurgence was Pilz, the global supplier of products, systems and services for automation technology. And, like Germany's social market economy, Pilz celebrated its 75th anniversary in 2023.

In 1948, as the rebuilding process was just beginning, Hermann Pilz and his wife, Herta, demonstrated courage and creativity by founding a glass-blowing workshop. They produced technical measuring instruments, precisely calibrated to a tenth of a millimetre, for use in hospitals, universities and chemicals companies. The product range soon expanded with the addition of mercury relays for industrial applications. This was the first chapter in the company's success story as a developer and manufacturer of industrial relays.

The couple's son, Peter Pilz, saw where the winds of time were blowing: the future lay in electronics.

He began working at his parents' company in the 1960s, expanded its product portfolio and assumed leadership of Pilz in 1968. He began working at his parents' company in the 1960s, expanded its product portfolio and assumed leadership of. He also instigated its internationalisation, founding the company's first three subsidiaries. In the 1970s, the company enjoyed dynamic growth. Pilz set new standards and evolved from a pioneer into a leading manufacturer of industrial electronic devices.

Following the sudden death of Peter Pilz in 1975, his wife Renate Pilz – who until then had been a housewife and mother of two – took over management of the company. She found her feet in the worlds of technology and business management, founding a further 33 inter-

THE SPIRIT OF SAFETY

Unternehmensname
PILZ GMBH & CO. KG

Industriezweig
AUTOMATISIERUNGSTECHNIK MIT DER KERNKOMPETENZ SICHERHEIT

Gründung
1948 IN ESSLINGEN

Vertrieb
42 TOCHTERGESELLSCHAFTEN WELTWEIT

Mitarbeitende
RD. 2500 WELTWEIT

Jahresumsatz
403 MIO. EURO (2022)

Automatisierungslösungen von Pilz sorgen weltweit für die Sicherheit von Mensch, Maschine und Umwelt

Pilz automation solutions protect the safety of people, machinery and the environment around the world

Company name
PILZ GMBH & CO. KG

Industry
AUTOMATION TECHNOLOGY WITH CORE EXPERTISE IN SAFETY

Founded
1948 IN ESSLINGEN

Distribution
42 SUBSIDIARIES WORLDWIDE

Employees
APPROX. 2,500 WORLDWIDE

Annual sales
€ 403 MILLION (2022)

zuverlässigen Stopp von Maschinen im Gefahrenfall und ist bis heute Synonym für Sicherheitsschaltgeräte. Pilz ist seither Marktführer in diesem Bereich. Das innovationsfreudige Unternehmen erweiterte seine Kompetenzen und setzte früh auf die Digitalisierung. Am Stammsitz in Ostfildern bei Stuttgart entstand das Peter Pilz Entwicklungszentrum, und seit 1998 arbeitet die eigene Softwareentwicklung im irischen Cork.

Pilz ist heute ein führender Anbieter von Automatisierungslösungen mit der Kernkompetenz Sicherheit. Seine Sensoren, Steuerungen und Antriebstechnik gewährleisten reibungslose Abläufe und die Sicherheit von Mensch, Maschine und Umwelt, unter anderem in der Verpackungs- und Automobilindustrie, an Roboter-Applikationen, in der Intralogistik sowie in den Branchen Robotik und Bahntechnik. Entsprechende Softwaretools, Diagnose- und Visualisierungssysteme, Systeme für die industrielle Kommunikation sowie umfangreiche internationale Services komplettieren das Angebot. Da Digitalisierung und Vernetzung immer komplexere Anforderungen an die Industrial Security stellen, sichern Produkte und Dienstleistungen von Pilz heute auch die Verfügbarkeit von Maschinen und Anlagen sowie die Integrität und Vertraulichkeit von maschinellen Daten und Prozessen nach höchsten Standards.

Von Ostfildern bei Stuttgart aus agiert Pilz mit 42 Tochtergesellschaften und Niederlassungen auf allen Kontinenten, darunter Produktionsstandorte in Deutschland, der Schweiz, Frankreich und China. Der innovationsstarke Mittelständler hat sich immer wieder erfolgreich gewandelt: von der Glasbläserei zum Elektronikunternehmen, sodann zum Automatisierungsunternehmen und schließlich zum Digitalisierer. Pilz investiert beständig und auf hohem Niveau in die Zukunft. In den letzten Dekaden flossen jährlich bis zu 20 Prozent des Umsatzes in die Forschung und Entwicklung des Unternehmens.

Renate Pilz, die für ihr Lebenswerk mit dem Bundesverdienstkreuz und der Rudolf-Diesel-Medaille, Europas ältestem Innovationspreis, geehrt wurde, zog sich 2017 aus der Geschäftsführung zurück. Das Unternehmen, zu 100 Prozent in Familienbesitz, wird seither in dritter Generation geführt von Susanne Kunschert, geborene Pilz, und ihrem Bruder Thomas Pilz. Anlässlich des Firmenjubiläums 2023 betonten beide ihre große Wertschätzung für alle Mitarbeitenden, die Pilz seit seiner Gründung zu dem gemacht haben, was es heute ist: stets wandlungsfähig, innovationsfreudig und damit sehr erfolgreich.

national subsidiaries in Europe, North America, South America and Asia in the decades that followed. n 1987, Pilz developed a ground-breaking safety product: PNOZ was the world's first safety relay with an emergency stop function capable of reliably shutting down machines in case of danger – and remains a synonym for safety relays to this day. Pilz has been a market leader in this field ever since. The innovative company refined its expertise and embraced digitalisation at an early stage. The Peter Pilz Technology Centre was constructed at the company's headquarters in Ostfildern near Stuttgart, while its software development facility in Cork, Ireland, opened in 1998.

Today, Pilz is a leading provider of automation solutions, with core expertise in safety-related solutions. Its sensors, controllers and drive technology guarantee smooth processes and the safety of people, machinery and the environment, including in the packaging and automotive industries, in robot applications, in intralogistics and in relation to robotics and railway technology. Corresponding software tools, diagnostic and visualisation systems, industrial communication systems and extensive international services complete its product range. Digitalisation and networking present increasingly complex requirements for industrial security, so Pilz products and services now also aim to ensure the availability of plant and machinery and the integrity and confidentiality of machine data and processes to the highest standards.

Based in Ostfildern, near Stuttgart, Pilz has 42 subsidiaries and affiliated companies across all continents, including production sites in Germany, Switzerland, France and China. An innovative medium-sized company, Pilz has repeatedly and successfully embraced change, evolving from a glass-blowing workshop to an electronics firm, then an automation company and, finally, a driver of digitalisation. Pilz is continuously making large-scale investments in the future. In recent decades, it has invested up to 20% of its annual revenue in research and development.

Renate Pilz, who was honoured with the Federal Cross of Merit and the Rudolf Diesel Medal, Europe's oldest innovation award, handed over management of the company in 2017. Since then, the company – which remains 100% family-owned – has been led by third-generation Susanne Kunschert (née Pilz) and her brother, Thomas Pilz. On the occasion of the company's anniversary in 2023, the management duo emphasised their appreciation for all Pilz employees since its foundation, who have made the company what it is today: always adaptable, innovative and thoroughly successful.

»Mit allem, was
wir tun, wollen wir
die Welt sicherer
machen.«

Familienunternehmen in dritter Generation:
Die Geschwister Susanne Kunschert (links)
und Thomas Pilz (rechts) haben die Geschäftsführung 2017 von ihrer Mutte Renate Pilz
(Mitte) übernommen

A third-generation family company:
Susanne Kunschert (left) and her brother
Thomas Pilz (right) took over management of
the company from their mother Renate Pilz
(centre) in 2017

Hermann Pilz gründete 1948
das Unternehmen als Glas-
bläserei für medizintechnische
Apparate. Das Unternehmen
hat sich immer wieder
gewandelt bis zum Anbieter
von sicheren Automatisie-
rungslösungen heute

Hermann Pilz founded the
company in 1948 as
a glass-blowing workshop
specialising in technical
medical equipment.
The company has evolved time
and again over the years
to become the provider of safe
automation solutions
it is today

»In everything
we do, we want
to make the world
a safer place.«

Pilz ist weltweit mit Vertriebs- und
Tochtergesellschaften, Entwicklungs-
zentren und Produktionsstätten vertreten.
Am Stammsitz Ostfildern ist die gesamte
Wertschöpfungskette plus Entwicklung,
IT und HR beheimatet

Pilz is represented with sales companies,
subsidiaries, technology centres and
production sites around the world.
Its headquarters in Ostfildern covers
the entire value chain and is home to
its development, IT and HR operations

RHEIN-NADEL AUTOMATION

Die Region um die Kaiserstadt Aachen war seit dem 18. Jahrhundert bekannt für ihre zahlreichen Unternehmen der Nadelindustrie. Deren Ära endete, weil nahezu alle Hersteller den technologischen Anschluss verloren und asiatische Anbieter ihre Märkte übernahmen. Nur eine einzige Firma schaffte einen erfolgreichen Wandel – vom Unternehmen einer aussterbenden Sparte zu einem innovationsgetriebenen Industrieunternehmen der Zukunft. Bis heute ist die Rhein-Nadel Automation (RNA) als Sondermaschinenbauer Weltmarkt- und Technologieführer in der Zuführtechnik, die zur Industriesparte Automation und Industrieautomatisierung zählt.

Das familiengeführte Industrieunternehmen entwickelt und fertigt Zuführsysteme, die viele Industrien weltweit bei der lagerichtigen Zuführung von Werkstücken in ihren Montagelinien einsetzen. Sie sind – wie die Antriebstechnik und Steuerungen der Zuführtechnik von RNA – wichtige Anlagen in vollautomatisierten Produktions- und Montageprozessen.

Das Akronym RNA steht für den Standort (Rheinland), das Ursprungsprodukt (Nadeln) und die Branche (Automation). 1898 nahmen die Rheinischen Nadelfabriken in Aachen die Produktion und den Vertrieb von Näh-, Steck- und Anstecknadeln sowie von Haushaltsnähmaschinennadeln auf. Nach der Übernahme durch die Gebrüder Herbert und Horst Pavel im Jahr 1954 wurde das Fertigungssortiment zunächst stark erweitert. Vorübergehend produzierte das Unternehmen auch Kurzwaren wie Reißverschlüsse und Druckknöpfe für die Textilindustrie, Sicherheitsgefäße, Zapfsäulen und Verpackungsmaschinen sowie Großgeräte, zum Beispiel Luftdruckkammern für die Lufthansa. 1972 gründete Klaus Pavel, der Sohn von Herbert Pavel, die Rhein-Nadel Automation GmbH (RNA), die sich seither einzig und allein auf die Zuführtechnik konzentriert. Seit 2013 führt Christopher Pavel das Unternehmen in dritter

In the 18th century, the region around the imperial city of Aachen became renowned for its numerous companies in the needlemaking industry. This era came to an end because almost all these manufacturers failed to keep pace with technological advancements and Asian providers took over their markets. Only one company achieved a successful transformation, evolving from a firm in a dying sector to become an innovation-driven, future-ready industrial enterprise. To this day, the specialist engineering company Rhein-Nadel Automation (RNA) remains a world leader and technology leader in feeding systems technology, operating in the automation and industrial automation sector.

The family-owned industrial enterprise develops and manufactures feeding systems that numerous industries around the world rely on to supply workpieces to the correct positions in assembly lines. These feeding systems – like the drive technologies and feeding control systems also produced by RNA – are vital components in fully automated production and assembly processes.

The acronym RNA stands for the company's location (Rhineland), its original product (needles) and its sector (automation). In 1898, Rheinische Nadelfabriken was founded in Aachen and began to produce and sell sewing needles, pins and lapel pins as well as needles for domestic sewing machines. Following a takeover in 1954 by two brothers, Herbert and Horst Pavel, the company's product range was significantly expanded. For a time, the company also produced haberdashery goods such as zips and snap buttons for the textile industry, safety containers, fuel dispensers and packaging machines as well as large-scale equipment, such as compression chambers for Lufthansa. In 1972, Klaus Pavel – the son of Herbert Pavel – founded Rhein-Nadel Automation GmbH (RNA), which has focused exclusively on feeding systems technology ever since. In 2013, Christopher Pavel became the third generation of the

Unternehmensname
RHEIN-NADEL AUTOMATION GMBH

Industriezweig
AUTOMATION/ INDUSTRIEAUTOMATISIERUNG/ SONDERMASCHINENBAU

Gründung
1972

Gründer
KLAUS PETER PAVEL

Produkte
ZUFÜHRSYSTEME UND KOMPONENTEN FÜR DIE ZUFÜHRTECHNIK

Jahresumsatz
75 MIO. EURO

Company name
RHEIN-NADEL AUTOMATION GMBH

Industry
AUTOMATION/ INDUSTRIAL AUTOMATION/ SPECIALIST ENGINEERING

Founded
1972

Founder
KLAUS PETER PAVEL

Products
FEEDING SYSTEMS AND COMPONENTS FOR FEEDING SYSTEMS TECHNOLOGY

Annual sales
€75 MILLION

Lineares Zuführsystem
für die Pharmaindustrie

Linear feeding system
for the pharmaceutical
industry

Generation, gemeinsam mit Benedict Borggreve und Jack Grevenstein.

Weltweit steht RNA heute für einzigartige Technologie, Qualität und Zuverlässigkeit; die Produkte gelten als Industriestandard. Vom Engineering bis zur Inbetriebnahme ist alles darauf ausgerichtet, nur die besten und innovativsten Zuführsysteme zu offerieren. Die RNA Mitarbeitenden verfügen über eine einzigartige Expertise und Erfahrung aus vielzähligen Referenzlieferungen. Und sie kennen die spezifischen Anforderungen für den Einsatz der Anlagen in Branchen wie Automotive, Pharma und Medizintechnik, Elektroindustrie, Kosmetik, Lebensmittel, Konsumgüter, Verbindungstechnik sowie Möbel- und Schraubenindustrie. Das RNA Portfolio zeichnet sich aus durch innovative und leistungsstarke Anlagen für vielfältige Lösungen: von kosteneffizienten Systemen zum Einstieg in die Zuführtechnik über konventionelle Zuführsysteme – mit ihrem hohen Innovationsgrad die zuverlässigsten und leistungsstärksten auf dem Weltmarkt – bis zu zukunftsweisenden digitalen Zuführsystemen.

Der Technologieführer schuf Innovationen wie lineare Zuführsysteme, das Katamaran-Zuführsystem, Robotik-Zuführsysteme, 3-D-gedruckte Sortiertöpfe sowie eine KI-Plattform zur Lösungsfindung (SolutionFinder) und digitalen Speicherung von Expertenwissen. Weltweit einmalig ist die RNA Software zur Simulation der Teile im Zuführsystem, was die Schaffung eines echten digitalen Zwillings ermöglicht. Damit können Anlagen schon vor der Fertigung digital getestet und gegebenenfalls modifiziert werden. Digitalisierung ist weiterhin die treibende Kraft zum Ausbau der RNA Marktführerschaft. Wichtige Elemente der Wachstumsstrategie sind reproduzierbare, flexible und hoch standardisierte Zuführsysteme, webbasierte KI-Plattformen für Machbarkeitsstudien und Simulationsmodelle, aber auch die Erschließung neuer Märkte wie der USA.

RNA war Erstplatzierter des handling award 2020 (Handhaben und Montage) und des ife-Award 2021 „Innovationspreis Losgröße 1+ (Projekt-Dienstleister)" und zählt laut „Deutsche Standards – Aus Bester Familie" (2022) zu den Top 100 der deutschen Familienunternehmen.

Die RNA Holding beschäftigt in sieben Tochtergesellschaften über 450 Mitarbeitende, die am Unternehmensgewinn beteiligt sind. Acht Produktionsstätten in Deutschland, der Schweiz, Großbritannien und Spanien fertigen jährlich bis zu 2.000 Zuführsysteme. Die globale Präsenz gewährleistet ein internationales Netzwerk von über 20 Kooperationspartnern. Einst hatte sich das Industrieunternehmen konsequent für die Zukunft positioniert. Heute blickt nicht nur die weltweite Zuführtechnikbranche wieder voller Anerkennung auf Aachen und RNA.

Pavel family to lead the company together with Benedict Borggreve and Jack Grevenstein.

Today, RNA is renowned around the world for its unique technology, quality and reliability, with its products considered the industry standard. From engineering to commissioning, everything the company does is designed to deliver only the best, most innovative feeding systems. RNA employees possess unparalleled expertise and experience from an array of past projects. They are also familiar with the specific requirements for machinery in areas such as the automotive industry, the pharmaceutical industry, medical devices, the electrical industry, cosmetics, food production, consumer goods, connection technology, the furniture industry and the screw and bolt industry. The RNA portfolio is characterised by innovative, high-performance systems for a variety of solutions, ranging from cost-efficient, entry-level feeding technology systems to conventional feeding systems – with a high degree of innovation that makes them the most reliable, high-performance systems on the global market – through to advanced digital feeding systems.

As a technology leader, RNA has produced innovations such as linear feeding systems, the catamaran feeder system, robotic feeding systems, 3D-printed bowl feeders and an AI platform (SolutionFinder) to help users identify solutions and store expert knowledge digitally. RNA software to simulate parts in a feeding system is unique around the world and makes it possible to create a genuine digital twin. This means that systems can be tested digitally and modified as needed before they are actually manufactured. Digitalisation remains the driving force behind efforts to consolidate RNA's market-leading position. Key elements of its growth strategy include reproducible, flexible and highly standardised feeding systems, web-based AI platforms for feasibility studies and simulation models, and opening up new markets, like the USA.

RNA finished in first place in the handling award 2020 (Handling and Assembly) and the ife Award 2021 (Innovation Prize Batch 1+ (Project Contractor)) – and, according to a previous German Standards compendium from 2022, is among the 100 leading family-owned companies in Germany.

RNA Holding has seven subsidiaries and over 450 employees, who benefit from a share of the company's profits. Its eight production sites in Germany, Switzerland, the United Kingdom and Spain produce up to 2,000 feeding systems per year. Meanwhile, the company's global presence is ensured by an international network of over 20 cooperation partners. Long ago, this industrial enterprise worked systematically to position itself for the future. Today, many again look to Aachen – and RNA – with respect and appreciation, both in the global feeding systems technology sector and beyond.

»RNA ist Technologie- und Marktführer in der Zuführtechnik und bekannt für seine innovativen und leistungs-starken Anlagen.«

Blick in die neue Fertigungshalle

The new production hall

Die RNA Hauptniederlassung in Aachen

RNA head office in Aachen

CHRISTOPHER PAVEL

»RNA is the technology and market leader for feeding technology systems and is renowned for its innovative, high-performance systems.«

Jack Grevenstein verantwortet den Geschäftsbereich Maschinenbau (Entwicklung und Bau der Zuführ-systeme), F&E, Standardisierung und Digitalisierung

Jack Grevenstein is responsible for the Mechanical Engineering division (i.e. development and production of feeding systems), R&D, standar-disation and digitalisation

Christopher Pavel verantwortet den Geschäftsbereich Komponen-ten, Vertrieb Maschinenbau, Marketing und Digitalisierung

Christopher Pavel is responsible for the Components division, machine sales, marketing and digitalisation

Benedict Borggreve ist verantwortlich für Finanzen, Personal, IT sowie die Betreuung der Tochterunternehmen

Benedict Borggreve is responsible for the areas of finance, HR, IT and supervising the compa-ny's subsidiaries

RHV-TECHNIK

Für manche Unternehmen kann keine Nummer groß genug sein: die Anzahl der Mitarbeitenden, die Höhe des Umsatzes, die produzierten Stückzahlen oder der Vertrieb in mindestens die halbe Welt. Für rhv-Technik war Quantität noch nie der Antrieb. Qualität dagegen schon. Als erfahrener Experte für thermische Beschichtungen hat sich das Familienunternehmen in fünf Jahrzehnten eine beachtliche Marktposition erarbeitet: Es zählt zu den zehn führenden thermischen Spritzbetrieben in Deutschland.

Für namhafte Kunden aus der Dichtungs- und Pumpentechnik, dem Maschinenbau, der Verpackungs-, Lebensmittel- und Pharmaindustrie bearbeitet der Betrieb Bauteile mit der Spezialtechnik des thermischen Spritzens – ein Beschichtungsprozess, der zum Schutz vor Verschleiß, Korrosion und Erosion auf Oberflächen eingesetzt wird. Darüber hinaus lassen sich mit der Methode elektrisch oder thermisch leitende und isolierende Schichten auf funktionale Bauteile aufbringen. Die Dicke der Schichten kann von üblichen 50 bis 500 Mikrometern bis zu mehreren Millimetern variieren, je nach Beschaffenheit des zu beschichtenden Werkstoffs.

Begonnen hat die Erfolgsgeschichte des mittelständischen Familienunternehmens 1968 im schwäbischen Waiblingen. Dort gründete Jochen Rybak einen Betrieb für feinmechanischen Apparatebau. Schnell avancierte der gebürtige Osnabrücker, der ursprünglich nur in den Süden Deutschlands gekommen war, um die Meisterschule zu absolvieren, zum Fachmann für die präzise mechanische Bearbeitung von Bauteilen. Seine Expertise war besonders in der Kernenergie, in der Luft- und Raumfahrt und in der Dichtungstechnologie gefragt. Was als kleine Werkstatt begann, entwickelte sich ab 1977 zum Spezialbetrieb für thermisches Spritzen. Die damals noch weitgehend unbekannte Technik hatte Rybaks Geschäftspartner Horst Höschele ins Unter-

For some companies, nothing is ever big enough, no matter how many people they employ, how much revenue they generate, how many parts they produce or whether they sell their products around half the world. For rhv-Technik, however, quantity has never been the driving force. Quality, on the other hand, certainly is. As a seasoned expert in thermal coatings, the family company has secured an impressive market position over the last five decades. Today, it is one of Germany's ten leading providers of thermal spraying services.

The company serves prestigious clients in the fields of sealing and pump technology, mechanical engineering and in the packaging, food processing and pharmaceutical industries. It processes components using the specialist technique called thermal spraying – a coating process that protects surfaces against wear, corrosion and erosion. This method can also be used to apply electrical or thermal insulation or conduction coatings to functional components. The coating thickness can vary between 50–500 micrometres as standard up to several millimetres, depending on the characteristics of the material in question.

The success story of this medium-sized family business began in 1968 in the Swabian town of Waiblingen. It was here that Jochen Rybak established a company specialising in precision apparatus engineering. The Osnabrück-born innovator – who had only moved to southern Germany to gain his qualifications from a technical college – soon became a specialist in the precise mechanical processing of components. His expertise was particularly sought after in relation to nuclear energy, the aerospace industry and sealing technology. From 1977 onwards, what began as a small workshop became a specialist provider of thermal spraying services. This technique, which was still largely unknown at the time, was introduced to the company by Rybak's business partner, Horst Höschele, with the enterprise

Unternehmensname
RYBAK + HOFMANN
RHV-TECHNIK GMBH + CO. KG

Industriezweig
OBERFLÄCHENVEREDELUNG

Gründung
1968

Gründer
JOCHEN RYBAK

Produkt
THERMISCHE BESCHICHTUNGEN

Jahresumsatz
6,5 MIO. EURO (2022)

Company name
RYBAK + HOFMANN
RHV-TECHNIK GMBH + CO. KG

Industry
SURFACE TREATMENTS

Founded
1968

Founder
JOCHEN RYBAK

Product
THERMAL COATINGS

Annual sales
€6.5 MILLION (2022)

Thermisches Spritzen im
Lichtbogenverfahren

Thermal spraying using
the arc spraying method

nehmen gebracht, das fortan unter dem Namen „Rybak + Höschele Verschleißschutz GmbH" firmierte.

Alleinstellungsmerkmal war und ist bis heute die Kombination von thermischen Beschichtungen und mechanischer Vor- und Fertigbearbeitung. Als Höschele 2003 aus der Firma ausschied, übernahm Rybaks Tochter Claudia dessen Anteile und führte das Unternehmen wieder vollständig in die Familie zurück. Seit Jochen Rybaks Tod im Jahr 2010 zeichnen Claudia und Steffen Hofmann für den Betrieb verantwortlich und bieten neben dem thermischen Spritzen heute auch Laserschweißen und 3D-Druck als Dienstleistungen an.

Das Bestimmen der Güte von Oberflächen und thermisch gespritzten Schichten erfordert eine genaue Analyse. Dazu hat rhv-Technik im Jahr 2002 ein eigenes metallografisches Labor eingerichtet, wo fortwährend qualitätssichernde Schliffpräparationen und Härtemessungen vorgenommen werden. Überdies erstellen die Metallografie-Expert*innen Schichtanalysen und Porositätsmessungen im Kundenauftrag. Zusammen mit wissenschaftlichen Einrichtungen, Hochschulen und Universitäten forscht das Waiblinger Unternehmen fortwährend an innovativen Oberflächentechniken, galt es in den Anfängen des Hochgeschwindigkeitsspritzens doch als Pionier in dieser Technologie. Inzwischen gehört das Verfahren zum Standard, wird aber beständig weiterentwickelt. Neu zum Beispiel ist das „High-Velocity Suspension Flame Spraying" – eine Methode, die hauchdünne und extrem dichte Keramikschichten ermöglicht, indem in Hochgeschwindigkeit ein feinpulvriger Werkstoff als Suspension auf ein Bauteil aufgetragen wird.

Für seine Innovationskraft wurde rhv-Technik bereits mehrfach ausgezeichnet und unter anderem 2018 und 2022 beim Deutschen Mittelstands-Summit mit dem TOP 100-Siegel geehrt. Darüber hinaus gewann das Unternehmen die von der Hochschule Neu-Ulm ausgerufene Deutsche 3D-Druck Challenge für innovative Lösungen in der additiven Fertigung.

Bereits vor 25 Jahren hat rhv-Technik damit begonnen, seine Kunden in die innovativen Prozesse miteinzubeziehen und mit der rhv-Akademie ein Kompetenzzentrum für Oberflächentechnik gegründet. In Seminaren und Praxisschulungen erhalten Interessierte Einblick in die rhv-Fertigungswelt. Auch die eigenen insgesamt 50 Mitarbeitenden werden regelmäßig weiterbefähigt und in den Aufgaben und Anforderungen der Zukunft geschult. Zur Motivation der Beschäftigten fördert rhv-Technik auch außerbetriebliche Projekte und Initiativen. Bietet Pilates-Kurse während der Arbeitszeit an, unterstützt lokale Sportvereine, in denen die Mitarbeitenden aktiv sind – und hält auf dem Betriebsgelände Bienenvölker zur Honigproduktion, um den Arbeitsalltag zu versüßen.

then renamed Rybak + Höschele Verschleißschutz GmbH.

Its unique selling point was, and remains to this day, its ability to combine thermal coatings and mechanical preprocessing and finishing. When Höschele left the company in 2003, Rybak's daughter Claudia acquired his shares and returned full control of the company back to the Rybak family. Since Jochen Rybak's death in 2010, Claudia and Steffen Hofmann have been responsible for running the company. In addition to thermal spraying, it now offers laser welding and 3D printing services.

Determining the quality of surfaces and thermally sprayed coatings requires precise analysis. So, in 2002, rhv-Technik established its own metallographic laboratory, where the company's specialists work tirelessly to prepare samples and conduct hardness measurements for quality assurance purposes. Its in-house metallographers also conduct coating analyses and porosity measurements on its customers' behalf. Together with scientific institutes, universities and other higher education institutions, the Waiblinger-based company continuously researches innovative surface technologies. It was also a pioneer of high-velocity spraying when this technology was in its infancy. Although this method has since become standard, it is subject to constant development. A new development, for example, is high-velocity suspension flame spraying – a method capable of achieving ultra-thin, extremely dense ceramic coatings, with a fine powdered material in suspension applied to the component at high velocity.

rhv-Technik has been recognised for its innovative strength on numerous occasions, including receiving the TOP 100 seal at the German SME Summit in 2018 and 2022. Furthermore, the company won the German 3D Printing Challenge hosted by the Neu-Ulm University of Applied Sciences (HNU), in which competitors put forward innovative solutions in additive manufacturing.

Even 25 years ago, rhv-Technik began to integrate its customers into its innovative processes and founded the rhv Academy – a centre of excellence for surface technology. Seminars and practical training sessions give interested parties insights into the world of manufacturing at rhv-Technik. The company's 50 employees regularly engage in professional development activities and receive training in the tasks and requirements of the future. In order to motivate its employees, rhv-Technik also support external projects and initiatives. These include pilates courses during working hours, sponsoring local sports clubs of which employees are members – and even housing bee colonies on company premises to produce honey and make the working day a little sweeter.

JOCHEN RYBAK († 2010), UNTERNEHMENSGRÜNDER

»Nur durch die eigene Überzeugung von einer Sache kann dein Gegenüber begeistert sein.«

Laserschweißen
von Spindelkegeln

Laser welding
of spindle cones

Sitz der rhv-Technik
in Waiblingen

rhv-Technik headquarters in Waiblingen

Claudia Hofmann,
geschäftsführende
Gesellschafterin

Claudia Hofmann,
Managing Partner

JOCHEN RYBAK (DIED 2010), COMPANY FOUNDER

»Only if you believe something with conviction can you inspire someone else with it.«

RITTAL

Es ist der 1. April 1961, als eine internationale Erfolgsgeschichte in einer kleinen Weberei in Mittelhessen beginnt: die Standardisierung von Schaltschränken. Rudolf Loh gründet die Firma Rittal und verändert mit einer Idee die Industrie. Was anfangs belächelt wurde, ist heute ein Phänomen: Der Standard-Schaltschrank steckt in Millionen von Produktlösungen weltweit. Rittal ist heute global führender Anbieter für Schaltschranksysteme, Automatisierung und Infrastruktur in den Bereichen Industrie, IT, Energy & Power, Cooling und Service. Mehr als 9200 Beschäftigte arbeiten weltweit an Innovationen, neuen Branchenlösungen und neuen Geschäftsmodellen. Aus einem kleinen blechverarbeitenden Betrieb ist ein globales Digitalunternehmen mit mehr als acht Produktionsstätten auf der ganzen Welt geworden. Nicht verändert hat sich: Rittal ist ein Familienunternehmen – Verantwortung, Gemeinschaft und soziales Engagement werden seit jeher großgeschrieben.

Im Zuge der Industrieautomatisierung entwickelte Rittal den Schaltschrank zu einem standardisierten Schaltschranksystem. Die Produkte sollten gleich mehrere Probleme der Kunden beheben, zum Beispiel mit Klimatisierungs- und Stromverteilungslösungen. Bis heute ist die Unternehmenskultur geprägt von Standardisierung, dem Systemgedanken sowie dem Anspruch, Veränderung voranzutreiben statt nur auf sie zu reagieren.

Rittal mit Sitz in Herborn (Hessen) ist das größte Unternehmen der Friedhelm Loh Group. Produkte und Lösungen von Rittal sind in über 90 Prozent aller Branchen weltweit im Einsatz – standardisiert, kundenindividuell, in bester Qualität –, etwa im Maschinen- und Anlagenbau, der Nahrungs- und Genussmittelindustrie sowie in der IT- und Telekommunikationsbranche – auf der Meyer Werft ebenso wie in der Vatikanischen Bibliothek oder im CERN. Energieeffizienz, Klimawandel oder die ausfallsichere Stromverteilung sind mehr

On 1 April 1961, in a small weaving mill in Middle Hesse, one man wrote the first chapter in an international success story: the standardisation of electrical enclosures. Rudolf Loh founded Rittal and transformed the industry with a single idea. Though it was derided at first, his concept has since become a phenomenon, with the standard enclosure incorporated in millions of products around the world. Today, Rittal is a world-leading supplier of enclosure systems, automation solutions and infrastructure in the fields of industry, IT, energy and power, cooling and technical services. The company has over 9,200 employees worldwide working on innovations, new industry solutions and new business models. A small sheet processing business has grown to become a global digital enterprise with over eight production sites around the world. Some things, however, have not changed: Rittal remains a family-owned company and places a strong emphasis on responsibility, community and social engagement – just as it always has.

As industrial automation progressed, Rittal developed its enclosure into a standardised enclosure system. Its products aimed to solve multiple problems for its customers simultaneously; its air-conditioning and power distribution solutions are just one example. To this day, the company's culture is shaped by the concept of standardisation, systems thinking and the desire to drive change rather than simply reacting to it.

Based in Herborn (Hesse), Rittal is the largest company in the Friedhelm Loh Group. Rittal products and solutions are in use in over 90% of all industrial sectors around the world – standardised, customised and of the highest quality – including in mechanical and plant engineering, in the food and beverage industry and in the telecommunications sector, from the Meyer Werft shipyards to the Vatican Library to CERN. With the topics of energy efficiency, climate change and fail-safe power distribution more pertinent now than ever,

Unternehmensname
RITTAL GMBH & CO. KG

Industriezweig
ELEKTROTECHNIK UND AUTOMATISIERUNG

Gründung
1961

Gründer
RUDOLF LOH

Vertrieb
ÜBER 65 TOCHTER-GESELLSCHAFTEN

Mitarbeitende
ÜBER 9200 WELTWEIT

Jahresumsatz
3 MRD. EURO (FRIEDHELM LOH GROUP INTERNATIONAL)

Company name
RITTAL GMBH & CO. KG

Industry
ELECTRICAL ENGINEERING AND AUTOMATION

Founded
1961

Founder
RUDOLF LOH

Distribution
OVER 65 SUBSIDIARIES

Employees
OVER 9,200 WORLDWIDE

Annual sales
€3 BILLION (FRIEDHELM LOH GROUP INTERNATIONAL)

Produktion von Klein- und Kompaktgehäusen im digital integrierten Werk im mittelhessischen Haiger

Small and compact housings in production in the digitally integrated factory in Haiger, Middle Hesse

denn je hochrelevante Themen, bei denen Rittal seine Kunden mit innovativen Lösungen für Industrie- und IT-Infrastrukturen jeglicher Größe erfolgreich macht.

Mit der Kombination aus Hardware- und Softwarekompetenzen optimieren und digitalisieren die Schwestergesellschaften Rittal, Rittal Software Systems (Eplan, Cideon und German Edge Cloud) und Rittal Automation Systems die Prozesse entlang der gesamten Wertschöpfungskette des Kunden: vom Steuerungs- und Schaltanlagenbau über den Maschinenbau bis hin zu Fabrikbetreibern oder der Energiebranche. Auch den schnellen Aufbau der IT-Infrastruktur unterstützt Rittal mit seiner Systemplattform.

Die Steigerung von Effizienz und Produktivität mithilfe von Automatisierung und Digitalisierung ist eine der größten Herausforderungen der Rittal Kunden. Dafür braucht es tiefgehendes Domänenwissen, die Kombination von Hardware und Software und übergreifende Zusammenarbeit. Zentrale Überzeugung und Kompetenz bei Rittal: Datenräume zu schaffen und zu verbinden ist entscheidend für das Gelingen der industriellen Transformation.

2023 wurden die Friedhelm Loh Group als „Best Place to Learn" und Rittal mit dem TOP 100-Siegel als eines der innovativsten mittelständischen Unternehmen in Deutschland ausgezeichnet. Über Jahrzehnte haben die Mitarbeitenden des Unternehmens Veränderungen gestaltet – vom Azubi bis zur erfahrensten Fachkraft, von der Entwicklung von Innovationen bis hin zur Integration von Geflüchteten. In der Region Mittelhessen ist Rittal der größte Arbeitgeber und hat jüngst über 250 Millionen Euro in den Neubau eines komplett digital integrierten Werks am Standort Haiger investiert.

Die Neugier auf Neues treibt Inhaber Prof. Friedhelm Loh an: Er ist Ehrenpräsident des Verbands der Elektro- und Digitalindustrie (ZVEI), Ehrenprofessor des Landes Hessen, Ehrendoktor der TU Chemnitz und Preisträger der Dieselmedaille für die „Erfolgreichste Innovation". Er ist leidenschaftlicher Macher, sozial vielfältig engagiert und bekennender Christ. Das alles prägt Prof. Friedhelm Loh als Unternehmer und als Mensch. Gesellschaftliche Verantwortung ist für den Inhaber keine Floskel, sondern ein Wert an sich. Verantwortung zu tragen und zu übernehmen gehört ebenso zur Rittal DNA wie die Innovationskraft und wird vom Inhaber, seiner Frau, seiner Familie sowie den Mitarbeitenden aktiv gelebt. Ein wichtiger Baustein des sozialen Engagements ist die Rittal Foundation. Die gemeinnützige Stiftung fördert seit 2011 Soziales, Bildung und Kultur. Über 6,4 Millionen Euro spendete die Unternehmensgruppe in den letzten Jahren für gute Zwecke. „Wir alle tragen gemeinsam eine Verantwortung für das Umfeld, in dem wir leben und arbeiten", sagt der Unternehmer.

Rittal offers its customers innovative solutions for industrial and IT infrastructure on every scale.

Drawing on its combination of hardware and software expertise, Rittal and its sister companies Rittal Software Systems (Eplan, Cideon and German Edge Cloud) and Rittal Automation Systems optimise and digitalise entire value chains. Their customers range from switching and control system manufacturers and mechanical engineering firms to factory operators and the energy industry. Rittal also provides a system platform that facilitates the rapid setup of IT infrastructure.

One of the largest challenges Rittal's customers face is increasing their efficiency and productivity with the help of automation and digitalisation. This requires extensive expertise, comprehensive cooperation and an intelligent combination of hardware and software. Rittal's core belief is that creating and connecting data rooms is crucial to the success of the industrial transformation – and this is exactly where its expertise lies.

In 2023, the Friedhelm Loh Group was named "Best Place to Learn", while Rittal received the Top 100 seal in recognition its achievements as one of the most innovative companies in the German Mittelstand. As the decades have passed, the company's employees have shaped change – from new apprentices to the most experienced specialists, and from developing innovations to supporting the integration of refugees. Rittal is the largest employer in the Middle Hesse region and recently invested over €250 million in the construction of a fully digitally integrated factory at its site in Haiger, Hesse.

The company's owner, Prof. Friedhelm Loh, is driven by a curiosity to explore new ideas. He is Honorary President of the German Electro and Digital Industry Association (ZVEI) and has received an honorary professorship from the State of Hesse, an honorary doctorate from TU Chemnitz and the Rudolf Diesel Medal for "Most Successful Innovation". In addition, he is a passionate self-starter, engages in a variety of social initiatives and is a professing Christian. All of these factors shape Prof. Friedhelm Loh as an entrepreneur and as a person. To him, social responsibility is more than a tick-box exercise and instead holds intrinsic value. Accepting and shouldering responsibility is as much a part of the Rittal DNA as innovative power and is a principle actively practised by its owner, his wife, his family and the company's employees. The Rittal Foundation is an important element in the company's social engagement. This charitable foundation has supported social, educational and cultural initiatives since it was established in 2011. The corporate group has made donations in excess of €6.4 million to good causes in recent years. "We all share a responsibility for the community in which we live and work," says Friedrich Loh.

PROF. FRIEDHELM LOH

»Man kann auf die Zukunft warten – oder sie gestalten.«

Rittal, Eplan, Cideon und German Edge Cloud verfügen über das nötige Domänenwissen, um für Anlagen, Produkte und Fertigungsprozesse je einen vollständigen digitalen Zwilling zu erzeugen und sie miteinander zu vernetzen – für optimierte Prozesse in einer smarten Fertigung

Rittal, Eplan, Cideon and German Edge Cloud possess the specialist expertise required to generate and network complete digital twins for plant, products and production processes – for optimised processes in smart manufacturing systems

Prof. Friedhelm Loh ist Unternehmer, Mutmacher und Visionär der digitalen Transformation

Prof. Friedhelm Loh is an entrepreneur, motivator and visionary of the digital transformation

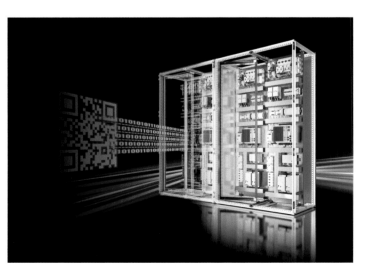

PROF. FRIEDHELM LOH

»You can either wait for the future to happen – or you can shape it yourself.«

Ökosysteme verbinden: Rittal ist der Spezialist für Systemtechnik in Industrie und IT

Connecting ecosystems: Rittal specialises in systems technology in industrial and IT contexts

RÖSLER OBERFLÄCHENTECHNIK

Auf ein perfektes Oberflächenfinish kann heutzutage kaum eine Branche verzichten – egal, ob aus ästhetischen Gründen oder um zum Beispiel die Sicherheit und Langlebigkeit des Produktes zu erhöhen. Bei der industriellen Veredelung von Oberflächen aller Art setzt seit Jahrzehnten ein fränkisches Unternehmen den Maßstab: die Rösler Oberflächentechnik GmbH mit ihren 15 Standorten und rund 150 weltweiten Handelsvertretungen.

Der Name Rösler steht seit mehr als 80 Jahren industrieübergreifend für höchste Qualität bei der Herstellung von Maschinen und Anlagen für die Bereiche Gleitschlifftechnik sowie Strahltechnik und alle dafür nötigen Verfahrensmittel. Zusätzlich produziert das Unternehmen Industriewaschanlagen, die höchsten technischen Standards entsprechen, und ist mit diesem umfangreichen Produktportfolio Weltmarktführer im Bereich Oberflächenbearbeitung. Produziert werden fast alle Anlagen sowie alle Verfahrensmittel in Deutschland.

Mit der Gründung der Marke AM Solutions bewies die Rösler Oberflächentechnik GmbH im Jahr 2018 strategischen Weitblick. Diese bündelt alle Aktivitäten der Rösler-Gruppe zum Thema 3-D-Druck und ist in kürzester Zeit zu einem selbstbewussten dritten Standbein – neben der Strahl- und Gleitschlifftechnik – geworden. Dabei profitiert AM Solutions gleichermaßen von den rund 80 Jahren Erfahrung in der industriellen Oberflächenbearbeitung des Mutterkonzerns und dem Nimbus des jungen, dynamischen und agilen Start-up-Unternehmens innerhalb dieser gefestigten Strukturen.

Zur Oberflächenbearbeitung kam die Familie Rösler, die ihre Ursprünge in der Porzellanherstellung hat, eher durch Zufall: Ende der 1940er-Jahre erkannte der Firmengründer Richard Stephan Rösler den Wert des Porzellanbruchs als Schleifkörper für die Oberflächen-

Nowadays, perfect surface finishing has become essential in just about every sector – whether for aesthetic reasons or to improve a product's safety or durability. Rösler Oberflächentechnik GmbH has been setting standards for industrial finishing of all surface types for decades. The Franconian company has a network of 15 locations and around 150 sales agents worldwide.

For more than 80 years, the name Rösler has been a byword throughout the industry for outstanding quality in the manufacture of plant and machinery for the fields of mass finishing and shot blasting as well as all associated consumables. The company also produces industrial cleaning systems that meet the highest technical standards and, with its comprehensive portfolio, is the world market leader for surface finishing. It manufactures almost all of its machinery and consumables in Germany.

In 2018, Rösler Oberflächentechnik GmbH demonstrated strategic foresight by founding the AM Solutions brand. It consolidates all of the Rösler Group's activities in relation to 3D printing and, in a short space of time, became a self-assured third pillar for the company – alongside mass finishing and shot blasting. AM Solutions benefits in equal measure from its parent company's roughly 80 years of experience in industrial surface treatment and the aura of a young, dynamic and agile start-up operating within these established structures.

The Rösler family – which has its origins in porcelain manufacturing – came to surface treatment rather by chance. In the late 1940s, the company's founder, Richard Stephan Rösler, identified the value of damaged porcelain as an abrasive for surface treatment. The next generation, led by Roland Rösler, focused increasingly on mass finishing. In 1998, the company also entered the field of shot blasting technology.

Unternehmensname
RÖSLER OBERFLÄCHENTECHNIK GMBH

Industriezweig
OBERFLÄCHENTECHNIK

Gründung
1933 IN DESSENDORF

Hauptfertigungsstätte
UNTERMERZBACH/MEMMELSDORF

Jahresumsatz
302 MIO. EURO

Gleitschliff- und Strahl-
anlagen von Rösler setzen
weltweit Standards

Rösler's mass finishing and
shot blasting systems set
global standards

Company name
RÖSLER OBERFLÄCHENTECHNIK GMBH

Industry
SURFACE TECHNOLOGY

Founded
1933 IN DESSENDORF

Main manufacturing facility
MEMMELSDORF, UNTERMERZBACH

Annual sales
€302 MILLION

bearbeitung. Die nächste Generation legte dann unter Roland Rösler den Fokus immer stärker auf das Geschäft mit der Gleitschlifftechnik. 1998 stieg das Unternehmen zusätzlich in die Strahltechnik ein. Mittlerweile beschäftigt die Rösler Oberflächentechnik GmbH weltweit 1556 Mitarbeitende und wird vom geschäftsführenden Gesellschafter Stephan Rösler in dritter Generation als Familienunternehmen mit übergeordneter Holding und operativen Tochtergesellschaften geführt.

Als regional verwurzeltes Unternehmen und als einer der größten Arbeitgeber in der Region ist sich Rösler seiner sozialen Verantwortung jederzeit bewusst. Eine langfristig orientierte und nachhaltige Denkweise geht über ein kurzfristig orientiertes Gewinnstreben: Nach dieser Maxime handelt das Unternehmen im fränkischen Untermerzbach jeden Tag aufs Neue – zusammen mit einem starken Team aus motivierten Mitarbeitenden. Damit das auch in Zukunft so bleibt, investiert die Rösler-Gruppe seit Jahren konsequent in eine hocheffiziente Unternehmensinfrastruktur und eine moderne Arbeitsumgebung, etwa durch weitreichende Automatisierungs- und Digitalisierungsmaßnahmen, New-Work-Konzepte und die Schaffung einer starken Arbeitgebermarke.

Das stetige Wachstum von Rösler spricht für den Erfolg der nachhaltigen Unternehmensausrichtung – und spiegelt sich auch in den aktuellen Geschäftszahlen wider: Im Jahr 2022 erzielte die Rösler-Gruppe einen weltweiten Umsatz von 302 Millionen Euro – und schreibt damit ihre Erfolgsgeschichte in dritter Generation weiter. Den Titel des Technologieführers untermauert das Unternehmen mit zahlreichen Patenten im Bereich Oberflächentechnik und Verfahrensmittel. Viele davon zielen auf eine umweltfreundlichere und ressourcenschonendere Art der Oberflächenbearbeitung ab und bieten ganz neue Lösungen für die Industrie auf dem Weg in eine klimaneutrale Produktion.

Die Rösler-Gruppe hat in den letzten Jahrzehnten viel erreicht und dankt es den Menschen in der Region durch ihr vielfältiges Engagement, zahlreiche Sponsorings und das klare Bekenntnis zu den deutschen Standorten. Gleichzeitig richtet sich Rösler weiter international aus und nutzt das vorhandene Potenzial, um global neue Märkte zu erschließen – getreu dem Firmenmotto „finding a better way".

Today, Rösler Oberflächentechnik GmbH has 1,556 employees. It remains a family business, now under third-generation ownership with Stephan Rösler as President and CEO, with a superordinated holding company and operational subsidiaries.

As a company with deep local roots, and as one of the largest employers in the region, Rösler never loses sight of its social responsibility. A sustainable mindset with a long-term focus is more important than the short-term pursuit of profit: this maxim guides the company, based in the Franconian municipality of Untermerzbach, in its day-to-day activities – together with a strong team of motivated employees. In an effort to ensure this remains the same in future, the Rösler Group has made consistent investments in building highly efficient internal infrastructure and a modern work environment for a number of years, including far-reaching automation and digitalisation measures, New Work concepts and creating a strong employer brand.

Rösler's continued growth is testament to the success of the company's sustainable orientation. This is also reflected in the company's latest financial results, with the Rösler Group achieving global sales of €302 million in 2022 – thereby continuing its success story under third-generation ownership. Rösler further underpins its reputation as a technology leader with numerous patents in the field of surface technology and consumables. Many of these innovations target a more environmentally friendly, resource-efficient form of surface processing and offer novel solutions to industrial customers on the road to climate-neutral production.

The Rösler Group has achieved a great deal in recent decades and shows its gratitude to the region's people through wide-ranging social engagement, numerous sponsorship arrangements and a clear commitment to its German locations. At the same time, Rösler is adopting an increasingly international approach and using existing potential to tap into new markets around the world – true to the company's motto, "finding a better way".

»Wir wollen
das weltbeste
Unternehmen
in der Branche sein,
höchste Qualität
liefern sowie
maximal service-
orientiert und
innovativ sein.«

Die Zukunft der Oberflächenbearbeitung: Produktionshalle
von AM Solutions, der Rösler-Marke
für die Nachbearbeitung additiv
gefertigter Werkstücke

The future of surface treatment:
the production hall of AM Solutions,
the Rösler brand for post-processing
of additively manufactured
components

Familienunternehmer in dritter
Generation: Stephan Rösler,
geschäftsführender Gesellschafter
der Rösler Oberflächentechnik GmbH

A third-generation entrepreneur:
Stephan Rösler, President and CEO at
Rösler Oberflächentechnik GmbH

STEPHAN RÖSLER, PRESIDENT AND CEO

»We want to be
the world's best
company in the
sector, deliver the
highest quality
and be as service-
oriented and inno-
vative as possible.«

Blick auf den Haupt-
produktionsstandort
von Rösler im fränkischen
Untermerzbach

A view of Rösler's
main production site in
Untermerzbach, Franconia

SCHAEFFLER

Die Schaeffler AG – The Motion Technology Company – ist ein weltweit führender Anbieter von Technologie für Bewegung. Das Unternehmen wurde 1946 von den Brüdern Wilhelm und Georg Schaeffler gegründet und hat seitdem eine beeindruckende Entwicklung durchlaufen. Schaeffler hat seinen Hauptsitz in Herzogenaurach und eine reiche Geschichte geprägt von einer besonders starken Innovationskultur. Heute ist Schaeffler ein global agierendes, börsennotiertes Familienunternehmen und gilt als Pionier im Bereich der Technologie für Bewegung.

Am Beginn der Unternehmensgeschichte steht eine revolutionäre Erfindung: das käfiggeführte Nadellager. Auch heute ist das Kernelement aller Produktfamilien die Bewegung. Die Schaeffler Gruppe bietet innovative Produkte und Services, die Bewegung führen, übertragen, erzeugen, antreiben, in Energie überführen und langfristig erhalten. Eine wesentliche Eigenschaft von Schaeffler ist die Fähigkeit, technologische Brücken zwischen Produktfamilien zu schlagen. Gleichermaßen ist das ausgeprägte Systemverständnis ein entscheidendes Werteversprechen und ein Mehrwert für Kunden. Durch Innovationsstärke und technologische Expertise ist Schaeffler in der Lage, seinen Kunden innovative Technologien für unterschiedliche Anwendungen in verschiedenen Märkten anzubieten. Schaeffler zählt Unternehmen in den vier Marktclustern Transport & Mobilität, Maschinen & Materialien, Industrial Automation und Erneuerbare Energien zu seinen Kunden. Diese Diversifizierung ermöglicht Synergien und macht das Unternehmen gleichzeitig resilient. Bei Schaeffler weiß man, wie exzellente Produkte entwickelt und gefertigt werden, in hoher Stückzahl und von höchster Qualität. Produkte, die die Bewegung in Produktionsmaschinen steuern oder beispielsweise den reibungslosen Betrieb von Windkraftanlagen gewährleisten.

Bewegung ist ein Schlüsselfaktor, um die globalen Herausforderungen zu bewältigen. Der Erfolg hängt dabei

Schaeffler AG – The Motion Technology Company – is a world-leading technology provider. The company was founded in 1946 by two brothers, Wilhelm and Georg Schaeffler, and has developed impressively ever since. Schaeffler has its headquarter in Herzogenaurach and can look back on a rich history shaped by a strong innovation culture. Today, Schaeffler is a listed family company with global operations and is considered a pioneer of motion technologies.

The company's history began with a revolutionary invention: the cage-guided needle roller bearing. Even today, motion remains a crucial element of all its product families. The Schaeffler Group offers innovative products and services that guide, transmit, generate, drive, energise and sustain motion. One of Schaeffler's key qualities is its ability to build technological bridges between product families. At the same time, its extensive systems expertise creates a decisive value proposition and provides added value for customers. Thanks to its innovative power and technological expertise, Schaeffler is able to offer its customers innovative technologies for wide-ranging applications in different markets. Schaeffler groups its customers into four market clusters: Transportation and Mobility, Machinery & Materials, Industrial Automation and Renewables. This diversification creates synergies and also supports the company's resilience. Schaeffler's experts know how to develop and manufacture excellent products in high quantities and to the highest quality standards. These include products that control motion in production machinery or ensure that wind turbines operate flawlessly.

Motion is a key factor in overcoming the global challenges we face. Our success will depend to a significant extent on our ability to rethink motion and develop progressive solutions. For companies to retain a pioneering position in increasingly dynamic and complex

SCHAEFFLER

Unternehmensname
SCHAEFFLER AG

Industriezweig
TECHNOLOGIEKONZERN

Gründung
**1946 ALS INDUSTRIE GMBH
IN HERZOGENAURACH**

Vertrieb
WELTWEIT

Mitarbeitende
CA. 84 000 (2022)

Jahresumsatz
CA. 15,8 MRD. EURO (2022)

Company name
SCHAEFFLER AG

Industry
TECHNOLOGY COMPANY

Founded
**1946 AS INDUSTRIE GMBH
IN HERZOGENAURACH**

Distribution
WORLDWIDE

Employees
APPROX. 84,000 (2022)

Annual sales
APPROX. €15.8 BILLION (2022)

1950 meldet Dr.-Ing. E. h. Georg Schaeffler den Nadelkäfig mit achsparallel geführten Wälzkörpern als Patent an und führt ihn vom Prototyp zum serienreifen Wälzlager. Heute finden Nadellager Anwendung im Maschinen- und Getriebebau sowie im Automobilbereich. Für die Funktion zahlreicher elektrifizierter Getriebe in der E-Mobilität sind sie unverzichtbar

In 1950, Dr Georg Schaeffler filed a patent application for a needle cage with axially parallel guided roller elements, turning it from a prototype into a roller bearing ready for series production. Today, needle bearings are used in mechanical engineering, gear manufacturing and the automotive industry. They are an essential component of numerous electrified gearboxes in the e-mobility industry

im besonderen Maße von der Fähigkeit ab, Bewegung neu zu denken und fortschrittlich zu gestalten. Um in zunehmend dynamischeren und komplexeren Umgebungen mit sich verändernden Kundenbedürfnissen Pionier zu bleiben, müssen sich Unternehmen kontinuierlich weiterentwickeln, innovativer, agiler und effizienter werden. Bei Schaeffler stehen die Kunden im Mittelpunkt. Das Unternehmen konzentriert sich bei seinem Produkt- und Serviceportfolio auf Bewegung als das Element, das alle Sparten verbindet und alle Aspekte der Bewegungstechnologie vereint. Als Motion Technology Company bietet die Schaeffler Gruppe ihren Kunden sechs Produktfamilien, deren verbindendes Element die Bewegung ist: Guide Motion, Transmit Motion, Generate Motion, Drive Motion, Energize Motion und Sustain Motion. Mit diesem Portfolio konzentriert sich die Schaeffler Gruppe auf das Element, das ihr Angebot über alle Geschäftsbereiche hinweg verbindet: die Bewegung.

Schaeffler ist ein globales Unternehmen mit einer starken Präsenz in allen wichtigen Märkten. Mit Produktionsstätten, Forschungs- und Entwicklungszentren sowie Vertriebsniederlassungen in über 50 Ländern ist das Unternehmen weltweit bei seinen Kunden vor Ort präsent. Diese globale Ausrichtung ermöglicht es Schaeffler, auf lokale Bedürfnisse einzugehen und gleichzeitig eine weltweite Lieferkette aufzubauen, die Effizienz und Flexibilität gewährleistet.

Nachhaltigkeit ist ein integraler Bestandteil der Unternehmensstrategie von Schaeffler. Das Unternehmen übernimmt ökologische und soziale Verantwortung entlang der gesamten Wertschöpfungskette. Vor allem das Thema „Klimaneutralität" nimmt eine zentrale Rolle bei der Umsetzung der Nachhaltigkeitsstrategie ein. Schaeffler hat sich zum Ziel gesetzt, ab dem Jahr 2040 klimaneutral zu wirtschaften und Emissionen sowohl in der eigenen Produktion als auch in der Lieferkette zu reduzieren.

Bewegung ist bei Schaeffler der Schlüssel zum Erfolg. Mit einem klaren Fokus auf Innovation, Digitalisierung und Nachhaltigkeit wird Schaeffler auch weiterhin eine führende Rolle in seinen vier Marktclustern spielen und sich noch stärker darauf konzentrieren, sowohl Synergie- als auch Skaleneffekte über Produkte, Anwendungen und Märkte hinweg zu realisieren. Als Motion Technology Company wird Schaeffler aktiv seine Stärken und Chancen nutzen und gemeinsam mit Kunden, Partnern und der Gesellschaft die Bewegung der Zukunft gestalten – getreu dem Motto „We pioneer motion".

environments with changing customer requirements, they must continuously evolve and become more innovative, more agile and more efficient. Customers are at the heart of what Schaeffler does. The company's portfolio of products and services focuses on motion as the element that connects all industries and brings all aspects of motion technology together. As the Motion Technology Company, the Schaeffler Group offers its customers six product families, all of which are connected by motion: Guide Motion, Transmit Motion, Generate Motion, Drive Motion, Energize Motion and Sustain Motion. The Schaeffler Group's portfolio revolves around the element that connects its service offering across all business segments: motion.

Schaeffler is a global company with a strong presence in all key markets. With research and development centres, production facilities and sales subsidiaries in over 50 countries, the company is close to its customers around the world. This global footprint enables Schaeffler to address local needs while also building a global supply chain that ensures efficiency and flexibility.

Sustainability is an integral component of Schaeffler's corporate strategy. The company assumes environmental and social responsibility throughout the entire value-creation chain. Above all, the concept of climate neutrality plays an important role in the implementation of its sustainability strategy. Schaeffler has set itself the goal of becoming climate-neutral by 2040 and reducing emissions both in its own production activities and throughout its supply chain.

Motion is the key to success at Schaeffler. By maintaining a clear focus on innovation, digitalisation and sustainability, Schaeffler will continue to play a leading role in its four market clusters, concentrating even more strongly on generating synergies and scaling effects across products, applications and markets. As the Motion Technology Company, Schaeffler will actively exploit its strengths and opportunities, working together with its customers, partners and wider society to shape the motion of the future in line with its claim: "We pioneer motion".

»Wir sind mehr als Automotive und Industrial: Wir sind die Motion Technology Company.«

Schaeffler AG Firmenzentrale
in Herzogenaurach

Schaeffler AG headquarters
in Herzogenaurach

Maria-Elisabeth Schaeffler-Thumann,
Gesellschafterin der INA-Holding Schaeffler
GmbH & Co. KG und Geschäftsführerin
der IHO Verwaltungs GmbH

Maria-Elisabeth Schaeffler-Thumann,
Shareholder of the INA-Holding Schaeffler
GmbH & Co. KG and Managing Director
of IHO Verwaltungs GmbH

Georg F. W. Schaeffler,
Vorsitzender des Aufsichtsrats
der Schaeffler AG | Gesell-
schafter der INA-Holding
Schaeffler GmbH & Co. KG

Georg F. W. Schaeffler,
Chairman of the Supervisory
Board of Schaeffler AG |
Shareholder of INA-Holding
Schaeffler GmbH & Co. KG

Klaus Rosenfeld,
Vorstandsvorsitzen-
der der Schaeffler AG

Klaus Rosenfeld,
Chief Executive
Officer Schaeffler AG

»We are more than automotive and industrial: we are the Motion Technology Company.«

Schaeffler OPTIME ist eine preisgekrönte
Condition-Monitoring-Lösung, welche
ungeplante Stillstände reduziert und für
beinahe alle Maschinen einsetzbar ist

Schaeffler OPTIME is an award-winning
condition-monitoring solution that reduces
unplanned breakdowns and can be used
with almost all machines

SCHNIEWINDT

Das weltweit agierende Elektrotechnikunternehmen Schniewindt begann 1829 als kleiner Familienbetrieb für Schusterwerkzeuge im Sauerland. Mit der Erfindung des Schniewindt-Heizgitters im Jahr 1902 begann die erfolgreiche Positionierung im auch heute noch bespielten Markt. Das Heizgitter wurde zum Patent angemeldet und weltweit in Widerstandsgeräten eingesetzt.

Neben der Beheizungstechnik sind die beiden weiteren Schwerpunkte im Bereich der elektrischen Widerstands- und Energieübertragungstechnik zu finden. Schniewindt bietet im Sektor Beheizungstechnik individuelle Lösungen für Industriekunden vom einzelnen Element bis hin zur schlüsselfertigen Lösung an. In den anderen beiden Sektoren Widerstandstechnik und Energieübertragungssysteme vertreibt das Familienunternehmen Filter-, Brems-, Dämpfungs- und Erdungswiderstände und hält Mess- und Sensortechnik für Stromnetze bereit.

Das Unternehmen ist auf prozessindividuelle Lösungen für die Industrie spezialisiert und bedient sowohl den chemischen Anlagenbau, die Petrochemie, die Energietechnik als auch Kunden im Bereich Bahn und Schiff, Maschinen- und Anlagenbau. Ebenso sind Schniewindt-Anwendungen bei thermischen Verfahren, in der Forschung und bei der Power-to-Heat-Technologie im Einsatz.

Entsprechend dem Firmen-Slogan „The Power of Electrifying Ideas" hat Schniewindt vom Spannungsteiler (1964) über die Entwicklung von Bremswiderständen für Schiffe (2004), leistungsstarken Durchlauferhitzern (2017) und Hochtemperatur-Gaserhitzern (2023) immer wieder Produktinnovationen erfolgreich auf den Markt gebracht und hält mittlerweile 14 Patente. In einigen Bereichen ist das märkische Unternehmen quantitativer Marktführer mit beispielsweise einem Weltmarktanteil von mehr als 50 Prozent bei Bremswiderständen

The global electrical engineering company Schniewindt dates back to 1829, when it was launched as a small family business producing tools for cobblers in Sauerland. The invention of the Schniewindt grid in 1902 marked the start of the company's success in the market segment it serves to this day. The grid was subsequently patented and used in resistors around the world.

In addition to heating technology, the company also has two further focus areas, namely resistor technology and energy transmission technology. In its heating technology segment, Schniewindt offers bespoke solutions for industrial customers, ranging from individual components to turnkey solutions. In terms of its resistor technology and energy transmission systems, the family company offers filtering, braking, damping and earthing resistors and supplies measurement and sensor technology for power grids.

The company specialises in developing process-specific solutions for industrial applications, serving the chemical plant engineering, petrochemical and energy engineering industries. Its customers also include mechanical and plant engineering firms and the rail and maritime industries. Schniewindt solutions are also used in thermal process applications, research projects and in power-to-heat technology.

In keeping with its slogan – The Power of Electrifying Ideas – Schniewindt has developed successful innovations time and again, from the voltage divider (1964) to braking resistors for ships (2004), high-performance flow heaters (2017) and high-temperature gas heaters (2023). At present, it holds 14 patents. Based in the Märkischer Kreis district of North Rhine-Westphalia, Schniewindt is a market leader by sales volume in certain fields. For example, its share of the global market for medium-voltage braking resistors is over 50%. Its

Unternehmensname	
SCHNIEWINDT GMBH & CO. KG	

Industriezweig
ELEKTROINDUSTRIE

Gründung
1829

Gründer
CARL SCHNIEWINDT

Hauptfertigungsstätte
NEUENRADE

Vertrieb
WELTWEIT

Mitarbeitende
200 WELTWEIT

Jahresumsatz
28 MIO. EURO

Company name
SCHNIEWINDT GMBH & CO. KG

Industry
ELECTRICAL INDUSTRY

Founded
1829

Founder
CARL SCHNIEWINDT

Main manufacturing facility
NEUENRADE

Distribution
WORLDWIDE

Employees
200 WORLDWIDE

Annual sales
€28 MILLION

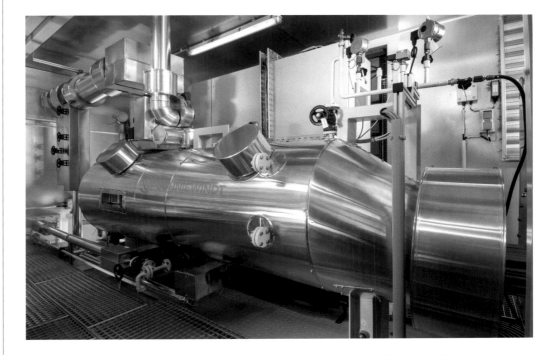

CSN® Dampfkessel:
elektrisch, CO_2-frei und
prozessindividuell

CSN® steam generators:
electric, carbon-free,
process-specific systems

aus Mittelspannung. Die luft- und wassergekühlten Bremswiderstände dienen dem kontrollierten Abbremsen und werden bei elektrisch betriebenen Containerschiffen und großen Personenschiffen eingesetzt. Ebenfalls von großer Bedeutung sind die Spannungsteiler, bei denen Schniewindt einen Marktanteil von mehr als 40 Prozent für sich reklamiert und sowohl in der EU als auch auf dem Weltmarkt Spitzenreiter ist. Die Spannungsteiler werden zur Spannungsmessung in der Regel- und Schutztechnik von Hochspannungs-Gleichstromübertragungsanlagen sowie an Forschungsinstituten eingesetzt. Technologieführer ist Schniewindt bei Flanschheizkörpern oder auch Durchlauferhitzern, die im Offshore-Umfeld zum Beispiel bei Ölbohrinseln oder auf Anlagen zur Gasförderung eingesetzt werden. Wichtig für die Produktpalette des Unternehmens sind zudem Ex-Gasvorwärmer zur Erwärmung von Brenngasen in Öl- und Gasversorgungsanlagen der Petrochemie und Patronenheizkörper für die direkte Erwärmung von Flüssigkeiten oder Gasen. Zukünftig will man sich im Bereich Elektrifizierung der Prozesswärme engagieren und bei der Lieferung von Komponenten für den weltweiten Ausbau von Energieübertragungsanlagen.

Das Unternehmen hat seinen Stammsitz noch immer in Neuenrade, wo es von Carl Schniewindt gegründet wurde, und beschäftigt dort 180 Mitarbeitende. Bei der Tochtergesellschaft in Pinghu (China) werden weitere 20 Mitarbeitende beschäftigt. Der Vertrieb erfolgt in Deutschland per Direktvertrieb und darüber hinaus mit 22 Vertriebspartnern weltweit. Der erwirtschaftete Jahresumsatz belief sich zuletzt auf 28 Millionen Euro. Die Geschäftsführung verantwortet Dr. Sarah Schniewindt, die kaufmännische Leitung hält Gerhard Barth.

Schniewindt investiert gerne in seine zukünftigen Leistungsträger, bildet die Fachkräfte selbst aus, bietet Tarifgehälter und flexible Arbeitszeitmodelle an. Ein duales Studium und Weiterbildungsmaßnahmen runden das Angebot ab. Das Unternehmen erhielt das Prädikat „familienfreundlich" von Competentia NRW, was unter anderem bedeutet, dass sich die Mitarbeitenden bei Betreuungsengpässen kurzfristig und flexibel um ihren Nachwuchs kümmern können. Ebenso gibt es Hilfen bei der Pflege von Angehörigen oder beim Wiedereinstieg nach der Familienpause oder Krankheit. Für das Unternehmen ist dieses Maßnahmenpaket ein deutlicher Pluspunkt bei der Fachkräftesuche und Mitarbeiterbindung. Zudem beteiligt sich Schniewindt an der Klima-Initiative der SIHK zu Hagen mit dem Ziel der Klimaneutralität bis 2030. Schniewindt unterstützt aus Verbundenheit mit dem Standort die lokalen Sportvereine und Schulen und beteiligt sich an der Bürgerstiftung zur Heimatpflege Neuenrade.

air-cooled and water-cooled braking resistors facilitate controlled braking and are used in electric container ships and large passenger vessels. Voltage dividers are also important products for the company: Schniewindt has secured a 40% market share and is the leading provider in the EU and in the global market. These devices are used for voltage measurement in control and protection systems in high-voltage direct current (HVDC) links and at research institutes. Schniewindt is also a technology leader when it comes to flange heaters and flow heaters, which are used in offshore settings such as oil rigs and gas production facilities. Other important elements of the company's product portfolio include its explosion-proof gas preheaters, which heat fuel gases in oil and gas supply facilities in the petrochemical industry, and cartridge heaters for direct heating of liquids and gases. In the future, Schniewindt hopes to engage with the electrification of process heating and the supply of components for the global expansion of energy transmission systems.

The company still has its headquarters in Neuenrade, where it was founded by Carl Schniewindt, and has 180 employees. Its Chinese subsidiary in Pinghu has 20 employees. It distributes its products through direct sales in Germany and with the help of 22 distribution partners around the world. The company's most recent accounts showed sales totalling €28 million. Dr Sarah Schniewindt oversees the company's overall management, while Gerhard Barth is responsible for commercial affairs.

Schniewindt readily invests in the specialists of the future, provides in-house training, offers wages in line with collective agreements and facilitates flexitime models. Dual work-study programmes and professional development services round off its range of employee benefits. The family has been certified as "family friendly" by Competentia NRW, in part because Schniewindt employees have the flexibility to look after their children if their arrangements fall through, even at short notice. The company also provides support to employees who care for relatives or return to work following a period of parental leave or illness. This benefits package gives the company a clear advantage in relation to recruitment and employee retention. Schniewindt has signed up to the climate initiative launched by the South Westphalia Chamber of Commerce and Industry at Hagen (SIHK zu Hagen) with the aim of achieving carbon neutrality by 2030. And, building on its affinity with the local area, Schniewindt supports nearby sports teams, schools and a community foundation to protect the culture and heritage of Neuenrade.

DR. SARAH SCHNIEWINDT

»Die Zukunft
ist elektrisch,
und Schniewindt
gestaltet diese
aktiv mit.«

Einzigartiger 1100 kV
CSN® Spannungsteiler für
Hochspannungsnetze

Unique 1100 kV CSN®
voltage divider for
high-voltage grids

CSN® Flanschheiz-
körper für verfahrens-
technische Prozesse

CSN® flange heater for
process engineering
applications

Geschäftsführerin
Dr. Sarah Schniewindt

Managing Partner
Dr Sarah Schniewindt

DR SARAH SCHNIEWINDT

»The future is
electric – and
Schniewindt is
actively shaping it.«

SCHWANK

Wärme im großen Stil, so lässt sich die Leidenschaft der Familie Schwank beschreiben. Die Kunst, so effizient und effektiv wie möglich für angenehme Temperaturen zum Arbeiten und Leben auch in schwierigen Umgebungen zu sorgen, zieht sich durch alle Stationen des Familienunternehmens.

Ihren Anfang nahm diese Erfolgsgeschichte im elsässischen Fegersheim. Im Jahr 1933 produzierte der junge Ingenieur Günther Schwank hier Gasherde und arbeitete an einer neuartigen keramischen Platte, die als Flammträger Infrarotstrahlung erzeugen sollte. Patentiert wurde diese Technik im Jahr 1939. Sie diente als Basis für die erste gasbetriebene Infrarot-Strahlungsheizung für Hallen, den sogenannten Hellstrahler. Die Produktion und der Vertrieb erfolgten zunächst über Lizenzverträge mit internationalen Partnern, erst 1951 startete die eigene Herstellung in Günther Schwanks Heimatstadt Hamburg. Doch schon 1952 stand ein Ortswechsel an – Schwank bezog seinen heutigen Standort in Köln.

War die Reise des Unternehmens geografisch erst einmal beendet, ging sie technologisch gerade erst los. Aus Herden wurden Heiz- und Klimasysteme, und der kleine Familienbetrieb wuchs rasant. Die effizienten Infrarotstrahler von Schwank, mit denen man selbst große Fabrik- oder Lagerhallen energiesparend heizen kann, trafen den Nerv der Zeit, wie die große Nachfrage bewies. Bis heute nutzt das Unternehmen die Infrarottechnologie, die nicht die Luft, sondern Oberflächen erwärmt. Denn mit ihr lässt sich mit wenig Energieeinsatz viel Wärme erzeugen.

Jedoch fußt der Erfolg nicht nur auf Technologien, sondern auch auf Führungspersönlichkeiten. So war es Professor Bernd H. Schwank, dem 1970 ins Unternehmen eingetretenen Sohn des Gründers, zu verdanken, dass das zwischenzeitlich angeschlagene Unternehmen wie-

Heating on a grand scale – that's the best way to describe the Schwank family's passion. The art of creating pleasant temperatures as efficiently and effectively as possible in both domestic and professional settings, even in difficult environments, pervades every aspect of this family company.

The company's history began in the town of Fegersheim in Alsace. In 1933, the young engineer Günther Schwank started producing gas stoves and worked on a new type of ceramic plate to serve as a burner by providing infrared radiation. He patented this technology in 1939. It served as the basis for the first gas infrared radiator for halls, known as a plaque heater. It was initially produced and sold via licence agreements with international partners before the company started manufacturing its own products in Günther Schwank's home town of Hamburg in 1951. A relocation followed in 1952, with Schwank moving to its current site in Cologne.

Yet, while the company's geographical journey was over, its technological journey was only just beginning. It expanded from stoves to heating and cooling systems, and the small family business enjoyed rapid growth. Schwank's efficient infrared heater, which offers an energy-saving way to heat even expansive factory halls and warehouses, struck a chord – as evidenced by the strong demand. While the company still uses infrared technology to this day, Schwank uses it to heat surfaces rather than the air. This presents a way to generate a lot of heat with relatively little energy input.

However, the company's success is based not only on technologies but also on its leaders. Professor Bernd H. Schwank, the founder's son, joined the company in 1970, guiding it through a difficult period and pushing Schwank back into the black. Thanks to continuous investment and shrewd management decisions, Bernd

Unternehmensname	Company name
SCHWANK GMBH	**SCHWANK GMBH**

Unternehmensname
SCHWANK GMBH

Industriezweig
HEIZ-, KLIMA- UND LÜFTUNGSSYSTEME

Gründung
1933

Gründer
GÜNTHER SCHWANK

Vertrieb
WELTWEIT

Mitarbeitende
337

Jahresumsatz
68 MIO. EURO (2022)

Ausstellungsmodell der weltweit ersten zu 100 Prozent mit Wasserstoff betriebenen Industrieheizung geniumSchwank auf der ISH 2023

Display model of the world's first 100% hydrogen-powered industrial heating solution, the geniumSchwank, at ISH 2023

Company name
SCHWANK GMBH

Industry
HEATING, COOLING AND VENTILATION SYSTEMS

Founded
1933

Founder
GÜNTHER SCHWANK

Distribution
WORLDWIDE

Employees
337

Annual sales
€68 MILLION (2022)

der in die Gewinnzone kam. Mit stetigen Investitionen und klugen Managemententscheidungen baute Bernd Schwank die Firma zum Weltmarktführer für energiesparende Infrarot-Heizsysteme aus.

Seit 2004 ist mit Oliver Schwank die nunmehr dritte Generation im Unternehmen aktiv. Oliver Schwank initiierte die Expansion in vielversprechende neue Märkte wie beispielsweise Großbritannien oder Kanada und erweiterte das Leistungsspektrum um zukunftsweisende Produkte und Lösungen. Seit 2016 führt er das Unternehmen gemeinsam mit dem Geschäftsführer Prof. Dr.-Ing. Friedhelm Schlößer. Die Unternehmensanteile sind nach wie vor zu 100 Prozent im Besitz der Familie Schwank, die über einen Beirat auch die Geschäftsleitung kontrolliert.

Schwank ist als Holding mit 15 Tochtergesellschaften organisiert. Produziert wird neben Deutschland in den USA, Kanada und China. Für den Vertrieb unterhält das Unternehmen 15 eigene Niederlassungen weltweit und arbeitet darüber hinaus in weiteren Märkten mit Distributionspartnern zusammen. Insgesamt beschäftigt Schwank rund 340 Mitarbeitende, die nicht nur für einen gruppenweiten Jahresumsatz von rund 68 Millionen Euro im Jahr 2022 sorgten, sondern auch kontinuierlich den großen Erfindungsreichtum des Unternehmens demonstrieren.

Das jüngste Beispiel dieser Innovationskraft ist eine neuartige und weltweit einzigartige zu 100 Prozent wasserstoffbetriebene Industrieheizung aus dem Hause Schwank. Das neue Dunkelstrahler-Heizsystem mit dem Namen geniumSchwank schafft erstmals die Symbiose aus moderner, umweltschonender sowie CO_2-freier Infrarot-Heiztechnik für Hallen und industrielle Gebäude weltweit. Was vor über 80 Jahren im Elsass begann und heute in dritter Generation in Köln fortgesetzt wird, ist zu einer globalen Erfolgsgeschichte geworden, die in der Heiz- und Klimabranche ihresgleichen sucht.

Im Sinne der Nachwuchsförderung unterhält Schwank den Lehrstuhl für Cost Engineering an der Fachhochschule Südwestfalen zur Ausbildung von Masterstudent*innen des Studiengangs Wirtschaftsingenieurwesen. Weiter wird mit der Technischen Hochschule Köln im Bereich Technische Gebäudeausrüstung zusammengearbeitet. Auch der Verein Deutscher Ingenieure (VDI) wird von Schwank gezielt gefördert. Neben dem deutschen Industriepreis und den Auszeichnungen als Weltmarktführer durch das Manager Magazin sowie als Top-100-Innovator, wurde Schwank wiederholt von der WirtschaftsWoche als Weltmarktführer geehrt.

Schwank became a global market leader in energy-saving infrared heating systems.

In 2004, Oliver Schwank became the third generation of the family to join the company. He instigated an expansion into promising new markets, such as the United Kingdom and Canada, and supplemented the company's service portfolio with pioneering products and solutions. Oliver Schwank has led the company since 2016 alongside Managing Director Prof. Friedhelm Schlößer. As has always been the case, the company remains fully owned by the Schwank family, who monitor the company's management through an Advisory Board.

Schwank is a holding company with 15 subsidiaries. It manufactures its products in Germany as well as in the USA, Canada and China. The company markets its products through 15 subsidiaries around the world and also cooperates with distribution partners in other markets. In total, Schwank has around 340 employees who not only achieved Group-wide turnover of approximately €68 million in 2022 but also continue to demonstrate the company's spirit of ingenuity.

The most recent example of its innovative strength is a novel, globally unique Schwank industrial heating system that is powered 100% by hydrogen. Named geniumSchwank, this new dark emitter is the first solution to successfully provide modern, environmentally friendly, CO_2-free infrared heating for halls and industrial buildings. From its beginnings in Alsace over 80 years ago to its current base in Cologne under third-generation management, Schwank has become a global success story that is unmatched in the heating and cooling industry.

In the interests of supporting talented young people, Schwank funds the Chair of Cost Engineering at the South Westphalia University of Applied Sciences to assist Master's students on the Engineering Management programme. It also cooperates with the TH Köln University of Applied Sciences in the field of technical building services. Schwank also provides targeted support for the Association of German Engineers (VDI). In addition to the German Industry Award and being named a Global Market Leader by Manager Magazin and a Top 100 Innovator, Schwank has also been named a Global Market Leader by WirtschaftsWoche on several occasions.

OLIVER SCHWANK

»Wir wissen nicht, wie alt unsere Systeme werden. Wir machen das erst seit 90 Jahren.«

Produktion am
Standort Köln

Production underway
at the company's
Cologne site

Firmengründer Günther
Schwank neben einem
industriellen Gasherd,
Fegersheim 1933

The company's founder,
Günther Schwank, beside
an industrial gas stove in
Fegersheim, 1933

OLIVER SCHWANK

»We don't know how old our systems will become. We've only been doing this for 90 years.«

Oliver Schwank (links) in
dritter Generation an der Spitze
des Familienunternehmens,
gemeinsam mit Prof. Dr.-Ing.
Friedhelm Schlößer (Geschäftsführer seit 2016)

Oliver Schwank (left) is the
third generation of the family
to lead the company, sharing
management responsibility
with Prof. Friedhelm Schlößer
(Managing Director since 2016)

SEW-EURODRIVE

SEW-EURODRIVE ist mit seinem umfassenden und vielfältigen Portfolio einer der führenden Spezialisten für Antriebstechnologie. Einst als Hersteller von Elektromotoren gestartet, nahm SEW-EURODRIVE eine dynamische Entwicklung. Heute fertigt und vertreibt das global agierende Unternehmen Getriebemotoren, Getriebe, Motoren, dezentrale Technologie, Software und Softwaremodule, Industriegetriebe für schwere Lasten, Energie-Effizienz-Lösungen, Automatisierungslösungen und entwickelt Antriebslösungen mit hohem Engineering-Anteil. Komplettiert wird das breite Angebotsspektrum durch zahlreiche Dienstleistungen und Services. Seine Kernkompetenzen machen SEW-EURODRIVE zum bevorzugten Technologiepartner von Unternehmen der Branchen Transport und Logistik, Automotive, Food and Beverage, Prozessindustrie, Hafenlogistik, Bergbau und vieler weiterer. Dank seines modularen Baukastensystems kann das Unternehmen flexibel auf spezifische Anforderungen eingehen und gewährleistet stets optimale Leistungswerte und höchste Effizienz. Bei SEW-EURODRIVE erhält jeder Kunde seine individuelle Antriebslösung.

Dezentrale Fertigungsstandorte, ausgedehnte Werksanlagen, bewährte Vertriebsstrukturen und erfahrene Serviceteams sind die Basis des eigenen, unabhängigen Logistiknetzwerks. Von besonderer Bedeutung ist das engmaschige internationale Vertriebs- und Servicenetz, das die Kunden rund um den Globus betreut. Neben 17 Fertigungswerken verfügt das SEW-EURODRIVE-Netzwerk derzeit über 90 Drive Technology Center in 55 Ländern, weitere sind in Planung. Die internationalen Niederlassungen gewährleisten die weltweite Präsenz von SEW-EURODRIVE bei gleichzeitig lokaler Nähe in allen Regionen. Sie engagieren sich je nach Region in verschiedenen Industrien und Märkten, denen sie gemäß der spezifischen Anforderungen maßgeschneiderte Lösungen bieten. Auf allen fünf Kontinenten präsent, profitiert das Unternehmen

With its comprehensive, wide-ranging portfolio, SEW-EURODRIVE is a leading specialist in drive technology. Originally established as a manufacturer of electric motors, SEW-EURODRIVE enjoyed dynamic growth. Today, the company operates on a global scale, manufacturing and distributing gear motors, gear units, motors, decentralised technology, software and software modules, industrial gear units for heavy loads, solutions to enhance energy efficiency and automation solutions. It also develops drive solutions that involve a lot of engineering. This broad product range is complemented by an extensive service portfolio. Thanks to its core competencies, SEW-EURODRIVE is the preferred technology partner for companies in various industries, including transport and logistics, the automotive industry, the food and beverage industry, the process industry, port logistics and mining. Thanks to its modular design system, the company can approach company-specific requirements with flexibility while always ensuring optimal performance and maximum efficiency. SEW-EURODRIVE provides every customer with a customised drive solution.

Decentralised manufacturing sites, sprawling factory facilities, tried-and-tested distribution structures and experienced service teams form the basis of its own independent logistics network. Its close-knit international sales and service network, which serves customers around the globe, is particularly important in this context. In addition to 17 manufacturing sites, the SEW-EURODRIVE network currently comprises over 90 drive technology centres in 55 countries, with more in the pipeline. Its international subsidiaries ensure that SEW-EURODRIVE has a global presence while also remaining close to its customers in every region. The company operates in various industries and markets, which differ from region to region, offering tailored solutions in line with customers' specific requirements. Present across all five continents, the company

Unternehmensname
SEW-EURODRIVE GMBH & CO KG

Industriezweig
ANTRIEBSTECHNIK, ANTRIEBSAUTOMATISIERUNG, MASCHINENBAU

Gründung
1931 IN BRUCHSAL

Vertrieb
WELTWEIT IN 55 LÄNDERN

Mitarbeitende
22 000 WELTWEIT

Jahresumsatz
4,2 MRD. EURO (GJ 2022)

So umfassend und umfangreich wie die antriebstechnischen Anforderungen der Industrie: die Produkt- und Lösungspalette von SEW-EURODRIVE

The SEW-EURODRIVE product and solution portfolio is as extensive and wide-ranging as industrial requirements for drive technology

Company name
SEW-EURODRIVE GMBH & CO KG

Industry
DRIVE TECHNOLOGY, DRIVE AUTOMATION, MECHANICAL ENGINEERING

Founded
1931 IN BRUCHSAL

Distribution
IN 55 COUNTRIES WORLDWIDE

Employees
22,000 WORLDWIDE

Annual sales
€4.2 BILLION (2022)

vom direkten Austausch vor Ort und erweitert so seinen globalen Reichweitenvorsprung.

Der große Innovationsvorsprung von SEW-EURODRIVE beruht auf seiner technologischen Expertise und dem konzertierten Zusammenwirken aller Mitarbeitenden im Unternehmen. Es ist erklärter Anspruch des Unternehmens, mit Pionierleistungen die Grenzen des Machbaren zu verschieben. SEW-EURODRIVE fördert Teamarbeit und die impulsgebende Kreativität der Mitarbeitenden, um weiterhin gemeinsam technologische Benchmarks zu setzen. Das Unternehmen ist überzeugt, dass es nur mit hochmotivierten Mitarbeitenden gelingt, erfolgreich technologische Standards zu etablieren und die Marktposition weiter auszubauen.

Mit leistungsstarken Elektronikprodukten und hochmodernen Steuerungssystemen hat sich der Antriebs- und Automatisierungsexperte bereits frühzeitig auf immer komplexere Anforderungen eingestellt und die Herausforderungen der Zukunft angenommen. Das Unternehmen investiert fortlaufend in seine Infrastruktur, Technologien und Produkte. Es forciert alle erforderlichen Maßnahmen, die Ökologie, Ökonomie und soziale Verantwortung in Einklang bringen. Der Global Player agiert erfolgreich mit agilen Ländergesellschaften und trotzt so selbst gesellschaftlich oder wirtschaftlich herausfordernden Zeiten. Das auch von Shareholder-Interessen unabhängige Unternehmen hat seinen Hauptsitz im baden-württembergischen Bruchsal. Im Geschäftsjahr 2022 erwirtschaftete die SEW-EURODRIVE GmbH & Co KG mit weltweit 22 000 Mitarbeitenden, davon allein über 800 in Forschung und Entwicklung, einen Umsatz von 4,2 Milliarden Euro.

„Driving the world" – seit 1931 dreht sich bei SEW-EURODRIVE alles um Bewegung.

Die Unternehmensgeschichte war immer geprägt von immenser Innovationskraft und dem beständigen Streben nach neuen, progressiven Lösungen. Seit der Erfindung des ersten bahnbrechenden SEW-Getriebemotors entwickelte sich das Unternehmen über drei Generationen zu einem Global Market Leader im Bereich Antriebstechnik und Antriebsautomatisierung. „Unsere Kunden sollen nicht nur zufrieden sein, sondern begeistert von dem, was wir ihnen bieten können." Zum Credo von Jürgen Blickle, geschäftsführender Gesellschafter von SEW-EURODRIVE, gehört neben der individuellen, uneingeschränkten Kundenorientierung insbesondere die Wertschätzung aller Mitarbeitenden. Deshalb bestimmt der Wertekodex des inhabergeführten Familienunternehmens, stets das technologisch Machbare anzustreben, doch dabei immer den Menschen in den Mittelpunkt zu stellen.

benefits from the ability to communicate directly with customers on the ground, thereby enhancing its global reach.

The major innovative advantage SEW-EURODRIVE enjoys is based on its technological expertise and concerted cooperation between all its employees. The company's stated aim is to push the boundaries of technological possibility through pioneering achievements. SEW-EURODRIVE promotes teamwork and fosters its employees' inspiring creativity so that, together, they can continue to set new technological benchmarks. The company firmly believes that a highly motivated workforce is the only way to establish successful technological standards and further expand its market position.

By providing high-performance electronic products and state-of-the-art control systems, the drive system and automation expert adapted to increasingly complex requirements at an early stage, facing up to the challenges of the future. The company is continuously investing in its infrastructure, technology and products. It is pressing ahead with all necessary measures to reconcile environmental and economic factors with its social responsibilities. As a global player, it operates successfully with its agile national subsidiaries, despite the significant social and economic challenges of our time. The company, which is independent of any shareholder interests, has its headquarters in Bruchsal, Baden-Württemberg. In the 2022 financial year, SEW-EURODRIVE GmbH & Co. KG and its 22,000 employees worldwide, 800 of whom are in research and development roles, achieved turnover of €4.2 billion.

True to its motto – "Driving the world" – everything at SEW-EURODRIVE has revolved around movement since its foundation in 1931.

Its history has always been characterised by immense innovative power and an unwavering pursuit of new, progressive solutions. Since the invention of the first groundbreaking SEW gearmotor, the company has grown to become a global market leader in the field of drive technology and drive automation over three generations. "What we offer shouldn't merely satisfy our customers, it should delight them." The credo of Jürgen Blickle, Managing Partner at SEW-EURODRIVE, includes an individual, unequivocal customer focus as well as appreciation for all employees. So, while the owner-operated family company's code of values targets the limits of technological possibility, it always puts people at its heart.

»Menschen wollen keine Produkte, sie wollen Lösungen.«

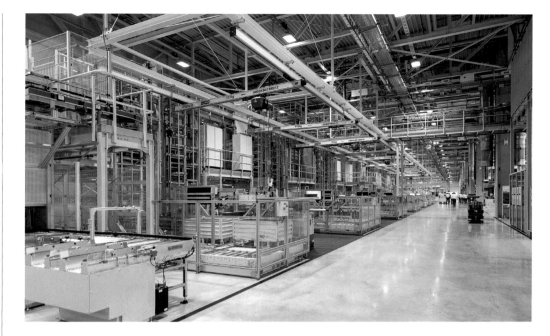

Moderne Produktionsanlagen prägen das Bild des Unternehmens mit klarer Verpflichtung zu Umweltschutz und zur Vermeidung von Umweltbelastungen

Modern production facilities shape the company's image, with a clear commitment to environmental protection and avoiding pollution

Ernst Blickle, Schwiegersohn des Gründers der Süddeutschen Elektromotoren-Werke (SEW)

Ernst Blickle, son-in-law of the founder of Süddeutsche Elektromotoren-Werke (SEW)

Die Hauptverwaltung der SEW-EURODRIVE in Bruchsal

SEW-EURODRIVE headquarters in Bruchsal

»People don't want products, they want solutions.«

SIEMENS HEALTHINEERS

1844 setzte Werner Siemens eine seiner Erfindungen, den Voltainduktor mit heilenden elektrischen Strömen, erstmals medizinisch ein und behandelte die Zahnschmerzen seines Bruders Friedrich. Damit beginnt eine unvergleichliche Geschichte, bei der sich aus kleinen Werkstätten große Unternehmen entwickeln. Und 2016 aus dem Unternehmensbereich Medizintechnik der Siemens AG die Marke Siemens Healthineers hervorgeht.

Heute ist Siemens Healthineers ein weltweit führendes Unternehmen der Medizintechnik und unterstützt das gesamte Spektrum der Gesundheitsversorgung. Es stattet Gesundheitsdienstleister in den Bereichen diagnostische und therapeutische Bildgebung, Labordiagnostik und Molekularmedizin sowie Digital Health Solutions mit innovativen Technologien und weiteren Produkten aus. Und auch Arztpraxen, Notaufnahmen und klinische Fachabteilungen vertrauen auf für sie entwickelte Lösungen. Das Portfolio enthält Systeme für Computertomographie, Magnetresonanztomographie, molekulare Bildgebung, Röntgenprodukte, Ultraschallsysteme, Point-of-Care-Testsysteme, Lösungen für Labordiagnostik und vieles mehr. Siemens Healthineers unterstützt medizinisches Fachpersonal bei der Erreichung bestmöglicher Behandlungsergebnisse sowie der Versorgung von Patient*innen mit wegweisenden Innovationen, umfassenden Beratungsleistungen und Services. Gesundheitsanbieter profitieren von Digitallösungen, die ihre Produktivität steigern und ihnen ermöglichen, standortunabhängig eine hochwertige Versorgung zu gewährleisten. Mit seinen Stärken in den Bereichen digitale Patienten-Zwillinge und Präzisionstherapie sowie Digitales, Daten und Künstliche Intelligenz forciert Siemens Healthineers den Wandel im Gesundheitswesen und ermöglicht so zum Beispiel den sicheren Austausch von Patientendaten unter Leistungserbringern.

Siemens Healthineers prägt die Medizintechnik seit über 175 Jahren, was rund 23 000 technische Schutz-

In 1844, Werner Siemens used the Volta inductor – with healing electrical currents – to treat his brother, Friedrich, who was suffering from toothache. This was the first time he used one of his inventions for medical purposes. In doing so, he penned the first chapter in an unparalleled story that would lead from small workshops to a number of major enterprises. In 2016, Siemens AG spun off its medical technology business – and Siemens Healthineers was born.

Today, Siemens Healthineers is a world-leading medical technology business and supports the entire healthcare spectrum. It equips healthcare providers in the fields of diagnostic and therapeutic imaging, laboratory diagnostics, molecular medicine and digital health solutions with innovative technologies and other products. Medical practices, emergency departments and specialist clinical departments also place their trust in the company's solutions. Its portfolio includes computer tomography (CT), magnetic resonance imaging (MRI) and molecular imaging systems as well as X-ray products, ultrasound systems, point-of-care test systems, laboratory diagnostic solutions and much more besides. Siemens Healthineers helps medical professionals to achieve the best possible treatment outcomes and provide patients with pioneering innovations, comprehensive consultations and extensive services. Healthcare providers benefit from digital solutions that boost their productivity and enable them to ensure high-quality healthcare provision at different locations. With particular strengths in patient twinning and precision therapy as well as digital, data and artificial intelligence, Siemens Healthineers is driving forward the transformation of healthcare, including by facilitating the secure exchange of patient data between service providers.

Siemens Healthineers has been shaping medical technology for over 175 years, as evidenced by 23,000 tech-

Unternehmensname
SIEMENS HEALTHINEERS AG

Industriezweig
MEDIZINTECHNIK

Hauptfertigungsstätten
DEUTSCHLAND, USA UND CHINA

Mitarbeitende
WELTWEIT RD. 70 000 (JUNI 2023)

Jahresumsatz
21,7 MRD. EURO (2022)

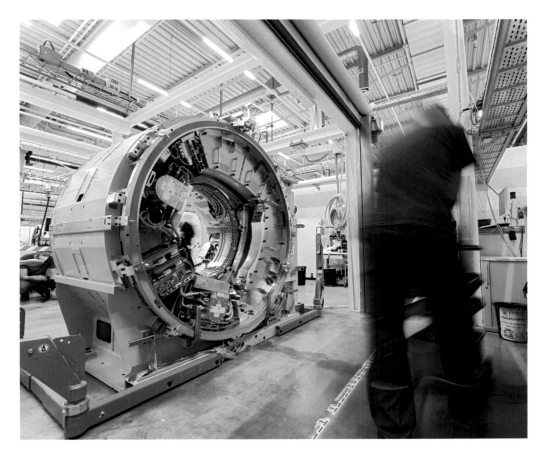

Seit Jahrzehnten ist Siemens Healthineers Innovationsführer in der Computertomographie. Zahlreiche CTs verlassen jährlich die Fertigung am Unternehmensstandort Forchheim

Siemens Healthineers has been an innovation leader in the field of computer tomography for decades. The company's Forchheim site produces numerous CT scanners every year

Company name
SIEMENS HEALTHINEERS AG

Industry
MEDICAL TECHNOLOGY

Main production facilities
GERMANY, USA AND CHINA

Employees
APPROX. 70,000 WORLDWIDE (JUNE 2023)

Annual sales
€21.7 BILLION (2022)

BEST OF GERMAN INDUSTRY

rechte, davon mehr als 14 000 erteilte Patente, eindrucksvoll belegen. Zu den bedeutendsten Innovationen zählen der voll implantierbare Herzschrittmacher, das weltweit erste Realtime-Ultraschallgerät und der Dual-Source-Computertomograph für die extrem schnelle Bildgebung. Den Technologieführer zeichnen auch die Nominierungen für den renommierten Deutschen Zukunftspreis aus: 2021 für den weltweit ersten und bisher einzigen photonenzählenden Computertomographen, der revolutionäre Bilder liefert sowie niedrigere Strahlen- und Kontrastmitteldosen ermöglicht, und 2023 für die neue Niedrigfeld-MRT-Plattform, die gemeinsam mit dem Uniklinikum Erlangen entwickelt wurde.

Siemens Healthineers betreibt seine größten Produktionsstätten in Deutschland – wo umfassend in Standorterweiterungen investiert wird –, in den USA und China. Das Unternehmen ist in mehr als 70 Ländern der Welt vertreten. Seine globale Expertise und die Kundennähe gewährleisten, dass Produkte, Lösungen und Dienstleistungen stets optimal auf die regionalen Märkte zugeschnitten sind.

Das Unternehmen hat klare strategische Ziele. Die bedrohlichsten Krankheiten sollen durch vielfältige Fortschritte der Medizintechnik noch effektiver bekämpft und Gesundheitsdienstleister in die Lage versetzt werden, mehr Patient*innen besser zu versorgen, unter anderem durch deren erweiterten Zugang zur Gesundheitsversorgung. Siemens Healthineers will als vertrauenswürdiger Partner der Gesundheitssysteme dazu beizutragen, allen Menschen eine bessere Gesundheitsversorgung zu ermöglichen. Das Unternehmen fördert humanitäre Organisationen wie das Kinderhilfswerk der Vereinten Nationen UNICEF und dessen Projekt zur Stärkung der Gesundheitssysteme in Subsahara-Afrika.

Siemens Healthineers wurde auch als Arbeitgeber international ausgezeichnet und bietet seinen Mitarbeitenden umfassende Leistungen wie eine präventive Gesundheitsvorsorge, ein Anerkennungs- und Belohnungssystem, vergünstigte Aktienprogramme und vieles mehr. Wie die Weiterbildung wird die Fachkräftegewinnung gefördert in drei globalen Schulungszentren für Auszubildende und dual Studierende, auch in neuen Studiengängen wie Data Science und Cybersecurity.

Die weltweite Gesundheitsversorgung wird auch zukünftig nur durch anhaltende Pionierarbeit Fortschritte machen. Siemens Healthineers verfügt über alle Kompetenzen, um dabei weiterhin die Benchmarks zu setzen.

nical property rights, including more than 14,000 granted patents. Its most significant innovations include fully implantable pacemakers, the world's first real-time ultrasound device and the dual-source computer CT scanner for ultra-fast imaging. The technology leader has also been nominated for the prestigious German Future Prize on multiple occasions. In 2021, it was nominated for the world's first – and, to date, only – photon-counting CT scanner, which produces revolutionary images and enables practitioners to work with lower doses of radiation and contrast media. A further nomination followed in 2023 for the new low-field MRI platform developed together with Uniklinikum Erlangen.

Siemens Healthineers has its main manufacturing facilities in Germany – where it is investing heavily in expanding its locations – as well as in the USA and China. The company is active in over 70 countries around the world. Its global expertise and proximity to its customers ensures that its products, solutions and services are always optimally tailored to regional markets.

The company has clear strategic goals. These include combating the most threatening diseases even more effectively through wide-ranging advances in medical technology and empowering healthcare providers to care better for more patients, including by extending access to healthcare services. As a trustworthy partner to healthcare systems, Siemens Healthineers strives to play its part in enabling all people to access better healthcare. The company supports humanitarian organisations, such as UNICEF and its project to strengthen healthcare systems in Sub-Saharan Africa.

Siemens Healthineers has received international employer awards and offers its employees comprehensive benefits packages, including preventive healthcare, an appreciation and reward system, subsidised equity programmes and much more. Siemens Healthineers conducts professional development activities and attracts skilled professionals at three global training centres for apprentices and dual students, including in new fields such as data science and cybersecurity.

Global healthcare systems will only progress in the future through continued pioneering work. Siemens Healthineers has the capabilities required to continue setting benchmarks.

BERND MONTAG, CEO VON SIEMENS HEALTHINEERS

»Das Gesundheitswesen ist eine Basis für Stabilität und Wohlstand ganzer Gesellschaften. Wir leisten Pionierarbeit im Gesundheitswesen – für jeden Menschen, überall.«

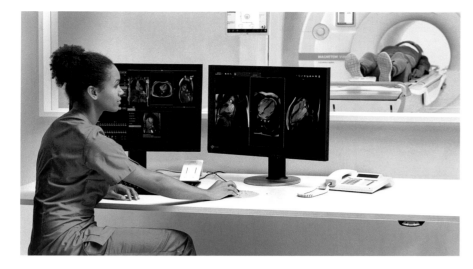

Siemens Healthineers treibt die Digitalisierung des Gesundheitswesens mithilfe von Technologien, Daten und KI voran. Neue Arbeitsmodelle wie das Remote Scanning sollen das medizinische Personal entlasten

Siemens Healthineers is advancing the digitalisation of healthcare with the help of technology, data and AI. New working models, such as remote scanning, aim to relieve the burden on medical staff

Das neu eröffnete Aus- und Weiterbildungszentrum für 240 Auszubildende und dual Studierende in Erlangen unterstreicht die Position von Siemens Healthineers als führendes Ausbildungsunternehmen

The newly opened Education & Development Centre (EDC) in Erlangen, which offers space for 240 apprentices and dual students, underscores Siemens Healthineers' position as a leading training company

BERND MONTAG, CEO OF SIEMENS HEALTHINEERS

»Healthcare is a foundation for the stability and prosperity of entire societies. We pioneer breakthroughs in healthcare – for everyone, everywhere.

Die Unternehmenszentrale von Siemens Healthineers am Traditionsstandort Erlangen bietet ein modernes Büroumfeld für bis zu 1000 Mitarbeitende

The headquarters of Siemens Healthineers, at the tradition-steeped Erlangen site, offers a modern office environment for up to 1,000 employees

SÜSS MICROTEC

Zur Vermeidung von Lieferkettenproblemen und wegen der teils angespannten geopolitischen Lage forcieren viele Nationen die subventionierte Ansiedlung von Mikrochip-Produzenten. Allein in Deutschland sind drei Halbleiterfabriken führender Unternehmen wie Wolfspeed, TSMC und Intel geplant. Das bietet enorme Wachstumspotenziale für SÜSS MicroTec, und das in der globalen Halbleiterindustrie etablierte Unternehmen weiß sie konstant für sich zu nutzen.

SÜSS MicroTec entwickelt und fertigt Anlagen und Prozesslösungen für die Produktion von Mikrochips, Sensoren und Mikrolinsen, wobei Strukturanwendungen im Mikrometer- und Nanometerbereich (ein Nanometer entspricht einem Milliardstel Meter) möglich sind. Auf engstem Raum potenziert sich die Leistungsfähigkeit heutiger Mikrosysteme in immer kürzeren Zeitintervallen. Als Technologieführer, der in einigen Bereichen zudem Weltmarktführer ist, leistet SÜSS MicroTec einen maßgeblichen Beitrag zur globalen Halbleiterherstellung der weltweit bedeutendsten Produzenten. Zunehmend nachgefragt sind temporäre Bonder und UV-Projektionsscanner zur Fertigung von Logik- und Speicherchips für Künstliche Intelligenz, deren rasante Verbreitung die Nachfrage nach Lösungen von SÜSS MicroTec dynamisch steigert. Weitere Systeme von SÜSS MicroTec dienen zur Herstellung von Reifendruck- oder Drehsensoren für Smartphones sowie von Leistungshalbleitern – den sogenannten Siliziumkarbid-Chips – für Elektrofahrzeuge und Industrien, in denen eine effiziente Energieübertragung unabdingbar ist. Auch Mikrolinsen, zum Beispiel für Smartphone-Kameras oder autonome Fahrzeuge, werden mit Technologien von SÜSS MicroTec gefertigt. Weitere verwandte Marktsegmente wie Advanced Packaging, mikroelektromechanische Systeme (MEMS) und LED-Anwendungen vertrauen auf SÜSS MicroTec Lösungen wie Maskenbelichtungsgeräte, Belacker, Wafer-Bonder und Fotomasken-Equipment.

Due to certain fraught geopolitical situations and in order to avoid supply chain problems, many countries have been forced to provide subsidies in an effort to encourage microchip producers to settle domestically. Leading companies such as Wolfspeed, TSMC and Intel have announced plans for three semiconductor factories in Germany alone. This offers enormous growth potential for SÜSS MicroTec, which is an established force in the global semiconductor industry and knows the importance of seizing such opportunities.

SÜSS MicroTec develops and produces systems and process solutions for the fabrication of microchips, sensors and micro-optics, with structural applications in the micrometre and nanometre range (i.e. one millionth of a metre). The capabilities of modern microsystems, which are incredibly compact, are developing at an increasingly rapid pace. As a technology leader – and, in some areas, a global market leader – SÜSS MicroTec makes a significant contribution to global semiconductor production by the world's largest manufacturers. Temporary bonders and UV projection scanners are increasingly sought after for use in the production of logic and memory chips, which are an essential part of artificial intelligence solutions. The rapid proliferation of AI has generated dynamic growth in demand for SÜSS MicroTec solutions. SÜSS MicroTec systems are used to manufacture tyre pressure sensors and gyro sensors for smartphones, while others fabricate power semiconductor devices – highly prized silicon carbide chips – for electric vehicles and industries in which efficient energy transfer is vital. SÜSS MicroTec technologies are also used in the manufacture of micro-optics, including for smartphone cameras or autonomous vehicles. Related market segments such as advanced packaging, micro-electromechanical systems (MEMS) and LED applications also rely on SÜSS MicroTec solutions such as mask aligners, coaters, wafer bonders and photomask equipment.

Unternehmensname
SÜSS MICROTEC SE

Industriezweig
**MASCHINENBAU/
HALBLEITER-EQUIPMENT**

Gründung
1949 IN MÜNCHEN

Produkte
**ANLAGEN UND PROZESSLÖSUNGEN
FÜR DIE HALBLEITERINDUSTRIE**

Vertrieb
WELTWEIT

Jahresumsatz
299,1 MIO. EURO (GJ 2022)

Mitarbeitende und Anlagen von
SÜSS MicroTec im Reinraum

SÜSS MicroTec employees and
systems in a clean room

Company name
SÜSS MICROTEC SE

Industry
**MECHANICAL ENGINEERING/
SEMICONDUCTOR EQUIPMENT**

Founded
1949 IN MUNICH

Products
**SYSTEMS AND PROCESS SOLUTIONS
FOR THE SEMICONDUCTOR
INDUSTRY**

Distribution
WORLDWIDE

Annual sales
**€299.1 MILLION
(2022 BUSINESS YEAR)**

Neben dem Hauptsitz in Garching bei München unterhält SÜSS MicroTec Fertigungsstandorte in Sternenfels nahe Pforzheim, im schweizerischen Neuchâtel und in Hsinchu, Taiwan. Weltweit beschäftigt das Unternehmen rund 1250 Mitarbeitende. Anlagen und Prozesslösungen von SÜSS MicroTec werden international über 35 Vertriebs- und Serviceniederlassungen vertrieben. Allein in Asien, mit den wichtigsten Einzelmärkten China und Taiwan, werden deutlich mehr als 50 Prozent des globalen Umsatzes erwirtschaftet. SÜSS MicroTec ist als SDAX-Wert seit 1999 im Prime Standard an der Frankfurter Wertpapierbörse gelistet.

Die 1949 vom Namensgeber in München gegründete Karl SÜSS KG begann mit drei Mitarbeitenden und dem Vertrieb von Produkten der „Ernst Leitz Wetzlar, Optische Werke". Mit dem weltweit ersten Mask Aligner für die Fotolithografie in der Mikrochipherstellung, dem 1963 für Siemens entwickelten MJB3, begann die Erfolgsgeschichte des Maschinenbauers in der Halbleiterindustrie. Heute ist SÜSS MicroTec ein anerkannter strategischer Partner für global agierende Halbleiterhersteller und -auftragsfertiger. In der Forschung und Entwicklung zukunftsweisender Innovationen profitiert SÜSS MicroTec von seiner exzellenten Vernetzung mit renommierten internationalen Forschungsinstituten und Universitäten. Das Unternehmen hält rund 110 aktive strikte Patentfamilien mit über 400 aktiven erteilten Patenten. Die Tochtergesellschaft SUSS MicroOptics erhielt 2021 den Swiss Manufacturing Award der Universität St. Gallen.

Für seinen Beitrag zu einer nachhaltigen Halbleiter-Wertschöpfungskette hat SÜSS MicroTec klare Ziele definiert. So sollen unter anderem die direkten und indirekten energie- und wärmebedingten Klimaemissionen (Scope 1 und 2) bis 2030 auf Netto-Null sinken. Zukünftige Fachkräfte fördert SÜSS MicroTec durch drei Ausbildungsgänge an den deutschen Standorten und betreibt eine intensive Talent-Akquise, die Bewerber*innen und Absolvent*innen von technologischen Studiengängen europaweit anspricht.

SÜSS MicroTec etabliert sich verstärkt als Anbieter ganzheitlicher, innovativer Prozesslösungen, der Anlagen nicht nur produziert und liefert, sondern bereits die Entwicklung individuell und kundenspezifisch abstimmt, um gemeinsam den technologischen Fortschritt voranzutreiben. Bis 2025 strebt SÜSS MicroTec ein Umsatzniveau von 400 Millionen Euro an – was in etwa der Verdoppelung des Umsatzes von 2018 entspricht –, bei einer EBIT-Marge von mindestens 15 Prozent. Dieses ambitionierte Ziel rückt mit jeder neuen Chipfabrik näher.

In addition to its headquarters in Garching, near Munich, SÜSS MicroTec has manufacturing facilities in Sternenfels, near Pforzheim, in Neuchâtel, Switzerland, and in Hsinchu, Taiwan. The company has roughly 1,250 employees around the world. SÜSS MicroTec markets its systems and process solutions internationally through 35 sales and service subsidiaries. It generates well over 50% of its global revenue in Asia alone, with China and Taiwan its most important markets. SÜSS MicroTec has been listed in the SDAX index, part of the Prime Standard segment on the Frankfurt Stock Exchange, since 1999.

Founded in Munich in 1949 by the man who gave the company its name, Karl SÜSS KG initially had three employees and sold optical instruments manufactured by Ernst Leitz GmbH in Wetzlar. The machine builder's success story in the semiconductor industry began with the world's first mask aligner for photolithography in microchip fabrication, the MJB3, which it developed for Siemens in 1963. Today, SÜSS MicroTec is a well-regarded strategic partner for global semiconductor fabricators and foundries. In terms of the research and development required to produce pioneering innovations, SÜSS MicroTec benefits from excellent networking with renowned international research institutes and universities. The company has around 110 active stringent patent families with over 400 active patents. Its subsidiary, SUSS MicroOptics, received the Swiss Manufacturing Award from the University of St. Gallen in 2021.

SÜSS MicroTec has set out clear objectives for its efforts to establish a sustainable value-creation chain in the semiconductor industry. This includes reducing its direct and indirect climate emissions due to energy and heating use (Scope 1 and 2 emissions) to net zero by 2030. SÜSS MicroTec offers three training pathways to support prospective employees at its German sites and conducts intensive talent acquisition activities to appeal to applicants and graduates in technical subjects across Europe.

SÜSS MicroTec is increasingly establishing itself as a supplier of innovative, holistic process solutions. Rather than simply producing and delivering solutions, it conducts bespoke, customer-specific development activities to drive forward technological progress together. By 2025, SÜSS MicroTec aspires to break the €400 million sales threshold – roughly double its 2018 sales figure – with an EBIT margin of at least 15%. And, with every chip factory that opens, this ambitious target comes another step closer.

»Zusammen mit unseren Kunden treiben wir die technologische Entwicklung immer weiter voran.«

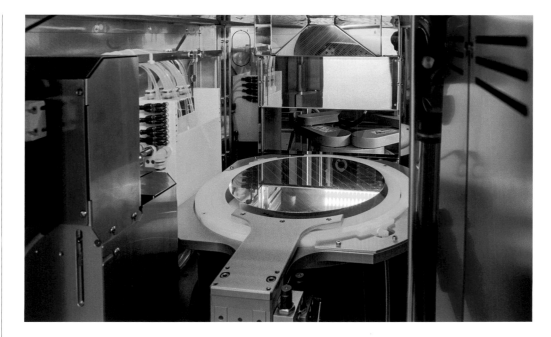

Detailaufnahme
eines Belackers für
die Herstellung von
Mikrochips

A close-up view of
a coater for microchip
fabrication

Arbeit an einem
Wafer im Reinraum

Working on a wafer
in a clean room

Der Hauptsitz von
SÜSS MicroTec in
Garching bei München

SÜSS MicroTec
headquarters in
Garching, near Munich

»Together with our customers, we continue to drive forward technological development.«

Burkhardt Frick,
CEO von SÜSS
MicroTec

Burkhardt Frick,
CEO of SÜSS
MicroTec

SUTCO

Die Sutco RecyclingTechnik GmbH ist weltweit einer der größten Hersteller von Anlagen zur Sortierung und Aufbereitung von Abfällen für deren Wiederverwertung. Bereits 1985 erkannte der damalige Student der Ingenieurswissenschaften Thomas Schmitz das Potenzial und gründete die Schmitz Umwelttechnik & Co., kurz Sutco. Die Nachfrage nach Sekundärrohstoffen wuchs und innovative Ideen in diesem Bereich waren gefragt. Zunächst bot man kleine Sortiereinheiten für Baustellenabfälle und Gewerbeabfälle an. In der Folge entwickelte sich das Unternehmen rasch und spezialisierte sich auf Konzeption und Konstruktion, Produktion, Montage und Inbetriebnahme, After Sales und Wartung von Sortier- und Aufbereitungsanlagen. Mit schlüsselfertigen Anlagen kommt bei Sutco alles aus einer Hand.

Kunden von Sutco sind unter anderem kommunale und private Abfallentsorger. Die Anlagen bereiten schwerpunktmäßig Hausmüll, Verpackungsabfälle, Kunststoffe, Gewerbeabfälle und organische Abfälle auf. Über verschiedene technische Kompostierungsverfahren verwerten die Sutco-Anlagen die organischen Bestandteile aus dem Abfall und tragen auch mit ihrer effizienten Technik maßgeblich zur Ressourcenschonung bei. Darüber hinaus erstellt Sutco für jeden Bereich das passende Recycling-Konzept. Ob es um Kunststoffe, Verpackungs-, Haushalts-, Gewerbe- und Industrieabfälle, Altpapier, Baustellenmischabfälle oder Schlacken aus der Müllverbrennung geht: Die Kunden erhalten am Ende eine schlüsselfertige Anlage. Mit der Herstellung von Ersatzbrennstoffen und dem Waste-to-Energy-Konzept tragen Sutco-Anlagen auch zu einer umweltschonenden Energieerzeugung bei.

Hochqualifizierte Mitarbeitende und modernste Fertigungsanlagen garantieren ein breites Spektrum an differenzierten Verwertungslösungen. Denn Voraussetzung für eine ökonomisch sinnvolle Verwertung von

Sutco RecyclingTechnik GmbH is among the world's largest manufacturers of systems for sorting and treating waste for recycling. Back in 1985, an engineering student by the name of Thomas Schmitz identified the potential of this industry and founded Schmitz Umwelttechnik & Co. – or Sutco for short. As demand for recycled products grew, companies increasingly sought innovative ideas in this field. To begin with, Sutco offered small-scale sorting systems for construction and commercial waste. The company then developed rapidly and specialised in the conception, design, production, assembly and commissioning of waste sorting and treatment systems as well as after-sales and maintenance services. Sutco delivers turnkey systems, providing everything from a single source.

Its customers include municipal and private waste disposal companies. Its treatment systems are predominantly designed for household waste, packaging waste, plastics, commercial waste and organic waste. Using a variety of composting techniques, Sutco systems utilise the organic components from waste and, through their efficient technology, also make a significant contribution to resource conservation. In addition, Sutco creates tailored recycling concepts for each sector. Whether designed to handle plastics, packaging waste, household waste, commercial waste, industrial waste, waste paper, mixed construction waste or slag from waste incineration, Sutco's customers ultimately receive a turnkey system. By producing substitute fuels and through their waste-to-energy concept, Sutco systems also contribute to environmentally friendly energy generation.

Highly qualified employees and state-of-the-art manufacturing systems guarantee a broad range of differentiated recycling solutions. Ultimately, automating the sorting and treatment processes wherever possible is essential for waste recycling to be economically viable.

Unternehmensname
SUTCO RECYCLINGTECHNIK GMBH

Industriezweig
ANLAGENBAU

Gründer
THOMAS SCHMITZ

Hauptfertigungsstätten
**HAREN (DEUTSCHLAND),
KATTOWITZ (POLEN)**

Vertrieb
WELTWEITES VERTRIEBSNETZ

Jahresumsatz
CA. 80 MIO. EURO

Sortieranlage für Hausmüll zur Gewinnung von Wertstoffen in Stockholm, Schweden

A sorting system to extract recyclable materials from household waste in Stockholm, Sweden

Company name
SUTCO RECYCLINGTECHNIK GMBH

Industry
PLANT CONSTRUCTION

Founder
THOMAS SCHMITZ

Main production facilities
**HAREN (GERMANY),
KATOWICE (POLAND)**

Distribution
GLOBAL DISTRIBUTION NETWORK

Annual sales
APPROX. €80 MILLION

Abfällen ist eine möglichst automatisierte Sortierung und Aufbereitung. Seine Expertise kann das Unternehmen ständig erweitern: Sutco ist mit sieben Tochtergesellschaften international vertreten und kennt und berücksichtigt die Besonderheiten des jeweiligen Landes. Die Tochtergesellschaften befinden sich in Großbritannien und Polen, mit Sutco Iberica in Barcelona wird der iberische und spanischsprachige Raum betreut, mit Sutco Brasil Südamerika. Die Asienvertretung erfolgt über Sutco Singapore und die Skandinavien-Präsenz über die Sutco Schweden. Dank dieses Engagements konnte Sutco im Jahr 2023 vermelden, dass im schwedischen Motala die ersten Wertstoffballen vom Band liefen und Sutco die erste automatisierte Abfallbehandlungsanlage Chiles baut. Mehr als 500 Referenzanlagen weltweit sprechen für sich. Zudem kümmert sich seit September 2023 die Sutco Romania um den südosteuropäischen Markt.

Seit 2003 gehört Sutco der familiengeführten Ludden + Mennekes GmbH. Sutco ist Teil der LM Group, eines Verbundes aus vier Unternehmen, der den Kunden den Vorteil bietet, Gesamtkonzepte für alle relevanten Bereiche der Abfallwirtschaft bereitzuhalten. Zum Verbund gehören neben Sutco die L&M Entsorgungssysteme, die Presstechnik für recycelbare Materialien und Wertstoffe anbieten, das auf die Entwicklung und Herstellung von Ballenpressen spezialisierte Unternehmen unoTech sowie die TIG Automation, Komplettanbieter für industrielle Automatisierungslösungen. Auf diese Weise bietet die LM Group die gesamte Verwertungskette aus Aufbereitung, Sortierung, Pressung und Reststoffverwertung an.

Für Sutco arbeiten am Firmensitz in Bergisch Gladbach 50, in Meppen 30, in Haren 25 und in Kattowitz 190 Mitarbeitende. Für junge Bewerber*innen ist das Unternehmen aufgrund seiner Nachhaltigkeit und Klimafreundlichkeit attraktiv. Mit Weiterbildungsangeboten werden Qualifizierung und Wohlbefinden der Mitarbeitenden unterstützt.

In der Zukunft möchte das Unternehmen seine Technologie in Ländern vertreiben, die bisher im Bereich Abfallrecycling noch Nachholbedarf haben, und so deren Klimabilanz verbessern. Und auch für das digitale Zeitalter ist die Firma längst gerüstet: Sie hält mit ProDIGIT digitale Lösungen für Sortieranlagen bereit. Die Software bietet stoffstromoptimierte Abfallbehandlung und steigert die Effizienz der verschiedenen Anlagenkomponenten. Sutco punktet mit vier Bausteinen zur cleveren Digitalisierung der Prozesse: Bunkermanagement, Durchsatzoptimierung, aktuelle Massenbilanz und automatische Ballenauszeichnung. Die ProDIGIT-Software wird bereits vielfach erfolgreich eingesetzt und stetig weiterentwickelt.

The company is also in a position to continuously further its expertise: Sutco has seven international subsidiaries and is therefore familiar with the characteristics and requirements of each country. It has subsidiaries in the United Kingdom and Poland. Barcelona-based Sutco Iberica serves the Iberian Peninsula and the Spanish-speaking world, while Sutco Brasil renders services in South America. The company is represented in Asia by Sutco Singapore and in Scandinavia by Sutco Sweden. In 2023, Sutco announced that the first bales of recycled material had rolled off its production line in Motala, Sweden, and construction of the first automated waste treatment plant in Chile had begun. A total of over 500 reference systems around the world speaks for itself. In addition, as of September 2023, Sutco Romania serves the Balkan market.

In 2003, Sutco was acquired by family-owned Ludden + Mennekes GmbH. Sutco is part of the LM Group, a network of four companies with the ability to offer customers overall concepts covering all relevant areas of waste management. Besides Sutco, the other group companies are: L&M Entsorgungssysteme, which supplies compaction systems for recyclable materials; unoTech, which specialises in the development and manufacture of baling presses, and TIG Automation, a full-service provider for industrial automation solutions. The LM Group therefore covers the entire recycling chain, from treatment and sorting to compaction and waste recycling.

Sutco has 50 employees at its headquarters in Bergisch Gladbach along with a further 30 in Meppen, 25 in Haren and 190 in Katowice. The company is a particularly attractive choice for young applicants thanks to its focus on sustainability and being environmentally friendly. It also helps its employees to upskill and promotes their well-being by offering professional development services.

In the future, the company aims to market its technology in countries where waste recycling processes are lacking in order to improve their climate footprint. The company is also well equipped for the digital age, including through its ProDIGIT software, which provides digital solutions for sorting plants. It facilitates flow-optimised waste treatment and increases the efficiency of various system components. Sutco relies on four building blocks to ensure intelligent process digitalisation: bunker management, throughput optimisation, up-to-date weight readings and automatic bale labelling. Its ProDIGIT software has been successfully deployed on numerous occasions and is subject to constant improvement.

MICHAEL LUDDEN

»Als Familien-
unternehmen
ist uns Circular
Economy
ein besonderes
Anliegen.«

Produkt aus einer
Sutco-Anlage

A product from a
Sutco system

Leiten Sutco (von links): Norbert Gravel
(Geschäftsführer), Naemi Denz (Geschäftsführerin)
und Michael Ludden (geschäftsführender
Gesellschafter)

Sutco management (from left): Norbert Gravel
(Managing Director), Naemi Denz (Managing Director)
and Michael Ludden (Managing Partner)

MICHAEL LUDDEN

»As a family
company, the
circular economy
is particularly
important to us.«

2024 eröffnet Sutco
sein neues Headoffice
in Bergisch Gladbach

In 2024, Sutco
will open its
new head office in
Bergisch Gladbach

TER GROUP

Die Werte hanseatischer Kaufmannstradition und drei Generationen Hamburger Entrepreneure haben ein Unternehmen geprägt, das heute zu den anerkanntesten seines Industriezweiges zählt. Die TER Group ist spezialisiert auf die Branchenbereiche Chemiedistribution, Kunststoffdistribution und -compoundierung sowie Wachsformulierung und Klebstoffherstellung. Das weltweit agierende Unternehmen ist in drei Geschäftsdivisionen organisiert: TER Chemicals, TER Plastics und Paramelt. Sie vereinen erfolgreich ihre Logistikexpertise aus der Beschaffung und Distribution vielfältiger Materialien mit ihren Kompetenzen und Erfahrungen aus der Anwendungstechnik, Produktentwicklung und Produktion. Das macht die TER Group zum perfekten Technologiepartner. Weltweit wird der umfassende Service stets individuell abgestimmt auf Einsatzzweck, Qualität, Timing, Preis-Leistungs-Verhältnis, Menge und Lieferfrequenz, auch für divisionsübergreifende Produkte und Lösungen. Hauptschwerpunkte sind die Branchensegmente Klebstoff, Farben & Lacke, Kunststoff, Gummi, Beschichtung, Konstruktion, Schmiermittel, Reinigungsmittel, Kosmetik und Nahrungsmittel. Die TER Group liefert ihren Kunden zudem passgenaue Vorprodukte zur Verarbeitung und Produktion. Die Unternehmensgruppe beschäftigt 1150 Mitarbeitende in 41 Tochterunternehmen, und zwar an 32 Büro- und 9 Produktionsstandorten. 2022 erwirtschaftete die TER Group einen Umsatz von 1,08 Milliarden Euro. Sie wird geführt von CEO Christian Westphal.

Die Ursprünge der TER Group gehen zurück auf das Jahr 1908 und ein seinerzeit gegründetes Handelsunternehmen. 1938 übernahm der Hamburger Kaufmann Walter Westphal die Anteile von seinem Gründungspartner Hermann ter Hell. Als Westphal 1976 verstarb, trat sein Sohn Klaus-Christian Westphal die Nachfolge an. 2005 wurde dessen Sohn Christian Gesellschafter, übernahm die Führung des Familienunternehmens und schuf die heutige Struktur.

The values of Hanseatic mercantile tradition and three generations of Hamburg-based entrepreneurs have shaped a company that is today one of the most prominent companies in its sector. The TER Group specialises in chemical distribution, plastics distribution, plastics compounding, wax finishing and adhesives production. The company, which has global operations, is organised into three divisions: TER Chemicals, TER Plastics and Paramelt. These divisions successfully combine their logistics expertise, gained through the procurement and distribution of various materials, with their skills and experience in the application technology, product development and production. These factors make the TER Group a perfect technology partner. It tailors its comprehensive service around the world, taking account of specific applications, quality requirements, timings, price-performance ratios, quantities and delivery frequency, including for inter-divisional products and solutions. Its primary focuses are adhesives, paints and lacquers, plastics, rubber, coatings, construction, lubricants, detergents, cosmetics and food products. The TER Group also supplies precisely manufactured primary products to its customers for subsequent processing and production. The corporate group has 1,150 employees across its 41 subsidiaries, based at 32 office locations and nine production sites. In 2022, the TER Group generated sales of €1.08 billion. It is led by CEO Christian Westphal.

The TER Group's origins date back to 1908, when it was founded as a commercial enterprise. In 1938, Hamburg-based entrepreneur Walter Westphal acquired the shares of his founding partner, Hermann ter Hell. When Westphal died in 1976, he was succeeded at the head of the company by his son, Klaus-Christian Westphal. In 2005, his son Christian became a partner in the company, assumed leadership of the family business and created the structure in place today.

Unternehmensname
TER HELL & CO. GMBH

Industriezweig
CHEMIEDISTRIBUTION, KUNSTSTOFFDISTRIBUTION UND -COMPOUNDIERUNG, WACHSFORMULIERUNG UND KLEBSTOFFHERSTELLUNG

Gründung
1908

Gründer
HERMANN TER HELL

Mitarbeitende
1150

Jahresumsatz
1,08 MRD. EURO (2022; NICHT KONSOLIDIERT)

Company name
TER HELL & CO. GMBH

Industry
CHEMICAL DISTRIBUTION, PLASTICS DISTRIBUTION, PLASTICS COMPOUNDING, WAX FINISHING AND ADHESIVES PRODUCTION

Founded
1908

Founder
HERMANN TER HELL

Employees
1,150

Annual sales
€1.08 BILLION (2022; UNCONSOLIDATED)

Produktansicht Spezialchemikalien als Beispiel der Firmendivision TER Chemicals

An example of the speciality chemical products offered by the TER Chemicals division

TER Chemicals, die umsatzstärkste Division der Gruppe, ist spezialisiert auf die Distribution von Spezialchemie. Als ganzheitlich handelnder Partner übernimmt TER Chemicals deren Beschaffung, die Logistik und Produktentwicklung sowie den Vertrieb. Das weite Netz mit 18 Niederlassungen in Europa, China und den USA garantiert, dass Kunden die Produkte stets zuverlässig, in konstant hoher Qualität, preisstabil und termingenau erhalten. TER Chemicals ist seit mehr als 100 Jahren über ein breites Produktspektrum eng mit der chemischen Industrie verbunden: von Zusatzstoffen für Reinigungsmittel, Feinchemikalien, Tensiden und Additiven bis zu Lösungen im chemisch-technischen Bereich oder für die Automobilindustrie. Von Anbeginn prosperierte diese Division als verlässlicher und ebenbürtiger Vertriebspartner namhafter Produzenten. TER Chemicals ist heute einer der führenden Akteure des europäischen Chemiehandels. Unter der Leitung von CEO Andreas Früh erwirtschaftete diese Sparte mit 360 Mitarbeitenden 2022 einen Umsatz von 480 Millionen Euro.

TER Plastics verantwortet in der TER Group die Distribution von Kunststoffen in ganz Europa. Daneben fertigt die Division eigene Compounds unter der Marke TEREZ®, deren Portfolio fokussiert ist auf Tribologie, Blends und Farbcompounds sowie hochmodulige Polymere für Metallersatzlösungen. Komplementär angeboten werden Produkte der Langfasertechnologie (LFT). TER Plastics profitiert von über 50 Jahren Erfahrung, großer Innovationskraft und konsequenter Kundenorientierung. Die hohe Reputation beruht auf jahrzehntelanger Zusammenarbeit mit international führenden Kunststoffproduzenten. 2022 betrug der Umsatz 330 Millionen Euro. TER Plastics beschäftigt 225 Mitarbeitende und wird geleitet von CEO Wolfgang Siegel.

Der dritte Geschäftsbereich der TER Group wird repräsentiert von Paramelt. Das global agierende, hochspezialisierte Unternehmen mit 215 Mitarbeitenden produziert auf hohem Qualitätsniveau Wachsmischungen, Klebstoffe und Spezialdispersionen. Paramelt entwickelt an acht Produktionsstandorten in den Niederlanden, Großbritannien, den USA und China innovative und verlässliche Lösungen für diverse Industriesparten. Das von CEO Mikael Dahlström geführte Unternehmen erzielte 2022 einen Umsatz von 270 Millionen Euro.

Mit ihrem starken Verbund zukunftsfester Geschäftsdivisionen baut die TER Group ihre Position im internationalen Markt führender Chemiespezialisten weiter aus.

TER Chemicals, the corporate group's highest-grossing division, specialises in the distribution of speciality chemicals. As an all-round partner for speciality chemicals, TER Chemicals oversees their procurement, logistics, product development and distribution. Its extensive network, which includes 18 subsidiaries in Europe, China and the USA, guarantees that customers can always rely on receiving their products in consistently high quality, at stable prices and on schedule. TER Chemicals has been closely connected to the chemicals industry for over 100 years through its broad product spectrum, from additives for detergents, fine chemicals and surfactants to solutions for chemical-technical applications and the automotive industry. This division prospered from the outset as a dependable, worthy sales partner to high-profile producers. Today, TER Chemicals is one of the leading players in the European chemicals market. Under the leadership of CEO Andreas Früh, this division and its 360 employees achieved sales of €480 million in 2022.

Another of the TER Group's divisions, TER Plastics, is responsible for the distribution of plastics throughout Europe. It also produces its own compounds under the brand TEREZ®, with a portfolio focused on tribology, blends and colour compounds as well as high-modulus polymers for metal substitutes. In addition, it offers complementary products based on long fibre technology (LFT). TER Plastics benefits from over 50 years of experience, vast innovative ability and a systematic customer focus. Its strong reputation is based on decades of cooperation with internationally leading plastics producers. In 2022, it achieved sales of €330 million. TER Plastics has 225 employees and is led by CEO Wolfgang Siegel.

The third division in the TER Group is Paramelt. This highly specialised company operates worldwide, has 215 employees and produces high-quality speciality waxes, adhesives and dispersions. Paramelt develops innovative, reliable solutions for various industrial sectors at its eight production sites in the Netherlands, the United Kingdom, the USA and China. Led by CEO Mikael Dahlström, the company achieved sales of €270 million in 2022.

With its robust combination of future-proof business divisions, the TER Group continues to consolidate its position as an international market leader for speciality chemicals.

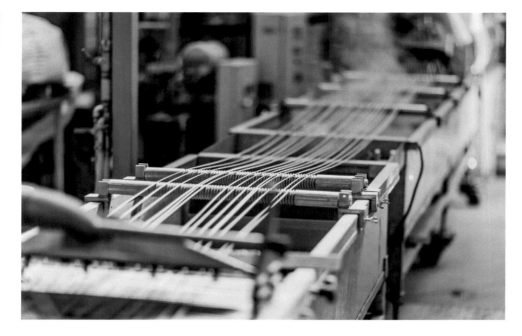

CHRISTIAN WESTPHAL, CEO TER GROUP

»Hohes technisches Know-how und professioneller Service für Kunden und Lieferanten: Die TER Group setzt weiter auf Wachstum.«

Stranggranulierung als Teil des Compoundierungs-prozesses in der Firmen-division TER Plastics

Strand granulation, part of the compounding process at TER Plastics

Produktionsbetrieb der Firmendivision Paramelt in Heerhugowaard, Niederlande

The Paramelt production site in Heerhugowaard, the Netherlands

CHRISTIAN WESTPHAL, CEO OF THE TER GROUP

»Extensive technical expertise and professional services for customers and suppliers: the TER Group has targeted further growth.«

Christian Westphal, geschäftsführender Gesellschafter der TER Group

Christian Westphal, Managing Partner of the TER Group

THERMIK

In nahezu jedem Haushalt weltweit gibt es Industrieprodukte, die so gut wie nie wahrgenommen werden – obwohl sie unverzichtbar sind. Thermik ist der Weltmarktführer in der Entwicklung und Fertigung von Temperaturbegrenzern sowie der führende Spezialist für Schutztemperaturbegrenzer auf Bimetallbasis. Temperaturbegrenzer werden unter anderem in Elektromotoren, Heizgeräten und Transformatoren verbaut und schützen elektrische Geräte wie Lüfter oder Wärmepumpen vor Überhitzung. Sie sind auch als Temperatursensoren oder Temperaturwächter bekannt. Neben dem Temperaturschutz dienen sie dem störungsfreien, anwendungssicheren Betrieb vieler Geräte. Zum Thermik Portfolio rund um die Temperatursicherung zählen außerdem PTC-Motorschutzfühler und -Kaltleiter sowie kundenspezifische PTC-Heizelemente und Sonderapplikationen. Insgesamt bietet das Industrieunternehmen seinen Kunden im Bereich Überhitzungsschutz das größte und fortschrittlichste Produktsortiment auf dem Weltmarkt.

Die Temperaturschutz-Produkte des Innovations- und Qualitätsführers werden hauptsächlich in der Hausgeräteindustrie, im Maschinenbau sowie in Spezialanwendungen für Automobile eingesetzt. Alle Produkte sind State of the Art in Konstruktion, Materialauswahl und -komposition, weshalb sich nicht nur zahlreiche namhafte Branchenführer immer wieder für sie entscheiden. Für die Fertigung werden nur Materialien verwendet, die höchsten Ansprüchen genügen, zum Beispiel Edelmetalle mit ihren einzigartigen elektromechanischen Eigenschaften. Die Qualität und die Wertigkeit der Feinwerktechnik sind außerhalb Europas erfahrungsgemäß nicht reproduzierbar. Den Wettbewerbsvorsprung untermauert das Unternehmen mit seinem Credo: Jeder Thermik Kunde erhält stets die weltweit besten, zuverlässigsten und sichersten Schutztemperaturbegrenzer.

Just about every household around the world has industrial products that are almost never noticed – despite being utterly indispensable. Thermik is the global market leader in the development and production of temperature limiters and the foremost specialist for bimetal thermal protectors. Temperature limiters are fitted in electric motors, heaters, transformers and an array of other appliances. Also known as thermal protectors, temperature controllers and temperature monitors, they protect electrical appliances such as fans and heat pumps against overheating. In addition to providing thermal protection, these devices ensure that an entire array of devices operate reliably and are safe to use. Thermik's portfolio of thermal protection products also includes PTC motor protection sensors and resistors as well as customised PTC heating elements and specialist applicators. Overall, the industrial manufacturer offers its customers the most extensive, advanced range of thermal protection-related products on the global market.

A pioneering innovator and quality leader, Thermik's thermal protection products are primarily used in the home appliance industry, mechanical engineering and in specialist automotive applications. All of its products are state-of-the-art in terms of their design, material selection and material composition – which is why a host of prestigious industry leaders choose Thermik products, time and again. The manufacturer relies exclusively on materials that meet its exacting standards, such as precious metals, which possess unique electromechanical properties. Experience has shown that providers outside of Europe cannot live up to the same precision engineering standards. The company's credo drives home this competitive advantage, ensuring that every Thermik customer receives the world's best, safest and most reliable thermal protector.

Thermik was founded by an inventor, Peter Hofsaess, in Pforzheim in 1968. His innovative design solved the

Unternehmensname
THERMIK GERÄTEBAU GMBH

Industriezweig
ELEKTROTECHNIK

Gründung
1968

Gründer
PETER HOFSAESS

Produkt
TEMPERATURBEGRENZER FÜR ÜBERHITZUNGSSCHUTZ ELEKTRISCHER GERÄTE

Mitarbeitende
ÜBER 800 WELTWEIT

Jahresumsatz
RD. 53 MIO. EURO (2023)

Company name
THERMIK GERÄTEBAU GMBH

Industry
ELECTRICAL ENGINEERING

Founded
1968

Founder
PETER HOFSAESS

Product
TEMPERATURE LIMITERS TO PROTECT ELECTRICAL APPLIANCES AGAINST OVERHEATING

Employees
OVER 800 WORLDWIDE

Annual sales
APPROX. €53 MILLION (2023)

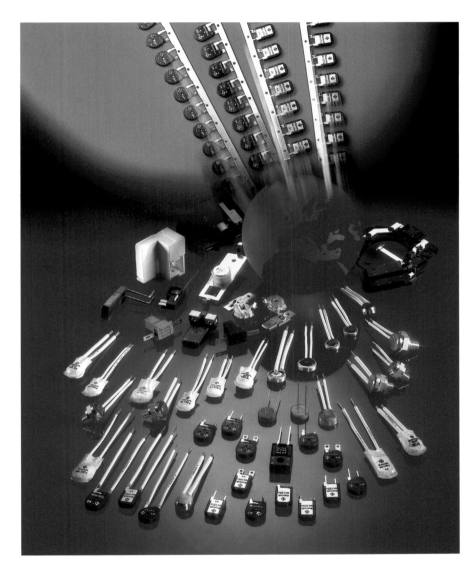

Thermik-Produkte sind weltweit über 4,5 Milliarden Mal im Einsatz

Thermik products are in use in over 4.5 million appliances worldwide

Thermik wurde 1968 von Peter Hofsaess in Pforzheim gegründet. Der Erfinder löste mit einer innovativen Konstruktion das Problem der Stromeigenerwärmung bei Bimetallschaltern und meldete sein erstes Patent an. Von da an setzte er alles daran, die besten und zuverlässigsten Temperaturbegrenzer der Welt zu entwickeln und zu produzieren. Zahlreiche weitere Erfindungen machten Thermik schnell zum Innovationstreiber der Branche. Die heutige Thermik Gerätebau GmbH ist ein Familienunternehmen der Hofsaess Holding GmbH & Co. KG mit vier Tochtergesellschaften. Marcel P. Hofsaess, ein Sohn des Gründers, ist in zweiter Generation Geschäftsführer von Thermik und der Unternehmensgruppe. Ein kreativer Visionär und leidenschaftlicher Erfinder, noch unangepasster und unkonventioneller als sein Vater, schreibt er die Erfolgsgeschichte des Unternehmens seit über 30 Jahren mit zahlreichen Innovationen fort. Als Nummer eins des weltweiten Erfinder-Rankings der Sparte Temperaturbegrenzer hält er mehr Schutzrechte als die sechs folgenden Platzierten. Gemessen an der Zahl seiner über 1000 patentierten Erfindungen zählt Marcel P. Hofsaess branchenübergreifend sogar zu den Top 5 aller in Deutschland lebenden Erfinder*innen, die ein eigenes Unternehmen gründeten und führen. Thermik hat rund 1600 nationale und internationale Patente für Temperaturbegrenzer und PTC-Thermistoren angemeldet – mehr Schutzrechte als alle Mitbewerber weltweit in der Summe halten. Mehr als 4,5 Milliarden Thermik Qualitätsprodukte sind rund um den Globus im Einsatz (Stand: September 2023) – und täglich werden es mehr.

In vier Thermik Werken auf drei Kontinenten – in den USA, in Malaysia und Rumänien – beschäftigt das Industrieunternehmen über 800 Mitarbeitende. Mehr als 30 internationale Vertragslagerhändler gewährleisten mit ihren Vertriebsaktivitäten, dass das Thermik Produktsortiment in aller Welt erhältlich ist. In Europa, Asien und Amerika liegt der Marktanteil gerundet schon bei 50 Prozent, in Deutschland sogar bei 70 Prozent. 2019 kürte die WirtschaftsWoche Thermik als Weltmarktführer zum „Future Champion". 2022 erhielt die Thermik Gerätebau GmbH zum elften Mal die CrefoZert-Auszeichnung von Creditreform als eines der führenden 1,7 Prozent unter den deutschen Unternehmen mit der besten Bonität. Für die technische Marktführerschaft und seinen Wettbewerbsvorsprung wurde Thermik 2023 zum vierzehnten Mal in Folge der „TOP 100 Innovationspreis" verliehen, wie stets zuvor wieder als einzigem Unternehmen der Temperaturbegrenzer-Branche. Thermik gilt als eines der erfolgreichsten mittelständischen Industrieunternehmen Europas. Es spricht alles dafür, dass sich daran so schnell nichts ändern wird.

problem of self-heating in bimetal switches and was registered as his first patent. From that point on, he did everything in his power to develop and produce the best, most reliable temperature limiters in the world. Many other inventions soon followed and made Thermik an innovation leader in the industry. Today, Thermik Gerätebau GmbH is a family company owned by Hofsaess Holding GmbH & Co. KG and has four subsidiaries. Marcel P. Hofsaess, a son of the company's founder, is the second generation of the family to lead Thermik and the corporate group. Another creative visionary and passionate inventor, with an even more unorthodox and unconventional approach than his father, Marcel P. Hofsaess has continued the company's success story for over 30 years, producing numerous innovations. As the undisputed leader of the global rankings for inventions in the temperature limiter segment, Thermik holds more patents than the next six highest-ranked companies combined. In fact, measured on the basis of his more than 1,000 patented inventions, Marcel P. Hofsaess is among the top five living German inventors across all industries to have founded and led their own company. Thermik has filed around 1,600 national and international patents for temperature limiters and PTC thermistors – more than the combined total of all patents held by its competitors around the world. As of September 2023, more than 4.5 billion high-quality Thermik products are in use around the globe – and this figure is rising every single day.

The industrial enterprise has over 800 employees at four factories that span three continents, located in the USA, Malaysia and Romania. More than 30 international contract warehouses ensure that the Thermik product range is available around the world. The company's market share in Europe, Asia and the USA is around 50% – and as high as 70% in Germany. In 2019, WirtschaftsWoche crowned Thermik a "Future Champion". In 2022, Thermik Gerätebau GmbH received the CrefoZert award from Creditreform for the eleventh time, placing it in the top 1.7% of German companies in terms of creditworthiness. And, in 2023, Thermik was awarded the TOP 100 Innovation Prize for the fourteenth year in succession in recognition of its technical leadership and competitive edge – once again as the only company in the temperature limiter sector to receive the accolade. Thermik is one of the most successful industrial SMEs in Europe. There is every indication that this success will continue into the future.

»Vor dem Erfolg
steht der Mut.
Nur so ist es
möglich,
Fortschritt zu
unternehmen.«

Hochautomatisierte Produktion
auf selbstkonstruierten
und -entwickelten Anlagen

Highly automated production
facility with systems designed
and developed in-house

Headquarter der
Thermik Gruppe in
Sondershausen/
Thüringen

Headquarters of
the Thermik Group
in Sondershausen,
Thuringia

Firmengründer Peter
Hofsaess am Beginn
seiner Tätigkeit 1968

The company's founder,
Peter Hofsaess, at the
start of his career in 1968

MARCEL P. HOFSAESS, MANAGING DIRECTOR
OF THERMIK

»Success is built
on courage.
It is the only way
to make progress.«

Geschäftsführer
Marcel P. Hofsaess

Managing Director
Marcel P. Hofsaess

WEBASTO

Die Webasto Gruppe ist als globaler Systempartner der Automobilindustrie seit Langem eine feste Größe in der Branche. Im Jahr 1901 gegründet, fertigte die „Eßlinger Draht- und Eisenwarenfabrik Wilhelm Baier" zunächst Stanzteile sowie Geräte für die Haus- und Feldarbeit. Sieben Jahre später zog die Firma nach Stockdorf bei München und erhielt ihren heutigen Namen. In den folgenden Jahren konzentrierte sich Webasto auf Zubehörteile für Fahrräder wie Schutzbleche und Gepäckträger.

Der Einstieg in die Automobilindustrie gelang dem Unternehmen in den 1930er-Jahren mit der Konstruktion und Herstellung von Faltdächern sowie Heizgeräten für Busse und Personenkraftwagen. In diesen beiden Produktbereichen setzt Webasto mit innovativen Lösungen seit Jahrzehnten wegweisende Trends. 2015 fiel die Entscheidung, sich mit den spezifischen Kernkompetenzen weitere Geschäftsfelder zu erschließen und in den Elektromobilitätsmarkt einzusteigen. Dort etablierte sich das Unternehmen schnell erfolgreich.

Heute entwickelt und produziert Webasto sowohl für verschiedene Fahrzeugarten Dächer sowie Heiz- und Kühllösungen als auch Batteriesysteme und elektrische Hochvoltheizer für hybride und elektrifizierte Pkw und Nutzfahrzeuge. Zudem gehören ergänzende Services rund um das Thermomanagement und die Elektromobilität zum Angebot des Unternehmens. Beispiele für technologische Besonderheiten sind in das Dachsystem integrierbare dynamische Lichtszenarien, eine schaltbare Verglasung, Solarzellen sowie Funktionalitäten für das autonome Fahren. Bei elektrischen Heizern ist Webasto derzeit der einzige Hersteller von Geräten mit einer Leistung von bis zu 800 Volt.

Mit mehr als 50 Standorten – davon mehr als 40 Produktionsstätten – ist der Zulieferer in allen wichtigen Automobilmärkten weltweit vertreten. Die frühe Inter-

As a global systems partner to the automotive industry, the Webasto Group has long since established itself as a key presence in the sector. Founded in 1901 under the name Eßlinger Draht- und Eisenwarenfabrik Wilhelm Baier, the company initially manufactured punched parts, domestic appliances and agricultural equipment. Seven years later, the company relocated to Stockdorf, a town near Munich, and rebranded with the name it bears to this day. In the years that followed, Webasto concentrated on bicycle accessories such as mudguards and pannier racks.

The company moved into the automotive industry in the 1930s, designing and manufacturing folding roofs and heating systems for buses and cars. Webasto and its innovative solutions have set the trend in these product areas for decades. In 2015, the company decided to apply its core competencies to tap into further business segments and enter the e-mobility market, where it soon achieved considerable success.

Today, Webasto develops and produces roofs, heating systems and cooling solutions for a variety of vehicle types, along with battery systems and electric high-voltage heaters for hybrid and electric cars and utility vehicles. The company's portfolio also includes supplementary services relating to thermal management and e-mobility. Technological highlights include its roof-integrated dynamic lighting systems, switchable glazing, solar cells and autonomous driving functions. In terms of electric heaters, Webasto is currently the only manufacturer that produces systems with an output of up to 800 volts.

With more than 50 locations – including over 40 production facilities – the supplier is represented in all key automotive markets around the world. Early internationalisation was a vital strategic step in achieving this. Starting in Europe, Webasto first expanded into the

Unternehmensname
WEBASTO SE

Industriezweig
AUTOMOBILINDUSTRIE

Gründung
1901 IN ESSLINGEN

Produkte
DACHSYSTEME, HEIZ- UND KÜHLLÖSUNGEN, BATTERIESYSTEME

Mitarbeitende
16 812 WELTWEIT

Jahresumsatz
4,3 MRD. EURO (2022)

Company name
WEBASTO SE

Industry
AUTOMOTIVE

Founded
1901 IN ESSLINGEN

Products
ROOF SYSTEMS, HEATING AND COOLING SOLUTIONS, BATTERY SYSTEMS

Employees
16,812 WORLDWIDE

Annual sales
€ 4.3 BILLION (2022)

Durch innovative Funktionen im Dach wird dieser Teil des Automobils immer mehr zum Hightech-System

Car roofs are increasingly becoming high-tech systems through the integration of innovative functions

nationalisierung war dafür ein wichtiger strategischer Schritt. Von Europa ausgehend, expandierte Webasto in den 1970ern zunächst in Richtung USA und Japan. 2001 startete das Unternehmen sein Geschäft in China. Zuletzt erweiterte der Automobilzulieferer seine Kapazitäten in Asien, unter anderem in Südkorea, Japan und Indien.

Die schnell voranschreitende Elektrifizierung von Fahrzeugen und anhaltende geopolitische Krisen haben den Druck in der Automobilindustrie in den letzten Jahren weiter erhöht. In dieser Situation profitiert Webasto nicht nur von seiner hohen Entwicklungskompetenz und Innovationskraft, sondern auch von seiner Organisationsstruktur: Das Unternehmen produziert grundsätzlich im Markt für den Markt und arbeitet überwiegend mit lokalen Zulieferern zusammen. Um seine Lieferketten noch resilienter zu gestalten, setzt Webasto auf einen breiten, ausgewogenen Footprint mit starken, möglichst eigenständigen Regionen.

Insgesamt beschäftigt Webasto mehr als 16 800 Mitarbeitende weltweit. Deren Zusammenarbeit ist geprägt von Offenheit, transparenter Kommunikation und einem aktiven Wissens- und Erfahrungsaustausch. Basis des konstruktiven Miteinanders von Kolleg*innen aus verschiedenen Ländern und Kulturen sind fünf weltweit gemeinschaftlich abgestimmte Werte: „Verantwortung mit Weitsicht", „Leidenschaft für Qualität und Innovation", „Herz und Verstand für unsere Kunden", „Freude an Zusammenarbeit und Verbesserung" und „zupackender Optimismus".

In Deutschland zählt Webasto rund 4000 Beschäftigte. Das Engagement des Unternehmens in den Bereichen Aus- und Weiterbildung ist traditionell hoch. Die firmeneigene Akademie bietet unter anderem fachliche Fortbildungen, interkulturelle Trainings und Sprachkurse an. Vertrauensarbeitszeit und Mobile-Work-Regelungen für Tätigkeiten außerhalb der Produktion sowie Kinderbetreuungsangebote an einigen Standorten unterstützen die Vereinbarkeit von Familie und Beruf. Das Headquarter in Stockdorf verfügt zum Beispiel über einen eigenen Hort und lädt die Kinder der Mitarbeitenden regelmäßig zu Ferienprogrammen ein.

Wesentlicher Treiber für Webasto ist die Nachhaltigkeit im Dreiklang von Ökonomie, Ökologie und Sozialem. Mit seinem Produktangebot trägt der Automobilzulieferer zu einer klimaschonenden Mobilität bei und verfolgt an seinen Standorten und in seiner Lieferkette ambitionierte Klimaschutzziele. Eine besondere Rolle spielt für das Unternehmen in Familienbesitz die Übernahme gesellschaftlicher Verantwortung über das Betriebliche hinaus. Zahlreiche soziale Aktivitäten sind seit 2019 in der Webasto Foundation gebündelt.

USA and Japan in the 1970s before entering the Chinese market in 2001. Most recently, the automotive supplier expanded its activities in Asia, including in South Korea, Japan and India.

In recent years, the rapid electrification of vehicles and persistent geopolitical crises have exacerbated existing pressures in the automotive industry. In these circumstances, Webasto benefits not only from its extensive development expertise and innovative power but also from its organisational structure. As a fundamental rule, the company only produces in each market for that market, working predominantly with local suppliers. And, in an effort to make its supply chains more resilient, Webasto relies on a broad, balanced footprint of robust regions with the greatest possible degree of autonomy.

In total, Webasto has more than 16,800 employees worldwide. Their collaboration is characterised by openness, transparent communication and an active exchange of knowledge and experience. Constructive cooperation between employees in different countries and from different cultures is built on five global values that aim to foster a sense of community: "responsibility with a long-term view", "passion for quality and innovation", "hearts and minds for our customers", "embracing cooperation and improvement", and "courageously optimistic".

Webasto employs around 4,000 people in Germany and has a long-standing tradition of promoting training and development. Its in-house academy offers a range of specialist training programmes, intercultural training sessions and language courses. Trust-based working hours, remote working for staff in non-production-related roles and childcare services at certain sites support the compatibility of family life and work. For example, Webasto's headquarters in Stockdorf features a dedicated daycare centre and regularly invites employees' children to holiday programmes.

A key driver for Webasto is ensuring sustainability in line with its economic, ecological and social responsibilities. The automotive supplier's product portfolio contributes to the development of climate-friendly mobility, with ambitious climate protection targets set for the company's locations and its supply chain. As a family-owned company, shouldering social responsibility within the company and beyond is particularly important to Webasto. Since it was established in 2019, the Webasto Foundation has supported a wide range of social activities.

»Mit unseren innovativen Produkten tragen wir zu einer sichereren und klimafreundlicheren Mobilität bei, die begeistert.«

2019 begann Webasto in seinem Dachwerk Schierling Batteriesysteme zu produzieren – der Standort ist inzwischen Batterie-Kompetenzzentrum für die gesamte Unternehmensgruppe

In 2019, Webasto started producing battery systems at its Schierling roof production site. The facility has since become the centre of excellence in battery technology for the entire Webasto Group

Die Zentrale von Webasto, die ein Entwicklungszentrum für Dachsysteme ist und zugleich hochmoderne Prüfeinrichtungen beherbergt, befindet sich im Landkreis Starnberg

Webasto's headquarters, which includes a development centre for roof systems and state-of-the-art testing facilities, is located in Starnberg, near Munich

DR. HOLGER ENGELMANN, CHAIRMAN OF THE
MANAGEMENT BOARD, WEBASTO SE

»With our innovative products we contribute to a safer, more enjoyable and climate-friendly mobility.«

Am Standort Neubrandenburg werden seit mehr als 30 Jahren Standheizungen und seit 2015 Hochvoltheizer für Elektrofahrzeuge hergestellt

The company's Neubrandenburg site has manufactured parking heaters for 30 years and, as of 2015, also produces high-voltage heaters for electric cars

WEIDMÜLLER

Unsichtbar sind sie auf den ersten Blick und zugleich allgegenwärtig – die hochwertigen Produkte und Lösungen von Weidmüller kommen überall dort zum Einsatz, wo Energie, Daten und Signale erfasst und verarbeitet werden: in Windkraft- und Photovoltaikanlagen, Ladestationen für Elektroautos oder auch in Maschinen der Konsumgüterherstellung. Die elektrische Verbindungstechnik von Weidmüller sorgt dafür, dass unterschiedliche Systeme und Anwendungen miteinander kommunizieren können.

Die über 170-jährige Geschichte von Weidmüller ist geprägt von Pionierleistungen – von der Erfindung des Druckknopfes über die Herstellung der ersten Reihenklemme bis hin zu neuen Technologien und Anschlusstechniken. Mit Erfindergeist und Mut ist Weidmüller bis heute industrieller Vorreiter für Automatisierungs- und Digitalisierungslösungen. Das Unternehmen ist gleichermaßen Anbieter und Anwender zukunftsweisender Produkte und Lösungen wie webbasierter KI-Anwendungen und Komponenten für die Geräteherstellung und den Schaltschrankbau. „Weidmüller ist Gestalter in den dynamischsten Märkten der Welt: Elektrifizierung, Automatisierung und Digitalisierung", definiert Aufsichtsratsvorsitzender Christian Gläsel, dessen Familie Eigentümer des Unternehmens ist, den eigenen Wirkungskreis.

Weidmüller fährt seinen Wachstumskurs mit offenem Ende: Derzeit zählt das Unternehmen knapp 6000 Mitarbeitende an über 30 Standorten und 60 Vertretungen weltweit. Das Portfolio von Weidmüller umfasst über 45 000 Produkte. Im Geschäftsjahr 2022 erwirtschaftete das Familienunternehmen 1,175 Milliarden Euro Umsatz. Dem Industriepionier ist seine ostwestfälisch-bodenständige Haltung eigen geblieben. So steht der Name Weidmüller zugleich für ein erfolgreiches Familienunternehmen sowie für Innovation in der Industrie 4.0 und der Digitalisierung.

Although invisible at first glance, they are in fact ubiquitous: Weidmüller's high-quality products and solutions are used wherever energy, data and signals are captured and processed – from wind turbines and photovoltaic systems to charging stations for electric vehicles and machinery used to manufacture consumer goods. Electrical connectivity solutions from Weidmüller ensure that different systems and applications can communicate with each other.

Stretching back over 170 years, Weidmüller's history has been peppered with pioneering achievements – from inventing the press fastening and producing the first terminal block to new technologies and connection systems. Demonstrating both ingenuity and courage, Weidmüller remains a pioneer of industrial automation and digitalisation solutions to this day. It is both a provider and an adopter of pioneering products and solutions, including web-based AI applications and components for device manufacturing and control cabinet construction. "Weidmüller is shaping the world's most dynamic markets: electrification, automation and digitalisation," is how Christian Gläsel, who is Chairman of Weidmüller's Supervisory Board and whose family own the company, described the company's sphere of influence.

Weidmüller has charted a course for growth without a final destination. At present, the company has almost 6,000 employees at over 30 locations and 60 representative offices worldwide. The Weidmüller portfolio comprises over 45,000 products. In the 2022 business year, the family company generated sales of €1.175 billion. Nevertheless, the industrial pioneer has stayed true to its down-to-earth, East Westphalian identity. Consequently, the name Weidmüller has come to stand for both a successful family company and innovation in the context of Industry 4.0 and digitalisation.

Weidmüller ⟫⟫

Unternehmensname
WEIDMÜLLER INTERFACE GMBH & CO. KG

Industriezweig
ELEKTROTECHNIK UND MASCHINENBAU

Gründer
CARL AUGUST WEIDMÜLLER

Produkte
LÖSUNGEN FÜR ELEKTRISCHE VERBINDUNGSTECHNIK, AUTOMATISIERUNG UND DIGITALISIERUNG

Vertrieb
WELTWEIT

Mitarbeitende
CA. 6000

Company name
WEIDMÜLLER INTERFACE GMBH & CO. KG

Industry
ELECTRICAL AND MECHANICAL ENGINEERING

Founder
CARL AUGUST WEIDMÜLLER

Products
ELECTRICAL CONNECTIVITY, AUTOMATION AND DIGITALISATION SOLUTIONS

Distribution
WORLDWIDE

Employees
APPROX. 6,000

Mit innovativen Produkten und Technologien ist Weidmüller ein wesentlicher Mitgestalter der Energiewende

With its innovative products and technologies, Weidmüller plays a vital role in shaping the energy transition

Von jeher durch einen ausgeprägten Nachhaltigkeitsgedanken getragen, werden hier zukunftsweisende Lösungen in zahlreichen Industriezweigen realisiert. So verbindet das Unternehmen Nachhaltigkeit mit fortwährendem Wachstum und Investitionen. Diese tätigt Weidmüller nicht zuletzt ganz gezielt an den deutschen Standorten und leistet damit einen signifikanten Beitrag zur Wettbewerbssicherung in Deutschland. „Weidmüller ist ein Familienunternehmen, das als solches seine gesellschaftliche Verantwortung in vielerlei Hinsicht übernimmt", erläutert Gläsel das Engagement des Elektronikherstellers.

Seit über 70 Jahren bildet Weidmüller in zukunftsorientierten Berufen aus, um mit gezielter Mitarbeiter- und Nachwuchsförderung dem Fachkräftemangel entgegenzuwirken. Das soziale Engagement von Weidmüller steht ganz im Zeichen der Zukunftssicherung beziehungsweise Resilienz. Das Zusammenwirken mit der Peter Gläsel Stiftung auf dem gemeinsamen Campus des Bildungsdorfes Detmold unterstreicht die Arbeitgeberattraktivität durch das Angebot von Kita- und Schulplätzen in anerkannten und zukunftsweisenden Bildungseinrichtungen. „Wir investieren entsprechend in die Zukunft – in neue Technologien, Produktion, Logistik und vor allem in Menschen. Know-how-Erweiterung sowie Aus- und Weiterbildung mit dem Ziel des lebenslangen Lernens bilden das Fundament für ein gesundes Wachstum", betont Gläsel. Gemeinsame Projekte von Schule und Ausbildungsstätte fördern die Verantwortungsübernahme junger Menschen und deren Kreativität.

Neben der sozialen Nachhaltigkeit hat sich das Unternehmen schon früh und vor vielen anderen auch der ökologischen Nachhaltigkeit angenommen. Seit über 50 Jahren recycelt Weidmüller Kunststoffabfälle. Bis heute ist zirkuläre Wertschöpfung ein ganzheitliches Fokusthema im Unternehmen. Eine Schonung von Ressourcen bei immer weiter steigender Performance wird bei Weidmüller etwa durch Möglichkeiten der Digitalisierung erreicht. Seit mehr als zehn Jahren Mitglied im Verband der Klimaschutz-Unternehmen, nimmt sich Weidmüller der Themen an, die unsere Gegenwart und Zukunft prägen. Mit Technologien und Innovationen ist der Pionier der industriellen Verbindungstechnik ein wesentlicher Mitgestalter der Energiewende. „Mit Eigeninitiative und Begeisterung für neue Technologien gestalten bei uns Menschen eine nachhaltige Zukunft." Technologien sind hierbei kein Widerspruch, im Gegenteil: „Technologie und Innovation sind unabdingbar für eine lebenswerte Welt. Wir leisten einen Beitrag und ermöglichen unseren Kunden nachhaltige und fortschrittliche Lösungen", fasst Gläsel die Mission des Unternehmens zusammen.

Its pioneering solutions have always been characterised by a pronounced commitment to sustainability and are used in numerous industries. This way, the company combines sustainability with continued growth and investment. In fact, Weidmüller has made targeted investments at its German sites, thereby making a significant contribution to preserving the country's competitive position. "Weidmüller is a family company and, as such, lives up to its responsibility to society in many different respects," said Gläsel, describing the electronics manufacturer's social engagement.

For more than 70 years, Weidmüller has provided training in future-oriented professions, thereby promoting the development of its employees and young people in a targeted effort to counter the shortage of skilled workers. Weidmüller's social engagement is fully focused on safeguarding the future and fostering resilience. It underscores its attractiveness as an employer through its cooperation with the Peter Gläsel Foundation at the Detmold Education Village, offering childcare and school places in recognised, trend-setting educational institutions. "We are investing in the future – in new technologies, production, logistics and, above all, in people. Expanding our expertise and our training and development activities with the aim of facilitating lifelong learning lays the foundations for healthy growth," emphasises Gläsel. Joint projects between schools and the training facility encourage young people to shoulder responsibility and fosters their creativity.

In addition to social sustainability, the company identified the importance of environmental sustainability at an early stage, before many others. For example, Weidmüller has been recycling plastic waste for over 50 years. Circular value creation is an integrated focus in the company to this day. Weidmüller strives to conserve resources while achieving further performance enhancements, including by leveraging the possibilities of digitalisation. It has been a member of Klimaschutz-Unternehmen, an association of companies committed to climate protection, for over a decade, thereby engaging with issues that shape our world today and in the future. With its technologies and innovations, Weidmüller is a pioneer of industrial connection technology and plays a vital role in shaping the energy transition. "By applying their initiative and their passion for new technologies, our people are creating a sustainable future," outlines Gläsel, who does not believe that a technological focus is contradictory to this. "Technology and innovation are essential for a liveable world. We are contributing and helping our customers to develop sustainable, advanced solutions," he says, neatly summarising the company's mission.

»Mit Eigen-
initiative und
Begeisterung für
neue Technologien
gestalten bei uns
Menschen
eine nachhaltige
Zukunft.«

Weidmüller beschäftigt knapp
6000 Mitarbeitende an über 30 Standorten und 60 Vertretungen weltweit

Weidmüller employs almost
6,000 people at over 30 locations and
60 representative offices worldwide

Auch im Detmolder Bildungsdorf
gestaltet die Peter Gläsel Stiftung
nachhaltige Bildungsprozesse

The Peter Gläsel Foundation
also promotes sustainable
educational processes at the
Detmold Education Village

CHRISTIAN GLÄSEL,
CHAIRMAN OF THE SUPERVISORY BOARD

»By applying
their initiative and
their passion for
new technologies,
our people are cre-
ating a sustainable
future.«

Der Sprecher der
Eigentümerfamilie und
Aufsichtsratsvorsitzende
Christian Gläsel

The owning family's
spokesperson and Chairman
of the Supervisory Board,
Christian Gläsel

WEMHÖNER SURFACE TECHNOLOGIES

„Wer aufhört, besser sein zu wollen, hat aufgehört, gut zu sein." Unter diesem Credo hat ein Industrieunternehmen aus Ostwestfalen die globale Spitzenposition seines Marktes erobert: Mit Kurztaktpressen-Anlagen zur Melamindirektbeschichtung und 3-D-Variopressen ist Wemhöner der unangefochtene Weltmarktführer für die Veredelung von Holzwerkstoffen und innovativer Technologieführer.

Heinrich Wemhöner schuf 1925 in Herford die Basis des Unternehmens mit einem Handwerksbetrieb für Metallarbeiten. Dieser fertigte bereits erste Eigenentwicklungen wie Tellerschleifmaschinen und Wurstmaschinen. Heute ist Wemhöner global die erste Adresse bei der Planung, Herstellung und Inbetriebnahme von Produktionslinien für die Holzwerkstoff- und Möbelindustrie sowie die Laminatfußbodenindustrie und deren Zulieferer. Doch bei Wemhöner denkt man weit über Oberflächen und ihre perfekte Veredelung hinaus. Für die vielfältigen komplexen Produktionsprozesse seiner Kunden schafft das Unternehmen Kurztaktpressen-Anlagen, Druck- und Lackieranlagen, 3-D-Membran- und Vakuumpressen, Laborpressen, Durchlaufpressen-Anlagen und Sonderanlagen: führende Wemhöner Technologie für die Fertigung hochwertiger Investitionsgüter.

Alle Produktionslinien zeichnen sich aus durch ein Maximum an Leistung, Flexibilität und nachhaltiger Effizienz. Die Wemhöner Ingenieur*innen und Verfahrenstechniker*innen arbeiten ebenso unentwegt an der Maschinen- und Anlagenoptimierung wie an originären Ideen und Entwicklungen. Im Wemhöner Technikum werden diese intensiv getestet und zur Fertigungsreife gebracht. Zu den herausragenden Innovationen zählen die Kurztakt-Durchlaufpresse mit Bandtablettbeschickung, die erste vollständig verkettete Maschinenstraße, das Wemhöner VARIOPIN-System und die doppelseitige Synchronpore (EIR) in der Melamindirektbeschichtung. Für 30 seiner Entwicklungen hält Wemhöner die Patente.

"If you stop striving to become better, you stop being good." This is the credo that Wemhöner followed to become a global market leader: the East Westphalian industrial enterprise manufactures short-cycle press lines for melamine direct lamination and 3D Variopress lines. It is an innovative technology leader and the undisputed global market leader in finishing systems for wood-based materials.

Heinrich Wemhöner laid the foundations for the company in 1925, opening a metalworking business in the town of Herford. Even then, the company developed its own devices, such as disc sanders and sausage machines. Today, Wemhöner is the world's first choice when it comes to planning, manufacturing and commissioning production lines for the wood-based materials and furniture industry, the laminate flooring industry and their suppliers. However, Wemhöner's focus extends far beyond surfaces and applying the perfect finish. To cater for its customers' wide-ranging and complex production processes, the company produces short-cycle press lines, printing and lacquering lines, 3D membrane and vacuum presses, laboratory presses, throughfeed press lines and special systems – all using pioneering Wemhöner technology to produce high-quality capital assets.

All Wemhöner production lines are characterised by unsurpassed performance, flexibility and sustainable efficiency. Wemhöner technicians and process engineers work just as tirelessly to optimise existing machinery and systems as they do to produce novel ideas and developments. New concepts undergo intensive testing at the Wemhöner technology centre to develop them to series maturity. The company's outstanding innovations include the short-cycle throughfeed press with tray belt feeding system, the first fully integrated production line, the Wemhöner VARIOPIN system and double-sided Synchronpore (EIR) technology in the

Unternehmensname
WEMHÖNER SURFACE TECHNOLOGIES GMBH & CO. KG

Industriezweig
MASCHINEN- UND ANLAGENBAU (METALL UND ELEKTRONIK) FÜR DIE HOLZWERKSTOFFINDUSTRIE

Gründung
1925 IN HERFORD

Vertrieb
WELTWEIT DURCH REPRÄSENTANTEN, IN SÜDOSTASIEN DURCH WEMHÖNER CHINA

Mitarbeitende
500 WELTWEIT

Jahresumsatz
150 MIO. EURO

Company name
WEMHÖNER SURFACE TECHNOLOGIES GMBH & CO. KG

Industry
MACHINERY AND PLANT ENGINEERING (METAL AND ELECTRONICS) FOR THE WOOD-BASED MATERIAL INDUSTRY

Founded
1925, HERFORD

Distribution
WORLDWIDE THROUGH SALES AGENCIES, INCL. WEMHÖNER CHINA IN SOUTH-EAST ASIA

Employees
500 WORLDWIDE

Annual sales
€150 MILLION

Wemhöner Kurztaktpressen-Anlagen setzen weltweit Standards

Wemhöner short-cycle press lines set global standards

Der Maschinen- und Anlagenbauer betreibt neben dem Standort in Herford mit 300 Mitarbeitenden zwei weitere in China mit zusammen 200 Beschäftigten. Weltweit sind Repräsentanten des Unternehmens vor Ort im Einsatz, der globale Vertrieb erfolgt über eigene Vertretungen und internationale Distributionspartner. Die Exportquote beträgt über 90 Prozent. Die Wemhöner Unternehmenskultur bietet allen Mitarbeitenden flache Hierarchien mit festen Strukturen und größtmögliche Eigenverantwortung – unabhängig von Geschlecht, Ethnie oder Religionszugehörigkeit. Um auch die Fachkräftepotenziale des Unternehmens besser zu nutzen, ist die Ausbildungsquote mit rund zehn Prozent überdurchschnittlich hoch.

Wemhöner hat früh auf die Entwicklung von nachhaltigen und ressourcenschonenden Technologien gesetzt und fertigt Maschinen und Anlagen mit hoher Verfügbarkeit und minimalem Ausschuss. Sie entstehen im intensiven Dialog mit den Kunden und festigen die Alleinstellung von Wemhöner als Weltmarkt- und Technologieführer. Heiner Wemhöner hält als geschäftsführender Gesellschafter 100 Prozent der Holdinganteile des Anlagen- und Maschinenbauers und wird das von ihm geprägte Unternehmen an die vierte Generation der Familie übergeben. Er ist zudem Vorsitzender des Kuratoriums der Wemhöner Stiftung, die vorrangig Kunst- und Kulturprojekte fördert.

Herausragende Leistungen, Innovationskraft und internationale Reputation sind wichtige Kriterien für zahlreiche namhafte Auszeichnungen des Unternehmens. So wurde Wemhöner als „Die beste Fabrik" von der WHU – Otto Beisheim School of Management geehrt (2006, 2007) und erhielt den Axia Award für seine Corporate Governance (Deloitte, 2007) sowie den China Trader Award for Sustainable Business (2008). Heiner Wemhöner wurde 2009 zum Ehrenbürger der chinesischen Metropole Changzhou ernannt. „Innovator des Jahres" (2019) und der PSI Competence Customer Award (2019), die Nominierungen zum „EY Entrepreneur of the Year 2021" und der Titel „Marke des Jahrhunderts" (2022) sind weitere Prädikate des Unternehmens. Bereits zum fünften Mal in Folge wurde Wemhöner 2023 von der WirtschaftsWoche/Universität St. Gallen als „WELTMARKTFÜHRER – CHAMPION" im Segment Maschinen- und Anlagenbau gewürdigt. Heiner Wemhöner ist seit Juni 2022 Ehrenbürger der Stadt Herford und hat 2023 für sein Engagement das Bundesverdienstkreuz verliehen bekommen.

Wemhöners Auftraggebende zählen in ihren Märkten zu den Besten. Deshalb entscheiden sie sich für die Expertise und Erfahrung des Weltmarkt- und Technologieführers. Gemeinsam mit ihnen will Wemhöner auch in Zukunft die Grenzen des technisch Machbaren verschieben.

melamine direct lamination process. Wemhöner holds patents for over 30 of its developments.

In addition to its site in Herford, where it has 300 employees, the machinery and plant engineering firm also has two locations in China where it has a further 200 employees. The company has field representatives around the world, with global sales handled through its own agencies and international distribution partners. Its export ratio is in excess of 90%. The culture at Wemhöner offers all employees flat hierarchies with robust structures and the highest possible level of autonomy – regardless of their gender, ethnicity or faith. The company has an above-average training ratio of 10% in an effort to make the best possible use of the available skilled labour.

Wemhöner focused its attention on developing sustainable, resource-conserving technologies at an early stage, producing machinery and plants with high availability and minimal rejects. Its products are the result of intensive dialogue with its customers and set Wemhöner apart as a global market and technology leader. As managing partner, Heiner Wemhöner owns 100% of the holding shares in the machinery and plant engineering firm and plans to pass the company he has shaped onto a fourth generation of the family. He is also Chair of the Board of Trustees at the Wemhöner Foundation, which primarily supports artistic and cultural projects.

Outstanding achievements, innovation and an international reputation are key criteria for the numerous prestigious awards the company has received. For instance, Wemhöner was named The Best Factory by WHU – Otto Beisheim School of Management (2006, 2007) and received the Axia Award for Corporate Governance (Deloitte, 2007) and the China Trader Award for Sustainable Business (2008). In 2009, Heiner Wemhöner was made an honorary citizen of the Chinese city of Changzhou. The company's other accolades include Innovator of the Year (2019), the PSI Competence Customer Award (2019), a nomination for EY Entrepreneur of the Year 2021 and the title of Brand of the Century (2022). In 2023, Wemhöner was named WORLD MARKET LEADER – CHAMPION for the fifth time in a row by the magazine WirtschaftsWoche and the University of St. Gallen in the Machinery and Plant Engineering category. Heiner Wemhöner was granted the freedom of the town of Herford in June 2022 and received the Federal Cross of Merit in 2023 in recognition of his dedication.

Wemhöner's customers are among the best in their respective markets – which is precisely why they rely on Wemhöner's expertise and experience as a global market and technology leader. Together with its customers, Wemhöner wants to continue pushing the limits of what is technically possible into the future.

»Wir erfinden leidenschaftlich gerne wegweisende Innovationen.«

Blick in die Fertigungshalle 5 und 6

A look inside Production Halls 5 and 6

Geschäftsführer Heiner Wemhöner

Heiner Wemhöner, Managing Director

Der neue Hallenkomplex in der Abenddämmerung

The new hall complex at dusk

»We are passionate about creating pioneering innovations.«

WÖHNER

Um energetische Zukunftslösungen entscheidend voranzubringen, brauchen wir Unternehmen mit Mut zur Transformation und exzellentem Innovationsmanagement. Wie Wöhner, führender und international renommierter Spezialist für innovative Energieverteilung. Das Unternehmen hat sich in den vergangenen 100 Jahren vom Komponentenhersteller zum umfassenden Lösungsanbieter entwickelt. Neben elektromechanischen Produkten und Energieverteilungssystemen umfassen die Leistungen das ganzheitliche Energiemanagement inklusive Messung, Monitoring und datenbasierter Optimierung bestehender Strukturen. Software-Services runden das Angebot ab.

Alfred Wöhner gründete das Familienunternehmen 1929 in Rödental (Oberfranken). Seine erste bahnbrechende Erfindung war ein dreipoliger, besonders kompakter Sicherungssockel, der sich ausgesprochen leicht montieren ließ. In den 1980er-Jahren setzte der Mittelständler neue Maßstäbe mit seinem 60Classic Basissystem. Dieses 60-Millimeter-Sammelschienensystem ist heute faktischer Industriestandard im Bereich der Niederspannungsverteilung sowie Steuerungstechnik und brachte Wöhner 2022 die Auszeichnung als „Marke des Jahrhunderts" in der Kategorie „Sammelschienensystemtechnik" ein. Auch weitere Wöhner Innovationen gelten in der Elektrotechnik als State of the Art, etwa das berührungsgeschützte Energieverteilungssystem CrossBoard® oder das modular aufgebaute Sammelschienensystem 185Power für die Niederspannungsverteilung.

Solche Neuerungen sind nicht für die Ewigkeit. Mit immer neuen Ideen begegnet Wöhner den Anforderungen einer Welt im Wandel und setzt immer wieder neue Standards in einer Branche, die entscheidend zur Energiewende und damit zur Zukunftsfähigkeit des Landes beiträgt. Dazu gehören beispielsweise Gleichstrom-Technologien oder eine intelligente, KI-gestützte Stromverteilung.

If we are to make decisive advances on the energy solutions of the future, we need companies with the courage to initiate transformation and conduct excellent innovation management. We need companies like Wöhner – a leading, internationally renowned specialist in innovative power distribution. Over the last 100 years, the company has developed from a component manufacturer to a comprehensive solutions provider. In addition to electromechanical products and power distribution systems, its services consist of comprehensive energy management, including measurement, monitoring and data-based optimisation of existing structures. Software services round off its portfolio.

Alfred Wöhner founded the family company in Rödental, Upper Franconia, in 1929. Its first ground-breaking invention was a three-pole, highly compact fuse-base that was particularly ease to install. In the 1980s, the medium-sized enterprise set new benchmarks with its 60Classic basic system. Today, this 60 mm busbar system is the de facto industry standard for low-voltage distribution and control technology. It also won Wöhner the title of "Brand of the Century" in 2022 in the category of "Busbar System Technology". Wöhner also offers further state-of-the-art innovations in the electrical engineering industry, such as the CrossBoard® touch-protected power distribution system and the 185Power modular busbar system for low-voltage distribution.

Of course, such innovations are not intended to last forever. This is why Wöhner continuously generates new ideas to meet the requirements of a changing world, setting new standards time and again in an industry of crucial importance to the energy transition and, therefore, to the future-readiness of our country. These new concepts include direct current technologies and intelligent, AI-assisted power distribution.

Unternehmensname
WÖHNER GMBH & CO. KG

Industriezweig
ELEKTROTECHNIK

Gründung
1929

Gründer
ALFRED WÖHNER

Vertrieb
IN ÜBER 80 LÄNDERN WELTWEIT

wöhner

Company name
WÖHNER GMBH & CO. KG

Industry
ELECTRICAL ENGINEERING

Founded
1929

Founder
ALFRED WÖHNER

Distribution
IN OVER 80 COUNTRIES WORLDWIDE

Das elektronische
Messtechnik-Modul CrossMT
treibt die Digitalisierung des
Schaltschranks voran

The CrossMT electronic
measurement technology
module is driving
the digitalisation
of control cabinets

Wöhner steht für Innovationen, die die Verwendung von Ressourcen transparenter machen und so die Effizienz und Nachhaltigkeit einer fortschrittlichen und zukunftssicheren Energienutzung steigern. Als vollelektronisches Messtechnik-Modul ermöglicht etwa das CrossMT die komfortable Messung wichtiger Parameter an den verschiedensten Stellen im Schaltschrank und gewährt so tiefgehende Einblicke in entscheidende Prozesse.

Seit 2023 ist Wöhner CEO Philipp Steinberger Mitglied im Gesamtvorstand des Verbandes der Elektro- und Digitalindustrie in Deutschland (ZVEI). Dem Verband gehören Hightech-Unternehmen und Innovatoren an, die wie Wöhner entscheidende Beiträge zur Transformation und zu einer CO_2-neutralen Industriegesellschaft leisten und dadurch den Wirtschaftsstandort Deutschland nachhaltig stärken. Im Projekt „PCF@ Control Cabinet" des ZVEI ist Wöhner einer der Vorreiter bei der Rückverfolgbarkeit von Produkten und der Kennzeichnung ihres ökologischen Fußabdruckes.

Die zukunftsweisenden Entwicklungen und Produkte von Wöhner fördern klimafreundliche sowie leistungsstarke Systeme. So gewährleistet das offene Energieverteilungssystem CrossBoard® das optimale Zusammenwirken unterschiedlicher Lösungen, selbst von verschiedenen Herstellern. Kunden profitieren zudem über die Messtechnik von intelligenten bis hin zu KI-basierten smarten Lösungen für eine zuverlässige, effiziente und nachhaltige Energieverteilung.

Neben der innovativ-technologischen Leistungskraft misst Wöhner Marke und Design einen besonderen Stellenwert bei. Beide sind Schlüsselthemen des unternehmerischen Erfolges und essenziell, um die Faszination der Produkte und die Leidenschaft für Energie erlebbar zu machen. Die systematische Markenarbeit zahlt sich aus. Das beweisen die vielen Auszeichnungen – sowohl für die technischen Innovationen als auch für das Produkt- und Kommunikationsdesign: als „Marke des Jahrhunderts" (2022), mit dem Schaltschrankbau Innovation Award (2021 und 2022), dem German Design Award und dem German Brand Award (jeweils 2022 und 2023) sowie dem German Innovation Award (2023).

Wöhner strives to produce innovations that make resource consumption more transparent, thereby improving the efficiency and sustainability of advanced, future-proof energy use. The CrossMT, for example, is a fully electronic measurement technology module that provides convenient measurement of key parameters in every area of a control cabinet, thereby providing in-depth insights into crucial processes.

In 2023, Wöhner CEO Philipp Steinberger became a member of the German Electro and Digital Industry Association (ZVEI) Board of Directors. The ZVEI brings together high-tech companies and innovators that, like Wöhner, make decisive contributions to technological transformation and the transition to a carbon-neutral industrial society, thereby strengthening Germany's long-term position as a location for business. Wöhner has a key role in the ZVEI's "PCF@Control Cabinet" project, which aims to facilitate product traceability and clearly indicate a product's carbon footprint.

Forward-looking developments and products from Wöhner promote climate-friendly, high-performance systems. The CrossBoard® open power distribution system, for instance, ensures that different solutions can be combined effectively, even if they originate from different manufacturers. Customers also benefit from its measurement technology, ranging from intelligent solutions to AI-based, smart solutions for reliable, efficient and sustainable power distribution.

In addition to its innovative, technological strengths, Wöhner also attaches particular importance to brand and design. Both aspects are key to the company's success and are essential in making Wöhner's fascination with its products and passion for energy come alive. Its systematic branding activities have paid dividends. This is evidenced by numerous awards recognising Wöhner's technical innovation as well as its product and communication design, including Brand of the Century (2022), the Control Cabinet Innovation Award (2021 and 2022), the German Design Award (2022 and 2023), the German Brand Award (2022 and 2023) and the German Innovation Award (2023).

PHILIPP STEINBERGER, CEO

»Die Energiewende braucht Teamplay. Coopetition ist das Zauberwort. Kooperation und Konkurrenz gehen dabei Hand in Hand.«

Das Hochregallager am Stammsitz in Rödental ist vollautomatisiert

The high-bay warehouse at its headquarters in Rödental is fully automated

Philipp Steinberger, CEO von Wöhner

Philipp Steinberger, CEO of Wöhner

PHILIPP STEINBERGER, CEO

»The energy transition needs team play. Coopetition is the magic word. Cooperation and competition go therefore hand in hand.«

Philipp Steinberger bei der Podiumsdiskussion auf dem ZVEI-Jahreskongress zu den Themen Manufacturing-X, Gleichstrom-Technologien und KI

Philipp Steinberger at a panel discussion on Manufacturing-X, direct current technology and AI at the ZVEI Annual Congress

ZEUTSCHEL

Nationalbibliotheken, Nationalarchive und Museen rund um den Globus streben danach, die Kulturschätze in ihrer Obhut langfristig zu bewahren und möglichst weltweit zugänglich zu machen – am besten für die Ewigkeit. Aber auch Unternehmen und Kanzleien, Banken und Versicherungen weltweit müssen geschäftskritische Informationen über große Zeiträume archivieren, gebundene Dokumente schonend und wirtschaftlich digitalisieren oder großformatige Vorlagen einscannen. Sie alle vertrauen überwiegend auf die einzigartige Expertise von Zeutschel aus dem baden-württembergischen Tübingen. Zeutschel ist Weltmarktführer bei der Entwicklung und Fertigung von Buchscannern und Aufsichtscannern sowie deren Anwendungssoftware. Großformatscanner und Mikrofilmsysteme komplettieren das Produktportfolio. Hinzu kommen Softwarelösungen für den Scan-Workflow, die Qualitätssicherung und die Steuerung des kompletten Digitalisierungsprozesses sowie andere Applikationen.

1961 war Heinz Zeutschel der namensgebende Gründer eines Unternehmens in Stuttgart-Sielmingen, das anfänglich Mikrofilm-Lesegeräte entwickelte, produzierte und vertrieb. 1993 stellte das Unternehmen, nunmehr in Tübingen ansässig, gemeinsam mit Kodak den weltweit ersten Aufsichtscanner vor und avancierte vom Pionier zum Technologieführer. 1997 erfolgte die internationale Markteinführung des in Eigenregie entwickelten, weltweit ersten Graustufen-Buchscanners. Nur ein Jahr später feierte die nächste Zeutschel Innovation für den Weltmarkt Premiere: ein Farb-Buchscanner für breite Anwenderkreise, der erstmalig eine hohe Imagequalität mit großer Produktivität kombinierte. Heute nimmt Zeutschel eine global führende Rolle bei der Digitalisierung von Kulturgütern ein. Das Unternehmen bietet vielfältige Lösungen, die wertvolle Kulturgüter erhalten und weltweit recherchierbar und abrufbar machen. Die Mitarbeitenden schaffen hierfür mit großer Innovationsfreude die erforderliche

National libraries, national archives and museums around the world strive to preserve the cultural treasures in their possession for as long as possible while also making them as widely accessible as possible – ideally in perpetuity. However, companies, solicitors, banks and insurance providers around the world also need to store business-critical information over long periods, digitalise bound documents carefully and economically and scan large-format originals. These organisations predominantly place their trust in the unique expertise of Zeutschel, a company based in Tübingen, Baden-Württemberg. Zeutschel is a global market leader in the development and manufacture of book scanners and overhead scanners as well as their application software. Its product portfolio also includes large-format scanners and microfilm systems. The company also provides software solutions for scanning workflows, quality assurance and to control the entire digitalisation process, among other applications.

In 1961, Heinz Zeutschel founded the company bearing his name in the Stuttgart suburb of Sielmingen, initially focusing on the development, production and distribution of microfilm readers. In 1993, the company – by then based in Tübingen – teamed up with Kodak to launch the world's first overhead scanner, and advanced from a pioneer to a technology leader. In 1997, the company launched the world's first grey-scale book scanner, an in-house development, on the international market. Just one year later, Zeutschel unveiled its next innovation for the global market: a colour book scanner. Aimed at a wide group of users, it was the first such solution to combine high image quality with high productivity. Today, Zeutschel has a world-leading role in the digitalisation of cultural assets. The company offers wide-ranging solutions designed to preserve valuable cultural assets and make them available for users around the world to access and use. Its employees demonstrate a true passion for innovation, producing

Unternehmensname
ZEUTSCHEL GMBH

Industriezweig
**BUCHSCANNER,
GROSSFORMATSCANNER**

Gründung
1961

Produkt
**AUFSICHTSCANNER UND
MIKROFILMAUFNAHMETECHNIK
MIT PASSENDEN SOFTWARE-
ANWENDUNGEN**

Vertrieb
WELTWEIT IN ÜBER 60 LÄNDERN

Jahresumsatz
CA. 13 MIO. EURO

Company name
ZEUTSCHEL GMBH

Industry
**BOOK SCANNERS,
LARGE-FORMAT SCANNERS**

Founded
1961

Product
**OVERHEAD SCANNERS AND
MICROFILM SCANNING
TECHNOLOGY WITH
CORRESPONDING SOFTWARE**

Distribution
**IN OVER 60 COUNTRIES
WORLDWIDE**

Annual sales
APPROX. €13 MILLION

ZEUTSCHEL

Die Lösungen von Zeutschel
decken den gesamten Arbeits-
prozess bei der Digitalisierung
von Kulturgut ab

Zeutschel offers solutions
covering the entire process of
digitalising cultural assets

Hardware und flexible, leistungsstarke und anwenderfreundliche Softwarelösungen, die Standards setzen.

Zeutschel hat mit seinen Aufsichtscannern und Software-Entwicklungen eine international anerkannte und hoch angesehene Plattform etabliert. In nahezu jeder Nationalbibliothek und in jedem Nationalarchiv auf der Welt arbeitet ein Zeutschel System. Dazu zählen renommierte Institutionen wie die Staatsbibliothek Berlin, die Bayerische Staatsbibliothek, die British Library, das Nationalarchiv der USA sowie die Nationalbibliotheken Brasiliens, Chinas und Südafrikas. Zugleich gewinnt Zeutschel mit dem Prinzip des Scans von oben immer mehr Kunden aus den Bereichen Industrie und Office.

Viele Objekte, deren Digitalisierung ansteht, haben einen unschätzbaren Wert oder sind nicht zu ersetzen. Zeutschel verfügt neben seinem Technologievorsprung auch über die erforderliche Expertise – von der individuellen Beratung über kundenspezifische Lösungen bis zum umfassenden Service. Zuverlässigkeit, Funktionalität, Flexibilität und die unkomplizierte Anwendung aller Systeme inklusive ihrer Software haben höchste Priorität. Die Scanner – wie alle Zeutschel Produkte ausnahmslos „made in Germany" – bieten eine bisher unerreichte Bildqualität und optimale Leistungsdaten für effiziente Digitalisierungsprozesse, die zur Einhaltung von Kosten- und Zeitrahmen beitragen.

Für die Distribution pflegt Zeutschel über Jahrzehnte gewachsene Partnerschaften. Erfahrene Digitalisierungsspezialist*innen unterstützen die Kunden von der Planung bis zur Inbetriebnahme der für sie optimalen Systeme. Die Produktlinien werden weltweit in über 60 Ländern inklusive der DACH-Region vertrieben, in Teilen Deutschlands auch direkt. Für seine Produkte erhielt Zeutschel Auszeichnungen wie den Red Dot Award, den MLA Award, den Designpreis FOCUS Open oder den iF Design-Award.

Nachhaltigkeit definiert Zeutschel als ganzheitliches Konzept für Ökonomie, Ökologie und soziales Engagement, die Unternehmensstrategie ist auf langfristiges, organisches Wachstum ausgerichtet. Alle Produkte werden am Stammsitz in Tübingen entwickelt und gefertigt. Die Gerätekomponenten stammen größtenteils von Zulieferern aus der Region. Seit 2021 wirtschaftet Zeutschel klimaneutral, 2023 wurde ein anerkanntes Umweltmanagementsystem implementiert. Zeutschel hegt eine in jeder Hinsicht verantwortungsvolle Leidenschaft für Kulturgüter und macht mit seiner technologischen Performance Wissen weltweit digital verfügbar.

the necessary hardware along with flexible, high-performance, user-friendly software solutions that set standards.

With its overhead scanners and software developments, Zeutschel has built an internationally recognised, highly regarded platform. Zeutschel systems are in use in almost every national library and national archive around the globe. These include prestigious institutions such as the Berlin State Library, the Bavarian State Library, the British Library, the US National Archives and the national libraries of Brazil, China and South Africa. At the same time, Zeutschel is winning over growing numbers of customers in its industry and office segments thanks to overhead scanning.

Many objects that are set to be digitalised are invaluable and cannot be replaced. In addition to its technological advantages, Zeutschel also possesses the necessary expertise – from individual consultancy to customer-specific solutions to comprehensive services. Reliability, functionality, flexibility and ease of use are top priorities in all Zeutschel systems and their software. Its scanners – which, like all Zeutschel products, are exclusively made in Germany – offer unparalleled image quality and optimal performance data for efficient digitalisation processes, thereby helping users to stay on budget and on schedule.

Zeutschel relies on partnerships that it has nurtured over decades to distribute its products. Experienced digitalisation specialists support customers from the planning phase through to commissioning the perfect systems for their needs. The company markets its product lines in over 60 countries around the world, including in the DACH region. It also sells its products directly in some parts of Germany. Zeutschel's products have received numerous accolades, including the Red Dot Award, the MLA Award, the FOCUS Open Design Award and the iF Design Award.

Zeutschel regards sustainability as a holistic concept comprising economic and environmental factors as well as social engagement. Its business strategy is based on long-term, organic growth. The company develops and manufactures all its products at its headquarters in Tübingen, with the components in its devices predominantly sourced from companies in the surrounding region. Zeutschel became a climate-neutral company in 2021 and implemented an accredited environmental management system in 2023. Zeutschel harbours a passion for cultural assets based on a sweeping sense of responsibility and, through its technological achievements, makes knowledge digitally available around the world.

CHRISTIAN HOHENDORF UND MARKUS WAGNER, GESCHÄFTSFÜHRER

»National-bibliotheken und Nationalarchive weltweit setzen auf unsere Digita-lisierungslösungen made in Germany.«

In Produktion: der zeta – Aufsicht-scanner für den Freihandbereich von Bibliotheken und Archiven

In production: the zeta – an overhead scanner for self-service use in libraries and archives

Zeutschel bildet junge Leute zu Industriekaufleuten und Mechatroniker*innen aus

Zeutschel trains young people to become industrial business assistants and mechatronic engineers

Firmengebäude in Tübingen, Stadt der Dichter und Denker

The company's offices in Tübingen, a city of poets and thinkers

CHRISTIAN HOHENDORF AND MARKUS WAGNER, MANAGING DIRECTORS

»National libraries and national archives around the world rely on our digitalisation solu-tions, which are made in Germany.«

Seit Juli 2023 Eigentümer und Geschäftsführer von Zeutschel: Christian Hohendorf und Markus Wagner (rechts)

Zeutschel's owners and Managing Directors since July 2023: Christian Hohendorf and Markus Wagner

ZIEHL-ABEGG

Der Feingeist und Visionär Emil Ziehl profitierte während des ingenieurwissenschaftlichen Studiums von seinem zeichnerischen und erfinderischen Talent. 1897 meldete er sein erstes Patent an: einen elektrischen Kreiselkompass, der auf Basis eines von ihm gezeichneten Außenläufermotors entstand – die Geburtsstunde moderner Ventilatorenantriebe. Der hochbegabte Kreative und studierte Techniker wurde zielstrebig Unternehmer und gründete im Jahr 1910 den Maschinenbauer ZIEHL-ABEGG. Damit legte er den Grundstein für ein global agierendes Unternehmen, das stets dem Credo seines Gründers folgte: „Produkte und Industriedesign müssen funktional und ästhetisch höchsten Ansprüchen genügen."

Heute zählt ZIEHL-ABEGG weltweit zur Königsklasse seines Industriezweiges und entwickelt kundenorientierte Systemlösungen für die Luft-, Antriebs- und Regeltechnik. Gefertigt werden unter anderem Elektromotoren für Aufzüge und medizintechnische Geräte sowie Industrie-Ventilatoren der neuesten Generation. Der innovative Technologieführer steht für effiziente und emissionsreduzierende Produkte mit hoher Fertigungstiefe. So produziert ZIEHL-ABEGG aus einem Spezialverbundkunststoff Ventilatoren, die aufgrund ihres einzigartigen Schaufeldesigns extremen Belastungen standhalten und hohe Wirtschaftlichkeit bieten.

Die Entwickler*innen von ZIEHL-ABEGG nutzten für Innovationen schon früh die Erkenntnisse der Bionik, die technische Probleme nach dem Vorbild biologischer Strukturen oder Funktionen löst. So inspirierten sie die Flügel der Schleiereule zum Design der Lüfterflügel des Ventilators FE2owlet. Mit progressiven Forschungs- und Entwicklungsmethoden arbeitet auch das ZIEHL-ABEGG Technologiezentrum in Künzelsau mit seinem weltweit beispiellosen Prüfstand für Ventilatoren. Das ZIEHL-ABEGG Produktsortiment umfasst rund 30 000 Artikel, die über eigene Vertriebsstandorte

While studying to become an engineer, the aesthete and visionary Emil Ziehl benefited from his talent for draughtsmanship and invention. In 1897, he filed for his first patent: an electrically driven gyroscope, which was based on an external rotor motor he had drawn – marking the birth of modern fan drive systems. A trained engineer with a gift for creativity, Ziehl became an ambitious entrepreneur and, in 1910, founded the mechanical engineering firm ZIEHL-ABEGG. In doing so, he laid the foundation stone for a global company that would unflinchingly follow its founder's credo: "Products and industrial design must satisfy the highest functional and aesthetic standards."

Today, ZIEHL-ABEGG is among the world's leading providers in its field, developing customer-oriented system solutions for ventilation, control and drive technology. It manufactures products including electric motors for lifts and medical devices as well as cutting-edge industrial fans. The innovative technology leader is known for its efficient, emission-reducing products with a high degree of vertical integration. For example, ZIEHL-ABEGG fabricates fans from a special composite plastic and using a unique blade concept, which enables them to withstand extreme stresses and offers high cost efficiency.

From an early stage, the development specialists at ZIEHL-ABEGG drew on insights from the field of bionics to produce innovations, solving technical problems based on examples in biological structures and functions. For example, a barn owl's wings inspired the design for the blades of the FE2owlet fan. At its technology centre in Künzelsau, ZIEHL-ABEGG uses advanced research and development methods, including its unparalleled test stand for fans. The ZIEHL-ABEGG product range comprises around 30,000 items, which it sells through its own sales offices in over 100 countries. In the 2022 business year, the company generated sales

Unternehmensname
ZIEHL-ABEGG SE

Industriezweig
MASCHINENBAU

Gründung
1910

Produkte
**ELEKTROMOTOREN
UND VENTILATOREN**

Mitarbeitende
**5100 WELTWEIT, DAVON 2800
IN DEUTSCHLAND**

Jahresumsatz
873 MIO. EURO (2022)

Company name
ZIEHL-ABEGG SE

Industry
MECHANICAL ENGINEERING

Founded
1910

Products
**ELECTRIC MOTORS
AND FANS**

Employees
**5,100 WORLDWIDE, INCLUDING
2,800 IN GERMANY**

Annual sales
€873 MILLION (2022)

ZIEHL-ABEGG

Die Fassade des Entwicklungszentrums am Firmensitz prägt das Stadtbild von Künzelsau

The façade of the development centre at the company's headquarters is a feature of the Künzelsau townscape

in 100 Länder verkauft werden. Im Geschäftsjahr 2022 erwirtschaftete das Unternehmen einen Umsatz von 873 Millionen Euro. ZIEHL-ABEGG verfügt über drei deutsche Standorte in Künzelsau, Schöntal-Bieringen und Kupferzell und betreibt insgesamt 16 weitere Werke in Europa, den USA, Asien und Australien. Dazu zählen die drei neuesten Produktionsstätten in Polen, den USA und Vietnam, die die globale Expansion des Unternehmens weiter vorantreiben. Deren Nähe zu den Kunden der jeweiligen Region trägt durch kürzere Transportwege auch zu einer optimierten Klimabilanz bei und verringert den CO_2-Fußabdruck.

ZIEHL-ABEGG ist eine nicht börsennotierte europäische Aktiengesellschaft. Das von einem familienfremden Management geführte Unternehmen ist in vierter Generation im Besitz der Familie Ziehl, die auch Aufsichtsratsmitglieder entsendet. Der Aufsichtsratsvorsitzende Dennis Ziehl wird unterstützt von seiner Schwester, Aufsichtsrätin Sindia Ziehl, und seinem Vater Uwe Ziehl, Enkel des Gründers und Ehrenvorsitzender des Aufsichtsrats, dem 2015 die Wirtschaftsmedaille des Landes Baden-Württemberg verliehen wurde.

Fachkräfte spricht ZIEHL-ABEGG mit einer Reihe von Maßnahmen an. Die Mitarbeitenden profitieren unter anderem von attraktiven Weiterbildungsprogrammen, Sportangeboten und JobRädern. Jährlich wird mehr als 70 dual Studierenden und Auszubildenden eine Zukunftsperspektive geboten und allen Absolvent*innen die Übernahme garantiert. Darüber hinaus nutzt ZIEHL-ABEGG unkonventionelle Strategien zur Gewinnung neuer Mitarbeitender: Die Willkommenskultur für Fachkräfte aus Süd- und Osteuropa wurde von der Standortinitiative „Deutschland – Land der Ideen" mit einer Auszeichnung gewürdigt. Dabei wurde Mitarbeitenden in spe die Lebensqualität im ländlichen Raum nähergebracht, Sprachkurse und weitere Angebote unterstützten sie beim Start in neuer Umgebung. Auch mit Social-Media-Aktivitäten wie Kurzvideos auf dem eigenen TikTok Channel ist ZIEHL-ABEGG erfolgreich und wurde dafür mit dem „Deutschen Preis für Onlinekommunikation" geehrt.

Der Maschinenbauer übernimmt gesellschaftliche Verantwortung und unterstützt ein Albert-Schweitzer-Kinderdorf sowie das Freilandmuseum Wackershofen. Ihm liegt die Förderung des technischen Verständnisses der Jüngsten besonders am Herzen, weshalb er mit Kindergärten, Grundschulen und weiterführenden Schulen zusammenarbeitet. Der Gründer Emil Ziehl würde es zweifelsohne wertschätzen, dass ZIEHL-ABEGG heute in etlichen Bereichen höchsten Ansprüchen genügt.

of €873 million. ZIEHL-ABEGG has three locations in Germany – in Künzelsau, Schöntal-Bieringen and Kupferzell – and operates a further 16 manufacturing facilities in Europe, the USA, Asia and Australia. These include its three newest production facilities in Poland, the USA and Vietnam, forging ahead with the company's global expansion. The sites' proximity to the company's customers in each region means shorter transport routes, thereby optimising its products' climate impact and reducing its carbon footprint.

ZIEHL-ABEGG is a privately held European company. While ownership has now passed to the fourth generation of the Ziehl family, responsibility for company management lies outside the family, with members of the Ziehl family on the Supervisory Board. The Chairman of the Supervisory Board, Dennis Ziehl, is supported by his sister and fellow board member, Sindia Ziehl. His father, Uwe Ziehl, is the grandson of the company's founder, Honorary Chairman of the Supervisory Board and also received the Business Medal of the State of Baden-Württemberg in 2015.

ZIEHL-ABEGG offers an array of measures for its specialist workforce. Its employees benefit, for example, from attractive professional development programmes, sporting activities and a company bicycle scheme. Every year, the company offers professional prospects to more than 70 dual students and apprentices, guaranteeing employment to all young people who complete their training. Furthermore, ZIEHL-ABEGG uses unconventional strategies to attract new employees. Its welcoming culture towards professionals from Southern and Eastern Europe was recognised by the 'Germany – Land of Ideas' initiative. The company has sought to give prospective employees an idea of the quality of life in rural areas of Germany, offering language courses and other services to help them find their feet in their new surroundings. ZIEHL-ABEGG has also achieved success with its social media activities, such as the short videos on its TikTok channel, for which it received the German Award for Online Communication.

The mechanical engineering firm also fulfils its social responsibilities, including by supporting an Albert Schweitzer village for foster families and the open-air museum in Wackershofen. It is particularly passionate about promoting an understanding of technology among young people and therefore cooperates with nurseries, primary schools and secondary schools. The company's founder, Emil Ziehl, would undoubtedly appreciate the high standards ZIEHL-ABEGG sets today in every area of its work.

DENNIS ZIEHL, AUFSICHTSRATSVORSITZENDER

»Technologischer Vorsprung, stetiges Wachstum und Profitabilität machen uns zum führenden unabhängigen Unternehmen unserer Branche.«

Die hohe Fertigungstiefe – wie hier die Leiterplattenbestückung – kennzeichnet die Produktion von ZIEHL-ABEGG

The high degree of vertical integration – including in the assembly of printed circuit boards – is a feature of ZIEHL-ABEGG's production activities

Das Werk in Kupferzell beherbergt im Tower das öffentliche Restaurant DeSi

The tower at the factory in Kupferzell is home to DeSi, a restaurant open to the public

DENNIS ZIEHL, CHAIRMAN OF THE SUPERVISORY BOARD

»Technological progress, constant growth and profitability make us a leading independent company in our industry.«

Der Vorstand von ZIEHL-ABEGG (von links): Joachim Ley, Olaf Kanig, Dr. Sascha Klett und Dr. Marc Wucherer

The Executive Board of ZIEHL-ABEGG (from left): Joachim Ley, Olaf Kanig, Dr Sascha Klett and Dr Marc Wucherer